Fodor's

New FOURTH EDITION

Virginia & Maryland

Fodor's Travel Publications, Inc.
New York • Toronto • London • Sydney • Auckland
http://www.fodors.com/

Virginia & Maryland

Editor: Amy McConnell
Contributors: Steven Amsterdam, Robert Andrews, David Brown, Laura M. Kidder, Heidi Sarna, Helayne Schiff, Mary Ellen Schultz, M. T. Schwartzman (Gold Guide Editor), Dinah Spritzer, Greg Tasker, Bruce Walker
Creative Director: Fabrizio La Rocca
Associate Art Director: Guido Caroti
Photo Researcher: Jolie Novak
Cartographer: David Lindroth
Cover Photograph: Catherine Karnow/Woodfin Camp
Design: Between the Covers

Copyright

Fourth Edition

ISBN 0–679–03297–5

"The Road to Appomattox," by Geoffrey C. Ward with Ric Burns and Ken Burns, is excerpted from *The Civil War.* Copyright © 1990 by American Documentaries, Inc.

"Pleasures of the Islands" is excerpted from *Bay Country,* by Tom Horton. Copyright © 1987 Johns Hopkins University Press, Baltimore and London.

Special Sales

Fodor's Travel Publications are available at special discounts for bulk purchases for sales promotions or premiums. Special editions, including personalized covers, excerpts of existing guides, and corporate imprints, can be created in large quantities for special needs. For more information, contact your local bookseller or write to Special Marketing, Fodor's Travel Publications, 201 East 50th Street, New York, NY 10022. Inquiries from Canada should be directed to your local Canadian bookseller or sent to Random House of Canada, Ltd., Marketing Department, 1265 Aerowood Drive, Mississauga, Ontario L4W 1B9. Inquiries from the United Kingdom should be sent to Fodor's Travel Publications, 20 Vauxhall Bridge Road, London SW1V 2SA, England.

PRINTED IN THE UNITED STATES OF AMERICA

10 9 8 7 6 5 4 3 2 1

CONTENTS

Maps

ON THE ROAD WITH FODOR'S

WE'RE ALWAYS THRILLED to get letters from readers, especially one like this:

It took us an hour to decide what book to buy and we now know we picked the best one. Your book was wonderful, easy to follow, very accurate, and good on pointing out eating places, informal as well as formal. When we saw other people using your book, we would look at each other and smile.

Our editors and writers are deeply committed to making every Fodor's guide "the best one"—not only accurate but always charming, brimming with sound recommendations and solid ideas, right on the mark in describing restaurants and hotels, and full of fascinating facts that make you view what you've traveled to see in a rich new light.

About Our Writers

Our success in achieving our goals—and in helping to make your trip the best of all possible vacations—is a credit to the hard work of our extraordinary writers.

Greg Tasker, who updated the Maryland half of the book, is a frequent contributor to the *Baltimore Sun*'s travel section and *Frederick Magazine*. As the former Western Maryland correspondent for the *Baltimore Sun* and a longtime resident of Western Maryland, Tasker was more than qualified to write a new chapter on Western Maryland.

Bruce Walker has lived in the Washington, DC area, including parts of Northern Virginia, since 1958. He currently works at the *Washington Post* on the staff of the Weekend section, a weekly guide to arts and entertainment.

New This Year

This year we've reformatted our guides to make them easier to use. Each chapter of *Virginia & Maryland* begins with brand-new recommended itineraries to help you decide what to see in the time you have; a section called When to Tour points out the optimal time of day, day of the week, and season for your journey. You may also notice our fresh graphics, new in 1996. More readable and more helpful than ever? We think so—and we hope you do, too.

Greg Tasker has also added a new chapter on Frederick and Western Maryland, the second most visited part of the state.

On the Web

Also check out Fodor's Web site (http://www.fodors.com/), where you'll find travel information on major destinations around the world and an ever-changing array of travel-savvy interactive features.

How to Use This Book

Organization

Up front is the **Gold Guide.** Its first section, **Important Contacts A to Z,** gives addresses and telephone numbers of organizations and companies that offer destination-related services and detailed information and publications. **Smart Travel Tips A to Z,** the Gold Guide's second section, gives specific information on how to accomplish what you need to in Virginia and Maryland, as well as tips on savvy traveling. Both sections are in alphabetical order by topic.

Chapters in *Virginia & Maryland* are arranged geographically, counterclockwise (Virginia) and clockwise (Maryland). The city chapter begins with an Exploring section that's subdivided by neighborhood; each subsection recommends a walking or driving tour and lists sights in alphabetical order. Each regional chapter is divided by geographical area; within each area, towns are covered in logical geographical order, and attractive stretches of road and minor points of interest between them are indicated by the designation *En Route*. Throughout, Off the Beaten Path sights appear after the places from which they are most easily accessible. And within town sections, all restaurants and lodgings are grouped together. The A to Z section that ends each chapter covers getting there, getting around, and helpful contacts and resources.

At the end of the book you'll find Portraits, wonderful essays about the Civil War and the islands of the Chesapeake Bay.

Icons and Symbols

★ Our special recommendations
✕ Restaurant
🏠 Lodging establishment
✕🏠 Lodging establishment whose restaurant warrants a detour
☺ Good for kids (rubber duckie)
☞ Sends you to another section of the guide for more information
✉ Address
☎ Telephone number
FAX Fax number
☉ Opening and closing times
🎟 Admission prices (those we give apply only to adults; substantially reduced fees are almost always available for children, students, and senior citizens)

Numbers in white and black circles (e.g., ② and ❷) that appear on the maps, in the margins, and within the tours correspond to one another.

Dining and Lodging

The restaurants and lodgings we list are the cream of the crop in each price range. Price categories are as follows.

For restaurants:

CATEGORY	COST*
$$$$	over $30
$$$	$20–$30
$$	$10–$20
$	under $10

Price categories represent the average cost of a three-course dinner for one person, not including beverages, tip, and state tax (4.5% in Virginia, 5% in Maryland).

For hotels:

CATEGORY	NON-CITIES*	BALTIMORE*
$$$$	over $120	over $175
$$$	$90–$120	$140–$175
$$	$50–$90	$115–$140
$	under $50	under $115

All prices are for a double room, excluding state tax (9.045% in Virginia, 10% in Maryland).

Hotel Facilities

We always list the facilities that are available—but we don't specify whether they cost extra. When pricing accommodations, always ask what's included. Unless otherwise specified, most hotels and inns have individual bathrooms.

Restaurant Reservations and Dress Codes

Reservations are always a good idea; we note only when they're essential or when they are not accepted. Book in advance, and reconfirm when you get to town. Unless otherwise noted, the restaurants listed are open daily for lunch and dinner. We mention dress only when men are required to wear a jacket or a jacket and tie.

Credit Cards

The following abbreviations are used: **AE**, American Express; **D**, Discover; **DC**, Diners Club; **MC**, MasterCard; and **V**, Visa.

Please Write to Us

All prices and opening times are based on information supplied to us at press time, March, 1997; Fodor's cannot accept responsibility for any errors. Time inevitably brings changes, so always confirm information when it matters. In addition, when making reservations, be sure to mention if you have a disability or are traveling with children, if you prefer a private bath or a certain type of bed, or if you have specific dietary needs or any other concerns.

Did our hotel picks exceed your expectations? Did you find a museum we recommended a waste of time? If you have complaints, we'll look into them and revise our entries when the facts warrant it. If you've discovered a special place that we haven't included, we'll have our correspondents check it out. So send your feedback, positive *and* negative, to the *Virginia & Maryland* editor at 201 East 50th Street, New York, New York 10022—and have a wonderful trip!

Karen Cure
Editorial Director

Virginia and Maryland

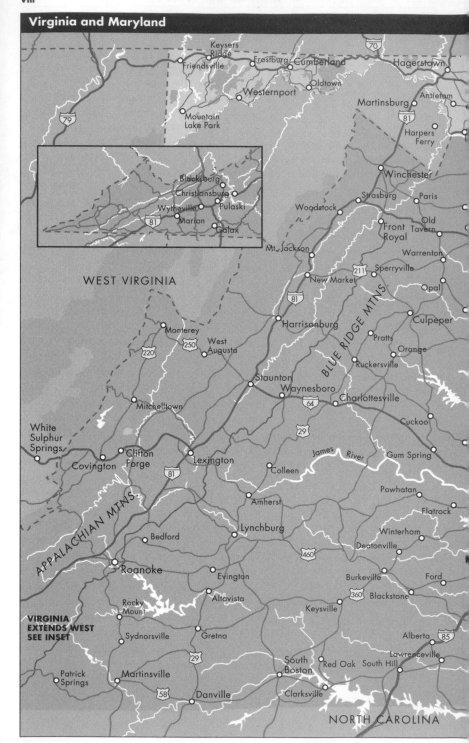

Keysers Ridge
Friendsville
Frostburg
Cumberland
Hagerstown
70
Westernport
Oldtown
Martinsburg
Antietam
81
Mountain Lake Park
Harpers Ferry
79
Winchester
Blacksburg
Christiansburg
Strasburg
Paris
Wytheville
Pulaski
Woodstock
Old Tavern
Marion
Front Royal
81
Galax
Warrenton
Mt. Jackson
Sperryville
WEST VIRGINIA
New Market
211
Opal
81
Culpeper
Monterey
Harrisonburg
BLUE RIDGE MTNS.
250
West Augusta
Pratts
220
Orange
Ruckersville
Staunton
Waynesboro
Charlottesville
64
Mitchelltown
29
Cuckoo
White Sulphur Springs
James
River
Gum Spring
Clifton Forge
Lexington
Covington
81
Colleen
Powhatan
Amherst
Flatrock
APPALACHIAN MTNS.
Lynchburg
Winterham
Bedford
Deatonville
Roanoke
Evington
460
Burkeville
Ford
Rocky Mount
Altavista
Blackstone
360
VIRGINIA EXTENDS WEST SEE INSET
Keysville
Sydnorsville
Gretna
Alberta
85
29
Lawrenceville
Patrick Springs
Martinsville
South Boston
Red Oak
South Hill
58
Danville
Clarksville
NORTH CAROLINA

The United States

IMPORTANT CONTACTS A TO Z

An Alphabetical Listing of Publications, Organizations, and Companies That Will Help You Before, During, and After Your Trip

A

AIR TRAVEL

The major gateways to Virginia and Maryland include **Richmond International Airport** (☎ 804/226–3000) in Virginia, and **Baltimore-Washington International (BWI) Airport** (☎ 410/859–7100), in Maryland, about 25 mi northeast of Washington.

FLYING TIME

Flying time to BWI is one hour from New York, two hours from Chicago, and five hours, 40 minutes from Los Angeles. Flying time to Richmond is approximately 1½ hours from New York, three hours from Chicago, and 6½ hours from Los Angeles.

CARRIERS

TO RICHMOND➤ Contact **American Airlines** (☎ 800/433–7300), **Continental** (☎ 800/525–0280), **Delta** (☎ 800/221–1212), **Eastwind** (☎ 800/644–3500), **Midway** (☎ 800/446–4392), **Northwest** (☎ 800/225–2525), **TWA** (☎ 800/221–2000), **United** (☎ 800/241–6522), or **USAir** (☎ 800/428–4322).

TO BWI➤ Contact **America West** (☎ 800/235–9292), **American Airlines** (☎ 800/433–7300), **Continental** (☎ 800/525–0280), **Delta** (☎ 800/221–1212),

Northwest (☎ 800/225–2525), **Southwest** (☎ 800/435–9792), **TWA** (☎ 800/221–2000), **United** (☎ 800/241–6522), or **USAir** (☎ 800/428–4322).

For inexpensive, no-frills flights to Richmond, contact **Air Trans Airways** (☎ 800/247–8726) or **Eastwind** (☎ 800/644–3592). **Midwest Express** (☎ 800/452–2022) serves BWI.

FROM THE U.K.

Continental (☎ 0800/776–464) flies to Richmond, Virginia, from Gatwick and Manchester. **Delta** (☎ 0800/414–767) flies from Gatwick to Atlanta, where connections can be made to Virginia and Maryland.

COMPLAINTS

To register complaints about charter and scheduled airlines, contact the U.S. Department of Transportation's **Aviation Consumer Protection Division** (✉ C-75, Washington, DC 20590, ☎ 202/366–2220). Complaints about lost baggage or ticketing problems and safety concerns may also be logged with the **Federal Aviation Administration (FAA) Consumer Hotline** (☎ 800/322–7873).

PUBLICATIONS

For general information about charter carriers, ask for the Department of Transportation's free

brochure **"Plane Talk: Public Charter Flights"** (✉ Aviation Consumer Protection Division, C-75, Washington, DC 20590, ☎ 202/366–2220). The Department of Transportation also publishes a 58-page booklet, **"Fly Rights,"** available from the Consumer Information Center (✉ Supt. of Documents, Dept. 136C, Pueblo, CO 81009; $1.75).

WITHIN VIRGINIA AND MARYLAND

USAir links the major airports in the region. For those who establish a vacation home on Maryland's Eastern Shore, commuter flights to and from Baltimore-Washington International Airport is a viable option.

COMMUTER SERVICES

Cumberland Municipal Airport (☎ 304/738–0002) serves Western Maryland; **Easton Municipal Airport** (☎ 410/822–8560), with Maryland Airlines, services Maryland's middle Eastern Shore; **Ocean City Municipal Airport** (☎ 410/213–2471) offers private facilities to Maryland's Atlantic seashore; **Salisbury/Wicomico County Regional Airport** (☎ 410/548–4827) provides service to Maryland's lower Eastern Shore; **Washington County/Hager-**

stown Airport (☎ 301/791–3333) has flights throughout midwestern Maryland.

B
BETTER BUSINESS BUREAU

For local contacts, consult the **Council of Better Business Bureaus** (✉ 4200 Wilson Blvd., Suite 800, Arlington, VA 22203, ☎ 703/276–0100, 𝐅𝐀𝐗 703/ 525–8277).

BUS TRAVEL

Greyhound Lines (☎ 800/231–2222) serves the following locations in Maryland: Baltimore, Cambridge, Easton, Salisbury, and Ocean City. In Virginia it serves: Abingdon, Charlottesville, Fairfax, Fredericksburg, Hampton, Lexington, Newport News, Norfolk, Richmond, Roanoke, Springfield, Staunton, Virginia Beach, and Williamsburg.

C
CAR RENTAL

The major car-rental companies represented in Virginia and Maryland are **Alamo** (☎ 800/327–9633; in the U.K., 0800/272–2000), **Avis** (☎ 800/331–1212; in Canada, 800/879–2847), **Budget** (☎ 800/ 527–0700; in the U.K., 0800/181181), **Dollar** (☎ 800/800–4000; in the U.K., 0990/565656, where it is known as Eurodollar), **Hertz** (☎ 800/ 654–3131; in Canada, 800/263–0600; in the U.K., 0345/555888), and **National InterRent** (☎ 800/227–7368; in the U.K., where National is known as Europcar InterRent, 0345/ 222525). Rates

in Virginia and Maryland begin at $40 a day and $130 a week for an economy car with unlimited mileage. This does not include tax on car rentals, which is 8% in Virginia and 11½% in Maryland.

RENTAL WHOLESALERS

Contact **Auto Europe** (☎ 207/828–2525 or 800/223–5555).

CHILDREN & TRAVEL

BABY-SITTING

Several local baby-sitting services in the two states are: **Babysitters of Tidewater** (☎ 804/489–1622) in Norfolk, Virginia; **Harbor City Sitter Service** (☎ 410/462–2977) in Baltimore, Maryland; **Durham Sitters Agency** (☎ 804/296–8732) in Charlottesville, Virginia; and **Nanny Connection** (☎ 804/379–9314) in Richmond, Virginia.

FLYING

Look into **"Flying with Baby"** (✉ Third Street Press, Box 261250, Littleton, CO 80163, ☎ 303/595–5959; $4.95 includes shipping), cowritten by a flight attendant. **"Kids and Teens in Flight,"** free from the U.S. Department of Transportation's Aviation Consumer Protection Division (✉ C-75, Washington, DC 20590, ☎ 202/366–2220), offers tips on children flying alone. Every two years the February issue of **Family Travel Times** (☞ Know-How, *below*) details children's services on three dozen airlines. **"Flying Alone, Handy Advice for Kids Traveling**

Solo"** is available free from the American Automobile Association (AAA) (✉ send stamped, self-addressed, legal-size envelope: Flying Alone, Mail Stop 800, 1000 AAA Dr., Heathrow, FL 32746).

KNOW-HOW

Family Travel Times, published quarterly by Travel with Your Children (✉ TWYCH, 40 5th Ave., New York, NY 10011, ☎ 212/477–5524; $40 per year), covers destinations, types of vacations, and modes of travel.

CUSTOMS

CANADIANS

Contact **Revenue Canada** (✉ 2265 St. Laurent Blvd. S, Ottawa, Ontario K1G 4K3, ☎ 613/993–0534) for a copy of the free brochure **"I Declare/Je Déclare"** and for details on duty-free limits. For recorded information (within Canada only), call 800/461–9999.

U.K. CITIZENS

HM Customs and Excise (✉ Dorset House, Stamford St., London SE1 9NG, ☎ 0171/202–4227) can answer questions about U.K. customs regulations and publishes a free pamphlet, **"A Guide for Travellers,"** detailing standard procedures and import rules.

D
DISABILITIES & ACCESSIBILITY

COMPLAINTS

To register complaints under the provisions of the Americans with

THE GOLD GUIDE / IMPORTANT CONTACTS

Disabilities Act, contact the U.S. Department of Justice's **Disability Rights Section** (✉ Box 66738, Washington, DC 20035, ☎ 202/514–0301 or 800/514–0301, FAX 202/307–1198, TTY 202/514–0383 or 800/514–0383). For airline-related problems, contact the U.S. Department of Transportation's **Aviation Consumer Protection Division** (☞ Air Travel, *above*). For complaints about surface transportation, contact the Department of Transportation's **Civil Rights Office** (✉ 400 7th St., SW, Room 10215, Washington DC, 20590, ☎ 202/366–4648).

ORGANIZATIONS

TRAVELERS WITH HEARING IMPAIRMENTS➤ The **American Academy of Otolaryngology** (✉ 1 Prince St., Alexandria, VA 22314, ☎ 703/836–4444, FAX 703/683–5100, TTY 703/519–1585) publishes a brochure, "Travel Tips for Hearing Impaired People."

TRAVELERS WITH MOBILITY PROBLEMS➤ Contact **Mobility International USA** (✉ Box 10767, Eugene, OR 97440, ☎ and TTY 541/343–1284, FAX 541/343–6812), the U.S. branch of a Belgium-based organization (☞ *below*) with affiliates in 30 countries; **MossRehab Hospital Travel Information Service** (☎ 215/456–9600, TTY 215/456–9602), a telephone information resource for travelers with physical disabilities; the **Society for the Advancement of Travel for the Handicapped** (✉ 347 5th Ave., Suite 610, New York, NY 10016, ☎ 212/447–7284, FAX 212/725–8253; membership $45); and **Travelin' Talk** (✉ Box 3534, Clarksville, TN 37043, ☎ 615/552–6670, FAX 615/552–1182) which provides local contacts worldwide for travelers with disabilities.

TRAVELERS WITH VISION IMPAIRMENTS➤ Contact the **American Council of the Blind** (✉ 1155 15th St. NW, Suite 720, Washington, DC 20005, ☎ 202/467–5081, FAX 202/467–5085) for a list of travelers' resources or the **American Foundation for the Blind** (✉ 11 Penn Plaza, Suite 300, New York, NY 10001, ☎ 212/502–7600 or 800/232–5463, TTY 212/502–7662), which provides general advice and publishes "Access to Art" ($19.95), a directory of museums that accommodate travelers with vision impairments.

IN THE U.K.

Contact the **Royal Association for Disability and Rehabilitation** (✉ RADAR, 12 City Forum, 250 City Rd., London EC1V 8AF, ☎ 0171/250–3222) or **Mobility International** (✉ rue de Manchester 25, B-1080 Brussels, Belgium, ☎ 00–322–410–6297, FAX 00–322–410–6874), an international travel-information clearinghouse for people with disabilities.

PUBLICATIONS

Several publications for travelers with disabilities are available from the **Consumer Information Center** (✉ Box 100, Pueblo, CO 81009, ☎ 719/948–3334). Call or write for its free catalog of current titles. The Society for the Advancement of Travel for the Handicapped (☞ Organizations, *above*) publishes the quarterly magazine **"Access to Travel"** ($13 for 1-year subscription).

Fodor's **Great American Vacations for Travelers with Disabilities** (available in bookstores, or ☎ 800/533–6478; $18 plus $4 shipping) details accessible attractions, restaurants, and hotels in U.S. destinations. The 500-page **Travelin' Talk Directory** (✉ Box 3534, Clarksville, TN 37043, ☎ 615/552–6670, FAX 615/552–1182; $35) lists people and organizations who help travelers with disabilities. For travel agents worldwide, consult the **Directory of Travel Agencies for the Disabled** (✉ Twin Peaks Press, Box 129, Vancouver, WA 98666, ☎ 360/694–2462 or 800/637–2256, FAX 360/696–3210; $19.95 plus $3 shipping). The Sierra Club publishes **Easy Access to National Parks** (✉ Sierra Club Store, 85 2nd St., San Francisco, CA 94105, ☎ 415/977–5630 or 800/935–1056 FAX 415/977–5795; $16 plus $4 shipping).

TRAVEL AGENCIES & TOUR OPERATORS

The Americans with Disabilities Act requires that all travel firms serve the needs of all travelers. That said, you should note that some agencies and operators specialize in making travel arrangements for individuals and groups with disabilities, among them **Access Adventures** (✉ 206 Chestnut Ridge Rd., Rochester, NY 14624, ☎ 716/889–9096), run by a former physical-rehab counselor.

TRAVELERS WITH MOBILITY PROBLEMS➤ Contact **Hinsdale Travel Service** (✉ 201 E. Ogden Ave., Suite 100, Hinsdale, IL 60521, ☎ 630/325–1335), a travel agency that benefits from the advice of wheelchair traveler Janice Perkins; and **Wheelchair Journeys** (✉ 16979 Redmond Way, Redmond, WA 98052, ☎ 206/885–2210 or 800/313–4751), which can handle arrangements worldwide.

TRAVELERS WITH DEVELOPMENTAL DISABILITIES➤ Contact the nonprofit **New Directions** (✉ 5276 Hollister Ave., Suite 207, Santa Barbara, CA 93111, ☎ 805/967–2841).

TRAVEL GEAR

The **Magellan's** catalog (☎ 800/962–4943, FAX 805/568–5406), includes a section devoted to products designed for travelers with disabilities.

DISCOUNTS & DEALS

AIRFARES

For the lowest airfares to Virginia or Maryland, call 800/FLY–4–LESS. Also try 800/FLY–ASAP.

CLUBS

Contact **Entertainment Travel Editions** (✉ Box 1068, Trumbull, CT 06611, ☎ 800/445–4137; $28–$53, depending on destination), **Great American Traveler** (✉ Box 27965, Salt Lake City, UT 84127, ☎ 800/548–2812; $49.95 per year), **Moment's Notice Discount Travel Club** (✉ 7301 New Utrecht Ave., Brooklyn, NY 11204, ☎ 718/234–6295; $25 per year, single or family), **Privilege Card International** (✉ 3391 Peachtree Rd. NE, Suite 110, Atlanta, GA 30326, ☎ 404/262–0222 or 800/236–9732; $74.95 per year), **Travelers Advantage** (✉ CUC Travel Service, 49 Music Sq. W, Nashville, TN 37203, ☎ 800/548–1116 or 800/648–4037; $49 per year, single or family), or **Worldwide Discount Travel Club** (✉ 1674 Meridian Ave., Miami Beach, FL 33139, ☎ 305/534–2082; $50 per year for family, $40 single).

PUBLICATIONS

Consult *The Frugal Globetrotter,* by Bruce Northam (✉ Fulcrum Publishing, 350 Indiana St., Suite 350, Golden, CO 80401, ☎ 800/992–2908; $16.95 plus $4 shipping). For publications that tell how to find the lowest prices on plane tickets, *see* Air Travel, *above.*

STUDENTS

Members of Hostelling International–American Youth Hostels (☞ Students, *below*) are eligible for discounts on car rentals, admissions to attractions, and other selected travel expenses.

DRIVING

MAPS

The state tourist offices of Maryland and Virginia (☞ Visitor Information, *below*) publish official state road maps, free for the asking, that contain directories and other useful information.

G
GAY & LESBIAN TRAVEL

ORGANIZATIONS

The **International Gay Travel Association** (✉ Box 4974, Key West, FL 33041, ☎ 800/448–8550, FAX 305/296–6633), a consortium of more than 1,000 travel companies, can supply names of gay-friendly travel agents, tour operators, and accommodations.

PUBLICATIONS

The 16-page monthly newsletter **"Out & About"** (✉ 8 W. 19th St., Suite 401, New York, NY 10011, ☎ 212/645–6922 or 800/929–2268, FAX 800/929–2215; $49 for 10 issues and quarterly calendar) covers gay-friendly resorts, hotels, cruise lines, and airlines.

Also consult Fodor's *Gay Guide to the USA* by Andrew Collins (available in bookstores, or ☎ 800/533–6478; $19.50 plus $4 shipping).

TOUR OPERATORS

Toto Tours (✉ 1326 W. Albion Ave., Suite 3W, Chicago, IL 60626, ☎ 773/274–8686 or 800/565–1241, FAX 773/274–8695) offers group tours to worldwide destinations.

TRAVEL AGENCIES

The largest agencies serving gay travelers are **Advance Travel** (✉ 10700 Northwest Fwy.,

THE GOLD GUIDE / IMPORTANT CONTACTS

Suite 160, Houston, TX 77092, ☎ 713/682–2002 or 800/292–0500), **Club Travel** (⌧ 8739 Santa Monica Blvd., W. Hollywood, CA 90069, ☎ 310/358–2200 or 800/429–8747), **Islanders/Kennedy Travel** (⌧ 183 W. 10th St., New York, NY 10014, ☎ 212/242–3222 or 800/988–1181), **Now Voyager** (⌧ 4406 18th St., San Francisco, CA 94114, ☎ 415/626–1169 or 800/255–6951), and **Yellowbrick Road** (⌧ 1500 W. Balmoral Ave., Chicago, IL 60640, ☎ 773/561–1800 or 800/642–2488). **Skylink Women's Travel** (⌧ 2460 W. 3rd St., Suite 215, Santa Rosa, CA 95401, ☎ 707/570–0105 or 800/225–5759) serves lesbian travelers.

I
INSURANCE

IN THE U.S.

Travel insurance covering baggage, health, and trip cancellation or interruption is available from **Access America** (⌧ 6600 W. Broad St., Richmond, VA 23230, ☎ 804/285–3300 or 800/334–7525), **Carefree Travel Insurance** (⌧ Box 9366, 100 Garden City Plaza, Garden City, NY 11530, ☎ 516/294–0220 or 800/323–3149), **Tele-Trip** (⌧ Mutual of Omaha Plaza, Box 31716, Omaha, NE 68131, ☎ 800/228–9792), **Travel Guard International** (⌧ 1145 Clark St., Stevens Point, WI 54481, ☎ 715/345–0505 or 800/826–1300), **Travel Insured International** (⌧ Box 280568, East Hartford, CT 06128, ☎ 203/528–7663 or 800/243–3174), and **Wallach & Com-**

pany (⌧ 107 W. Federal St., Box 480, Middleburg, VA 22117, ☎ 540/687–3166 or 800/237–6615).

IN CANADA

Contact **Mutual of Omaha** (⌧ Travel Division, 500 University Ave., Toronto, Ontario M5G 1V8, ☎ 800/465–0267 [in Canada] or 416/598–4083).

IN THE U.K.

The **Association of British Insurers** (⌧ 51 Gresham St., London EC2V 7HQ, ☎ 0171/600–3333) gives advice by phone and publishes the free pamphlet **"Holiday Insurance and Motoring Abroad,"** which sets out typical policy provisions and costs.

L
LODGING

APARTMENT & VILLA RENTAL

Among the companies to contact are **Property Rentals International** (⌧ 1008 Mansfield Crossing Rd., Richmond, VA 23236, ☎ 804/378–6054 or 800/220–3332, FAX 804/379–2073), and **Rent-a-Home International** (⌧ 7200 34th Ave. NW, Seattle, WA 98117, ☎ 206/789–9377 or 800/488–7368, FAX 206/789–9379, rentahomeinternational@msn.com). Members of the travel club **Hideaways International** (⌧ 767 Islington St., Portsmouth, NH 03801, ☎ 603/430– 4433 or 800/843–4433, FAX 603/430–4444, info@hideaways. com; $99 per year) receive two annual guides plus quarterly newsletters

and arrange rentals among themselves.

HOME EXCHANGE

Some of the principal clearinghouses are **HomeLink International/Vacation Exchange Club** (⌧ Box 650, Key West, FL 33041, ☎ 305/294–1448 or 800/638–3841, FAX 305/294–1148; $78 per year), which sends members five annual directories, with a listing in one, plus updates; and **Loan-a-Home** (⌧ 2 Park La., Apt. 6E, Mount Vernon, NY 10552, ☎ 914/664–7640; $40–$50 per year), which specializes in long-term exchanges.

M
MONEY

ATMS

For specific **Cirrus** locations in the United States and Canada, call 800/424–7787. For U.S. **Plus** locations, call 800/843–7587 and enter the area code and first three digits of the number from which you're calling (or of the calling area in which you want to locate an ATM).

N
NATIONAL AND STATE PARKS

Passes for travelers with disabilities or frequent visitors can be purchased at any park that charges admission or obtained by mail from the **National Park Service** (⌧ Dept. of the Interior, Washington, DC 20240). Passes for senior citizens (age 62 or older) must be applied for in person at the parks. Proof of age is required.

In Maryland, the **Division of Tourism and Promotion** (✉ 217 E. Redwood St., Baltimore 21202, ☎ 800/543–1036) and the **State Forest and Park Service** (✉ MD Dept. of Natural Resources, Tawes State Office Bldg., 580 Taylor Ave., Annapolis, MD 21401, ☎ 410/974–3771; TTY 410/974–3683) can provide information about each of the state parks.

The **Division of Conservation and Recreation** (✉ 203 Governor St., Richmond 23219, ☎ 804/786–1712) can provide information on all of Virginia's state parks.

PACKING

For strategies on packing light, get a copy of *The Packing Book,* by Judith Gilford (✉ Ten Speed Press, Box 7123, Berkeley, CA 94707, ☎ 510/559–1600 or 800/841–2665, FAX 510/524–4588; $7.95 plus $3.50 shipping).

PASSPORTS & VISAS

U.K. CITIZENS

For fees, documentation requirements, and to request an emergency passport, call the **London Passport Office** (☎ 0990/210410). For U.S. visa information, call the **U.S. Embassy Visa Information Line** (☎ 01891/200–290; calls cost 49p per minute or 39p per minute cheap rate) or send a self-addressed, stamped envelope to the **U.S. Embassy Visa Branch**

(✉ 5 Upper Grosvenor St., London W1A 2JB). If you live in Northern Ireland, write to the **U.S. Consulate General** (✉ Queen's House, Queen St., Belfast BTI 6EO).

PHOTO HELP

The **Kodak Information Center** (☎ 800/242–2424) answers consumer questions about film and photography. The *Kodak Guide to Shooting Great Travel Pictures* (available in bookstores; or contact Fodor's Travel Publications, ☎ 800/533–6478; $16.50 plus $4 shipping) explains how to take expert travel photographs.

S

SAFETY

"Trouble-Free Travel," from the AAA, is a booklet of tips for protecting yourself and your belongings when away from home. Send a stamped, self-addressed, legal-size envelope to Trouble-Free Travel (✉ Mail Stop 75, 1000 AAA Dr., Heathrow, FL 32746).

SENIOR CITIZENS

CLUBS

Sears's **Mature Outlook** (✉ Box 10448, Des Moines, IA 50306, ☎ 800/336–6330; annual membership $14.95) includes a lifestyle/travel magazine and membership in ITC-50 travel club, which offers discounts of up to 50% at participating hotels and restaurants. (☞ Discounts & Deals *in* Smart Travel Tips A to Z, *below*).

EDUCATIONAL TRAVEL

The nonprofit **Elderhostel** (✉ 75 Federal St., 3rd Floor, Boston, MA 02110, ☎ 617/426–7788), for people 55 and older, has offered inexpensive study programs since 1975. Courses cover everything from marine science to Greek mythology and cowboy poetry. Fees for programs in the United States and Canada, which usually last one week, run about $300, not including transportation.

ORGANIZATIONS

Contact the **American Association of Retired Persons** (✉ AARP, 601 E St. NW, Washington, DC 20049, ☎ 202/434–2277; annual dues $8 per person or couple). Its Purchase Privilege Program secures discounts for members on lodging, car rentals, and sightseeing, and the AARP Motoring Plan (☎ 800/334–3300) furnishes domestic trip-routing information and emergency road-service aid for an annual fee of $39.95 ($59.95 for a premium version). Senior citizen travelers can also join the AAA for emergency road service and other travel benefits (☞ Discounts & Deals *in* Smart Travel Tips A to Z, *below*).

SPORTS

BIKING

For information on biking in Virginia, contact the **State Bicycle Coordinator** (✉ VA Dept. of Transportation, 1401 E. Broad St., Richmond, VA 23219, ☎ 804/786–2964).

THE GOLD GUIDE / IMPORTANT CONTACTS

"Best Bike Routes in Maryland," a series of 10 maps covering scores of Maryland's touring and off-road routes, is printed on sturdy waterproof and tearproof paper (✉ Box 16388, Baltimore, MD 21210, ☎ 410/685–3626). The cost is $9.95 for one and $29.95 for the series. Also helpful is the **Maryland State Highway Administration** (✉ Bicycle Affairs Coordinator, Room 218, State Hwy. Adm., 707 N. Calvert St., Box 717, Baltimore, MD 21203, ☎ 800/252–8776), which can provide details concerning statewide bike routes.

CANOEING & KAYAKING

For information, contact the **Virginia Tourism Development Group** (✉ 1021 E. Cary St., Richmond 23219, ☎ 804/786–2051) or the **Maryland Division of Tourism and Promotion** (✉ 217 E. Redwood St., Baltimore 21202, ☎ 800/543–1036).

FISHING

Virginia does not require a license for saltwater fishing in the ocean, in the bay, or in rivers up to the freshwater line. A license is required for freshwater fishing in rivers, lakes, and impoundments; a license valid for one year costs $30.50 for nonresidents, $12.50 for residents. The **Virginia Commission of Game and Inland Fisheries** (✉ Box 1104, Richmond 23230, ☎ 804/367–1000) can provide further information.

Maryland fishing licenses valid for one year are $7 from the **Department of Natural Resources** (Box 1869, Annapolis 21404, ☎ 410/974–3211). Fishing licenses can also be obtained at many sporting-goods stores; these licenses are valid for one week and cost $7 or more.

SAILING

Because demand is heavy from mid-May through October, it's a good idea to reserve boats as soon as you know your plans. The **Chesapeake Bay Yacht Racing Association** (✉ Box 4022, Annapolis, MD 21403, ☎ 410/269–1194) prepares a list of charter companies on the bay. *Chesapeake Bay Magazine* (✉ 1819 Bay Ridge Ave., Suite 200, Annapolis, MD 21403, ☎ 410/263–2662) publishes the thorough **Guide to Cruising Chesapeake Bay** for $34.50 plus $3 postage. The **Maryland Department of Natural Resources** publishes the **Cruising Guide to Maryland Waters,** which costs $18.

SKIING

In the Shenandoah Valley, the Homestead Resort in Hot Springs started the southern ski industry in the 1950s and has since been joined by Wintergreen near Waynesboro, Massanutten near Harrisonburg, and other Virginia resorts. The **Division of Conservation and Recreation** (✉ 203 Governor St., Richmond, VA 23219, ☎ 804/786–1712) provides further information on skiing facilities and seasons.

Wisp Ski Area (✉ Deep Creek Lake, Marsh Hill Rd., Box 629, McHenry, MD 21541, ☎ 301/387–4911), in far Western Maryland, rises nearly 3,100 feet above sea level and overlooks Deep Creek Lake. It offers 23 slopes and 14 mi of trails, from novice to expert. It is easily accessible for weekenders from Baltimore and Washington. There are additional cross-country ski trails in the region.

STUDENTS

HOSTELING

In the United States, contact **Hostelling International–American Youth Hostels** (✉ 733 15th St. NW, Suite 840, Washington, DC 20005, ☎ 202/783–6161 for reservations worldwide or 800/444–6111 for reservations at U.S. hostels using a credit card, FAX 202/783–6171); in Canada, **Hostelling International–Canada** (✉ 205 Catherine St., Suite 400, Ottawa, Ontario K2P 1C3, ☎ 613/237–7884); and in the United Kingdom, the **Youth Hostel Association of England and Wales** (✉ Trevelyan House, 8 St. Stephen's Hill, St. Albans, Hertfordshire AL1 2DY, ☎ 01727/855215 or 01727/845 047). Membership (in the U.S., $25; in Canada, C$26.75; in the U.K., £9.30) gives you access to 5,000 hostels in 77 countries that charge $5–$40 per person per night.

ORGANIZATIONS

A major contact is the **Council on International Educational Exchange** (✉ mail orders only: CIEE, 205 E. 42nd St., 16th Floor, New York,

NY 10017, ☎ 212/822–2600, FAX 212/822–2699, info@ciee.org). The **Educational Travel Centre** (✉ 438 N. Frances St., Madison, WI 53703, ☎ 608/256–5551 or 800/747–5551, FAX 608/256–2042) offers rail passes and low-cost airline tickets, mostly for flights that depart from Chicago.

In Canada, also contact **Travel Cuts** (✉ 187 College St., Toronto, Ontario M5T 1P7, ☎ 416/979–2406 or 800/667–2887).

T
TOUR OPERATORS

Among the companies that sell tours and packages to Virginia and Maryland, the following are nationally known, have a proven reputation, and offer plenty of options.

GROUP TOURS

DELUXE➤ **Globus** (✉ 5301 S. Federal Circle, Littleton, CO 80123, ☎ 303/797–2800 or 800/221–0090, FAX 303/795–0962), **Maupintour** (✉ Box 807, 1515 St. Andrews Dr., Lawrence, KS 66047, ☎ 913/843–1211 or 800/255–4266, FAX 913/843–8351), and **Tauck Tours** (✉ Box 5027, 276 Post Rd. W, Westport, CT 06881, ☎ 203/226–6911 or 800/468–2825, FAX 203/221–6828).

FIRST-CLASS➤ **Brendan Tours** (✉ 15137 Califa St., Van Nuys, CA 91411, ☎ 818/785–9696 or 800/421–8446, FAX 818/902–9876), **Collette Tours** (✉ 162 Middle St., Pawtucket, RI 02860, ☎ 401/728–3805 or 800/832–4656, FAX 401/728–1380),

Gadabout Tours (✉ 700 E. Tahquitz Canyon Way, Palm Springs, CA 92262, ☎ 619/325–5556 or 800/952–5068), and **Mayflower Tours** (✉ Box 490, 1225 Warren Ave., Downers Grove, IL 60515, ☎ 708/960–3793 or 800/323–7604, FAX 708/960–3575).

BUDGET➤ **Cosmos** (☞ Globus, *above*).

PACKAGES

Independent packages are available from major tour operators. Contact **Adventure Vacations** (✉ 10612 Beaver Dam Rd., Hunt Valley, MD 21030-2205, ☎ 410/785–3500 or 800/638–9040, FAX 410/584–2771). **Gogo Tours,** based in Ramsey, New Jersey, sells packages only through travel agents.

Also contact **Amtrak**'s Great American Vacations (☎ 800/321–8684).

FROM THE U.K.

Tour operators offering packages to Virginia and Maryland include **Jetsave** (✉ Sussex House, London Rd., East Grinstead, West Sussex RH19 1LD, ☎ 01342/312–033), **Key to America** (✉ 1–3 Station Rd., Ashford Middlesex, TW15 2UW, ☎ 01784/248–777), **Premier Holidays** (✉ Premier Travel Center, Westbrook, Milton Rd., Cambridge CB4 1YG, ☎ 01223/516–688), and **Trailfinders** (✉ 42–50 Earl's Court Rd., London W8 6FT, ☎ 0171/937–5400; ✉ 58 Deansgate, Manchester M3 2FF, ☎ 0161/839–6969).

THEME TRIPS

BICYCLING➤ Bike tours throughout Virginia's Shenandoah Valley and along Maryland's eastern shores are available from **Back-roads** (✉ 1516 5th St., Berkeley, CA 94710-1740, ☎ 510/527–1555 or 800/462–2848, FAX 510/527–1444, goactive@Backroads.com).

LEARNING➤ **Smithsonian Study Tours and Seminars** (✉ 1100 Jefferson Dr. SW, Room 3045, MRC 702, Washington, DC 20560, ☎ 202/357–4700, FAX 202/633–9250) offers art, culture, and history seminars and tours.

PERFORMING ARTS➤ **Dailey-Thorp Travel** (✉ 330 W. 58th St., #610, New York, NY 10019-1817, ☎ 212/307–1555 or 800/998–4677, FAX 212/974–1420) specializes in classical music and opera programs, and offers one in Williamsburg.

WALKING/HIKING➤ For hike trips in the Shenandoah National Park, contact **New England Hiking Holidays** (✉ Box 1648, North Conway, NH 03860, ☎ 800/869–0949).

ORGANIZATIONS

The **National Tour Association** (✉ NTA, 546 E. Main St., Lexington, KY 40508, ☎ 606/226–4444 or 800/755–8687) and the **United States Tour Operators Association** (✉ USTOA, 211 E. 51st St., Suite 12B, New York, NY 10022, ☎ 212/750–7371) can provide lists of members and information on booking tours.

PUBLICATIONS

Contact the USTOA (☞ Organizations, *above*) for its **"Smart Traveler's Planning Kit."** Pamphlets in the kit include the "Worldwide Tour and Vacation Package Finder," "How to Select a Tour or Vacation Package," and information on the organization's consumer protection plan. Also get a copy of the Better Business Bureau's **"Tips on Travel Packages"** (✉ Publication 24-195, 4200 Wilson Blvd., Arlington, VA 22203; $2). The National Tour Association will send you **"On Tour,"** a listing of its member operators, and a personalized package of information on group travel in North America.

TRAIN TRAVEL

Amtrak (☎ 800/872–7245) trains run out of Baltimore, Maryland, north toward Boston and south toward Washington, DC, along the busy "northeast corridor." A rail station at BWI Airport serves both Baltimore (about 15 mi to the north) and Washington, DC (about 30 mi to the south). Some trains running between New York and Chicago stop at Charlottesville, Virginia, and at two locations in western Virginia. Trains run between Newport News, Virginia, and New York City, stopping in northern Virginia, Richmond, and Williamsburg in between. Stops in Richmond and northern Virginia are also made on runs between New York City and Florida.

The Maryland State Railroad Administration (☎ 800/325–7245), or MARC, operates 19 daily commuter trains between Baltimore's Penn Station and Washington, DC's Union Station. It also operates 11 trains from Baltimore's downtown Camden Station and from Union Station in Washington, DC There is free bus transportation between the BWI Airport Rail Station and the airport passenger terminal.

TRAVEL GEAR

For travel apparel, appliances, personal-care items, and other travel necessities, get a free catalog from **Magellan's** (☎ 800/962–4943, 🖷 805/568–5406), **Orvis Travel** (☎ 800/541–3541, 🖷 540/343–7053), or **TravelSmith** (☎ 800/950–1600, 🖷 415/455–0554).

TRAVEL AGENCIES

For names of reputable agencies in your area, contact the **American Society of Travel Agents** (✉ ASTA, 1101 King St., Suite 200, Alexandria, VA 22314, ☎ 703/739–2782), the **Association of Canadian Travel Agents** (✉ Suite 201, 1729 Bank St., Ottawa, Ontario K1V 7Z5, ☎ 613/521–0474, 🖷 613/521–0805) or the **Association of British Travel Agents** (✉ 55-57 Newman St., London W1P 4AH, ☎ 0171/637–2444, 🖷 0171/637–0713).

V

VISITOR INFORMATION

Contact the **Maryland Department of Economic and Employment/Tourism Development** (✉ Office of Tourist Development, 217 E. Redwood St., 9th Floor, Baltimore, MD 21202, ☎ 410/767–3400 or 800/543–1036, 🖷 410/333–6643)) and the **Virginia Division of Tourism** (✉ 901 East Byrd St., Richmond, VA 23219, ☎ 804/786–4484 or 804/847–4882, 🖷 804/786–1919). The **Virginia-Maryland Travel Center** (✉ 1629 K St. NW, Washington, DC 20017, ☎ 202/659–5523, 🖷 202/659–8646) can book accommodations at Virginia bed-and-breakfasts (☎ 800/934–9184).

If you're planning to visit the nation's capital, contact the **Washington, DC, Convention and Visitors Association** (✉ 1212 New York Ave. NW, 6th Floor, Washington, DC 20005, ☎ 202/208–1631, 🖷 202/208–1643) and the **DC Committee to Promote Washington** (✉ 1212 New York Ave. NW, 2nd Floor, Washington, DC 20005, ☎ 800/422–8644).

The **White House Visitor Center** (✉ Baldridge Hall, Department of Commerce, 1450 Pennsylvania Ave. NW, Washington, DC 20230, ☎ 202/208–1631) has information on White House tours and special events. **Dial-A-Park** (☎ 202/619–7275) is a recording of events at Park Service attractions in and around Washington. **Dial-A-Museum** (☎ 202/357–2020) is a recording of exhibits and special offerings at Smithsonian Institution museums.

The **National Park Service** (⊠ Office of Public Affairs, National Capital Region, 1100 Ohio Dr. SW, Washington, DC 20242, ☎ 202/619–7222, FAX 202/619–7302) has information about attractions and events in regional parks. The park service also operates information kiosks in Washington on the Mall, near the White House, next to the Vietnam Veterans Memorial, and at several other locations throughout the city.

IN THE U.K.

In the U.K., contact the tourism offices of Virginia (☎ 0181/651-4743, FAX 0181/651-5702) and Maryland (☎ FAX 01295/750789).

W
WEATHER

For current conditions and forecasts, plus the local time and helpful travel tips, call the **Weather Channel Connection** (☎ 900/932–8437; 95¢ per minute) from a Touch-Tone phone.

The *International Traveler's Weather Guide* (⊠ Weather Press, Box 660606, Sacramento, CA 95866, ☎ 916/974–0201 or 800/972–0201; $10.95 includes shipping), written by two meteorologists, provides month-by-month information on temperature, humidity, and precipitation in more than 175 cities worldwide.

THE GOLD GUIDE / IMPORTANT CONTACTS

SMART TRAVEL TIPS A TO Z

Basic Information on Traveling in Virginia and Maryland and Savvy Tips to Make Your Trip a Breeze

A

AIR TRAVEL

If time is an issue, **always look for nonstop flights.** If possible, **avoid connecting flights,** which stop at least once and can involve a change of plane, even though the flight number remains the same; if the first leg is late, the second waits.

For better service, **fly smaller or regional carriers,** which often have higher passenger satisfaction ratings. Sometimes they have such in-flight amenities as leather seats or greater legroom and they often have better food.

CUTTING COSTS

The Sunday travel section of most newspapers is a good place to look for deals.

MAJOR AIRLINES➤ The least-expensive airfares from the major airlines are priced for round-trip travel and are subject to restrictions. Usually, you must **book in advance and buy the ticket within 24 hours** to get cheaper fares, and you may have to **stay over a Saturday night.** The lowest fare is subject to availability, and only a small percentage of the plane's total seats is sold at that price. It's smart to **call a number of airlines,** and when you are quoted a good price, book it on the spot—the same fare may not be available on the same flight the next day. Airlines generally allow you to change your return date for a $25 to $50 fee. If you don't use your ticket, you can apply the cost toward the purchase of a new ticket, again for a small charge. However, most low-fare tickets are nonrefundable. To get the lowest airfare, **check different routings.** If your destination has more than one gateway, **compare prices to different airports.**

FROM THE U.K.➤ To save money on flights, **look into an APEX or Super-Pex ticket.** APEX tickets must be booked in advance and have certain restrictions. Super-PEX tickets can be purchased right at the airport.

ALOFT

AIRLINE FOOD➤ If you hate airline food, **ask for special meals when booking.** These can be vegetarian, low-cholesterol, or kosher, for example; commonly prepared to order in smaller quantities than standard fare, they can be tastier.

SMOKING➤ Smoking is not allowed on flights of six hours or less within the continental United States. Smoking is also prohibited on flights within Canada. For U.S. flights longer than six hours or inter-national flights, **contact your carrier regarding their smoking policy.** Some carriers have prohibited smoking throughout their system; others allow smoking only on certain routes or even certain departures of that route.

B

BUS TRAVEL

A bus excursion may be a practical way to visit Ocean City or Virginia Beach, but for most of the area bus travel would be an inconvenient alternative to the greater freedom of movement that driving allows.

C

CAMERAS, CAMCORDERS, & COMPUTERS

IN TRANSIT

Always **keep your film, tape, or disks out of the sun;** never put these on the dashboard of a car. Carry an extra supply of batteries, and **be prepared to turn on your camera, camcorder, or laptop computer for security personnel** to prove that it's real.

X-RAYS

Always **ask for hand inspection at security.** Such requests are virtually always honored at U.S. airports, and are usually accommodated abroad. Photographic film becomes clouded after successive exposure to airport x-ray machines. Videotape and computer disks are not harmed by X-rays, but **keep your tapes and disks away from metal detectors.**

CAR RENTAL

CUTTING COSTS

To get the best deal, **book through a travel agent who is willing to shop around.** When pricing cars, **ask where the rental lot is located.** Some off-airport locations offer lower rates—even though their lots are only minutes away from the terminal via complimentary shuttle. You also may want to **price local car-rental companies,** whose rates may be lower still, although service and maintenance standards may not be as high as those of a national firm. Ask your agent to **look for fly-drive packages,** which also save you money, and **ask if local taxes are included** in the rental or fly-drive price. These can be as high as 20% in some destinations. Don't forget to find out about required deposits, cancellation penalties, drop-off charges, and the cost of any required insurance coverage.

Also **ask your travel agent about a company's customer-service record.** How has it responded to late plane arrivals and vehicle mishaps? Are there often lines at the rental counter, and—if you're traveling during a holiday period—does a confirmed reservation guarantee you a car?

INSURANCE

When driving a rented car, you are generally responsible for any damage to or loss of the rental vehicle, as well as any property damage or personal injury that you cause. Before you rent, **see what coverage you already have** under the terms of your personal auto insurance policy and credit cards.

For about $14 a day, rental companies sell protection, known as a collision- or loss-damage waiver (CDW or LDW), that eliminates your liability for damage to the car; it's always optional and should never be automatically added to your bill.

In most states, the renter's personal auto insurance or other liability insurance covers damage to third parties. Only when the damage exceeds the renter's own insurance coverage does the car-rental company pay. However, companies renting cars in Maryland have the initial responsibility for damage caused to third parties, after which the renter's personal auto or other liability insurance covers the loss. This may seem like unlimited protection for the renter, but state law caps the amount that the car-rental company must pay. If you do not have auto insurance or an umbrella insurance policy that covers damage to third parties, consider purchasing CDW or LDW.

U.K. CITIZENS

In the United States you must be 21 to rent a car; rates may be higher if you're under 25. You'll pay extra for child seats (about $3 per day), compulsory for children under five, and for additional drivers (about $2 per day). To pick up your reserved car you will need the reservation voucher, a passport, a U.K. driver's license, and a travel policy that covers each driver.

SURCHARGES

Before you pick up a car in one city and leave it in another, **ask about drop-off charges or one-way service fees,** which can be substantial. Note, too, that some rental agencies charge extra if you return the car before the time specified on your contract. To avoid a hefty refueling fee, **fill the tank just before you turn in the car**—but be aware that gas stations near the rental outlet may overcharge.

CHILDREN & TRAVEL

Endowed with plenty of national parks, seashores, battlefields, and historic homes and restored towns—as well as theme parks and beach-town amusement piers—Virginia and Maryland make excellent destinations for family vacations. Driving distances are not wearisome and, outside of Virginia Beach and the northern Virginia suburbs of Washington, DC, there are plenty of simple, low-cost accommodations and restaurants where children are more than welcome.

THE GOLD GUIDE / SMART TRAVEL TIPS

BABY-SITTING

For recommended local sitters, **check with your hotel desk.**

DRIVING

If you are renting a car, don't forget to **arrange for a car seat when you reserve.** Sometimes they're free.

FLYING

As a general rule, infants under two not occupying a seat fly for free. If your children are two or older **ask about special children's fares.** Age limits for these fares vary among carriers. Rules also vary regarding unaccompanied minors, so again, check with your airline.

BAGGAGE➤ In general, the adult baggage allowance applies to children paying half or more of the adult fare.

SAFETY SEATS➤ According to the FAA, it's a good idea to **use safety seats aloft** for children weighing less than 40 pounds. Airline policies vary. U.S. carriers allow FAA-approved models but usually require that you buy a ticket, even if your child would otherwise ride free, since the seats must be strapped into regular seats. However, some airlines may require you to hold your baby during takeoff and landing—defeating the seat's purpose.

FACILITIES➤ When making your reservation, **request children's meals or freestanding bassinets** if you need them; the latter are available only to those seated at the bulkhead, where there's enough legroom. If you don't need a bassinet, **think twice before requesting bulkhead seats**—the only storage space for in-flight necessities is in inconveniently distant overhead bins.

LODGING

Most hotels allow children under a certain age to stay in their parents' room at no extra charge; others charge them as extra adults. Be sure to **ask about the cutoff age for children's rates.**

CUSTOMS & DUTIES

To speed your clearance through customs, **keep receipts for all your purchases abroad** and **be ready to show the inspector what you've bought.** If you feel that you've been incorrectly or unfairly charged a duty, you can **appeal assessments in dispute.** First ask to see a supervisor. If you are still unsatisfied, **write to the port director** at your point of entry, sending your customs receipt and any other appropriate documentation. The address will be listed on your receipt. If you still don't get satisfaction, you can take your case to customs headquarters in Washington.

ON ARRIVAL

Entering the United States, a visitor 21 or over can bring in 200 cigarettes or 50 cigars or 2 kilograms of tobacco; one liter of alcohol; and duty-free gifts to a value of $100. Restricted items include meat, meat products, fruits, vegetables, plants, and seeds. Never carry illegal drugs.

IN CANADA

If you've been out of Canada for at least seven days, you may bring in C$500 worth of goods duty-free. If you've been away for fewer than seven days but for more than 48 hours, the duty-free allowance drops to C$200; if your trip lasts between 24 and 48 hours, the allowance is C$50. You cannot pool allowances with family members. Goods claimed under the C$500 exemption may follow you by mail; those claimed under the lesser exemptions must accompany you.

Alcohol and tobacco products may be included in the seven-day and 48-hour exemptions but not in the 24-hour exemption. If you meet the age requirements of the province or territory through which you reenter Canada, you may bring in, duty-free, 1.14 liters (40 imperial ounces) of wine or liquor *or* 24 12-ounce cans or bottles of beer or ale. If you are 16 or older, you may bring in, duty-free, 200 cigarettes, 50 cigars or cigarillos, and 400 tobacco sticks or 400 grams of manufactured tobacco. Alcohol and tobacco must accompany you on your return.

An unlimited number of gifts with a value of up to C$60 each may be mailed to Canada duty-free. These do not affect your duty-free allowance on your return. Label the package "Unsolicited Gift— Value Under $60." Alcohol and tobacco are excluded.

IN THE U.K.

From countries outside the EU, including the United States, you may import, duty-free, 200 cigarettes, 100 cigarillos, 50 cigars, or 250 grams of tobacco; 1 liter of spirits or 2 liters of fortified or sparkling wine or liqueurs; 2 liters of still table wine; 60 milliliters of perfume; 250 milliliters of toilet water; plus £136 worth of other goods, including gifts and souvenirs.

D

DISABILITIES & ACCESSIBILITY

When discussing accessibility with an operator or reservationist, **ask hard questions.** Are there any stairs, inside *or* out? Are there grab bars next to the toilet *and* in the shower/tub? How wide is the doorway to the room? To the bathroom? For the most extensive facilities, meeting the latest legal specifications, **opt for newer accommodations,** which more often have been designed with access in mind. Older properties or ships must usually be retrofitted and may offer more limited facilities as a result. Be sure to **discuss your needs before booking.**

DISCOUNTS & DEALS

You shouldn't have to pay for a discount. In fact, you may already be eligible for all kinds of savings. Here are some time-honored strategies for getting the best deal.

LOOK IN YOUR WALLET

When you **use your credit card to make travel purchases,** you may get free travel-accident insurance, collision damage insurance, or medical or legal assistance, depending on the card and bank that issued it. American Express, Visa, and MasterCard provide one or more of these services, so **get a copy of your card's travel benefits.** If you are a member of the AAA or an oil-company-sponsored road-assistance plan, always **ask hotel or car-rental reservationists for auto-club discounts.** Some clubs offer additional discounts on tours, cruises, or admission to attractions. And don't forget that auto-club membership entitles you to free maps and trip-planning services.

SENIORS CITIZENS & STUDENTS

As a senior-citizen traveler, you may be eligible for special rates, but you should mention your senior-citizen status up front. If you're a student or under 26 you can also get discounts, especially if you **carry an official student ID card** (☞ Senior-Citizen Discounts *and* Students on the Road, *below*).

DIAL FOR DOLLARS

To save money, **look into "1-800" discount reservations services,** which often have lower rates. These services use their buying power to get a better price on hotels, airline tickets, and sometimes even car rentals. When booking a room, always **call the hotel's local toll-free number** (if one is available) rather than the central reservations number—you'll often get a better price. Ask the reservationist about special packages or corporate rates, which are usually available even if you're not traveling on business.

JOIN A CLUB?

Discount clubs can be a legitimate source of savings, but you must use the participating hotels and visit the participating attractions in order to realize any benefits. Remember, too, that you have to pay a fee to join, so **determine if you'll save enough to warrant your membership fee.** Before booking with a club, **make sure the hotel or other supplier isn't offering a better deal.**

GET A GUARANTEE

When shopping for the best deal on hotels and car rentals, **look for guaranteed exchange rates,** which protect you against a falling dollar. With your rate locked in, you won't pay more even if the price goes up in the local currency.

DRIVING

Unless you are visiting central Baltimore, a car is by far the most convenient means of travel throughout Maryland and Virginia, and in many areas it is the only practical way to get around. (Where it exists, public transportation is clean and comfortable, but too often it bypasses or falls short of travel high points.) The maximum speed limit is 55 mph on major highways in Maryland, 65 mph in Virginia. A right turn on red is permitted in Maryland (unless signed otherwise), once you've brought the vehicle to a complete stop.

HIGHWAYS

Interstate 95 runs north–south through Maryland and Virginia, carrying traffic to and from New England and Florida and intermediate points. U.S. 50 links I–95 with Annapolis and Maryland's Eastern Shore. U.S. 97 links Baltimore with Annapolis. I–64 intersects I–95 at Richmond and runs east–west, headed east toward Williamsburg, Hampton Roads, and the bridge-tunnel to Virginia's Eastern Shore, and west toward Charlottesville and the Shenandoah Valley. At Staunton, I–64 intersects I–81, which runs north–south. Interstate 70 runs west from Baltimore's Beltway I–695, to Hancock in Western Maryland. I–68 connects Hancock to Cumberland and Garrett County. Also, U.S. 40—The National Pike—travels east and west, the entire length of Maryland. Interstate 83 journeys south from Pennsylvania to the top of I–695, the Baltimore Beltway.

I

INSURANCE

Travel insurance can protect your monetary investment, replace your luggage and its contents, or provide for medical coverage should you fall ill during your trip. Most tour operators, travel agents, and insurance agents sell specialized health-and-accident, flight, trip-cancellation, and luggage insurance as well as comprehensive policies with some or all of these coverages. Comprehensive policies may also reimburse you for delays due to weather—an important consideration if you're traveling during the winter months. Some health-insurance policies do not cover preexisting conditions, but waivers may be available in specific cases. Coverage is sold by the companies listed in Important Contacts A to Z; these companies act as the policy's administrators. The actual insurance is usually underwritten by a well-known name, such as The Travelers or Continental Insurance.

Before you make any purchase, **review your existing health and homeowner's policies** to find out whether they cover expenses incurred while traveling.

BAGGAGE

Airline liability for baggage is limited to $1,250 per person on domestic flights. On international flights, it amounts to $9.07 per pound or $20 per kilogram for checked baggage (roughly $640 per 70-pound bag) and $400 per passenger for unchecked baggage. Insurance for losses exceeding the terms of your airline ticket can be bought directly from the airline at check-in for about $10 per $1,000 of coverage; note that it excludes a rather extensive list of items, shown on your airline ticket.

COMPREHENSIVE

Comprehensive insurance policies include all the coverages described above plus some that may not be available in more specific policies. If you have purchased an expensive vacation, especially one that involves travel abroad, comprehensive insurance is a must; **look for policies that include trip delay insurance,** which will protect you in the event that weather problems cause you to miss your flight, tour, or cruise. A few insurers will also sell you a waiver for preexisting medical conditions. Some of the companies that offer both these features are Access America, Carefree Travel, Travel Insured International, and Travel Guard International (☞ Insurance in Important Contacts A to Z, above).

FLIGHT

You should **think twice before buying flight insurance.** Often purchased as a last-minute impulse at the airport, it pays a lump sum when a plane crashes, either to a beneficiary if the insured dies or sometimes to a surviving passenger who loses his or her eyesight or a limb. Supplementing the airlines' coverage described in the limits-of-liability paragraphs on your ticket, it's expensive and basically unnecessary. Charging an airline ticket to a major credit card often automatically provides you with coverage that may also extend to travel by bus, train, and ship.

U.K. TRAVELERS

You can buy an annual travel insurance policy valid for most vacations during the year in which it's purchased. If you are pregnant or have a preexisting medical condition, make sure you're covered before buying such a policy.

TRIP

Without insurance, you will lose all or most of your money if you cancel your trip, regardless of the reason. Especially if your airline ticket, cruise, or package tour is nonrefundable and cannot be changed, it's essential that you **buy trip-cancellation-and-interruption insurance.** When considering how much coverage you need, look for a policy that will cover the cost of your trip plus the nondiscounted price of a one-way airline ticket should you need to return home early. Read the fine print carefully, especially sections that define "family member" and "preexisting medical conditions." Also **consider default or bankruptcy insurance,** which protects you against a supplier's failure to deliver. Be aware, however, that if you buy such a policy from a travel agency, tour operator, airline, or cruise line, it may not cover default by the firm in question.

L
LODGING

APARTMENT & VILLA RENTAL

If you want a home base that's roomy

enough for a family and comes with cooking facilities, **consider taking a furnished rental.** This can also save you money, but not always—some rentals are luxury properties (economical only when your party is large). Home-exchange directories list rentals—often second homes owned by prospective house swappers—and some services search for a house or apartment for you (even a castle if that's your fancy) and handle the paperwork. Some send an illustrated catalog; others send photographs only of specific properties, sometimes at a charge; up-front registration fees may apply.

BED-&-BREAKFASTS

The many 18th- and 19th-century houses in this region make it a natural area for bed-and-breakfast accommodations. The majority of B&Bs in Virginia and Maryland are Victorian structures with fewer than 10 rental units; a full or a Continental breakfast is typically included in the lodging rate, and rooms rarely have TV or telephone.

HOME EXCHANGE

If you would like to find a house, an apartment, or some other type of vacation property to exchange for your own while on holiday, **become a member of a home-exchange organization,** which will send you its updated listings of available exchanges for a year, and will include your own listing in at

least one of them. Arrangements for the actual exchange are made by the two parties involved, not by the organization (☞ Home Exchange *in* Important Contacts A to Z).

HOTELS & RESORTS

The large hotels of Baltimore, Richmond, Norfolk, and the Virginia suburbs of Washington, DC, are in competitive markets where standards and prices remain high. The beach and mountain resorts in the region are among the oldest, largest, and most expensive in the country.

M
MONEY

ATMS

CASH ADVANCES➤ Before leaving home, **make sure that your credit cards have been programmed for ATM use.**

TAXES

The sales tax in Virginia is 4.5%; in Maryland it is 5%.

N
NATIONAL PARKS

If you are a frequent visitor, senior citizen, or traveler with a disability, you can **save money on park entrance fees** by getting a discount pass. The Golden Eagle Pass can be a good deal if you plan to visit several parks during your travels. Priced at $25, it entitles you and your companions to free admission to *all* parks for a year. It does not cover additional park fees such as those for camping or parking.

Both the Golden Age Passport, for U.S. citizens or permanent residents 62 or older, and the Golden Access Passport, for travelers with disabilities, entitle holders to free entry to all national parks plus 50% off fees for the use of all park facilities and services except those run by private concessionaires. Both passports are free; you must show proof of age and U.S. citizenship or permanent residency (such as a U.S. passport, driver's license, or birth certificate) or proof of disability. All three passes are available at all national park entrances. Golden Eagle and Golden Access passes are also available by mail.

P
PACKING

Since porters and luggage trolleys can be hard to find, **pack light.** (Porters are, however, readily available for inbound international passengers at Baltimore Washington International Airport.)

Visitors to the mountains and the caverns of Virginia will want to prepare for colder than average temperatures. Hiking along the Appalachian Trail, even during spring and fall, frequently requires a coat. A sweater is in order for a visit to Luray Caverns or Shenandoah Caverns at all seasons of the year.

Where dress is concerned, Baltimore and Richmond are relatively conservative. In the more expensive restaurants, men are expected to wear jacket and tie;

in such public areas as art museums and theaters, patrons who are not neatly dressed and groomed are liable to feel conspicuous.

At the bay and ocean resorts, "formal" means long trousers and a collared shirt for men, and shoes for everybody. A tie might never get tied during a stay in these areas.

Bring an extra pair of eyeglasses or contact lenses in your carry-on luggage, and if you have a health problem, **pack enough medication** to last the trip. It's important that you **don't put prescription drugs or valuables in luggage to be checked,** as it could easily go astray.

LUGGAGE

Airline baggage allowances depend on the airline, the route, and the class of your ticket; ask in advance. In general, on domestic flights you are entitled to check two bags. A third piece may be brought on board, but it must fit easily under the seat in front of you or in the overhead compartment. In the United States, the FAA gives airlines broad latitude regarding carry-on allowances, and they tend to tailor them to different aircraft and operational conditions. Charges for excess, oversize, or overweight pieces vary.

SAFEGUARDING YOUR LUGGAGE➤ Before leaving home, **itemize your bags' contents** and their worth, and label them with your name, address, and phone number. (If you use your home address,

cover it so that potential thieves can't see it readily.) Inside each bag, **pack a copy of your itinerary.** At check-in, **make sure that each bag is correctly tagged** with the destination airport's three-letter code. If your bags arrive damaged—or fail to arrive at all—file a written report with the airline before leaving the airport.

PASSPORTS & VISAS

CANADIANS

No passport is necessary to enter the United States.

U.K. CITIZENS

British citizens need a valid passport to enter the United States. If you are staying for fewer than 90 days and traveling on a vacation, with a return or onward ticket, you probably will not need a visa. However, you will need to fill out the Visa Waiver Form, 1-94W, supplied by the airline.

It is advisable that you **leave one photocopy of your passport's data page** with someone at home and keep another with you, separated from your passport, while traveling. If you lose your passport, promptly call the nearest embassy or consulate and the local police; having the data page information can speed replacement.

S
SENIOR-CITIZEN DISCOUNTS

To qualify for age-related discounts, **mention your senior-**

citizen status up front when booking hotel reservations, not when checking out, and before you're seated in restaurants, not when paying the bill. Note that discounts may be limited to certain menus, days, or hours. When renting a car, **ask about promotional car-rental discounts**—they can net even lower costs than your senior-citizen discount.

STUDENTS ON THE ROAD

To save money, **look into deals available through student-oriented travel agencies.** To qualify, you'll need to have a bona fide student ID card. Members of international student groups are also eligible (☞ Students *in* Important Contacts A to Z, *above*).

T

TELEPHONES

LONG-DISTANCE

To avoid hotel surcharges, **use the long-distance services of AT&T, MCI, or Sprint.** Typically, you dial an 800 number in the United States.

TOUR OPERATORS

A package or tour to Virginia and Maryland can make your vacation less expensive and more hassle-free. Firms that sell tours and packages reserve airline seats, hotel rooms, and rental cars in bulk and pass some of the savings on to you. In addition, the best operators have local representatives available to help you at your destination.

A GOOD DEAL?

The more your package or tour includes, the better you can predict the ultimate cost of your vacation. Make sure you know exactly what is covered, and **beware of hidden costs.** Are taxes, tips, and service charges included? Transfers and baggage handling? Entertainment and excursions? These can add up.

Most packages and tours are rated deluxe, first-class superior, first class, tourist, or budget. The key difference is usually accommodations. If the package or tour you are considering is priced lower than in your wildest dreams, **be skeptical.** Also, **make sure your travel agent knows the accommodations** and other services. Ask about the hotel's location, room size, beds, and whether it has a pool, room service, or programs for children, if you care about these. Has your agent been there in person or sent others you can contact?

BUYER BEWARE

Each year a number of consumers are stranded or lose their money when operators—even very large ones with excellent reputations—go out of business. To avoid becoming one of them, take the time to **check out the operator**—find out how long the company has been in business and ask several agents about its reputation. Next, **don't book unless the firm has a consumer-protection program.** Members of the

USTOA and the NTA are required to set aside funds for the sole purpose of covering your payments and travel arrangements in case of default. Nonmember operators may instead carry insurance; look for the details in the operator's brochure—and for the name of an underwriter with a solid reputation. Note: When it comes to tour operators, **don't trust escrow accounts.** Although there are laws governing those of charter-flight operators, no governmental body prevents tour operators from raiding the till.

Next, **contact your local Better Business Bureau and the attorney general's offices** in both your own state and the operator's; have any complaints been filed? Finally, **pay with a major credit card.** Then you can cancel payment, provided that you can document your complaint. Always **consider trip-cancellation insurance** (☞ Insurance, *above*).

BIG VS. SMALL➤ Operators that handle several hundred thousand travelers per year can use their purchasing power to give you a good price. Their high volume may also indicate financial stability. But some small companies provide more personalized service; because they tend to specialize, they may also be more knowledgeable about a given area.

USING AN AGENT

Travel agents are excellent resources. In fact, large operators accept bookings made only through travel agents. But it's good to **collect brochures from several agencies** because some agents' suggestions may be skewed by promotional relationships with tour and package firms that reward them for volume sales. If you have a special interest, **find an agent with expertise in that area**; ASTA can provide leads in the United States. Don't rely solely on your agent, however; agents may be unaware of small-niche operators, and some special-interest travel companies only sell direct.

SINGLE TRAVELERS

Prices are usually quoted per person, based on two sharing a room. If traveling solo, you may be required to pay the full double-occupancy rate. Some operators eliminate this surcharge if you agree to be matched up with a roommate of the same sex, even if one is not found by departure time.

TRAVEL GEAR

Travel catalogs specialize in useful items that can **save space when packing** and make life on the road more convenient (☞ Travel Gear *in* Important Contacts A to Z). Compact alarm clocks, travel irons, travel wallets, and personal-care kits are among the most common items you'll find.

U
U.S.
GOVERNMENT

The U.S. government can be an excellent source of travel infor-

mation. Some of this is free and some is available for a nominal charge. When planning your trip, **find out what government materials are available.** For just a couple of dollars, you can get a variety of publications from the Consumer Information Center in Pueblo, Colorado (☞ Tour Operators *in* Important Contacts A to Z, *above*). Free consumer information also is available from individual government agencies, such as the Department of Transportation or the U.S. Customs Service.

W
WHEN TO GO

Spring brings horse racing to Baltimore, northern Virginia, and the Virginia Piedmont; the Preakness Stakes in Baltimore is a highly festive occasion, but many point-to-points and steeplechases are more interesting to watch and visit. Many public gardens are in full bloom and offer free visitations; garden clubs conduct tours of private properties throughout both states. In Shenandoah National Park, Skyline Drive overlooks a blooming panorama that is as stirring as the autumn colors. At Jarrettsville, north of Baltimore, visitors are welcomed at the Harvey Smith Ladew Topiary Gardens, nearly 20 acres of the finest sculpted gardens in the country. If you happen to travel to Baltimore in early May, don't miss Sherwood Gardens, well-known for hun-

dreds of thousands of tulips (planted freshly each year), azaleas, pansies, and blossoming trees.

Summer draws the largest numbers of visitors, particularly at Virginia Beach, Ocean City, and other popular resorts on the bay and the ocean. Historical buildings and museums in both states tend to schedule longer opening hours to serve the crowds. Baltimore's Inner Harbor has become an East Coast mecca for tourists and yachtsmen. On warm days, the promenade is filled with visitors from around the world.

Autumn brings spectacular colors in the foliage of the rolling Piedmont region of Virginia and the Catoctin Mountains west of Baltimore; the temperatures become more comfortable for hiking and biking. Equestrian events resume, and in Maryland the sailboat and powerboat shows in Annapolis and the Waterfowl Festival in Easton attract thousands of visitors in October and November.

Winter temperatures may make it too cold to swim, yet the major resorts continue to draw vacationers with seasonal peace and quiet at much lower off-season rates. Other travelers come for romantic seclusion at a bed-and-breakfast in a little town. Virginia was the first southern state to develop skiing commercially, and now both downhill and cross-country skiing are popular activities at resorts in the Shenandoah Valley and western Maryland. Elsewhere in the region heavy snow is rarely seen, and because local residents are unaccustomed to driving under such conditions, a snowfall is a serious traffic hazard in this area.

CLIMATE

Maryland enjoys a moderate climate with summer temperatures reaching into the 90s and winter days that usually stay in the 30s. The average temperature for the state is 64.4F°. The average rainfall is 41.6 inches, while snowfall is a modest 26.7 inches, except in the western Maryland mountains where it averages 82 inches. What follows are average daily maximum and minimum temperatures for major cities in Virginia and Maryland.

Climate

BALTIMORE

Jan.	43F	6C	May	74F	23C	Sept.	79F	26C
	29	− 2		56	13		61	16
Feb.	43F	6C	June	83F	28C	Oct.	67F	19C
	29	− 2		65	18		50	10
Mar.	52F	11C	July	86F	30C	Nov.	54F	12C
	36	2		70	21		40	4
Apr.	63F	17C	Aug.	85F	29C	Dec.	45F	7C
	45	7		67	19		31	− 1

NORFOLK

Jan.	49F	9C	May	76F	24C	Sept.	81F	27C
	34	1		58	14		65	18
Feb.	50F	10C	June	83F	28C	Oct.	70F	21C
	34	1		67	19		56	13
Mar.	58F	14C	July	88F	31C	Nov.	61F	16C
	40	4		72	22		45	7
Apr.	67F	19C	Aug.	85F	29C	Dec.	52F	11C
	49	9		70	21		36	2

1 Destination: Virginia & Maryland

THE PLANTER AND THE WATERMAN

THE PLANTER AND THE waterman are two curious human species—one long extinct, the other now endangered. Standing side by side, they evoke the histories and express the personalities of the bordering states of Virginia and Maryland, respectively.

Virginians have an extraordinary sense of place; a Virginian, if he lives in a house more than 50 years old, can tell you not only who built it but also about all the generations that have dwelt there up to his own. If the house is more than 150 years old, he will probably tell you Mr. Jefferson designed it (it's the spirit of history, not the letter, that Virginians cherish most).

The Virginia planter was very much connected to the land, at least to his own plantation. Many plantations in various stages of restoration, some of them still going concerns, can be toured today throughout the northern, eastern, and central parts of the state—Washington's august Mount Vernon, Jefferson's ingenious Monticello, and others less well-known but also memorable. The heirloom silver in their grand dining rooms and the dirt floors of their slave quarters are eloquent evocations of antebellum Virginia.

Two centuries of life on the plantation go far to explain the curious combination of hauteur and hospitality that marks the Virginian personality to this day. Eighteenth-century aristocrats such as William Byrd of Westover, or his friends the Carters (whose descendants still live at nearby Shirley) used to show off their wealth by throwing lavish parties and taking solicitous interest in the affairs of their dependents and other inferiors. The condescension of one class and the deference of another melded into a common courtesy that visitors can still hear echoes of, in the tone of gracious reserve used by museum docents and waitresses alike.

Of all the crops raised on Virginia plantations, the most abundant was tobacco; the least likely, liberty. Yet this paternalistic, slave-holding system cultivated the interests and ideas that promoted the American Revolution. The rising landed gentry of Virginia composed the House of Burgesses (its chamber is now on view inside the reconstructed capitol in Williamsburg), which gave the colonists a long preparatory exercise in self-government. Though ultimately the Revolution meant far more than the self-interest of a certain class, it was crucial that plantation owners, alienated from a Crown that coveted their landed wealth, formed the preeminent Virginia contingent of revolutionaries.

The hard-won liberty was inequitably distributed, of course. Although the "peculiar institution" of slavery was more peculiar to the Deep South states, such as South Carolina and Georgia, than to Virginia—James Madison and George Mason, both Virginians, included abolition in an early draft of the Constitution—when rancor over the issue erupted into the Civil War, the Old Dominion took the lead in the rebellion. The capital of the Confederacy was in Richmond; the top commander of the Confederate army was a Virginian, Robert E. Lee; and two-thirds of the battles in the Civil War were fought in this state. Petersburg and Richmond were especially ravaged, but few places lay untouched. Today every town has at least one amateur historian who can point out the scenes of skirmishes or tell which buildings survived and which burned down. As he talks, the listener hears the mournful tone of Virginia's rich historical consciousness; much of the lore takes the form of lamentation.

But though they revere the past, Virginians have decided they prefer building to brooding. Jamestown's scrappy Captain John Smith told the very first generation of Virginia gentlemen, "Who does not work does not eat," and in a gentler tone the defeated but resilient Lee, after Appomattox, wrote to his relations at Shirley, "There is nothing left for us but work." Such industry has brought about change, often of a nature that would have startled Lee.

Consequently, the physical landscape has been markedly altered, in many respects shamefully. On the rolling plains in Albemarle and Orange counties ("Mr. Jefferson's Country") and in the still-remote southwestern highlands (a region through which the Wilderness Road once coursed), the roadsides are littered with fast-food outlets and discount malls in dumbfounding profusion. Manassas, where nearly 29,000 men died in two Civil War battles, has only temporarily fended off the encroachment of luxury town homes. Yet many Virginians regard the landscape itself as their preeminent luxury, and violations of it offend their sense of place. Great tracts of Virginia are legally protected from such disfigurement: More than a million acres are dedicated to national and state parks, an official wilderness that includes mountains, marshes, forests, and seashore.

In the beginning, all of America was Virginia—even Plymouth Rock in Massachusetts Bay, where the Pilgrims landed in 1620, was officially in northern Virginia, for all of English North America had been so named, after Elizabeth I the Virgin Queen. Maryland, which was subtracted from Virginia and set up as its own colony in the 18th century, was named not for a reigning monarch but for a mere consort, Charles I's wife Queen Henrietta Maria. In the 3½ centuries since, it has lost border disputes with all its neighbors—Pennsylvania, West Virginia, and Virginia—to end up in its ungainly current shape, a quarter of the size of Virginia.

The map, however, shows only one aspect of history. Maryland's largest city, Baltimore, is almost three times as populous as any in Virginia, and Maryland has three-quarters the inhabitants of its grand southern neighbor. Though there is much less of it, Maryland has a terrain just as varied as Virginia's, from the mountains in the west through the central plateau to the jagged coast around the Chesapeake Bay. Virginia is also bounded by the bay, but the Chesapeake is by far the predominant feature in Maryland's geography, cleaving the Eastern from the Western shores. Divided by water, the inhabitants of the two shores have preserved quite different accents and customs. On the Western Shore itself, the Patuxent River separates Calvert and St. Mary's counties, which maintain subtly distinct identities and manners. On the Eastern Shore, the winding shoreline prolongs distance; in many cases it takes several times as long to drive to the next town as to sail to it across an inlet. If one were to straighten the shoreline of the Chesapeake Bay, it would stretch from Maryland to Hawaii with a few hundred miles to spare.

MOST MARYLANDERS lead terrestrial lives—they ride to work on subways and super-highways—but in spirit they are a waterborne people, bearing the legacy of a prominent maritime past. "Virginia is for lovers" was a hit promotional slogan in the 1970s; a Maryland T-shirt manufacturer matched it with a takeoff, "Maryland is for crabs." The second motto has the advantage, besides mild wit, of concrete truth, for crabs, along with oysters and other seafood from the Chesapeake Bay, remain a major Maryland industry.

Baltimore, on the Patapsco River, was an 18th- and 19th-century shipbuilding center, famous for the speedy Baltimore Clippers that were heavily employed in privateering, drawing the especial ire of the British in the early 1800s. When, in the War of 1812, British ships bombarded Fort McHenry in the harbor, Baltimoreans stood firm, and their flag-waving defiance inspired the "Star-Spangled Banner." Now Baltimore is the fifth-busiest port on the East Coast, and, since renovations and enhancements in the late '70s and early '80s, its Inner Harbor has been an attractive waterside recreation area, with shops, restaurants, and museums that draw millions of locals and out-of-towners alike each year.

Annapolis, on the banks of the Severn River, is one of the most important sailing cities in the world and home of the U.S. Naval Academy. All along both shores of the bay, towns such as St. Michaels, Tilghman's Island, and Solomons thrive on the weekend pleasures of yachtsmen.

Maryland's mythic hero—its cowboy, if you will—is the waterman, who prowls the Chesapeake in his skipjack, "drudging arshters" (dredging oysters) from the decks of America's last fleet of working sailboats. In the 1880s there were more than 1,500 of these native flat-bottomed sloops harvesting oysters with rakes and nets that were dragged over the oyster beds under sail power. Today, there are fewer than three dozen still plying the Chesapeake waters.

On one hand, in the great separateness of his life—spending days and nights on the water with his colleagues, and returning home to an isolated bay-side or island village—the waterman is an anomaly in a state where half the population is concentrated in the Baltimore metropolitan area. But in another respect, the waterman provides a rich symbol of contemporary Maryland society: not in the manner in which he sets off to work, but in the variety of the catch he hauls back to the dock. Maryland has always been a land of diversity.

It is said that Maryland was founded as a Catholic colony. In one sense this is true, in that Cecil Calvert, the second Lord Baltimore, who organized the first expedition of colonists in 1633, was a member of the Church of Rome; half the members of that expedition were also Catholic. But Puritans and Anglicans were made welcome, too, a courtesy that was not reciprocated in most of the other English colonies. Maryland was, in fact, the first colony to enact legislation guaranteeing freedom of religion.

Diversity has been cause for turmoil. During the Civil War the state was dangerously ambivalent. Sitting below the Mason–Dixon line, with an economy based equally on agriculture and industry, Maryland found its popular sentiment divided between the agrarian South and the industrial North. The consensus was, in the tradition of tolerance, for compromise: to preserve the Union somehow without coercing the South. There was rioting (and the first bloodshed of that war) when Union troops appeared in Baltimore, and President Lincoln saw fit to incarcerate some city officials, including the mayor of the city and Francis Scott Key's grandson, an action that was strategically effective but probably unconstitutional. The state faced itself on the field of battle when the First Maryland Regiment of the Union army fought the First Maryland Regiment of the Confederate army at Front Royal, Virginia.

The planter and the waterman: One is patrician, landed, and gregarious; the other plebeian, afloat, and solitary. Both are enterprising and jealous of their independence, but they have proved to be congenial neighbors.

Between Virginia and Maryland, nature carved out the Chesapeake Bay, and politics carved out the District of Columbia. Maryland teeters between the cultures of North and South; it has been called the northernmost southern state and the southernmost northern state, with the efficiency of the North and the graciousness of the South. Virginia, by contrast, is quintessentially southern. It is tempting to draw further distinctions: Virginians are gracious, Marylanders fractious; Virginians are tragic, Marylanders sassy; Virginians are stalwart, Marylanders mercurial. There is plenty of evidence to disprove all such generalizations. Nevertheless, such comparisons help us to understand both states. Virginia and Maryland are best visited in tandem.

WHAT'S WHERE

Northern Virginia

Much more than a satellite of the nation's capital, Northern Virginia is a virtual repository of Colonial and Civil War history. Alexandria's Old Town has an inordinate number of historic buildings; Fredericksburg has a 40-block National Historic District; and Arlington, Fairfax, and Loudon counties are sprinkled with historic sites and monuments such as Mount Vernon, Arlington Cemetery, and the Manassas battlefield.

Shenandoah Valley and the Highlands

Lovers of the outdoors, take note: Here lie Shenandoah National Park, the scenic Skyline Drive and Blue Ridge Parkway, and the isolated, rugged Highlands—site of seven state parks, three national parks, and six national forests. Purple-tinted mountain ranges, vast stands of multicolor hardwood trees, and stunning vistas characterize the valley; to the southwest, the Highlands are studded with gorges such as the Cumberland Gap. Also within the region are historic Lexington and quiet Roanoke and Abingdon—both cultural magnets on a small scale.

Richmond and the Piedmont

Richmond, capital of the commonwealth and former capital of the Confederacy, is not only full of historic sites; it is also one of the South's preeminent art cities and a major industrial center. West of Richmond, the Piedmont consists of Virginia's central section of rolling plains, dotted with small towns and vineyards. Aside from Richmond, the most prominent city in this region is Charlottesville, where Monticello stands as one of the many monuments left by Thomas Jefferson.

Williamsburg, Jamestown, Yorktown

Colonial Williamsburg, a recreated 18th-century American city complete with historic buildings, working shops, and costumed interpreters, is Virginia's most visited—and most unusual—attraction. Nearby are two other historical treasures: Jamestown Island, where the first permanent settlers made their home; and Yorktown, site of the final major battle in the American War of Independence. For anyone with limited time in Virginia, these are must-sees.

Hampton Roads Area and the Eastern Shore

This region is not easy to characterize: Hampton Roads—where the James, Elizabeth, and Nansemond rivers meet—is surrounded by small towns such as the historic settlements of Hampton and Portsmouth; Newport News, builder of the Navy's biggest nuclear ships; the port town of Norfolk; and the busy resort town of Virginia Beach. The Eastern Shore, which extends south from Maryland, is a largely undisturbed area of tiny towns and abundant wildlife, including wild ponies.

Baltimore

Known as the jewel of the Patapsco River, Baltimore is a busy port city with a newly revitalized tourist appeal. Lively Inner Harbor, with its constellation of attractions such as the National Aquarium, is in many ways the heart of the city, though historic Charles Street is the more established part of town.

Frederick and Western Maryland

Rugged, scenic mountains dominate the landscape of Western Maryland, framing cities such as Frederick and Cumberland; walling pastoral valleys, state forests, and parks; and even setting the stage for a popular train excursion, the Western Maryland Scenic Railroad. Once crossed by the nation's first pioneers on their westward journey, these mountains are rich with remnants of an earlier time; today you can still hike along a towpath that remains from the Chesapeake & Ohio (C&O) Canal—the region's main trade route in the mid-19th century.

Annapolis and Southern Maryland

Maryland traces its origins to the western shore of the Chesapeake Bay, where English colonists arrived in the 1600s. Today, Annapolis, the state capital, is rich with Colonial architecture and history. Tobacco fields, once the livelihood of early colonists, still blanket the gentle landscape of the southern part of the state.

Maryland's Eastern Shore

Separated from mainland Maryland by the Chesapeake Bay and bounded on the east by the Atlantic Ocean, this peninsula is a land apart. Here, marshy wildlife refuges, isolated islands, and rivers busy with fishermen and sailors set the stage for a quieter way of life.

PLEASURES AND PASTIMES

American History

As two of our nation's original colonies, Virginia and Maryland offer a vast assortment of historical attractions, from entire re-created colonial towns to Civil War battlefields to remnants of routes that the early pioneers followed on their westward treks. Explore Colonial beginnings in Virginia's Williamsburg or Maryland's Historic St. Mary's City; walk through neighborhoods that look virtually unchanged from the 18th and 19th century in Richmond, Fredericksburg, Baltimore, and Frederick; or stand on the battlefields of Yorktown, Antietam, or Manassas, where Americans gave their lives for their country. At Mount Vernon and Monticello you can step into the homes—and the minds—of two of the country's most important former presidents; in Maryland, you can follow the region's former trade route by walking the route of the historic C&O Canal, now a national park.

Biking and Hiking

The three regions of Maryland and Virginia—coastal plain, Piedmont, and mountains—present cyclists and hikers with an abundance of choices. National and regional trails such as the famed Appalachian Trail cross both states. In Virginia, the 500-mi section of the Trans-America Bicycle Trail extends from Breaks Interstate Park at the western fringe of the state to Yorktown on the coast; in addition, a 280-mi segment of the Maine-Richmond and Richmond-Florida coastal tracks crosses the state. In Maryland, trails, canal towpaths, and even old railroad routes are popular biking and hiking routes. Multiday treks are organized by several companies.

National Parks

From the mountains to the seashore, Virginia and Maryland are home to a plethora of scenic and historical national parks. In Virginia's Shenandoah Mountains lies Sykline Drive, a popular 105-mi route that winds through Shenandoah National Park. In Maryland's smaller Catoctin Mountains sits the aptly named Catoctin Mountain Park, home of Camp David, the presidential retreat. Virginia's massive George Washington National Forest is easily accessible from Washington, DC. The Potomac River, the waterway that divides Maryland and Virginia, is the route of the 185-mi linear park, the C&O Canal National Historical Park, popular with hikers and bikers.

Seafood

The Chesapeake Bay, the estuary that separates mainland Maryland and Virginia from their respective Eastern Shores, offers diners a cornucopia of seafood. Steamed hard-shell crabs cracked on paper-covered tables, to the accompaniment of plenty of beer, are as traditional as crab cakes, broiled or fried, and seasoned with Old Bay spices or garlic. Cream of crab soup, Maryland crab soup, crab balls, crab dip, and crab imperial are just a few of the other odes to this six-legged creature. Also on the menu, in season, are bluefish, rockfish, oysters, and mussels.

Wineries

Some of the East Coast's most prolific wine regions are bounded by Virginia and Maryland. The rolling landscape of the Piedmont plateau, which stretches from central Virginia through central Maryland, is dotted with small, family-owned wineries that offer tours and tastings. Both states celebrate autumn with wine festivals in which guests—with paid admission—receive a wine glass to sample wines. Maryland's Wine Festival, at the Carroll County Farm Museum, combines crafts, gourmet food, and entertainment in one bacchanalian weekend.

FODOR'S CHOICE

No two people will agree on what makes a perfect vacation, but it's fun and helpful to know what others think. We hope you'll have a chance to experience some of Fodor's Choices while visiting Virginia and Maryland. For detailed information about each entry, refer to the appropriate chapters in this guidebook.

Historic Buildings and Monuments

★ In Sharpsburg, Maryland, **Antietam National Battlefield**—setting of the bloody 1862 Civil War battle—remains largely free of modern intrusion and is a must-see for Civil War enthusiasts.

★ **Manassas National Battlefield (Bull Run)**, in Manassas, Virginia, was the site of two important Civil War battles—both victories for the Confederates.

★ In Richmond, Virginia, Thomas Jefferson modeled the **Virginia State Capitol** after a Roman temple in the South of France.

★ **Monticello,** the impressive home of Thomas Jefferson in Charlottesville, Virginia, reflects the varied interests of the president and statesman.

★ Overlooking the Potomac River and the Maryland shore, Fairfax County's **Mount Vernon** was the home of George Washington and is now the most visited historic house museum in the United States.

★ At Arlington National Cemetery, in Arlington, Virginia, the **Tomb of the Unknown Soldier** is the site of a solemn changing of the guard every half hour or hour, depending on the season.

★ In Annapolis, Maryland, the wooden dome of the **Maryland State House**—the oldest state capitol in continuous legislative use—dominates the colonial skyline of Annapolis.

★ Baltimore's early 19th-century brick and earthen **Fort McHenry** saw battle during the War of 1812 and was the setting from which Francis Scott Key wrote the "Star-Spangled Banner."

Historic Restorations

★ At the village of **Appomattox Court House,** in Appomattox County, Virginia, Confederate General Lee surrendered his troops to U.S. General Grant; the village has since been restored to its 1865 appearance.

★ Once the capital of Virginia, the restored village of **Colonial Williamsburg** is the next best step to turning back the hands of time.

★ With four genuine 18th-century farmsteads, the **Museum of American Frontier Culture** in Staunton, Virginia, recreates the beginnings of agrarian life in North America.

★ In St. Mary's County, archaeologists have been unearthing the 800-plus-acre remains of **Historic St. Mary's City,** Maryland's first capital.

Hotels

★ At **The Homestead,** a luxurious redbrick hotel nestled among the beautiful mountains in Hot Springs, Virginia, guests can still relax in a spa built in the late 19th century. $$$$

★ **Stone Manor,** a 19th-century stone house in Middletown, Maryland, offers guests a relaxing but elegant retreat in the rolling farmlands of Western Maryland. $$$$

★ Gracious service and a great location are the trademarks of the **Williamsburg Inn,** where the rooms are individually furnished in the English Regency style. $$$$

★ Adjacent to Baltimore's Inner Harbor, the eight-story, redbrick **Harbor Court Hotel** is known for its English country house decor and first-rate service. $$$

★ On the Miles River in St. Michaels, Maryland, the **Inn at Perry Cabin** has metamorphosed from a Colonial Revival farm into an elegant inn where guests can peruse books in a cozy library or stroll among spectacular gardens. $$$

★ On Kent Island, in Stevensville, Maryland, the 19th-century **Kent Manor Inn** sits on a 226-acre working farm whose ownership can be traced back to the mid-17th century. $$$

★ Private baths, maid service, and no curfew are among the unusual assets of the **YMCA of Tidewater,** a modest lodging in a residential and historic neighborhood of Norfolk, Virginia. $

Museums

★ At the new **American Visionary Art Museum** in Baltimore, some of the best creations of housewives, mechanics, people with disabilities, and other unconventional artists are displayed in seven galleries.

★ The history of the bay, boat building, fishing, and other traditions are explored at the **Chesapeake Bay Maritime Museum,** in St. Michaels, Maryland.

★ The **Chrysler Museum** in Norfolk, Virginia, is considered one of the best art museums in the nation, with a collection that includes works by Rubens, Gainsborough, Renoir, and Picasso.

★ Seagoing vessels and the people who occupied them are the focus of the **Mariners Museum** in Newport News, Virginia.

★ Among the important works on display at Richmond's **Virginia Museum of Fine Arts** are paintings by Goya, Renoir, Monet, and van Gogh.

★ The **Ward Museum of Wildfowl Art,** in Salisbury, Maryland, traces the evolution of decoys as an art form, with environmental exhibits and a recreated Eastern Shore marshland.

Restaurants

★ A view of Baltimore's Inner Harbor, an English country house ambience, and an innovative menu have earned **Hamptons** widespread acclaim. $$$$

★ Daily specials at **Eastern Standard,** in Charlottesville, Virginia, include rainbow trout stuffed with shiitake mushrooms, wild rice and fontina cheese, and oysters cooked in a champagne and caviar sauce. $$$

★Large urns, Corinthian columns, and an entire wall of frames and half frames lend a grand, Roman air to Norfolk's **La Galleria,** where the excellent food is—of course—Italian. *$$$*

★Near Johns Hopkins University campus in Baltimore, the dining room of the **Polo Grill** is decidedly masculine, and the food—grilled veal with wild mushrooms in Madeira sauce, for example—is superb. *$$$*

★Candles and whitewashed walls lend a mystical air to the cellar dining rooms of Baltimore's **Tio Pepe,** whose diverse Spanish menu consistently draws crowds. *$$$*

★With the atmosphere of a Napa Valley country inn, the **Trellis,** in Williamsburg, Virginia, offers guests a choice of five cozy dining rooms and a constantly changing selection of imaginative dishes; grilled seafood steals the limelight. *$$$*

★Decorated with Currier and Ives and Audubon prints, the **Waterwheel,** in Warm Springs, Virginia, is part of a complex of five restored buildings, including a gristmill that dates from 1700. *$$$*

★A Baltimore institution since 1926, **Haussner's** offers more than 100 menu choices—German and otherwise—in a restaurant-cum-gallery showcasing works by Rembrandt, Van Dyck, and Whistler, among others. *$$*

★Perhaps the best of the many Vietnamese restaurants in Arlington, **Queen Bee** has cordial service and such savory dishes as green-papaya salad with sausage and beef jerky. *$*

★At **Stoney's Seafood House** in Broomes Island, Maryland, the dining room overlooks Island Creek River, and the fist-size back-fin crab cakes are the best around. *$*

Sights

★Virginia's 105-mi-long **Skyline Drive** winds up the Blue Ridge in Shenandoah National Park, offering motorists multiple vantage points for spectacular scenery, especially in the fall.

★The **Natural Bridge of Virginia,** called the "Bridge of God" by Native Americans, is an impressive limestone arch that supports part of a highway and draws many tourists.

★One of the largest naval bases in the world, the **Norfolk Naval Base** in Norfolk, Virginia, is home to more than 115 ships of the Second Fleet.

★At the **C&O National Historical Park** in Great Falls, Maryland, a 185-mi towpath popular with hikers and cyclists was once trodden by mules pulling barges in the now-defunct C&O Canal.

★**Assateague Island National Seashore,** a 37-mi-long barrier island on the border of Virginia and Maryland, is home to pristine beaches, wild ponies, deer, and 300 species of birds and waterfowl.

★At **Calvert Cliffs State Park,** in Lusby, Maryland, visitors can scavenge for fossils that range in age from 15 to 20 million years old, against a spectacular backdrop of towering cliffs.

GREAT ITINERARIES

A week is ample time to cover the major attractions in Maryland and Virginia, including both the historical and coastal sites. If you're only planning to visit select attractions in either state, a few days will suffice. The best times to visit are fall and spring, when the temperature and humidity are down.

Because Civil War attractions are among the most compelling reasons to visit Virginia and Maryland, we have provided a customized Civil War itinerary that covers the standouts. You may tailor the tour to last 8 or 10 days, depending on your time frame.

Maryland

IF YOU HAVE 3 DAYS➤ ☷ **Baltimore,** the geographical and cultural center of Maryland, is a must-see for first-time visitors. At least a day is required to visit the major sites, many of which are clustered around the colorful Inner Harbor. Spend day two exploring Maryland's Colonial past in ☷ **Annapolis,** the state capital, and nearby **Londontown,** once a thriving tobacco port. Head farther south to view some of Maryland's earlier history at historic **St. Mary's City;** or cross the expansive Chesapeake Bay to witness the water-based lifestyle of the Eastern Shore, stopping in small towns such as **Easton** and **St. Michaels.**

IF YOU HAVE 5 DAYS➤ Spend two days in ⊞ **Baltimore** before heading south to ⊞ **Annapolis.** Historic **St. Mary's City,** ⊞ **Solomons Island,** and other towns in St. Mary's and Calvert counties will take care of day four. On your last day, either cross the Chesapeake Bay to visit the Eastern Shore or head west to ⊞ **Frederick,** a vibrant city nestled in the foothills of the Catoctin Mountains.

Virginia

IF YOU HAVE 3 DAYS➤ If you have only three days to visit Virginia, start in the northern part of the state. Spend a day exploring the sights of ⊞ **Alexandria** and **Mount Vernon,** then take a nighttime drive across the river for a glimpse of the illuminated monuments of Washington, DC. If you are a nature lover, head out toward the Shenandoah Valley on your second day (especially lovely in the fall, when the foliage is at its peak), then drive southwest along Skyline Drive. Leave early in the day so that you'll have time to end your drive in ⊞ **Charlottesville,** with enough time to see Monticello. Spend your third day visiting ⊞ **Richmond** and **Petersburg.** If history is more your passion than the great outdoors, head to Richmond on day two, then visit ⊞ **Williamsburg** and its surroundings on your third day.

IF YOU HAVE 5 DAYS➤ If you have five days, spend your first day in Northern Virginia, visiting the Shenandoah Valley and ⊞ **Charlottesville** on your second day. If you enjoy the mountains, you can use your third day to continue along the Blue Ridge Parkway to ⊞ **Roanoke.** Otherwise, head to ⊞ **Richmond** on day three. Spend day four in the ⊞ **Williamsburg** area. Visit ⊞ **Hampton** and the surrounding area on your final day or, if you feel like relaxing, head toward ⊞ **Chincoteague** on the Eastern Shore, cross the bridge, and kick back at the **Assateague Island** wildlife refuge.

Virginia and Maryland

IF YOU HAVE 7 DAYS➤ A week allows time to explore the Colonial and maritime pasts of Virginia and Maryland and to visit two major cities, Baltimore and Richmond. Spend your first two days exploring ⊞ **Baltimore,** with its Inner Harbor sights, art museums, and historic homes and neighborhoods. On day three visit Maryland's state capital, ⊞ **Annapolis,** rife with Colonial neighborhoods and home to the U.S. Naval Academy. Spend the next two days experiencing Virginia's Colonial past in ⊞ **Williamsburg, Jamestown** and **York.** Head farther south along the coast to **Norfolk,** home of the Norfolk Naval Base and a great place to explore Virginia's maritime history. ⊞ **Richmond,** Virginia's capital and the capital of the Confederacy, beckons on the last day, with its stately streets, mansions, museums, and monuments.

Civil War Tour

On April 17, 1861, Virginia seceded from the Union and doomed itself to become a major battleground. Thus, much of this tour is in Virginia, with a brief foray across the Mason–Dixon line into Maryland. Richmond is the tour's hub.

DURATION: 8 OR 10 DAYS➤ **1 Day:** Start at Hampton, on the Virginia Peninsula, where, in 1861, Union general George McClellan launched his drive toward Richmond. Across the channel is Fort Monroe—a Union stronghold, where Confederate president Jefferson Davis was imprisoned.

2 Days: Drive northwest on I–64 up the peninsula to Richmond and visit the Museum and White House of the Confederacy and the Richmond National Battlefield Park. Proceed 20 mi south on I–95 to Petersburg, the city that was under an extended siege by Grant's army. Visit Petersburg National Battlefield and the Siege Museum.

2 or 3 Days: From Richmond proceed north on I–95 to Fredericksburg. Detour to see four Civil War battlefields at Fredericksburg and Spotsylvania National Military Park. Then return to I–95 and drive northwest to Manassas National Battlefield (Bull Run), where the Confederates won two important victories. Return to Richmond.

2 Days: Take I–66 north from Richmond into Arlington and see Arlington National Cemetery and Arlington House (General Lee's home for 30 years, before the Union army confiscated it and turned the grounds into the cemetery). Then head north on I–270 into Maryland. North of Frederick catch Route 34 out of Boonsboro and follow it to the Antietam National Battlefield. Not far to the south, at Harpers Ferry, you can walk the historic streets and see the Federal Arsenal where John Brown and his band of followers attempted their uprising. Return to Richmond.

2 or 3 Days: Drive southwest from Richmond on Route 360 to Route 460. Proceed west into Appomattox and see the courthouse where Lee surrendered to Grant. From Appomattox you can continue west on Route 460 to Lynchburg's Monument Terrace, a Civil War memorial. Then take Route 29 north to Route 60 northwest into Lexington, where you can visit the Lee Chapel and Museum and the Virginia Military Institute Museum with its displays on Stonewall Jackson.

Information: ☞ Chapters 2, 3, 4, and 6.

FESTIVALS AND SEASONAL EVENTS

WINTER

EARLY DEC.➤ The **Virginia Thanksgiving Festival** (☎ 804/272–3226), at Berkeley Plantation in Charles City, reenacts the original Thanksgiving of December 4, 1619, with performances of period music and the participation of costumed colonists and Native Americans. The **Old Town Christmas Candlelight Tour** (☎ 703/838–4200) of Alexandria, Virginia, is a visit to historic houses for light refreshment and performances of period music of the season.

DEC. 31➤ **New Year's Eve** (☎ 410/332–4191) festivities in Baltimore include a concert at the Harborplace amphitheater and a midnight fireworks display over Inner Harbor. **First Night Annapolis** (☎ 410/268–8553) is a family-oriented, non-alcoholic, affordable celebration of the lively arts. The state capital is transformed into a stage with more than 150 performances by more than 40 local acts in historic homes, public buildings, schools, churches, and even shop windows.

LATE JAN.➤ **Lee-Jackson Day** (☎ 540/463–3777), the third Monday of the month, commemorates the birthdays of the Confederate generals Robert E. Lee (Jan. 19) and Stonewall Jackson (Jan. 21) with celebrations all over Virginia, especially in Lexington, where both men lived and taught. The **Annapolis Heritage Antiques Show** (☎ 410/222–1919), in Annapolis, Maryland, is one of the major mid-Atlantic events of its kind, and lasts three days.

MID-FEB.➤ The **ACC Crafts Fair** (☎ 410/659–7144) in Baltimore draws more than 800 exhibitors for three days of trading.

LATE FEB.➤ **George Washington's Birthday** (☎ 703/838–5005) is celebrated in Alexandria, Virginia, with a parade—175 floats and marching units—and a reenactment of a Revolutionary War skirmish at Ft. Ward nearby.

SPRING

MAR.➤ **Military Through the Ages** (☎ 804/229–1607), in Williamsburg, Virginia, uses authentic weapons in a series of reenactments of battles from the Middle Ages to the 20th century.

LATE MAR.➤ **Maryland Days Weekend** (☎ 410/862–0990) of St. Mary's City, Maryland, commemorates the founding of the colony at its original birthplace. A celebration (☎ 410/889–6060) on a smaller scale takes place at the courthouse in Baltimore.

MID-APR.➤ The **Azalea Festival** (☎ 804/622–2312) in Norfolk, Virginia, salutes NATO with battleship tours, a parade, an air show, outdoor concerts, a ball, and the crowning of a queen from the year's honored NATO member nation.

LATE APR.➤ **Historic Garden Week** (☎ 804/644–7776) throughout Virginia is a time when grand private homes, otherwise closed to the public, open their doors to visitors. **Southern Maryland Celtic Festival and Highland Gathering** (☎ 410/257–9003), which takes place in Calvert County, features piping and fiddling competitions, dancing, games, and the foods and crafts of Scotland, Wales, Ireland, and England.

EARLY MAY➤ **Virginia Gold Cup** (☎ 540/253–5001) steeplechase horse races, held near Middleburg, have been among the most prominent social and sporting events of Virginia since the 1920s.

MID-MAY➤ **Maryland Preakness Celebration** (☎ 410/542–9400) in Baltimore is a weeklong festival including, among the more than 100 events: parades, street parties, fund-raisers, and hot-air-balloon races. The celebration culminates in the annual running of the Preakness Stakes at Pimlico Racetrack in Baltimore, on the third Saturday in May. **Civil War Living History Weekend** (☎ 540/740–3101), a reenactment in New Market, Virginia, of a battle of 1864, is the oldest and possibly the largest event of its kind in the country.

LATE MAY➤ **Commissioning Week** (☎ 410/263–6933) at the United States Naval Academy in Annapolis, Maryland, is a time of dress parades, traditional stunts such as the Herndon Monument Climb, and a spectacular aerobatics demonstration by the Navy's famous **Blue Angels** precision flying team.

EARLY JUNE➤ **Folklore Week** (☎ 540/297–6066) at Smith Mountain Lake State Park near Roanoke, Virginia, brings demonstrations of Appalachian crafts and skills. The **Eastern Shore Chamber Music Festival** (☎ 410/745–2750) in Easton, Maryland, consists of two weekends of classical music performances at historical sites around town.

MID-JUNE➤ The **Deer Creek Fiddler's Convention** (☎ 410/876–2667), a twice-annual gathering at the Carroll County Farm Museum in Westminster, attracts some of the nation's finest bluegrass entertainers and fiddlers.

LATE JUNE➤ The **Hampton Jazz Festival** (☎ 804/838–4203) in Hampton, Virginia—an event of national importance—brings together top performers in the various styles of jazz. The **Virginia State Horse Show** (☎ 804/228–3200), with a full program of competitions among Arabians, Half-Arabians, Morgans, saddlebreds, and others, takes place in Richmond, Virginia.

JULY 4➤ **Independence Day** (☎ 410/837–4636) celebrations in Baltimore culminate in a major show of fireworks over the Inner Harbor.

LATE JULY➤ The **Pony Swim and Auction** (☎ 804/336–6161) in Chincoteague, Virginia, is the annual roundup of wild ponies from Assateague Island; the foals are auctioned off to support the volunteer fire department.

EARLY AUG.➤ The **Virginia Highlands Festival** (☎ 540/628–8141) in Abingdon celebrates Appalachia with displays and demonstrations of arts and crafts, exhibitions of animals, sales of antiques, and performances of country music. The **Governor's Cup** (☎ 301/862–0380) overnight yacht race, from Annapolis to St. Mary's City, Maryland, draws more than 300 sailboat participants and culminates in a day-long party at St. Mary's College. The **Seafood Feast-I-Val** (☎ 410/228–3575) in Cambridge, Maryland, is an all-you-can-eat extravaganza on the shore of the Choptank River.

LATE AUG.➤ The **Wine Festival** (☎ 410/269–5140) in the Plains features tastings of vintages from 20 Virginia wineries, plus grape stomping and musical entertainment. The **Maryland State Fair** (☎ 410/252–0200), in Timonium, is 10 days of horse racing, livestock judging, live entertainment, agricultural displays, farm implements, and plenty of food.

EARLY SEPT.➤ **Defender's Day** (☎ 410/962–4290) celebrations at Fort McHenry in Baltimore commemorate—with music, drilling, mock bombardment, and fireworks—the battle that led to the writing of the national anthem.

MID-SEPT.➤ The **Apple Harvest Festival** (☎ 540/665–8060) in Winchester, Virginia, is a weekend of arts and crafts to celebrate the traditions of an important regional crop.

LATE SEPT.➤ The **Virginia State Fair** (☎ 804/228–3200), in Richmond, is a classic conglomeration of carnival rides, livestock shows, displays of farm equipment, and lots of food for sale. The **Maryland Wine Festival** (☎ 410/876–2667), at the Carroll County Farm Museum, Westminster, brings representatives from nearly a dozen of Maryland's wineries to display their products, offer tastings, and give seminars on winemaking.

EARLY–MID-OCT.➤ The **Autumn Glory Festival** (☎ 301/334–1948), held at various western Maryland locations (Garrett County), is a celebration of the peak fall foliage, and includes state banjo and fiddle championships, a Tournament of Bands, firefighters' parades, Oktoberfest festivities, arts, crafts, and antiques. The **United States Sailboat and Powerboat Shows** (☎ 410/268–8828), the world's largest events of their kind, take place in Annapolis, Maryland.

LATE OCT.➤ **Yorktown Day** (☎ 804/898–3400) observances in Yorktown, Virginia, celebrate the Colonial victory in the American War of Independence (October 19,

1781) with 18th-century tactical demonstrations, patriotic exercises, and a stirring wreath-laying ceremony. The **Virginia Festival of American Film** (☎ 804/924–3378), in Charlottesville, Virginia, is becoming a major event in the motion picture industry, with screenings of important new movies and appearances by their stars.

EARLY NOV.➤ The **Waterfowl Festival** (☎ 410/822–4567) in Easton, Maryland, involves decoy exhibitions, carving demonstrations, duck-calling contests, and retriever exercises during a three-day weekend.

LATE NOV.➤ **Waterfowl Week** (☎ 804/336–6122) in Chincoteague, Virginia, is when the National Wildlife Refuge opens nature trails to motor vehicles, allowing visitors to watch the Canada and snow geese on their southward migration.

LATE NOV.–EARLY JAN.➤ The **Winter Festival of Lights** (☎ 301/699–2545), at Prince George's County (near Washington, DC), features a spectacular display of more than 150,000 multicolor lights in a drive-through setting. Also on the docket are a glittering giant tree, a lighted train station and carousel, and Santa and his reindeer in lights.

2 Northern Virginia

Historical treasures abound between the District of Columbia and the Blue Ridge Mountains. Star attractions include Mount Vernon, Arlington Cemetery, Manassas National Battlefield, and the Chesapeake & Ohio Canal National Historic Park; there are also several important historic homes and plantations. Old Town Alexandria boasts more than 2,000 18th- and 19th-century buildings; and Fredericksburg's pre-Revolutionary buildings attest to the lasting influence of the Washington family.

NORTHERN VIRGINIA, WHICH EXTENDS from the District of Columbia westward to the Blue Ridge Mountains, is unlike any other section of the state. Much of it has been subsumed into the official and residential life of the nation's capital—and has prospered as a result. The affluent and cosmopolitan northern Virginians may look more to Washington than to the rest of the commonwealth for direction, yet they take pride in being Virginians and in protecting the historic treasures they hold in trust for the rest of the nation.

Old Town Alexandria appears unsuburbanized; its more than 2,000 18th- and 19th-century buildings are listed collectively in the National Register of Historic Places. Fairfax and Arlington counties thrive as satellites of Washington (Tysons Corner in Fairfax County is said to have more commercial office space than Miami, Florida, and serves more than 400 corporations employing 70,000 people) and contain some of America's most precious acreage, Mount Vernon and Arlington Cemetery included. Fredericksburg, only an hour from the nation's capital, seems farther away: It's a quiet, well-preserved southern town, with a 40-block National Historic District. But Fredericksburg was once the scene of bloody conflict—as was Manassas (Bull Run), 26 mi from Washington, the site of some of the most significant battles of the Civil War. In 1994 this area almost became home to a Disney history theme park. It would have meant big business for this region (the state approved incentives to encourage the project), but opponents to the development prevailed, raising concerns about the Disney-scale traffic and questions about the company's cultural sensitivity to history. Instead, the gracious lifestyle of the Old South survives, and the diversions here still include fox hunting and steeplechasing.

Exploring Northern Virginia

Northern Virginia is generally defined as the area south of the Maryland border, running from Arlington westward to Leesburg and continuing south to the southern borders of Greene, Orange, Spotsylvania, and Caroline counties.

ALEXANDRIA

Numbers in the margin correspond to points of interest on the Old Town Alexandria map.

The city of Alexandria maintains an identity distinct from that of Washington, DC, across the Potomac. Established in 1749, the city dwarfed Georgetown—Washington's oldest neighborhood—in the days before the Revolution. Visitors today can glimpse remnants of its past in the historic district of Old Town Alexandria. The main arteries of this district are Washington Street (the parkway as it passes through town) and King Street. Most points of historic interest are on the east (Potomac) side of Washington Street. Visit them on foot if you are prepared to walk for 20 blocks or so; parking is usually scarce, but parking garages within walking distance of the Visitor's Bureau (☞ *below*) provide some relief. On Saturday, parking costs $2 all day; it's $3 after 6 PM.

1 The **Alexandria Convention and Visitor's Bureau,** where you should begin your tour, will issue a 24-hour parking permit for the two-hour metered zones and will provide a walking-tour map. The bureau also has a translation service and can issue tickets for museums and local events. The bureau is in Ramsay House, the home of the town's first postmaster and Lord Mayor, William Ramsay. The white clapboard structure was built in 1724 in Dumfries (about 25 mi south along the Potomac) and moved here in 1749, and is believed to be the oldest house in Alexandria. Ramsay was a Scot, as a swatch of his tartan on the door proclaims. ⊠ *221 King St.,* ☎ *703/838–4200.* ☉ *Daily 9–5.*

② The **Stabler-Leadbeater Apothecary Museum,** at the corner of Fairfax and King streets, is the second-oldest apothecary in the country and was patronized by George Washington and the Lee family. Here, on October 17, 1859, Lieutenant Colonel Robert E. Lee received the orders to move to Harpers Ferry, West Virginia, to suppress John Brown's insurrection. The shop now houses a small museum of 18th-century apothecary paraphernalia, including a fine collection of about 800 apothecary bottles. ⊠ *105–107 S. Fairfax St.,* ☎ *703/836–3713.* ▣ *$2.* ☉ *Mon.–Sat. 10–4, Sun. 1–5.*

③ Except for a six-decade hiatus, the redbrick **Old Presbyterian Meeting House** has been an active house of worship since 1774, when Scottish pioneers established the church; a Presbyterian congregation still meets at 8:30 and 11 on Sunday mornings. The **Tomb of the Unknown Soldier of the American Revolution** lies in a corner of the churchyard, where many prominent Alexandrians—including Dr. James Craik, physician to both Washington and Lafayette—are interred. If the church door is locked during visiting hours, walk around back to the office at the right rear of the churchyard to locate a staff member. ⊠ *321 S. Fairfax St.,* ☎ *703/549–6670.* ▣ *Free.* ☉ *Weekdays 9–5, weekends when staff available.*

④ The reddish-brown Greek Revival **Athenaeum** stands in contrast to its many redbrick Federal neighbors. Built in 1851 as a bank, it now houses the gallery of the Northern Virginia Fine Arts Association, which shows the work of local, national, and international artists. This block of Prince Street between Fairfax and Lee streets is known as **Gentry Row,** after the 18th- and 19th-century inhabitants of its imposing three-story houses. ⊠ *201 Prince St.,* ☎ *703/548–0035.* ▣ *Free.* ☉ *Wed.–Fri. 11–4, Sat. 11–1, Sun. 1–4.*

⑤ West of Gentry Row, the block of Prince Street between Lee and Union streets is lined with humble but very photogenic redbrick houses. Most of them were built by 19th-century sea captains—hence the name **Captain's Row.** According to legend, the cobblestones that pave the street were laid by Hessian mercenaries in the employ of the British, who were then being held as prisoners of war.

⑥ About 180 artists and craftspeople have their studios (and sell their wares) in the **Torpedo Factory Art Center,** a renovated waterfront building where torpedo parts were manufactured during the two world wars. The center also houses exhibits of the city's archaeology program (one of the nation's largest and oldest) and laboratories where you can observe work in progress. ⊠ *105 N. Union St.,* ☎ *703/838–4565.* ▣ *Free.* ☉ *Daily 10–5. Archaeology section (☎ 703/838–4399): Tues.–Fri. 10–3, Sat. 10–5, Sun. 1–5.*

⑦ The Georgian-style **Carlyle House** (1753) was the manor house of the riverside estate of John Carlyle, a Scottish merchant who was one of Alexandria's founders. General Edward Braddock met here with five royal governors in 1755 to plan the strategy and funding of the early campaigns in the French and Indian War. The decor of the house re-

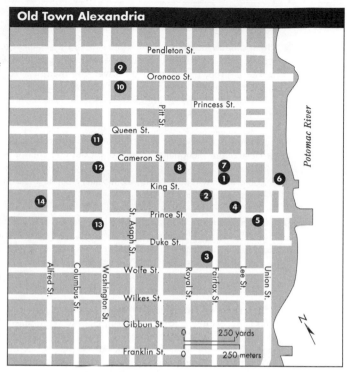

Old Town Alexandria

Alexandria
Convention
and Visitor's
Bureau, **1**

Athenaeum, **4**

Boyhood Home
of Robert E.
Lee, **9**

Captain's
Row, **5**

Carlyle
House, **7**

Christ
Church, **12**

Friendship Fire
House
Museum, **14**

Gadsby's
Tavern
Museum, **8**

Lee-Fendall
House, **10**

Lloyd
House, **11**

Lyceum, **13**

Old Presbyterian
Meeting
House, **3**

Stabler-
Leadbeater
Apothecary, **2**

Torpedo
Factory Art
Center, **6**

mains 18th-century, with the original woodwork, Chippendale furniture throughout, and decorative items that include Chinese export porcelain. An architectural exhibit on the second floor explains how the house was built. ⊠ *121 N. Fairfax St.,* ☎ *703/549–2997.* ⊑ *$3.* ☉ *Tues.–Sat. 10–4:30, Sun. noon–4:30.*

❽ Gadsby's Tavern Museum is a convincingly restored pair of buildings: a circa-1770 tavern, and a hotel that was built 22 years later. General Washington reviewed his troops for the last time from the steps of this building, and Lafayette was entertained here during his visit in 1824. The rooms in the tavern have been convincingly restored to look as they are believed to have looked in the 1770s. ⊠ *134 N. Royal St.,* ☎ *703/838–4242.* ⊑ *$3.* ☉ *Apr.–Sept., Tues.–Sat. 10–5, Sun. 1–5; Oct.–Mar., Tues.–Sat. 10–4, Sun. 1–4.*

❾ The **Boyhood Home of Robert E. Lee** is where Lee lived on and off for 13 years. The Georgian town house (1795) is furnished with antiques that reflect life in the 1820s. ⊠ *607 Oronoco St.,* ☎ *703/548–8454.* ⊑ *$3.* ☉ *Feb.–mid-Dec., Mon.–Sat. 10–4, Sun. 1–4.*

❿ Built in 1785 by an in-law of the Lee family, the **Lee-Fendall House** was the family's home until 1903. The interior reflects styles from a variety of periods and includes furniture that belonged to the family. The labor leader John L. Lewis lived here from 1937 to 1969. ⊠ *614 Oronoco St.,* ☎ *703/548–1789.* ⊑ *$3.* ☉ *Tues.–Sat. 10–4, Sun. noon–4.*

⓫ Lloyd House (1794) stands as a fine example of Georgian architecture. Now part of the Alexandria Library System, it houses a collection of rare books and documents related to city and state history. ⊠ *220 N.*

Washington St., ☎ *703/838–4577.* 🎫 *Free; tours on request if a docent is available.* 🕘 *Mon–Sat. 9–5.*

⑫ **Christ Church** looks much the same as it did when George Washington worshiped here. His pew and that of Robert E. Lee, who was confirmed in the church, are marked by silver commemorative plaques. The churchyard contains the graves of several Confederate dead. ✉ *118 N. Washington St.,* ☎ *703/549–1450.* 🎫 *Free; donation requested.* 🕘 *Mon.–Sat. 9–4, Sun. 2–4.*

NEED A
BREAK?
Sightseers may welcome the opportunity to stop for a pint of Guinness or Harp and a ploughman's lunch of pickles and cheese at **Murphy's Irish Pub** (✉ 713 King St., ☎ 703/548–1717). This brick-wall pub and restaurant, on two floors of an 18th-century building, resounds with an Irish sing-along at night.

⑬ The **Lyceum** is one of Alexandria's best examples of Greek Revival design. Since it was built in 1839, the structure has served as a library, a hospital, a residence, and an office building; in the 1970s it was restored and now houses three art galleries, a gift shop, and a museum of local history. ✉ *201 S. Washington St.,* ☎ *703/838–4994.* 🎫 *Free.* 🕘 *Mon.–Sat. 10–5, Sun. 1–5.*

⑭ The **Friendship Fire House Museum** occupies a building dating from 1855. According to local tradition, George Washington helped found the volunteer fire company in 1774 and served as its honorary captain. Among the early fire engines on display is one that Washington bought for the company for about $140—it was one of the finest of its time. ✉ *107 S. Alfred St.,* ☎ *703/838–3891.* 🎫 *Free.* 🕘 *Fri.–Sat. 10–4, Sun. 1–4.*

OFF THE
BEATEN PATH
GEORGE WASHINGTON MASONIC NATIONAL MEMORIAL – On display at Alexandria's George Washington Masonic National Memorial are furniture and regalia that Washington used while he was charter master of the local Masonic lodge. Exhibits demystify the international organization, explaining many of its traditions, aims, and activities. Every 45 minutes until 4 PM, an elevator tour takes visitors to the top of the 333-foot structure for a grand view of the town and nearby Washington. The memorial is a 15-minute walk from Washington Street, heading west on King Street; it can also be reached by DASH bus west on King Street (85¢ fare, exact change, includes transfer for return trip). ✉ 101 Callahan Dr., Alexandria, ☎ 703/683-2007. 🎫 Free. 🕘 Daily 9–5.

Dining and Lodging

$$$ ✗ **Gadsby's Tavern.** In the heart of Old Town Alexandria, this circa-1792 tavern gives visitors a taste of the decor, cuisine, and entertainment of Colonial days. As you dine, John Douglas Hall, dressed as a gentleman of the 18th century, performs on the lute and recounts the latest news and gossip of Colonial Virginia. The tavern was a favorite of George Washington, who is commemorated on the menu by George Washington's Favorite Duck, a cornbread-stuffed roast duck with fruit-and-Madeira sauce. Other period offerings include Colonial Game Pye (lamb, pork, and rabbit), Sally Lunn bread, and a rich English trifle. ✉ *138 N. Royal St.,* ☎ *703/548–1288. D, DC, MC, V.*

$$ ✗ **King Street Blues.** Not the place for power-lunching or princely wooing, this informal eatery just off King Street in the heart of Old Town is popular for its relaxed ambience and hearty but quirky southern menu. The whimsical neon and papier-mâché constructions create an ideal setting for the friendly, twentysomething waiters hustling around in T-shirts and shorts. Diners of all ages come to enjoy baked pecan-crusted catfish, Thai chicken and noodle salad, glazed pork chops, and the fish special of the day; wash your choice down with the excellent house beer. ⊠ *112 N. St. Asaph St.,* ☎ *703/836–8800. AE, D, DC, MC, V.*

$$ ✕ **Le Gaulois.** Scenes of southern France cover the white plaster walls
★ of this quiet country bistro. Gather around the dark-blue plastic-covered tables to sample pot-au-feu *gaulois* (a beef-and-chicken stew with whole vegetables) or cassoulet, a rich bean casserole with sausage and beef. More than half a dozen wines from France and California are available by the glass. ⊠ *1106 King St.,* ☎ *703/739–9494. AE, D, DC, MC, V. Closed Sun.*

$$ ✕ **Taverna Cretekou.** Whitewashed stucco walls and brightly colored
★ macramé tapestries bring a Mediterranean ambience to the center of Old Town. On the menu are lamb *exohikon* (baked in a pastry shell) and swordfish kabob. All the wines served are Greek, and in the warm months you can dine in the canopied garden. A buffet brunch is served on Sundays. ⊠ *818 King St.,* ☎ *703/548–8688. AE, D, MC, V. Closed Mon.*

$ ✕ **Hard Times Café.** Recorded country-and-western music and framed photographs of Depression-era Oklahoma set the tone at this casual, crowded, two-floor hangout. Three kinds of chili—Texas (spicy), Cincinnati (sweeter), and vegetarian—are served. Texas chili is typically served over spaghetti—a "Chili-mac"; Cincinnati comes with cheese, onions, beans, or all three. A tuna sandwich, chicken salad, and chicken wings are alternatives to the more combustive cuisine. About 30 domestic and Mexican beers are available. ⊠ *1404 King St.,* ☎ *703/683–5340. Reservations not accepted. AE, MC, V. No lunch Sun.*

$$$$ 🏨 **Holiday Inn Old Town.** The distinctive mahogany-paneled lobby of
★ this well-known chain hotel suggests a men's club in the city, and guest-room decor follows this motif, with hunting-and-horse prints on the walls. Bathrooms have a marble floor and tub, and the phones have computer-modem capabilities. The hotel chain has decreed this member to be one of its 20 best worldwide, in large part because of the extraordinary service: Staff will bring exercise bicycles to rooms on request and provide touring bicycles for use in the area without charge. Guests in some rooms on the fifth and sixth floors can enjoy a picturesque roofscape of 18th- and 19th-century buildings and the river beyond—but only in the winter, after the trees have shed their leaves. ⊠ *480 King St., 22314,* ☎ *703/549–6080 or 800/368–5047,* 𝔽𝔸𝕏 *703/684–6508. 227 rooms. Restaurant, lobby lounge, indoor pool, barbershop, beauty salon, sauna, parking (fee). AE, D, DC, MC, V.*

$$$$ 🏨 **Morrison House.** This small hotel in Old Town is decorated in Federal style throughout, the rooms are furnished with four-poster beds, and afternoon tea is served as it would have been 200 years ago—though the four-story redbrick building has been here only since 1985. English butlers will unpack guests' bags on request, and the marble bathrooms have telephones and hair dryers. ⊠ *116 S. Alfred St., 22314,* ☎ *703/838–8000,* 𝔽𝔸𝕏 *703/684–6283. 42 rooms, 3 suites. 2 restaurants, lobby lounge. AE, DC, MC, V.*

$$$ 🏨 **Holiday Inn Eisenhower Metro.** Location is this hotel's calling card: It's in a suburban area 1½ mi from the Amtrak station and within walking distance of the Eisenhower Metro station. Decor is standard modern: light-color walls and curtains with shades of mauve and teal. The rooms facing east overlook Old Town Alexandria. ⊠ *2460 Eisenhower Ave., 22314,* ☎ *703/960–3400,* 𝔽𝔸𝕏 *703/329–0953. 201 rooms, 1 suite. Restaurant, bar, indoor pool, exercise room. AE, D, DC, MC, V.*

Nightlife and the Arts

Bars and Pubs

Murphy's Irish Pub (⊠ 713 King St., ☎ 703/548–1717) has boisterous entertainment and, in winter, a blazing fire.

Jazz

Two Nineteen (⊠ 219 King St., ☎ 703/549–1141) has jazz upstairs and a bar in the basement.

Outdoor Activities and Sports

Biking

The **Mount Vernon Bicycle Trail** (☎ 703/285–2598), 19 mi of asphalt, runs along the shore of the Potomac and through Alexandria (bike maps sold at Ramsay House).

The **Alexandria Park Planning** office (☎ 703/838–5040) has maps for biking around Alexandria.

Shopping

Old Town Alexandria is dense with antiques shops—many of them quite expensive—that are particularly strong in the Federal and Victorian periods. The Visitor's Bureau (☞ *below*) has maps and lists of the dozens of stores.

Side Trip to Mount Vernon and Environs

Numbers in the margin correspond to points of interest on the Northern Virginia map.

⑮–⑱   *8 mi southwest of Alexandria; 48 mi northeast of Fredericksburg.*

First in war, first in peace, and first stop on a tour of the Virginia suburbs of Washington, DC, is George Washington—his house, that is, at **★ ⑮ Mount Vernon,** 16 mi south of the nation's capital. It is the most visited historic house museum in the United States after the White House. Washington considered himself a farmer, and although his farmhouse was a formal one, none of the embellishments disguised its working nature; in the ornate dining room, for example, guests ate at a simple trestle table assembled from boards and sawhorses. The long portico with its eight columns faces east across the Potomac; as the riverbank opposite remains forested, the views match the period authenticity of Mount Vernon's interior. About 25% of the furnishings are original; the others are carefully selected and authenticated antiques. The outbuildings, including kitchen and stable, have been precisely restored. Beyond them, George and Martha Washington were laid to rest in a tomb on the estate. ⊠ *Rte. 235 and George Washington Memorial Pkwy.,* ☎ *703/780–2000.* ☜ *$8.* ◷ *Apr.–Aug., daily 8–5; Sept.–Oct., daily 9–5; Nov.–Feb., daily 9–4; Mar., daily 9–5.*

The former home of Major Lawrence and Nellie Custis Lewis, the nephew and grandaughter of George and Martha Washington, the circa-**⑯** 1800 **Woodlawn Plantation** is appropriately grandiose. The Federal-style mansion was designed by William Thornton (architect of the Capitol) to resemble Kenmore, Lewis's boyhood home in Fredericksburg, and offers a commanding view of the river and countryside. Woodlawn Plantation stands atop Grey's Hill, 3 mi to the west of Mount Vernon, on land Washington gave as a wedding present to his nephew. Furnished to accommodate a growing family and to entertain notable guests, the house is now owned by the National Trust for Historic Preservation, and still has many original and period furnishings. The well-maintained formal gardens include the largest collection of Heritage Roses on the East Coast. ⊠ *U.S. 1 and Rte. 235,* ☎ *703/780–4000.* ☞ *$6.* ☉ *Mid-Feb.–Dec., daily 9:30–4:30; Jan. and early Feb., weekends 9:30–4:30. Closed Thanksgiving, Dec. 25.*

⓱ On the grounds of the Woodlawn Plantation, but having no connection with the Washington family, is Frank Lloyd Wright's **Pope-Leighey House,** a 1930s Usonian home constructed of cypress, brick, and glass. In contrast to Woodlawn mansion, the Pope-Leighey House was designed to satisfy the post–World War II housing needs of middle-class Americans. Scheduled to be torn down in 1964 for highway construction, it was dismantled by the National Trust for Historic Preservation, reassembled here, and furnished with original Wright pieces. A $600,000 restoration completed in 1996 included dismantling the house again and moving it 30 feet uphill to firmer ground, as well as adding air-conditioning to help preserve the original artwork and contents of the house. Linger awhile in order to appreciate the subdued beauty of this utilitarian home. Together, Woodlawn and Pope-Leighey houses offer a unique opportunity to compare two celebrated architects at the same site. ⊠ *U.S. 1 and Rte. 235,* ☎ *703/780–4000.* ☞ *$6. Woodlawn/Pope-Leighey combination: $10.* ☉ *Mar.–Dec., daily 9:30–4:30; Jan.–Feb., weekends 9:30–4:30.*

⓲ **Gunston Hall** was the home of George Mason, who helped frame the Constitution but then refused to sign it because it failed to prohibit slavery, to restrain adequately the powers of the federal government, and to include a bill of rights. The interior of the house, with its carved woodwork ranging from Chinese to Gothic style, has been meticulously restored, using paints made from the original formulas and with carefully carved replacements for the intricate mahogany medallions in the moldings. The grounds, whose formal gardens are filled with boxwood hedges, may look familiar; the last scene of the movie *Broadcast News* (1987) was filmed here, by the gazebo. Gunston Hall is on the Potomac River, 6 mi south of Mount Vernon, but unless you're traveling by boat it's a 15-mi drive via Routes 1 and 242. ⊠ *Rte. 242,* ☎ *703/550–9220.* ☞ *$5.* ☉ *Daily 9:30–5.*

En Route   Don't miss the stirring panorama of the famous buildings and monuments of Washington, DC, that can be seen on the short drive north from Alexandria to Arlington on the George Washington Memorial Parkway. At Memorial Bridge, cross the river into Washington and turn back again to Virginia to make the most impressive approach to the Arlington National Cemetery. Behind you in Washington is the Lincoln Memorial; ahead of you, high atop a hill, is Robert E. Lee's Arlington House; a little below it Jacqueline Kennedy Onassis is interred, next to the eternal flame marking the grave of John F. Kennedy.

ARLINGTON COUNTY

Numbers in the margin correspond to points of interest on the Northern Virginia map.

Connected to Washington, DC, by three bridges, Arlington is practically part of the nation's capital; in fact, much of what is now Arlington was originally planned by Congress to be part of DC. In the 18th century the Custis family (as in Martha Dandridge Custis, who later married George Washington) had extensive land holdings in the area. Since the end of World War I, Arlington has evolved from a farming community to headquarters for computer, communications, and defense industries.

Northern Virginia

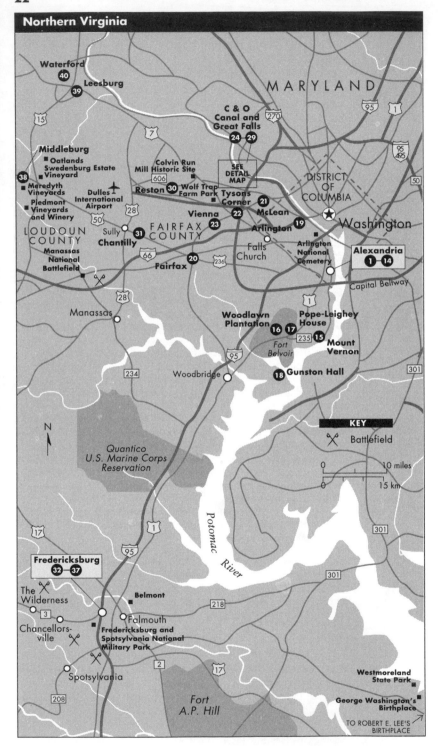

Waterford
40
Leesburg
39

MARYLAND

270
95
1

C & O
Canal and
Great Falls
24 29

15

7

Middleburg
■ Oatlands
Swedenburg Estate
Vineyard
38
■ Meredyth
Vineyards
■ Piedmont
Vineyards
and Winery

Colvin Run
Mill Historic Site
606
Reston 30
Wolf Trap
Farm Park

SEE
DETAIL
MAP

DISTRICT
OF
COLUMBIA

Dulles
International
Airport
50
28

Tysons
Corner
22
21
McLean
McLean

Washington

50

LOUDOUN
COUNTY
Manassas
National
Battlefield

Sully
Chantilly
31

FAIRFAX
COUNTY

Vienna
23
Arlington
19

Falls
Church
Arlington
National
Cemetery

Alexandria
1 14

66
236
Fairfax
20

Manassas

28

Woodlawn
Plantation

Pope-Leighey
House
16 17
235 15
Fort
Belvoir
Mount
Vernon

Capital Beltway

1

95

234

Woodbridge

Gunston Hall
18

301

N

Quantico
U.S. Marine Corps
Reservation

KEY

✂ Battlefield

0   10 miles
0   15 km

17

1

301

95

Fredericksburg
32 — 37

301

The
Wilderness
3
Chancellors-
ville

Belmont

Falmouth
Fredericksburg and
Spotsylvania National
Military Park

218

Potomac River

2

Spotsylvania

17

Westmoreland
State Park

208

Fort
A.P. Hill

George Washington's
Birthplace

TO ROBERT E. LEE'S
BIRTHPLACE

Arlington

⓳ *4 mi north of Alexandria (via George Washington Memorial Pkwy.).*

Once home to Robert E. Lee, the city of Arlington is now home to the Pentagon as well as the nation's most famous cemetery.

The **Pentagon,** headquarters of the Department of Defense, is a construction marvel. Completed in 1943 after only two years of construction, the immense, five-sided building is as wide as three Washington Monuments laid end to end. It has 17½ mi of corridors, 7,754 windows, 691 water (drinking) fountains, and a 5-acre interior courtyard. Twenty-three-thousand people, both military and civilian, work there. A 75-minute tour takes you down hallways lined with pictures of military leaders, scale models of Navy ships and Air Force craft, and to the Hall of Heroes, where you'll find the names of all recipients of the Congressional Medal of Honor. *Off I-395 (take Metro to the Pentagon station).* ☎ *703/695–1776.* ▣ *Free.* ☉ *Tours: Weekdays every ½ hr, 9:30–3:30. A photo ID is required. Closed federal holidays.*

Thousands of veterans are interred beneath simple white headstones at **Arlington National Cemetery** (☎ 703/607–8052). Among the many famous Americans who lie here are William Howard Taft, Oliver Wendell Holmes, George C. Marshall, Joe Louis, and the brothers John and Robert Kennedy. In and around the Tomb of the Unknowns are the graves of men and women who lost their lives in the two world wars, Korea, and Vietnam, as well as soldiers of the Gulf War. The tomb is guarded constantly by members of the Old Guard: First Battalion (reinforced), 3rd Infantry. The changing-of-the-guard ceremony takes place every half hour from 8 AM to 7 PM, April to September, and hourly October to March. ☎ 703/697–2131. ▣ *Free.* ☉ *Oct.–Mar., daily 8–5; Apr.–Sept., daily 8–7.*

Within Arlington National Cemetery is **Arlington House,** where Robert E. Lee lived for 30 years until his work obliged him to leave the proximity of the Union capital. During the Civil War, the Union confiscated the estate when Arlington began to function as a cemetery. The massive Greek Revival house, with its templelike appearance, is furnished with antiques and reproductions. The view of Washington from the portico is as magnificent as the sight of the house from the bridge. ☎ 703/557–0613. ▣ *Free.* ☉ *Oct.–Mar., daily 9:30–4:30; Apr.–Sept., daily 9:30–6.*

Perhaps the best way to see Arlington National Cemetery is by taking the **Tourmobile** narrated-tour buses, which set out from the visitor center and stop at Arlington House, the Tomb of the Unknowns, and the Kennedy graves. If you want to spend time at any one place, you can catch the next tour bus when you're ready to move on. ☎ 202/554–7020. ▣ *$4.* ☉ *Buses operate 8:30–6 in summer, 9:30–4:30 in winter.*

At press time (March 1997), a new museum, appropriately called the **Newsmuseum,** was scheduled to open in April 1997, with various news-related exhibits, video monitors, a theater, and a "News Café" with access to the Internet. The museum was expected to adjoin Freedom Park, where statues and historical artifacts honor journalists who have died in the line of duty and others who have overcome political, racial, and sexual oppression. ✉ *1101 Wilson Blvd.,* ☎ *703/284–3725. Call for details on admission and opening hrs.* ☉ *Park: Daily dawn–dusk.*

Dining and Lodging

$$$$ ✕ **The View.** Picture windows on three sides of this restaurant on the 14th floor of the Key Bridge Marriott Hotel more than fulfill the promise of its name: The Washington Monument and the spires of Georgetown University are among the most prominent landmarks to be seen across the Potomac. The interior is heavily burgundy—the carpeting, the leather banquettes, the wallpaper, even the ceiling. Prominent entrées have been broiled lobster, served out of its shell with an unusual cucumber flan; and New York strip steak, broiled in Jack Daniels sauce and served in medallions with hot peppers. This is a grazing restaurant; many of the entrées are also available as appetizers, in one form or another. A salad of seasonal fruit is served warm with chicken and quail. At the popular Sunday brunch buffet, swordfish and oysters are among the more than 50 items offered. ⊠ *Key Bridge Marriott, 1401 Lee Hwy.,* ☎ *703/524–6400. AE, D, DC, MC, V. No lunch.*

$$ ✕ **Queen Bee.** Arlington's Little Saigon area has many noteworthy Viet-
★ namese restaurants, but this is one of the best. The atmosphere is unassuming, the service is cordial, and the food is always excellent. Spring rolls are moist and delicately flavorful. The green-papaya salad with sausage and beef jerky, and the Saigon pancake—accented with a mix of crab, pork, and shrimp—are two other reasons that diners often wait in line for a table. ⊠ *3181 Wilson Blvd.,* ☎ *703/527–3444. MC, V.*

$ ✕ **Red Hot & Blue.** Photos of famous customers, such as John Grisham
★ and B. B. King, adorn the walls of this joint where patrons inhale (among other dishes) pork ribs and shoulders prepared Memphis-style—smoked over a pit, then spiced or sauced—or pulled-pig sandwiches, all served with a choice of beans, cole slaw, potato salad, or french fries. ⊠ *1600 Wilson Blvd.,* ☎ *703/276–7427. Reservations not accepted. AE, MC, V.*

$$$$ ⊟ **Holiday Inn National Airport.** This is your basic, familiar high-rise Holiday Inn, set just off the highway, with modern, cheerful decor and a convenient location a mile from the airport. Rooms have the standard furnishings in pastels or earth tones. The casual Fred's Place, suitable for family dining, has an American menu. ⊠ *1489 Jefferson Davis Hwy., 22202,* ☎ *703/416–1600 or 800/465–4329,* 🖷 *703/416–1615. 295 rooms, 11 suites. Restaurant, bar, pool, racquetball. AE, D, DC, MC, V.*

$$$$ ⊟ **Marriott Crystal Gateway.** This elegant, modern Marriott caters to the business traveler and those who want to be pampered. Its two towers rise 17 stories above the highway; inside you'll find marble, blond wood, Oriental touches, and lots of greenery. Rooms have contemporary styling. ⊠ *1700 Jefferson Davis Hwy., 22202,* ☎ *703/920–3230 or 800/228–9290,* 🖷 *703/271–5212. 563 rooms, 131 suites. 3 restaurants, lobby lounge, 1 indoor and 1 outdoor pool, sauna, spa, exercise rooms, nightclubs. AE, DC, MC, V.*

$$$$ ⊟ **Ritz-Carlton Pentagon City.** In the middle of a vast shopping mall, five minutes from National Airport, this hotel greets guests with Persian carpets and an 18th-century grandfather's clock. Upstairs, the rooms have either a rose or a blue color scheme, with silk drapes, silk floral-pattern wallpaper, and framed botanical prints. The furniture is reproduction Federal. The building's insulation from the noise of air traffic and its lavish appointments together make it a paragon among airport hotels. ⊠ *1250 S. Hayes St., 22202,* ☎ *703/415–5000,* 🖷 *703/415–5060. 345 rooms, 42 suites. 2 restaurants, bar, indoor pool, sauna, steam room, exercise room. AE, D, DC, MC, V.*

$$ ⊞ **Best Western Arlington.** There are essentially two hotels situated here on 6 acres: the three units of a 30-year-old low-rise building that was renovated in 1986, and an executive tower built in 1987. The tower combines shades of rose and light green in a typically modern decor; the rooms of the low-rise tend to be a bit darker, with rust carpeting and touches of mauve. All rooms have ample seating space, and some have pullout sofa beds. The hotel is just 2 mi from the District of Columbia, and there's easy access to I–395. Shuttle service to the nearby National Airport is free. ⊠ *2480 S. Glebe Rd., 22206,* ☎ *703/979–4400 or 800/426–6886,* FAX *703/685–0051. 325 rooms. Restaurant, pool, exercise room, laundry service. AE, D, DC, MC, V.*

Nightlife and the Arts

MUSIC

Whitey's (⊠ 2761 Washington Blvd., Arlington, ☎ 703/525–9825) is crowded, noisy, and irresistible—a blues dive with a loyal following of diverse ages and backgrounds.

Iota (⊠ 2832 Wilson Blvd., ☎ 703/522-8340) has a broad range of live music nightly. You'll hear everything from alternative rock to folk.

THEATER

Gunston Arts Center (⊠ 2700 S. Lang St., Arlington, ☎ 703/358–6960) is home to the Teatro de la Luna, American Century Theater, and other groups.

Outdoor Activities and Sports

The Arlington Parks and Recreation Bureau (☎ 703/358–4747, TTY 703/358–4743) has a free map of the **Arlington County Bikeway System,** available on request.

Shopping

The **Fashion Centre at Pentagon City** (⊠ 1100 S. Hayes St., at the Pentagon City Metro stop, ☎ 703/415–2400) has three shopping levels and a food court level. Stores include the department stores Macy's (☎ 703/418–4488) and Nordstrom (☎ 703/415–1121), as well as gift stores, such as the Disney Store (☎ 703/418–0310) and the Museum Company (☎ 703/415–3838).

Crystal City's street-level and underground stores, on the Metro line, include conventional shops as well as the more unusual, such as Geppi's (⊠ 1675 Crystal Square Arcade, ☎ 703/413–0618), which sells comic-book and baseball-card collectibles.

FAIRFAX COUNTY

Numbers in the margin correspond to points of interest on the Northern Virginia map.

In 1694 King Charles II of England gave the land that would become Fairfax County to seven English noblemen. It became a county in 1741 and was named after Thomas, sixth Lord of Fairfax. Widespread tobacco farming, the dominant industry in the 18th century, eventually depleted the land and helped steer the county toward a more industrial base. Today Fairfax County has one of the highest per capita incomes in the country.

The **Arts Council of Fairfax County** (☎ 703/642–0862) acts as a clearinghouse for information about performances and exhibitions throughout northern Virginia.

Outdoor Activities and Sports

BIKING

The **Washington & Old Dominion Railroad Regional Trail** (☎ 703/729–0596) follows the roadbed of the "Virginia Creeper" tracks from Shirlington (near I–95) to Purcellville, stretching 46 mi through the Allegheny foothills.

TENNIS

The **Fairfax County Park Authority** (☎ 703/246–5700) maintains a directory of tennis courts within its jurisdiction.

Fairfax

㉟ *10 mi west of Arlington.*

Its central location makes Fairfax a convenient place to stay while visiting Fairfax County's sights, as well as the rest of Northern Virginia.

Dining and Lodging

$$$$ ✕☷ **The Bailiwick Inn.** Red brick and green shutters distinguish this bed-and-breakfast in an 1812 building that stands opposite the historic Fairfax County Courthouse. The rooms, named for eminent Virginians, have antique and reproduction furniture, period detail, and 1990s bathrooms. Four rooms have a fireplace; two have a Jacuzzi. The location at the meeting of Routes 123 and 236 is particularly convenient for business travelers. The restaurant offers an expensive but tasty prix-fixe menu. Room rates include a full breakfast. ✉ *4023 Chain Bridge Rd., 22030,* ☎ *703/691–2266 or 800/366–7666,* 𝐅𝐀𝐗 *703/934–2112. 13 rooms, 1 suite. Restaurant. AE, MC, V.*

Nightlife and the Arts

George Mason University Center for the Arts (☎ 703/993–8888) frequently holds jazz, classical, opera, dance, and theater performances by premier artists.

THEATER

The Harris Theater (☎ 703/993–2503) of George Mason University presents student drama performances.

McLean

㉑ *15 mi northeast of Fairfax, 15 mi northwest of Alexandria.*

☀ At **Claude Moore Colonial Farm,** a family in costume re-creates the activities of a tenant farm in the 1770s—planting, cultivating, and harvesting crops, and tending the livestock. Seasonal harvest celebrations and 18th-century market fairs are among the special events. ✉ *6310 Georgetown Pike, McLean,* ☎ *703/442–7557.* ☷ *$2. (Fees slightly higher for special events.)* ☽ *Apr.–mid-Dec., Wed.–Sun. 10–4:30.*

Nightlife and the Arts

Sitting Duck (✉ Evans Farm Inn, 1696 Chain Bridge Rd., McLean, ☎ 703/356–8000), an English pub, has a piano bar Friday through Sunday.

Tysons Corner

㉒ *11 mi northwest of Alexandria.*

Essentially a commercial area with an assortment of office buildings, hotels, restaurants, shopping centers, and two major malls, Tysons Corner is a fashionable address in the Washington, DC, area.

Dining and Lodging

$$$ ✕ **Clyde's of Tysons Corner.** A branch of a popular Georgetown pub, Clyde's has four art deco dining rooms that offer a choice of styles. The Palm Terrace has high ceilings and lots of greenery; another room is a formal dining room. The long, eclectic menu always includes fresh fish, often in such preparations as trout Parmesan. The wine list is equally long. Quality is high, service attentive. ⊠ *8332 Leesburg Pike,* ☎ *703/734–1900. AE, D, DC, MC, V.*

$$$$ ⊡ **The Ritz-Carlton.** Rooms here are large, with antique furniture, 19th-century lithographs, and the trademark simplicity of Ritz-Carlton hotels. The lobby lounge feels like a men's club, with dark paneled walls and safari animal bronzes; the innovative bar menu includes pizzettes with goat cheese and smoked duck. The elegant restaurant, at the foot of a grand double staircase, serves contemporary American cuisine. On the third floor, the brand-new Eden Spa has everything from a juice bar to a pool with lap lanes. Concierge-level guests have access to an exclusive club with sweeping views of the Virginia countryside. ⊠ *1700 Tysons Blvd., McLean,* ☎ *703/506–4300,* FAX *703/506–4305. 366 rooms, 33 suites. Restaurant, lobby lounge, minibars, room service, indoor lap pool, spa, health club, business services, meeting rooms, parking (free). AE, D, MC, V.*

$$$ ⊡ **Doubletree Hotel.** Formerly a Ramada, this hotel 10 mi west of Arlington has a convention center and guest rooms with contemporary furnishings. The restaurant, Horizons, serves popular American fare; there's also an Au Bon Pain restaurant offering sandwiches and fresh baked bread. About half the rooms are especially suited for business travelers, with computer dataports and large work stations. ⊠ *7801 Leesburg Pike (Rte. 7 and I–495), Falls Church,* ☎ *703/893–1340,* FAX *703/847–9520. 405 rooms, 14 suites. 2 restaurants, lounge, indoor pool, sauna, exercise room. AE, D, DC, MC, V.*

Nightlife

Clyde's of Tysons Corner (⊠ 8332 Leesburg Pike, Vienna, ☎ 703/734–1900) is famous in the DC area as a gathering place for unattached professionals.

Shopping

Tysons Corner Center (⊠ 1961 Chain Bridge Rd.), at the junction of Routes 7 and 123, contains 240 retailers, including Bloomingdale's (☎ 703/556–4600), Nordstrom (☎ 703/761–1121), and Hecht's (☎ 703/893–4900) department stores. Kids flock to the Disney Store (☎ 703/448–8314) and F. A. O. Schwarz (☎ 703/917–9600).

The **Galleria at Tysons II** (2001 International Dr.), across the street from the Tysons Corner Center, has 125 stores, including Saks Fifth Avenue (☎ 703/761–0700) and Neiman Marcus (☎ 703/761–1600).

Vienna

㉓ *13 mi west of Alexandria.*

Ↄ At **Wolf Trap Farm Park,** a national park devoted to the performing arts, drama, dance, and music performances are given in a partially covered amphitheater during the warmer months, and in The Barns—two 18th-century barns transported from upstate New York—the rest of the year. Children's programs are emphasized, including mime, puppets, animal shows, music, drama, and storytelling. During the summer, free performances take place at the outdoor Theater in the Woods (☎ 703/255–1827) Monday through Friday in July, and Tuesday through Saturday in August; reservations are required. For several days in September, the International Children's Festival brings together performers from the United States and abroad. This is one of the major performing-arts venues in the greater Washington area. Picnicking is permitted at wood tables on the grounds. ⊠ *1551 Trap Rd., Vienna,* ☎ *703/255–1860.* 🎫 *Varies with event.*

Shopping

The first area branch of the New York jeweler **Tiffany & Co.** (⊠ 8045 Leesburg Pike, Rte. 7, ☎ 703/893–7700) is a few minutes from the mall in Fairfax Square.

The C&O Canal and Great Falls

Numbers in the margin correspond to points of interest on the C&O Canal and Great Falls map.

㉔–㉙ *20 mi northwest of Alexandria.*

In the 18th and early 19th centuries, the Potomac River was the main transport route between vital Maryland ports and the seaports of the Chesapeake Bay. But though it served as an important link with the country's western territories, the Potomac had a major drawback for a commercial waterway: Rapids and waterfalls along its 190 mi made navigation of the entire distance by boat impossible.

To make the flow of goods from east to west more efficient, engineers proposed that a canal with elevator locks be built parallel to the river. George Washington founded a company to build the canal, and in 1802 his firm opened the Patowmack Canal on the Virginia side of the river.

In 1828 Washington's canal was replaced by the Chesapeake & Ohio Canal, known as the C&O. Stretching from downtown Washington to Cumberland, Maryland, the C&O moved barges through 75 locks, and by the mid-19th century it carried a million tons of goods a year. But by the time it had opened, newer technology was already starting to make canal systems obsolete. The Baltimore & Ohio Railroad—which opened the same day as the C&O—finally put the canal out of business in 1924. After Palisades residents defeated a 1950s proposal to

★ build a highway over it, the canal was reborn as the **Chesapeake & Ohio National Historical Park.**

㉔ The towpath along the canal in **Georgetown** passes traces of that area's industrial past, such as the Godey Lime Kilns near the mouth of Rock Creek, as well as the fronts of numerous houses dating from 1810. From mid-April through early November, mule-drawn barges leave for 90-minute trips from the Foundry Mall on Thomas Jefferson Street NW, half a block south of M Street. No reservations are required for the public trips. At press time (March 1997), the barge trips had been canceled for the 1996 season due to flood damage in January 1996. It was unclear when operations would resume. *For information,* ☎ *202/653–5190 or 301/299–2026. For group reservations and rates,* ☎ *301/299–3613.* 🎫 *$6.*

㉕ **Fletcher's Boat House** (⊠ 4940 Canal Rd. NW, ☎ 202/244–0461) rents canoes and bicycles and sells fishing tackle and DC fishing licenses. Fishermen often congregate here to try their luck with shad, perch, catfish, striped bass, and other freshwater species. Be sure to call ahead; hours vary seasonally.

㉖ **Chain Bridge**—named for the chains that held up the original structure—links the District of Columbia with Virginia. The bridge was built to enable cattlemen to bring Virginia herds to the slaughterhouses on the Maryland side of the Potomac. The Virginia side of the river in the area around Chain Bridge is known for its good fishing and narrow, treacherous channel.

Glen Echo, on the Maryland side of the Potomac, is a charming village of Victorian houses that was founded in 1891 when brothers Edwin and Edward Baltzley fell under the spell of the short-lived Chautauqua movement, an organization that promoted liberal and practical education among the masses. Their compound served a stint as an amusement park and is now run by the National Park Service as **(27)** an arts and cultural center. **Glen Echo Park** (✉ 7300 MacArthur Blvd., ☎ 301/492–6282) is noted not only for its whimsical architecture, including a stone tower left from the Chautauqua period, but also for its splendid 1921 Dentzel carousel. The park is also the site of frequent folk festivals, and dances are held in the ornate Spanish Ballroom. For scheduling information, check the "Weekend" section in Friday's *Washington Post* or the free weekly *City Paper*.

The **Clara Barton House,** one of the most striking Victorian structures in Glen Echo, has been preserved as a monument to the founder of the American Red Cross. Barton moved here toward the end of her life, using the place for a while to store Red Cross supplies and as the organization's headquarters. Today the building is furnished with original period artifacts. ✉ *5801 Oxford Rd., Glen Echo, MD,* ☎ *301/492–6245.* 🎫 *Free.* ☉ *Daily 10–5; guided tours hourly on the ½ hr.*

The twin parks of **Great Falls**—on either side of the river, 13 mi west of Georgetown—are now part of the national park system. The 800-acre park on the Virginia side is a favorite spot for outings, not least because the steep, jagged falls roar into a narrow gorge, providing one of the most spectacular scenic attractions in the East.

Colvin Run Mill Historic Site dates from the first decade of the 19th century, although the country store, which is still open for business, was added in the early 20th century. In addition to the restored mill, there's a small museum inside the miller's home. The mill operates on an irregular schedule, so call ahead for opening times as well as information on interpretive programs. *Rte. 7 and Colvin Run Rd., Great Falls,* ☎ *703/759–2771.* 🎫 *$4.* ☉ *Wed.–Mon. 11–5.*

(28) **Great Falls Tavern,** on the Maryland side of Great Falls Park, has displays of canal history and a platform from which to view the falls. Better yet, walk over the Olmsted Bridges out to a small island in the middle of the river for a spectacular view. On the canal walls are "rope burns" caused by decade upon decade of friction from barge lines. Half a mile west, a flood marker shows how high the Potomac can go—after a hurricane in 1972 the river crested far above the ground where visitors stand. Canal barge trips start here between April and October. The tavern ceased being a hostelry long ago, so if you're hungry head for the snack bar a few paces north of the tavern. At press time (March 1997), the Olmsted Bridges had been closed and the barge trips cancelled, due to extensive flood damage in January 1996. The bridges were scheduled to reopen by the summer of 1996, but the barge trips were not expected to resume until at least 1997. *Park,* ☎ *301/299–2026.* 🎫 *$4 per vehicle, $2 per person without vehicle, good for 7 days for MD and VA sides of the park.* ☉ *Daily sunrise–sunset. Tavern, snack bar, and museum,* ☎ *301/299–3613.* ☉ *Daily 9–4:30.*

(29) On the Virginia side of **Great Falls Park,** a clifftop path looks down on Mather Gorge, the rocky narrows that make the Potomac River churn. Here you can follow trails past the old Patowmack Canal and among the boulders and forests lining the edge of the falls; or visit the one-

C&O Canal and Great Falls

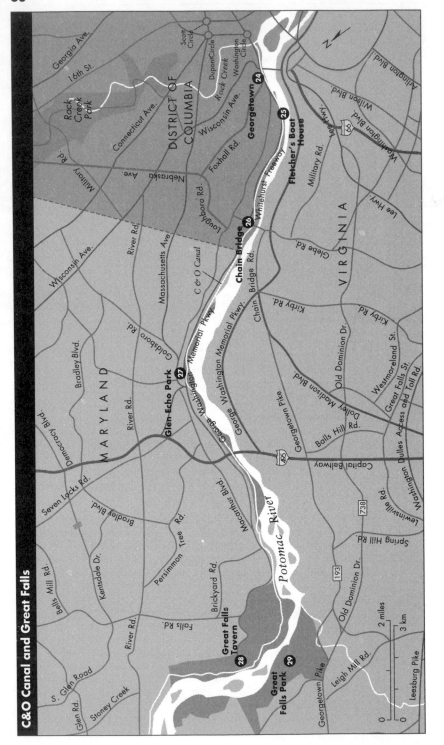

N

District of Columbia

Georgia Ave.

16th St.

Rock Creek Park

Connecticut Ave.

Military Rd.

Nebraska Ave.

Rock Creek

Scott Circle

Dupont Circle

Washington Circle

Wisconsin Ave.

Foxhall Rd.

Loughboro Rd.

Georgetown 24

25

Fletcher's Boat House

Whitehurst Freeway

Military Rd.

Lee Hwy.

Wilson Blvd.

Arlington Blvd.

Washington Blvd.

Virginia

Lee Hwy.

26 **Chain Bridge**

Chain Bridge Rd.

Glebe Rd.

Kirby Rd.

Kirby Rd.

Old Dominion Dr.

Westmoreland St.

Great Falls St.

Toll Rd.

Wisconsin Ave.

River Rd.

Massachusetts Ave.

Goldsboro Rd.

C & O Canal

George Washington Memorial Pkwy.

27 **Glen-Echo Park**

Maryland

Bradley Blvd.

River Rd.

Democracy Blvd.

Seven Locks Rd.

Bradley Blvd.

Kentsdale Dr.

Bells Mill Rd.

S. Glen Road

Glen Rd.

Stoney Creek

River Rd.

Falls Rd.

Brickyard Rd.

Persimmon Tree Rd.

MacArthur Blvd.

George Washington Memorial Pkwy.

Georgetown Pike

Balls Hill Rd.

Dolley Madison Blvd.

495

Capital Beltway

Washington Dulles Access and Toll Rd.

Lewinsville Rd.

738

Spring Hill Rd.

Old Dominion Dr.

193

Georgetown Pike

Leigh Mill Rd.

Leesburg Pike

Potomac River

28 **Great Falls Tavern**

29 **Great Falls Park**

2 miles
3 km
0
0

time town of Matildaville and look across to the Maryland side, where boats re-create canal rides. Horseback riding is permitted—maps are available at the visitor center—but you can't rent horses in the park. Swimming and wading are prohibited, but there are fine opportunities for fishing (a Virginia, Maryland, or DC license is required for anglers 16 and older), rock climbing (climbers must register at the visitor center beforehand), and white-water kayaking (*below* the falls only, and only by experienced boaters). A tour of the visitor center and museum takes 30 minutes. Staff members conduct special tours and walks year-round. ⊠ *Rte 193 (Exit 13 off Rte 495, the Capitol Beltway) to Rte 738, and follow the signs,* ☎ *703/285–2966.* ☟ *$4 per vehicle, good for 7 days.* ☉ *Year-round, daily 7–dusk. Visitor center: Apr.–Oct., daily 10–6; Nov.–Mar., daily 10–4.*

To reach the Virginia side of Great Falls Park, take the scenic and winding Route 193 (Exit 13 off Route 495, the Capitol Beltway) to Route 738, and follow the signs. It takes about 25 minutes to drive to the park from the Beltway. You can get to the Maryland side of the park by following MacArthur Boulevard from Georgetown or by taking Exit 41 off the Beltway, following the signs to Carderock.

Dining

$$$$ ✕ **L'Auberge Chez François.** Alsatian cuisine is served here, 12 mi west
★ of Tysons Corner, in a country-inn atmosphere. The building, of white stucco and dark exposed beams, is set on 6 acres, with a garden that can be seen from the dining room. Three fireplaces, flowered tablecloths, and stained glass set the mood for such specialties as salmon soufflé— a fillet of salmon topped with a mousse of scallops and salmon and a white-wine or lobster sauce. Reservations are required four weeks in advance. ⊠ *332 Springvale Rd. (Rte. 674), Great Falls,* ☎ *703/759– 3800. Reservations essential. Jacket required. AE, D, DC, MC, V. Closed Mon. No lunch.*

Nightlife and the Arts

The Old Brogue (⊠ 760-C Walker Rd., Great Falls, ☎ 703/759–3309) has lively music.

Reston

③⓪ *20 mi northwest of Alexandria.*

The planned community of Reston was the brainchild of Robert E. Simon, whose initials form the "Res" in "Reston."

☾ At the intersection of Routes 7 and 606, **Reston Animal Park** is inhabited by a gibbon, emus, giant tortoises, zebras, and other exotica as well as domestic farm animals. Children can take pony and elephant rides, and the entire family can go on a hayride. Special events every weekend are included in the admission price. ⊠ *1228 Hunter Mill Rd.,* ☎ *703/759–3636.* ☟ *$7.95 Wed.–Sun.; $5.95 Mon.–Tues.* ☉ *Late Mar.–mid-June and Labor Day–late Nov., weekdays 10–5, weekends 10–6; mid-June–Labor Day, daily 10–5.*

Outdoor Activities and Sports

Reston National Golf Course (⊠ 11875 Sunrise Valley Dr., Reston, ☎ 703/620–9333) has 18 holes.

Chantilly

③① *20 mi west of Alexandria.*

Chantilly is far enough from the metropolitan Washington area to harbor more trees and farms than office buildings.

The Federal-style home called **Sully** has changed hands many times since 1795, when it was built by Richard Bland Lee. Citizen action in the 20th century saved it from destruction during construction of nearby Dulles Airport. In the 1970s the house was restored to Federal style and today has an 18th-century-style garden. ⊠ *Rte. 28 near Chantilly,* ☎ *703/437–1794.* 🖃 *$4.* ◎ *Mar.–Dec., Wed.–Mon. 11–4; Jan.–Feb., Wed.–Fri. and Mon. 11–3, weekends 11–3:30.*

OFF THE
BEATEN PATH

MANASSAS NATIONAL BATTLEFIELD PARK – The Confederacy won two important victories—in July 1861 and August 1862—at Manassas National Battlefield Park, or Bull Run, earning Stonewall Jackson his nickname. The self-guided tour begins at the visitor center, where exhibits and audiovisual presentations greatly enhance a visit. It's a 26-mi drive from Washington; take I–66 west to Route 234 North (don't be fooled by the earlier Manassas exit for Route 28), and the visitor center is ½ mi north on the right. From Chantilly, drive 10 mi south on Route 28. ☎ *703/361–1339.* 🖃 *$2.* ◎ *Daily dawn–dusk. Visitor center, daily 8:30–5 (until 6, June–Aug.).*

FREDERICKSBURG

Numbers in the margin correspond to points of interest on the Fredericksburg map.

32–37 *48 mi southwest of Alexandria.*

Fredericksburg rivals Alexandria and Mount Vernon in the number of its associations with the Washington family. The first president lived across the Rappahannock River at Ferry Farm from age six to 16; later he bought a house for his mother here, near his sister and brother.

32 George Washington's only sister, Betty, married her cousin Fielding Lewis in 1750, and they built **Kenmore** a few years later. The plain exterior belies a lavish interior; these have been called some of the most beautiful rooms in America. The plaster moldings in the ceilings are even more ornate than those of Mount Vernon. Equally elegant are the furnishings, which include a large standing clock that belonged to Betty's mother. A snack of tea and ginger cookies is included in the tour. ⊠ *1201 Washington Ave.,* ☎ *540/373–3381.* 🖃 *$6.* ◎ *Mar.–Dec., Mon.–Sat. 10–5, Sun. 12–5; Jan.–Feb., Sat. and holidays 10–5, Sun. 12–5.*

33 In 1760 George Washington's brother Charles built as his home what became the **Rising Sun Tavern,** a watering hole for such revolutionaries as the Lee brothers, Patrick Henry, Washington, and Jefferson. An actress dressed in period costume and portraying the character of "wench" leads the tour, allowing you to observe the activity at this busy institution entirely from her perspective. Visitors are served spiced tea in the tap room. ⊠ *1306 Caroline St.,* ☎ *540/371–1494.* 🖃 *$3.* ◎ *Mar.–Nov., daily 9–5; Dec.–Feb., daily 10–4.*

34 In 1772 George Washington purchased the modest white **Mary Washington House** for his mother. Here she spent the last 17 years of her life, tending the charming garden where her boxwood still flourishes—and where many a bride and groom come today to exchange vows. ⊠ *Charles and Lewis Sts.,* ☎ *540/373–1569.* 🖃 *$3.* ◎ *Mar.–Nov., daily 9–5; Dec.–Feb., daily 10–4. Closed Thanksgiving, Dec. 24–25, and Dec. 31–Jan. 1.*

Dr. Hugh Mercer, a Scotsman who served as a brigadier general of the Revolutionary army, may have been more careful than most other Colo-

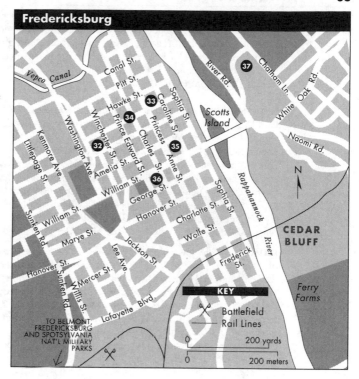

nial physicians, yet his methods make today's visitors cringe. A costumed hostess at the **Hugh Mercer Apothecary Shop** describes explicitly the procedures for amputations and cataract operations; she also tells about therapeutic bleeding and shows off the gruesome devices used in Colonial dentistry. This look at life two centuries ago is informative, if mildly nauseating. ⊠ *Caroline and Amelia Sts.,* ☎ *540/373–3362.* ⊠ *$3.* ⊘ *Mar.–Nov., daily 9–5; Dec.–Feb., daily 10–4.*

The **James Monroe Museum and Memorial Library,** a tiny one-story building where the man who would later be the nation's fifth president practiced law from 1787 to 1789, is the repository of many of Monroe's possessions, which were collected and preserved by his family. Here is the desk at which Monroe signed the nation's single most enduring declaration of foreign policy, the Monroe Doctrine. ⊠ *908 Charles St.,* ☎ *540/654–1043.* ⊠ *$3.* ⊘ *Daily 9–5.*

NEED A BREAK?

The **Virginia Deli** (⊠ 101 William St., ☎ 540/371-2233) is a good place to stop for a bread *boulé* (a hollowed-out loaf of bread filled with Brunswick stew or roast beef au jus) or a gourmet sandwich (the "Thomas Jefferson" is turkey and bacon). Fudge brownie cheesecake and other homemade sweets complete the menu.

Chatham Manor is a fine example of Georgian architecture, built between 1768 and 1771 by William Fitzhugh on a site overlooking the Rappahannock and the town of Fredericksburg. Fitzhugh, a plantation owner, frequently hosted such luminaries as Washington and Jefferson. At the time of the Civil War, Union forces commandeered the house and converted it into a headquarters and hospital. President Lin coln conferred here with his generals; Clara Barton, founder of the American Red Cross, and the poet Walt Whitman tended the wounded here. Later its owners restored the house and gardens and gave the property to the National Park Service. Concerts are performed here in summer. ⊠ *Chatham La.,* ☎ *540/371–0802.* ☜ *Free.* ⊙ *Daily 9–5, except Dec. 25 and Jan. 1.*

OFF THE
BEATEN PATH

FREDERICKSBURG AND SPOTSYLVANIA NATIONAL MILITARY PARK – Four Civil War battlefields in the Fredericksburg environs—Fredericksburg, Chancellorsville, the Wilderness, and the Spotsylvania Courthouse—together constitute the Fredericksburg and Spotsylvania National Military Park. All are in or within 17 mi of Fredericksburg. The in-town visitor center for the park has two floors of exhibits and a slide show on the fighting. On the fields, signs and exhibits recount details of the battles. ⊠ *1013 Lafayette Blvd. (Business Rte. 1),* ☎ *540/371-0802.* ☜ *Free.* ⊙ *Mid-June–Labor Day, daily 8:30–6:30; Sept.–Oct. and Apr.–mid-June, weekdays 9–5, weekends 9–6; Nov.–Mar., daily 9–5.*

BELMONT – In the town of Falmouth is the 18th-century estate of Belmont, also known as the Gari Melchers Estate and Memorial gallery. Belmont was acquired in 1916 by Detroit-born artist Gari Melchers, who returned from Europe at the outbreak of World War I. The house is furnished with antiques; the stone studio Melchers built in 1924 houses the largest collection of his works anywhere. ⊠ *224 Washington St., Falmouth (off U.S. 17 north of Fredericksburg),* ☎ *540/654-1015.* ☜ *$4.* ⊙ *Mar.–Nov., Mon.–Sat. 10–5, Sun. 1–5; Dec.–Feb., Mon.–Sat. 10–4, Sun. 1–4; closed major holidays.*

Dining and Lodging

$$$ ✕ **Le Lafayette.** Here you can expect well-prepared French cuisine made with fresh Virginia ingredients and served in the Colonial setting of a 1771 Georgian-style house. The menu includes both brook trout and Chesapeake Bay seafood, plus imaginative Continental dishes such as grilled breast of duck in red currant sauce over fresh, braised red cabbage; poached fillet of salmon in saffron broth with mussels, leeks, and tomatoes; and pecan-crusted rack of lamb. ⊠ *623 Caroline St.,* ☎ *540/373–6895. AE, D, DC, MC, V. Closed Mon.*

$$ ✕ **Ristorante Renato.** This unlikely Italian restaurant in the center of the Colonial town justifies its presence with a strong if conventional menu. "Romeo and Juliet" is veal and chicken topped with mozzarella and swimming in white-wine sauce; shrimp scampi Napoli has a lemon-butter sauce. White tablecloths and candles decorate the tables in the three quiet dining rooms, and the main dining room, with a view of the street corner, has red carpeting, stone walls, and a fireplace. ⊠ *422 Williams St.,* ☎ *540/371–8228. AE, MC, V.*

$ ✕ **Goolrick's Pharmacy.** This 1940s pharmacy with a soda fountain and Formica tables serves soft drinks in paper cups set in metal stands, and offers breakfast and light meals. ⊠ *901 Caroline St.,* ☎ *540/373–3411. Reservations not accepted. Closed Sun.*

$$ ▥ **Best Western Johnny Appleseed.** This family-oriented two-story motel, a five-minute drive from the battlefields, is on a commercial highway strip. Rooms are of the basic motel variety, and queen-size beds are available; efficiencies have a stove and microwave oven. The most pleasant views are of the pool. A truck stop across the street can be a source of predawn racket. ⊠ *543 Warrenton Rd. (U.S. 17 and I–95), Fredericksburg 22406,* ☎ *540/373–0000 or 800/528–1234,* 𝔽𝔸𝕏 *540/373–*

5676. 87 rooms. Restaurant, pool, volleyball, playground. AE, D, DC, MC, V.

$$ ⊡ **Hampton Inn.** On the interstate near the historic district, this cheerful motel has a U-shape layout, with rooms on two stories that face the parking spaces, and a pool at the center. The rooms have a pink-and-green color scheme and the basic furnishings. Seven restaurants are within walking distance. ⊠ *2310 Plank Rd., Fredericksburg 22401,* ☎ *540/371–0330,* 𝔽𝔸𝕏 *540/371–1753. 165 rooms, 2 equipped for guests with disabilities, 1 suite. Pool. AE, D, DC, MC, V. Rates include Continental breakfast.*

$$ ⊡ **The Richard Johnston Inn.** This is a three-story row house across the street from the visitor center, with parking in the rear under the magnolia trees. Empire-style and Chippendale antiques and polished wood floors with Oriental rugs show that care has gone into the restoration. Two suites, with wet bar and wall-to-wall carpeting, open onto a patio. ⊠ *711 Caroline St., Fredericksburg 22401,* ☎ *540/899–7606. 7 rooms. AE, MC, V.*

Outdoor Activities and Sports

The Fredericksburg Visitor Center (☎ 540/373–1776) has mapped rides of 3, 9, and 20 mi, highlighting the historical and natural beauty of the town.

Shopping

The Old Town area of Fredericksburg is teeming with antiques shops, from moderately priced to very expensive. The visitor center has maps and lists of many of the stores.

LOUDOUN COUNTY

Numbers in the margin correspond to points of interest on the Northern Virginia map.

Welcome to Virginia's horse country. The major towns in Loudoun County are Leesburg, Middleburg, and Waterford, where old Virginia still carries on, with gracious homes, fox hunts, and steeplechases.

Middleburg

38 *40 mi west of Alexandria.*

The area that is now Middleburg was surveyed by George Washington in 1763, when it was known as Chinn's Crossroads. Then it was considered strategic because of its location midway on the Winchester–Alexandria route (roughly what is now Route 50). The community, incorporated in 1787, has numerous horse events; polo matches are played Sundays June through Labor Day (☎ 703/777–0775).

OFF THE BEATEN PATH   **THE VINEYARDS** – Middleburg is in the midst of a constellation of wineries, all of which offer tours and tastings daily from 10 to 4. On Route 628, south of Middleburg, Meredyth Vineyards (☎ 540/687–6277), established in 1972, has been in the forefront of promoting the recent Virginian industry of wine growing. Also south of Middleburg but on Route 626 is Piedmont Vineyards and Winery (☎ 540/687–5528). East of Middleburg on Route 50 is the Swedenburg Estate Vineyard (☎ 540/687–5219).

Lodging

$$–$$$ 🏨 **Middleburg Country Inn.** This historic three-story structure, built in 1820 and enlarged in 1858, was the rectory of St. John's Parish Episcopal Church until 1907. Its medium-size rooms are furnished with antiques and period reproductions and have working fireplaces. A full country breakfast is served, and, when weather permits, guests can enjoy their meals alfresco. ⊠ *209 E. Washington St., Box 2065, Middleburg 22117,* ☎ *540/687–6082 or 800/262–6082,* 𝖥𝖠𝖷 *540/687–5603. 6 rooms, 2 suites. Hot tub. AE, D, MC, V.*

$$–$$$ 🏨 **Middleburg Inn and Guest Suites.** Though this is not a historic building, the atmosphere conveys 18th-century-style living. Large rooms are furnished with canopied beds, antiques, and period reproductions. ⊠ *105 W. Washington St., Middleburg 22117,* ☎ *540/687–3115 or 800/432–6125. 4 suites, 1 cottage. MC, V.*

En Route   Five mi south of Leesburg on Route 15, **Oatlands** is a former 5,000-acre plantation built by a great-grandson of Robert "King" Carter, one of the wealthiest planters in Virginia before the Revolution. The manor house was built in 1803 in Greek Revival style; a stately portico and half-octagonal stair wings were added in 1827. The house has been meticulously restored, and the manicured fields that remain host public and private equestrian events from spring to fall, among them the Loudoun Hunt Point-to-Point in April, a race that brings out the entire community for picnics on blankets and tailgates. A restored English garden of 4½ acres is bordered by terraced walls. ☎ *703/777–3174.* 🎫 *$6. Additional fee for special events.* ☉ *Apr.–Dec., Mon.–Sat. 10–4:30, Sun. 1–4:30. Closed Jan.–Mar., Dec. 25, Thanksgiving.*

Leesburg

39   *36 mi northwest of Alexandria.*

A staging area during the French and Indian War, Leesburg is one of the oldest towns in northern Virginia, with numerous fine Colonial and Revolutionary buildings that now house offices, shops, restaurants, and residences. When the British burned Washington during the War of 1812, James and Dolley Madison fled to Leesburg with many government records, including official copies of the Declaration of Independence and the U.S. Constitution.

The history of the Loudoun County area is detailed in exhibits at the **Loudoun Museum,** which displays art and artifacts of daily life from the time of the Native American tribes to the 20th century. ⊠ *16 W. Loudoun St. SW,* ☎ *703/777–7427.* 🎫 *Suggested $2 donation.* ☉ *Mon.–Sat. 10–5, Sun. 1–5.*

OFF THE   **MORVEN PARK** – This 1,200-acre estate is home to the Westmoreland
BEATEN PATH   Davis Equestrian Institute, a private riding school. Also on the grounds are the Morven Park Carriage Museum, with its collection of more than 100 horse-drawn vehicles, and the Museum of Hounds and Hunting. The mansion, the work of three architects in 1781, is a Greek Revival building that bears a striking resemblance to the White House and has been used as a stand-in for it in films. Two governors have lived here. The price of admission includes entrance to the two museums and to 16 rooms in the Morven Park mansion. ⊠ *Rte. 7, 1 mi north of Leesburg,* ☎ *703/777–2414.* 🎫 *$6.* ☉ *Apr.–Oct., Tues.–Fri. noon–5, Sat. 10–5, Sun. 1–5; Nov., weekends noon–5; special Christmas tours during the 1st 3 wks of Dec., Tues.–Sun. noon–5.*

Dining and Lodging

$$$$ ⊞ **Hyatt Dulles.** This 14-story hotel is linked to Dulles International Airport 3 mi away by a free shuttle service every half hour. Soundproof guest rooms are suite-size; the parlor area, which seats four, is separated from the bed by a credenza. Rooms currently have blond-wood furniture, floral paintings, and a mauve color scheme with liberal touches of gray, violet, and teal, but that will change after a renovation scheduled to begin in the winter of 1996–97. A pianist performs, morning and afternoon, near the fountain in the two-story atrium. This is warmer and more elegant than the standard airport hotel. ⊠ *2300 Dulles Corner Blvd., Herndon 22071,* ☎ *703/713–1234,* FAX *703/713–3410. 317 rooms. Restaurant, bar, indoor pool, sauna, exercise room. AE, D, DC, MC, V.*

$$$$ ✕⊞ **Lansdowne Conference Resort.** The windows of this modern retreat 45 minutes from Washington overlook the fields and rolling hills of the northern corner of Virginia. Polished wood furniture, carpets, handsome wall decorations, and marble-accented bathrooms evoke the classy feel of this property. Tall windows in the dining room, where regional cuisine is served, look toward Sugarloaf Mountain. Among the many menu specialties are hot smoked salmon with sage hollandaise sauce; Maine lobster tail with *arborio* (Italian rice) and spring vegetables; and cilantro-and-garlic-roasted leg of lamb. The pastry chef's buffet is an award winner. ⊠ *44050 Woodridge Pkwy., Leesburg 22075,* ☎ *703/729–8400 or 800/541–4801,* FAX *703/729–4111. 305 rooms. 3 restaurants, bar, 1 indoor and 1 outdoor pool, 18-hole golf course, tennis court, exercise room, racquetball, volleyball, billiards. Weekend packages available. AE, D, DC, MC, V.*

Waterford

40 *45 mi northwest of Alexandria.*

The historic community of Waterford was founded by a Quaker miller and for many decades has been synonymous with fine crafts; its annual early October Homes Tour and Crafts Exhibit attracts as many as 15,000 visitors. Festival activities include Revolutionary War military camps with marching fife and drum corps, Civil War skirmishing, and visits to 18th-century buildings. Waterford and more than 1,400 acres around it were declared a National Historic Landmark in 1970. For information on events, contact the Waterford Foundation (⊠ Main and 2nd Sts., Waterford, ☎ 540/882–3018).

NORTHERN VIRGINIA A TO Z

Arriving and Departing

By Bus

Greyhound Lines (☎ 800/231–2222) provides scheduled service to Fairfax (⊠ 4103 Rust Rd., ☎ 703/273–7770), Fredericksburg (⊠ 1400 Jefferson Davis Hwy., ☎ 540/373–2103), Arlington (⊠ 3860 S. Four Mile Run Dr., ☎ 703/998–6312), and Springfield (⊠ 6583 Backlick Rd., ☎ 703/451–5800).

By Car

I–95 runs north–south along the eastern side of the region. I–66 runs east–west, perpendicular to I–95, cutting off the top third of the region.

By Plane

Three major airports serve both northern Virginia and the Washington, DC, area. The busy and often crowded **Washington National Airport** (☎ 703/419–8000) in Arlington has scheduled daily flights by all major U.S. carriers. **Washington Dulles International Airport** (☎ 703/419–8000), in Loudoun County, 26 mi northwest of Washington, is a modern facility served by the major U.S. airlines and many international carriers. **Baltimore-Washington International Airport** (☎ 410/859–7111 for information and paging), 10 mi south of Baltimore off Route 295, also serves the metropolitan Washington area, including Northern Virginia. It is almost as close to some areas as Dulles.

By Train

Amtrak (☎ 800/872–7245) has scheduled stops in Alexandria (⊠ 110 Callahan Dr., ☎ 703/836–4339) and Fredericksburg (⊠ Caroline St. and Lafayette Blvd., no phone) as part of its East Coast service.

Contacts and Resources

B&B Reservation Agencies

Bed & Breakfast Accommodations Ltd. of Washington, DC (⊠ Box 12011, Washington, DC 20005, ☎ 202/328–3510) and **Princely Bed & Breakfast Ltd.** (⊠ Box 325, Port Haywood 23138, ☎ 804/725–9511 or 800/470–5588) will both arrange accommodations in historic homes in Alexandria.

Emergencies

Throughout the region, dial **911** for emergency assistance.

Alexandria Hospital (⊠ 4320 Seminary Rd., Alexandria, ☎ 703/504–3000) has a 24-hour emergency room.

National Hospital Medical Center (⊠ 2455 Army Navy Dr., Arlington, ☎ 703/553–2417) has a 24-hour emergency room.

Medic 1 Clinic (⊠ 3429 Jefferson Davis Hwy., Fredericksburg, ☎ 540/371–1664) is open Mon.–Fri. 8–9, Sat. 9–7, and Sun. 9–3.

Guided Tours

Doorways to Old Virginia (☎ 703/548–0100) and the **Old Town Experience** (☎ 703/836–0694) are two private companies that offer tours of historic Old Town Alexandria; many tours begin at the Ramsay House Visitor Center (⊠ 221 King St., ☎ 703/838–4200).

Visitor Information

Alexandria Convention and Visitor's Bureau (⊠ Ramsay House, 221 King St., Alexandria 22314, ☎ 703/838–4200, TTY 703/838–6494).
Arlington County Visitor Center (⊠ 735 S. 18th St., Arlington 22202, ☎ 703/358–5720 or 800/677–6267).
Fairfax County Convention and Visitors Bureau (⊠ 8300 Boone Blvd., Suite 450, Vienna 22182, ☎ 703/790–3329).
Fredericksburg Visitor Center (⊠ 706 Caroline St., Fredericksburg 22401, ☎ 540/373–1776 or 800/678–4748).
Loudoun Tourism Council (⊠ 108D South St. SE, Leesburg 22075, ☎ 703/777–0519 or 800/752–6118).

3 Shenandoah Valley and the Highlands

Dazzling vistas, rugged hiking trails, wild azaleas, hardwood trees that blaze with color in fall, and streams stocked with trout—these draw more visitors to the Shenandoah than any other national park. Just to the southwest, intrepid travelers venture to the Highlands, known for its rugged beauty and many gorges—among them the Cumberland Gap, which leads into Kentucky and Tennessee.

THE SHENANDOAH VALLEY IS BEST KNOWN as an outdoor destination—Shenandoah National Park is the most often visited park in the U.S. system—and the region's towns and cities, rich pockets of history and culture, are all too often bypassed by travelers skimming along the scenic Skyline Drive and Blue Ridge Parkway. In Staunton, you can visit the birthplace of Woodrow Wilson, the 28th president of the United States (and the eighth president from Virginia). Bath County, where the mineral waters flow, has been a fashionable resort for two centuries. Lexington, dense with historic sites, looks largely unchanged since the 19th century. Roanoke, nicknamed Star City of the South for an 88½-foot-high illuminated star atop a mountain within city limits, is the proud cultural and commercial center of western Virginia.

The Shenandoah Valley, about 150 mi long, lies between the Allegheny and Blue Ridge mountain ranges in northwestern Virginia, parallel to the western edge of the state and extending to Harpers Ferry in West Virginia. In the heights east of the valley, Shenandoah National Park's nearly 200,000 acres stretch more than 80 mi along the Blue Ridge, providing stunning vistas, hundreds of miles of hiking trails (including a section of the Appalachian Trail), and trout fishing in rushing streams. The park is a sanctuary for deer, bear, and red fox, and a botanical treasury whose most spectacular specimens are blooming wild azaleas in spring and hardwood trees that turn glorious colors in autumn.

The Highlands, or the Appalachian Plateau, in the state's southwest corner, lie at an average elevation of 2,000 feet. This is a region heavily wooded and incised with gorges, one of them the legendary Cumberland Gap that leads into Kentucky and Tennessee. Here, near the southern end of the Blue Ridge, is Virginia's highest peak, Mt. Rogers (5,729 feet). Often neglected by travelers, the Highlands have a peculiar, rugged beauty and plenty of indoor and outdoor recreation: Seven state parks, three national parks, and six national forests can be counted in the area. The town of Abingdon boasts well-preserved 18th- and 19th-century buildings, two major regional festivals, and the state theater of Virginia, the Barter Theatre.

Exploring Shenandoah Valley and the Highlands

Although there are other attractions in the Shenandoah Valley, most people come for the Shenandoah National Park—the most-visited park in the national park system—and the stunning scenic views along Skyline Drive and the Blue Ridge Parkway. Far from the valley, in the Highlands region, you can hike and camp in the George Washington and Jefferson national forests and the Mount Rogers National Recreation Area. Farther south, Newbern and Tazewell offer remnants of life in the pioneer days, while Abingdon draws crowds with its renowned Barter Theatre and its annual Virginia Highlands Festival.

SHENANDOAH VALLEY

Numbers in the margin correspond to points of interest on the Shenandoah Valley and the Highlands map.

In addition to Shenandoah National Park, Skyline Drive, and the Blue Ridge Parkway, the Shenandoah Valley is also home to the George Washington and Jefferson national forests and the Mount Rogers National Recreation Area, dominated by Virginia's highest mountain, Mt. Rogers (5,729 feet). All along the valley are historic, cultural, and geological places of interest, including Skyline, Luray, and Endless caverns; the New Market Battlefield Historic Park; Staunton, Woodrow Wilson's birthplace; and Bath County, famous for its hot mineral springs.

Middletown

❶ *140 mi northwest of Richmond (Rte. 11, west of I–81).*

In Middletown, **Belle Grove** is a fitting first stop on a tour of the Shenandoah. The elegant farmhouse is a monument to the rural and the refined, two qualities that exist in harmony in the architecture here and throughout the region. Completed in 1794 after consultation with Thomas Jefferson, the building bears such signature Jeffersonian touches as fan windows; the four chimneys that tower over the structure are made of Virginia limestone. This was the headquarters of the Union general Philip Sheridan during the Battle of Cedar Creek (1864), a crucial defeat for the Confederacy. Part of the battle was fought on the farm, and an annual reenactment is held in October with as many as 2,000 participants. Today it is a 165-acre working farm. ⊠ *Rte. 11,* ☏ *540/869–2028.* ⌷ *House: $5; Reenactment: varies.* ☉ *Mid-Mar.–Oct., Mon.–Sat. 10–4, Sun. 1–5. Christmas candlelight tours: call for schedule.*

Shenandoah National Park

Northern entrance 12 mi southeast of Middletown.

Its name Shenandoah means "Daughter of the Stars" in a Native American language, and the metaphor is apt indeed, for some 60 peaks of the Blue Ridge Mountains stretch skyward within this park's vast boundaries. The park extends more than 80 mi south along the Blue Ridge, with several gaps in the range forming passes between the Shenandoah Valley on the west and the Piedmont on the east. Hardwood and pine forests shroud the slopes, with mountain meadows rampant with wildflowers opening up to gorgeous panoramas that can be viewed at leisure from numerous turnoffs. Hikers and campers find deep natural environments just yards from the highway, trout fishers may wade into more than 25 streams in seven counties, horses can be rented for wilderness trail rides, and naturalists conduct daily guided hikes throughout the summer. The seasonal activities of the park, supervised by rangers, are outlined in the *Shenandoah Overlook,* a free newspaper you can pick up on entering the park. The town of Front Royal marks the northern limit of the park, which is easily reached from I–66 and I–81 (and I–64 farther south). ⊠ *Park Superintendent, Box 348, Rte. 4, Luray 22835,* ☏ *540/999–3500.* ⌷ *Park (and Skyline Drive): $5 car; $3 motorcycle, bicycle, or pedestrian.*

Outdoor Activities and Sports

CAMPING

The **Big Meadows Campground** (Mistix, ☏ 800/365–2267), at the approximate midpoint of Shenandoah National Park, accepts reservations; other campsites are available on a first-come, first-served basis. ⊠ *Shenandoah National Park, Box 727, Luray 22835,* ☏ *540/999–3500.* ⌷ *Park: $5 car.*

CANOEING

Many local outfitters rent canoes; try any of the following. **Front Royal Canoe** (⊠ Rte. 340 S, near Front Royal, ☏ 540/635–5440). **Downriver Canoe** (⊠ Rte. 613, near Front Royal, ☏ 540/635–5526).

Shenandoah River Outfitters (✉ Rte. 684, RD 3, Luray 22835, ☎ 540/743–4159).

FISHING

To take advantage of the trout that abound in some 50 streams of Shenandoah National Park, you will need a Virginia fishing license; it's available in season (early April to mid-October) at concession stands along Skyline Drive.

GOLF

Caverns Country Club Resort (✉ Rte. 211, Luray, ☎ 540/743–6551) has an 18-hole course along the Shenandoah.

HORSE RACING

Charles Town Races, in West Virginia, 30 minutes northwest of Front Royal, has Thoroughbred racing Friday and Saturday evenings at 7:15 and Wednesday and Sunday afternoons at 1. ✉ *Charles Town, WV,* ☎ *304/725–7001.* ✇ *$4 clubhouse, $2 grandstand.*

TENNIS

Caverns Country Club Resort (✉ Rte. 211, Luray, ☎ 540/743–6551) has four tennis courts.

Skyline Drive

★ *Entrance southeast of Front Royal (via Rte. 340).*

The most popular way to see Shenandoah National Park is by car on Skyline Drive, a spectacular route that winds 105 mi south from Front Royal to Waynesboro over the mountains of the park. The drive offers panoramas of the valley to the west and the rolling country of the Piedmont to the east; white-tailed deer are often seen along the route. But the fame of Skyline Drive has its drawbacks: The holiday and weekend crowds in high season—spring and fall—can slow traffic to much less than the maximum speed of 35 mph and strain the facilities of the few lodges, campsites, and eating places along the way. Winter brings further problems, for many facilities are closed from November through April, and treacherous road conditions can cause the closing of parts of the drive itself. Nevertheless, for easily accessible wilderness and exciting views, few routes can compete with this one. Just come during the fine weather—and bring a sweater, for temperatures can be brisk.

Outdoor Activities and Sports

HIKING

The 2,000-mi wilderness footpath from Maine to Georgia known as the **Appalachian Trail** is no relic of pioneer days but a creation of the 1920s and 1930s that provides challenging hiking opportunities. The stretch of the trail that runs the length of Shenandoah National Park takes hikers along the skyline of the Blue Ridge Mountains to views of some of the most stunning prospects of the Piedmont to the east and the valley to the west. Wildlife that auto traffic would scare away—such as the white-tail deer, for whom the park is a refuge—often step quietly into view. Because the trail's main pathway is never more than a few hundred yards from Skyline Drive (the two arteries intersect repeatedly), and there are parking lots every few miles, one can embark on any kind of hike. Maintained by the National Park Service, with the help of volunteers, the trail has a smooth surface and—given the steep terrain—a gentle grade. Three-sided emergency shelters offer protection from unexpected storms. Hiking neophytes and experienced backpackers will all set their own pace here, and deep-wilderness lovers will head farther into the backcountry by means of the 500 mi of marked side trails within the park. A number of walking trails at intervals along the parkway lead to historical relics such as pioneer farmsteads and natural phenomena such as geologic formations and forests. Park service information sheets show distances, degrees of difficulty, and other information.

En Route Two miles west of the entrance to Skyline Drive, **Skyline Caverns** is known for its anthodites, or spiked nodes that grow from ceilings at an estimated rate of one inch every 7,000 years, and for its chambers with appropriately descriptive names such as the Capitol Dome, Rainbow Trail, Fairytale Lake, and Cathedral Hall. ⊠ *Box 193, Front Royal 22630,* ☎ *540/635–4545 or 800/296–4545.* ⌑ *$10.* ⊘ *Mar. 15–June 14, weekdays 9–5, weekends 9–6; June 15–Labor Day, daily 9–6:30; Nov. 15–Mar. 14, daily 9–4.*

Luray Caverns, 9 mi west of Skyline Drive on Rte. 211, are the largest caverns in the state. For millions of years water has seeped through the limestone and clay to create a variety of suggestive rock and mineral formations. The world's only "stalacpipe organ" is composed of stalactites (calcite formations hanging from the ceilings of the caverns) that have been tuned to concert pitch and are tapped by electronically controlled rubber-tipped plungers. The organ is played electronically for every tour and may be played manually on special occasions. A one-hour tour begins every 20 minutes. ⊠ *Rte. 211, Luray,* ☎ *540/743–6551.* ⌑ *$12.* ⊘ *Mid-June–Labor Day, daily 9–7; mid-Mar.–mid-June and Labor Day–mid-Nov., daily 9–6; mid-Nov.–mid-Mar., weekdays 9–4, weekends 9–5.*

New Market

❷ *12 mi west of Luray (Rte. 211 off I–81); 35 mi southwest of Middletown.*

New Market marks the site of a costly Confederate victory late in the Civil War. Here 247 cadets from the Virginia Military Institute, some as young as 15 years old, were mobilized to improve the odds against superior Union numbers. Fighting under their cadet flag, 10 of the boys died on the field of honor.

At the Hall of Valor, focal point of the 260-acre **New Market Battlefield Historical Park,** the sacrifice of the Virginia cadets is commemorated in a stained-glass window mosaic, unconventional and dignified. This circular building contains a chronology of the war, and a short film deals with Stonewall Jackson's legendary campaign in the Shenandoah Valley. A farmhouse that figured in the fighting still stands on the premises; its outbuildings have been reconstructed and equipped to show a prosperous farm of the period. On the ridge over a precipitous 200-foot drop to the Shenandoah River are two overlooks with views of the nearby countryside and the Alleghenies. The battle is reenacted at the park each May. ⊠ *I–81 (Exit 264), New Market,* ☎ *540/740–3102.* ⌑ *Hall of Valor: $5. Farmhouse: Free with Hall of Valor admission.* ⊘ *Daily 9–5. Farmhouse: Mid-June–Labor Day, daily 9–5.*

The **New Market Battlefield Military Museum** stands in the area where the New Market battle began. The front of the building is a replica of Arlington, Robert E. Lee's house near Washington, DC. The museum has more than 1,500 artifacts from all American wars beginning with the Revolution and including Desert Storm; 60% deal with the Civil War. A movie on the Battle of New Market is shown. ⊠ *9500 Collins Pkwy, off Rte. 211, New Market 22844,* ☎ *540/740–8065.* ⌑ *$6.* ⊘ *Mar. 15–Dec. 1, daily 9–5.*

Shenandoah Valley and the Highlands

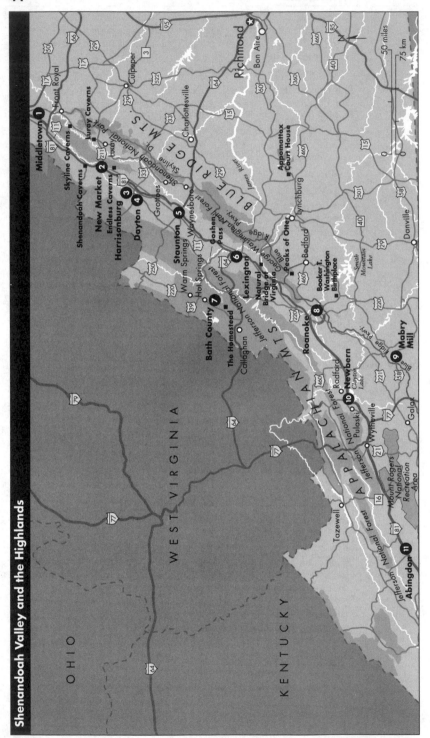

Dining and Lodging

$$–$$$ ✕ **Parkhurst Restaurant.** This redbrick building was built as a restaurant in the 1930s, gutted by fire in the 1940s, turned into a motel in the 1950s, and finally restored to its original function in 1978. In addition to a glass-enclosed porch where meals are served within sight of greenery all year long, there's a main dining room with white walls decorated with baskets and mirrors. Another dining room is finished in knotty pine, and still another is distinguished by a crystal chandelier. The menu, international in character, may include grilled quail; curried chicken accompanied by fresh-fruit condiments; beef strips sautéed with mushrooms, topped with a blue-cheese sauce, and baked; or veal Oscar (with Alaskan king crab, asparagus, and béarnaise). The commendable wine list is more heavily Virginian every year, and local vintages are available by the glass. ✉ *Rte. 211 W,* ☏ *540/743–6009. AE, DC, MC, V. No lunch.*

$$–$$$ 🏨 **Jordan Hollow Farm.** The oldest of the four buildings is the dining hall, originally created as a farmhouse in 1790; the youngest structure, built of hand-hewn logs almost 200 years later, contains the inn's most luxurious rooms, which include a fireplace, whirlpool, and TV. The inn's setting, on a 45-acre horse farm near the tiny town of Stanley, 6 mi from Luray, lets you gaze out over pastures full of horses toward a backdrop of the Blue Ridge Mountains. Guided tours on horseback are varied in length and terrain to match the rider's experience. ✉ *326 Hawksbill Park Rd., Stanley 22851,* ☏ *540/778–2285 or 888/418– 7000. 21 rooms. Restaurant, bar, horseback riding. D, DC, MC, V.*

OFF THE
BEATEN PATH

SHENANDOAH CAVERNS – Here you'll find spectacular calcite formations, among them a series resembling strips of bacon, formed by water dripping through long, narrow cracks in the limestone. The lighting effects are most noticeable where the sparkling calcite crystals are differentiated by colored lights. As at Luray, most of the formations are wet and shiny and continue to grow at an imperceptible rate. ✉ *261 Caverns Rd. (I–81, Exit 269),* ☏ *540/477–3115.* 🎫 *$9. Accessible for visitors with disabilities.* ☉ *Mid-June–Aug., daily 9–6:15; mid-Apr.–mid-June and Sept.–mid-Oct., daily 9–5:15; mid-Oct.–mid-Apr., daily 9–4:15.*

ENDLESS CAVERNS – These caverns were discovered in 1879 by two boys and a dog chasing a rabbit. Opened to the public in 1920, the seemingly endless configurations of the caverns have baffled numerous explorers. The tour is enhanced by lighting effects, especially at "Snow Drift," where a sudden illumination emphasizes the white powdery appearance of the "drift" in a brown and yellow tinted room. ✉ *3 mi south of New Market on Rte. 11 (Exits 264 or 257 off I–81),* ☏ *540/740–3993 or 800/544–2283.* 🎫 *$10 adults.* ☉ *Mid-Mar.–mid-June and Sept.–early Nov., daily 9–5; mid-June–Labor Day, daily 9–7; Sept.–Nov., daily 9–5; mid-Nov.–mid-Mar., daily 9–4.*

Harrisonburg

❸ *18 mi southwest of New Market (via Exit 251 from I–81).*

Though it is often bypassed as a workaday market town for the rich farmlands that surround it, Harrisonburg is worth a visit. Settled in 1739, it's a stronghold of Mennonites who wear plain clothes and drive horse-drawn buggies. The city is also a center of higher education, with James Madison University and Eastern Mennonite College in town and Bridgewater College nearby.

At the **Virginia Quilt Museum,** you can see examples of quilts made in the region and learn about the important role of quilts and quilting in the local culture. ✉ *301 S. Main St., Harrisonburg,* ☎ *540/433–3818.* 🖙 *$4.* ⊙ *Mon. and Thurs.–Sat. 10–4, Sun. 1–4.*

Lodging

$$$ 🏨 **Joshua Wilton House.** A row of trees guards the privacy of this late-19th-century house decorated in the Victorian style and set on a large yard at the edge of downtown. Guests relax in the sunroom and on the back patio. Ask for Room 4; it has a canopy bed and a view of the Blue Ridge Mountains looming over Main Street. Room 2 has a fireplace. ✉ *412 S. Main St., Harrisonburg 22801,* ☎ *540/434–4464,* ℻ *540/432–9525. 5 rooms. Restaurant. AE, MC, V. Rates include breakfast.*

Outdoor Activities and Sports

GOLF AND SKIING

Massanutten Resort (✉ Off Rte. 33, 10 mi east of Harrisonburg on Rte. 644; ☎ 540/289–9441) offers night skiing, equipment rental, and snow making. There's also an 18-hole golf course.

JOUSTING

Natural Chimneys Regional Park, in Mt. Solon, south of Harrisonburg, hosts jousting tournaments in June and August. The day's entertainment typically includes a parade and crafts exhibitions. Campsites are available. ☎ *540/350–2510.* 🖙 *Prices vary according to event.*

Shopping

The area around Harrisonburg once was a good place to find bargains on antiques and collectibles at estate sales and the like, but dealers have made this as impossible here as elsewhere in the country. Still, there are more than 25 antiques shops in the area—on or near Rte. 11. Contact the Harrisonburg-Rockingham Convention and Visitors Bureau (☞ Shenandoah Valley and the Highlands A to Z, *below*) for a list, or drive through communities such as Bridgewater, Dayton, Elkton, Mt. Crawford, Mt. Sydney, Verona, and Weyer's Cave.

OFF THE
BEATEN PATH

NATURAL CHIMNEYS – Near the town of Grottoes, these seven free-standing limestone pylons stand tall and slender like the pillars of an Egyptian temple ruin. The 500-million-year-old formations were created by some form of natural action, though their exact origins are unknown. Facilities include connecting nature trails and a swimming pool. Every June and August a jousting tournament is held at the site. ✉ *I–81 (Exit 240), west to Bridgewater and follow signs to Grottoes,* ☎ *540/249–5729.* 🖙 *$5 per car.* ⊙ *Daily 9–dusk.*

Dayton

❹ *2 mi west of Harrisonburg (Rte. 33 off I–81).*

For a dose of local culture, head to the **Shenandoah Valley Folk Art & Heritage Center,** where multimedia folk art reflects the culture of the valley. There is also a Civil War exhibit with an electric map that traces Stonewall Jackson's famous 1862 Valley Campaign, as well as other displays. ✉ *382 High St., Dayton,* ☎ *540/879–2681.* 🖙 *$4 adults.* ⊙ *Wed.–Sat. 10–4, Sun. 1–4.*

Fort Harrison (also known as the Daniel Harrison House), which dates from about 1749, is a fortified frontier home decorated in prosperous frontier style. Costumed interpreters discuss how the furnishings—beds with ropes as slats and hand-quilted comforters—were made. Restoration of the summer kitchen began in the fall of 1996 and was expected to take several years. *Route 42 (south of Harrisonburg), Dayton,* ☎ *540/879–2280.* ✉ *Free.* ☉ *Mid-May–Oct., weekends 1–4.*

Shopping

The **Dayton Farmers Market** (✉ Rte. 42, south of Dayton, Box 2-H, Dayton 22821, ☎ 540/879–9885), an 18,000-square-foot area, has everything from homemade baked goods and fresh fruits and vegetables to crafts, such as butter churns and speckleware made by the Mennonites. It's one place to mingle with the industrious and pleasant Mennonites who live in the vicinity, as well as with students from James Madison University in nearby Harrisonburg. ☉ *Thurs. 9–6, Fri. 9–8, Sat. 9–5.*

Staunton

❺ *27 mi south of Dayton; 11 mi west of southern end of Skyline Drive at Waynesboro (off I–64).*

Staunton (pronounced *Stan-*ton) is a town with a distinguished past. This was once the seat of government of the vast Augusta County, formed in 1738 and encompassing present-day West Virginia, Kentucky, Ohio, Illinois, Indiana, and the Pittsburgh area. Staunton was briefly the capital of Virginia, when the General Assembly fled here from the British in 1781. And here Woodrow Wilson was born in 1856.

The restored **Woodrow Wilson Birthplace and Museum** has period antiques, items from Wilson's political career, and some original pieces from when this museum was the residence of Wilson's father, a Presbyterian minister. Among the memorabilia exhibited is Wilson's presidential limousine, a 1919 Pierce-Arrow sedan, on display in the garage. ✉ *24 N. Coalter St., Staunton,* ☎ *540/885–0897.* ✉ *$6.* ☉ *Mar.–Nov., daily 9–5; Dec., daily 10–4; Jan.–Feb., Mon.–Sat. 10–4.*

★ The **Museum of American Frontier Culture,** an outdoor living museum, re-creates the beginnings of agrarian life in America in four genuine 18th-century farmsteads: American, Scots-Irish, German, and English. The attention to authenticity here is painstaking. Master craftsmen were brought from Ulster, Northern Ireland, to thatch the roofs on farm buildings transported from County Tyrone. Livestock have been backbred and ancient seeds germinated in order to create an environment accurate in all details. The museum is off I–81; take Exit 222 to Route 250 West. ✉ *1250 Richmond Rd., Staunton,* ☎ *540/332–7850.* ✉ *$8.* ☉ *Dec.–mid Mar., daily 10–4; mid-Mar.–Nov., daily 9–5.*

The **Statler Brothers Museum,** on the edge of downtown Staunton, about 2 mi from I–81, features memorabilia of more than 30 years, including awards, collected by the Staunton-born country-music singing group. The building that houses the museum is a former school the brothers attended. ✉ *501 Thornrose Ave.,* ☎ *540/885–7297.* ✉ *Free.* ☉ *Guided tours weekdays at 2* PM.

OFF THE BEATEN PATH

GRAND CAVERNS – One of the highlights of Augusta County's Grand Caverns is an underground room that's classified as one of the largest of its kind in the East. Since their discovery in 1806, the caverns have inspired artists such as Porte Crayon, whose drawings appeared in many 19th-century magazines. ✉ *I–81 (Exit 235).* ✉ *$9.* ☉ *Apr.–Oct., daily 9–5; Mar., weekends 9-5.*

Dining and Lodging

$ ✕ **Rowe's Family Restaurant.** A homey restaurant with a bright, comfortable dining room filled with booths, Rowe's has been operated by the same family since 1947. House specialties include Virginia ham, steak, chicken, and homemade pies—the mincemeat is a standout. ⊠ *I–81 (Exit 222), ☎ 540/886–1833. D, MC, V.*

$$–$$$ ✕▥ **Belle Grae Inn.** The sitting room and music room of a restored Victorian house have been converted into formal dining rooms appointed with brass wall sconces, Oriental rugs, and candles at the tables. The cook prepares breast of chicken with artichoke hearts, Bermuda onions, red peppers, and balsamic vinegar sauce. Classic entrées include pecan-crusted, smoked rack of lamb with balsamic vinaigrette; and pan-seared tuna with pepper relish. An adjacent bistro, more casual and less expensive, offers dinner entrées such as chicken Parmesan and London broil. Eighteen rooms available for overnight guests are furnished with rocking chairs and canopied or brass beds; the lodging rates are moderate and include breakfast. ⊠ *515 W. Frederick, 24401, ☎ 540/886–5151, ℻ 540/886–6641. 18 rooms. 2 dining rooms. AE, MC, V.*

$$ ▥ **Frederick House.** Three restored town houses dating from 1810 make up this inn in the center of the historic district. All rooms are decorated with antiques, and smoking is not allowed on the premises. A pub and a restaurant are adjacent. ⊠ *28 N. New St., 24401, ☎ 540/885–4220 or 800/334–5575. 14 rooms. AE, D, DC, MC, V. Rates include breakfast.*

Shopping

Virginia Made Shop (⊠ I–81 Exit 222, Staunton, ☎ 540/886–7180) specializes in English and Irish antique pine furniture.

Blue Ridge Parkway

470 mi from south end of Skyline Drive, parallel to I–81.

The 470-mi Blue Ridge Parkway, a continuation of Skyline Drive, extends south through the George Washington National Forest to Great Smoky Mountains National Park in North Carolina and Tennessee. Although the parkway is less pristine, the higher mountains offer even better views than those of Skyline Drive: **Peaks of Otter Recreation Area,** about 25 mi northeast of Roanoke, rewards drivers and hikers with a 360° panorama of old, soft-sloping mountains—the rougher Alleghenies are visible in the distance. Trails of varying difficulty lead the way up the two main peaks: Sharp Top and Flat Top (the higher of the two at 4,004 feet). The hills rise above the shores of Abbott Lake, a bucolic picnic spot. A pleasant lakeside lodge and campground below are an ideal base for local trekking. Like the drive, the parkway has a variety of lodges, waysides, and self-guided nature walks on a section of the Appalachian Trail; unlike the drive, admission to the parkway and its attractions is free. *Peaks of Otter Recreation Area: ☎ 540/586–4357; Peaks of Otter Lodge: ☎ 540/586–1081.*

Lodging

$$$ ▥ **Doe Run Lodge.** This resort at Groundhog Mountain, a rustic lodge
★   on the crest of the Blue Ridge, offers grand vistas of the Piedmont and proximity to golf, skiing, and hunting. Each unit has a fireplace, and floor-to-ceiling windows allow full appreciation of the view. Reserve well in advance to stay in the log cabin, which is more than 100 years old. ⊠ *Mile Post 189, Rte. 2, Box 338, Hillsville 24343, ☎ 540/398–*

2212 or 800/325–6189, FAX 540/398–2833. 39 chalets, 3 villas. Restaurant, pool, sauna, 3 tennis courts, hiking, fishing. AE, MC, V.

$$$ ⊞ **Wintergreen.** December through March, guests at this 11,000-acre resort may ski and golf on the same day for the price of a lift ticket; all year long there's an extensive choice of sports options. This makes Wintergreen a popular weekend getaway attraction for active Washingtonians, especially in summer, when temperatures in the mountains are significantly lower than elsewhere. Accommodations range from studio apartments to houses with seven bedrooms, and all buildings are wood structures built to blend in with the natural surroundings. The resort is proud of its award-winning environmental awareness; 6,700 acres are protected as natural forest area, and a staff biologist plans nature walks. Ask about discounted packages. ⊠ *Rte. 664, Wintergreen 22958, ☎ 804/325–2200 or 800/325–2200, FAX 804/325–8003. 350 units. 6 restaurants, bar, 1 indoor and 5 outdoor pools, lake, sauna, 2 18-hole golf courses, 25 tennis courts, exercise room, hiking, horseback riding, boating, bicycles, downhill skiing. AE, D, MC, V.*

$$ ⊞ **Peaks of Otter Lodge.** This unpretentious lodge is so popular that reservations are accepted beginning October 1 for the following year. Every room looks out on Abbott Lake from a private terrace or balcony, and the folksy decor adds to the peaceful ambience—unlike the suites, rooms have neither TVs nor phones. The restaurant serves the area's ubiquitous fried trout and offers a prix-fixe menu. ⊠ *Rte. 664, Box 489, Bedford 24523, ☎ 540/586–1081, FAX 540/586–4420. 59 rooms, 3 suites. Restaurant, hiking, fishing. MC, V.*

Outdoor Activities and Sports

GOLF

Wintergreen Resort (⊠ Rte. 664, Wintergreen, ☎ 804/325–2200 or 800/325–2200) offers 36 holes, half in the mountains, half in the valley.

SKIING

There are 17 downhill slopes and five chairlifts at **Wintergreen Resort** (⊠ Rte. 664, Wintergreen, ☎ 804/325–2200 or 800/325–2200).

TENNIS

Wintergreen (⊠ Rte. 664, Wintergreen, ☎ 804/325–2200 or 800/325–2200) maintains 25 outdoor tennis courts. Many hotels throughout the region provide courts or arrange for guests to use nearby facilities.

Lexington

6 *30 mi south of Staunton on I–81.*

Two deeply traditional Virginia colleges sit side by side in this town, each with a memorial to a soldier who was also a man of peace.

Washington and Lee University, the sixth-oldest college in the United States, was founded in 1749 as Augusta Academy and later renamed Washington College in gratitude for a donation from George Washington. After Robert E. Lee served as its president following the Civil War, it received its present name. Today, with 1,850 students, the university occupies a campus of white-column, redbrick buildings around a central colonnade. The Lee Chapel and Museum on campus contains many relics of the Lee family. Edward Valentine's statue of the recumbent general, behind the altar, is especially moving: The pose is natural and the expression gentle, a striking contrast to most monumental art. Here one can sense the affection and reverence that Lee inspired. ⊠ *Jefferson St. (Rte. 11), ☎ 540/463–8768. ☜ Free. ☉ Apr.–Oct., Mon.–Sat. 9–5, Sun. 2–5; Nov.–Mar., Mon.–Sat. 9–4, Sun. 2–5.*

Adjacent to Washington and Lee University are the imposing Gothic buildings of the **Virginia Military Institute,** founded in 1839 and home to about 1,300 cadets. The **Virginia Military Institute Museum** in the lower level of Jackson Memorial Hall displays Stonewall Jackson's stuffed and mounted horse, Little Sorrel, and the general's coat, pierced by the bullet that killed him at Chancellorsville. ☎ *540/464–7232. ⌨ Free.* ☉ *Daily 9–5.*

The **George C. Marshall Museum** preserves the memory of the World War II army chief of staff. Exhibits trace his brilliant career, which began when he was aide-de-camp to John "Black Jack" Pershing in World War I and culminated when, as secretary of state, he devised the Marshall Plan, a strategy for reviving postwar Western Europe. Marshall's Nobel Peace Prize is on display; so is the Oscar won by his aide Frank McCarthy, who produced the Academy Award–winning Best Picture of 1970, *Patton.* An electronically narrated map tells the story of World War II. ☎ *540/463–7103. ⌨ $3.* ☉ *Mar.–Oct., daily 9–5; Nov.–Feb., daily 9–4.*

<table>
<tr><td>NEED A BREAK?</td><td>**Sweet Things** (⌨ 106 W. Washington St., ☎ 540/463–6055) is one of those rare places that still make old-fashioned milk shakes, sundaes, and homemade ice cream and frozen yogurt in special flavors, served in homemade cones.</td></tr>
</table>

Jackson's private life is on display at the **Stonewall Jackson House,** where he is revealed as a man devoted to physical fitness and the Presbyterian faith, careful with money, musically inclined, and fond of gardening. The general lived here only two years, while teaching physics and military tactics to the cadets, until the Civil War put his tactical genius to bloody use. This is the only house he ever owned; it is furnished now with period pieces and some of his belongings. ⌨ *8 E. Washington St.,* ☎ *540/463–2552. ⌨ $5.* ☉ *Sept.–May, Mon.–Sat. 9–5, Sun. 1–5; June–Aug., Mon.–Sat. 9–6, Sun. 1–6.*

Cyrus McCormick, who invented the first mechanical wheat reaper, is honored at the **McCormick Museum and Wayside,** which sits about a mile off I–81. Follow the signs to Walnut Grove farm; now a livestock research center, this mill farmstead is where McCormick did his work. ⌨ *S.R. 606, a few mi north of Lexington,* ☎ *540/377–2255. ⌨ Free.* ☉ *Daily 8:30–5.*

Dining and Lodging

$$–$$$ ✕ **Wilson-Walker House.** This stately 19th-century Greek Revival house is the ideal setting in which to enjoy elegant regional cuisine. Seafood dishes are a specialty, particularly the crab-and-shrimp cakes—but additional offerings such as burgers and pasta are more mundane. The restaurant is surprisingly affordable, particularly during the $5 chef's-special luncheon. ⌨ *30 N. Main St.,* ☎ *540/463–3020. Reservations essential for dinner. AE, MC, V. Closed Sun. and Mon.*

$ ✕ **The Palms.** Once a Victorian ice-cream parlor, this property is now a full-service restaurant with indoor and outdoor dining. Wood booths line the walls of the plant-filled room whose pressed-metal ceiling is one of the original details of this 1890 building. Food is prepared and presented with care; specialties include broccoli-cheese soup, charbroiled meats, and teriyaki chicken. ⌨ *101 W. Nelson St.,* ☎ *540/463–7911. Reservations not accepted. D, MC, V.*

$$$ ✕⌂ **Maple Hall.** For a taste of southern history, spend a night at this country inn of 1850, formerly a plantation house, set on 56 acres 7 mi north of the Lexington historic district. All rooms have private baths,

period antiques, and modern amenities; most have gas log fireplaces as well. Dinner is served in three ground-floor rooms and on a glassed-in patio. Watercolors by local artists adorn the cream-color walls; the main dining room has a large decorative fireplace, and in one of the other rooms the fireplace is used in cold weather. Among notable entrées on the seasonal menu are beef fillet with green peppercorn sauce; veal sautéed with mushrooms in hollandaise sauce; and chicken Chesapeake, a chicken breast stuffed with spinach and crabmeat. ⊠ *Rte. 11, 24450,* ☎ *540/463–6693,* ꜰꜰ *540/463–7262. 21 rooms. Restaurant, pool, tennis court, hiking, fishing. MC, V.*

$$ ⊞ **Natural Bridge Hotel.** Within walking distance of the spectacular rock arch of the same name (there is also shuttle-bus service), the hotel has a beautiful setting as well as numerous family recreational facilities. Long porches with rocking chairs allow leisurely appreciation of the prospect of the Blue Ridge Mountains. Rooms have ersatz Colonial Virginia decor. ⊠ *U.S. 11, Box 57, Natural Bridge 24578,* ☎ *540/291–2121 or 800/533–1410,* ꜰꜰ *540/291–1896. 180 rooms. Restaurant, deli, pool, 2 tennis courts, hiking. AE, D, DC, MC, V.*

Nightlife and the Arts

Washington and Lee University's **Lenfest Center for the Performing Arts** (⊠ Lexington, ☎ 540/463–8000) sponsors a variety of concerts, recitals, and dramatic events during the school year.

The **Theater at Lime Kiln** (⊠ Lexington, ☎ 540/463–3074) performs in the ruins of a lime kiln whose solid rock walls create a dramatic backdrop for each performance. Original musicals are staged Tuesday through Saturday, and contemporary music concerts are given on Sunday throughout the summer. Previous visiting artists have ranged from Russian clowns to Vietnamese puppets.

Outdoor Activities and Sports

The **Virginia Horse Center** stages competitions—show jumping, hunter trials, multibreed shows—several days a week. An indoor arena permits year-round operation. ⊠ *Lexington,* ☎ *540/463–2194.* ꜰ *Varies with event.*

OFF THE
BEATEN PATH

NATURAL BRIDGE OF VIRGINIA – About 20 mi south of Lexington on I–81, this impressive limestone arch has been gradually carved out of rock by Cedar Creek, which rushes through 215 feet below. The Monocan Indians called it the Bridge of God, but today it is destined for less heavenly uses; in addition to being the popular tourist attraction of a private corporation, the bridge supports part of U.S. 11. Surveying the structure for Lord Halifax, George Washington carved his own initials in the stone; Thomas Jefferson bought it (and more than 150 surrounding acres) from George III. The after-dark sound-and-light show may be overkill, but viewing and walking under the bridge itself and along the wooded pathway beyond are worth the price of admission. The bridge complex also includes dizzying caverns that descend 34 stories into the earth and a wax museum that gives a factory tour of the state-of-the-art process by which the figures are made. ⊠ *Exit 180 off I–81 south, Exit 175 off I–81 north,* ☎ *540/291–2121 or 800/533–1410.* ꜰ *Single attraction $8; any two attractions $12; all three attractions $15. Sound-and-light show $8.* ☺ *May–Aug., daily 8–8; Sept., Nov., Mar.–Apr., daily 8–6; Dec.–Feb., Wed.–Sun. 8–4.*

En Route   The drive to Bath County on the 35-mi stretch of Route 39 north and west from Lexington provides a scenic side trip whose most prominent feature is the 3-mi **Goshen Pass,** which follows the Maury River through the mountains. Before the coming of railroads, it was the principal stagecoach route into Lexington. The sunlight shining through the thick, variegated foliage creates a brilliant kaleidoscope at any time of year. Starting in May, the scene becomes lush with rhododendrons and other flowering plants. A day-use park enables picnickers to bask in this still underused sylvan refuge, where visitors can fish, swim, and inner-tube in the river.

Bath County

❼ *20 mi northwest of Lexington, on Rte. 39.*

As residents are proud to point out, there are no traffic lights in all of Bath County, just four billboards and only 10 year-round inhabitants per square mile. For more than 200 years this peaceful area has been a popular resort. Visitors came originally for the healing thermal springs, whose treatments are less fashionable today—though the sulfur waters still flow at **Warm Springs, Hot Springs,** and **Bolar Springs,** their temperatures ranging from 77°F to 104°F. On Route 645, in Warm Springs, you may want to stop by **Gristmill Square,** where five restored historic buildings have been converted into a gift shop, inn, and the Waterwheel Restaurant (☞ Dining and Lodging, *below*).

★ Of the numerous resorts in Bath County, the **Homestead** has long been an attraction in its own right. The sprawling redbrick main building, which looks almost like a movie-set version of a Colonial mansion grown to fantastic size, was built in 1891 and is still owned by the founding M. E. Ingalls family. Every imaginable luxury and diversion is available to its guests, whose number at any one time may reach 1,000. You can still drink from the springs around which the spa was built in the 19th century, when wealthy vacationers from the North traveled here on private rail cars. The oldest of the resort's three golf courses was laid out in 1892, making it the oldest course in Virginia—the first tee is the oldest in continuous use in the United States. It was here that famed golfer Sam Snead got his start. In addition to golf, the resort offers tennis, horseback riding, carriage riding, fishing, lawn bowling, skeet, trap, and archery; this is also where the first downhill skiing in the South took place in 1959–60. ⊠ *Hot Springs, 5 mi south of Warm Springs on Rte. 39,* ☎ *540/839–5500 or 800/336–5771,* 𝔽𝔸𝕏 *540/839–7670.*

Dining and Lodging

$$$ ✕ **Waterwheel Restaurant.** Part of a complex of five restored build-
★ ings, this restaurant is in a gristmill that dates from 1700. A walk-in wine cellar, set among the gears of the original waterwheel, has 100 varieties of wine; diners may step in and make their own selections. The dining area is decorated with Currier and Ives and Audubon prints. The changing menu includes such favorites as salmon fillet with béarnaise sauce and chicken Fantasio (breast of chicken stuffed with wild rice, sausage, apple, and pecans). Desserts include such Old Virginny recipes as apple brown Betty, a deep-dish apple pie baked with bourbon. On Sundays, look for the hearty but affordable brunch. ⊠ *Grist Mill Sq., Warm Springs,* ☎ *540/839–2231. D, MC, V. Closed Mon. Nov.–Apr. No lunch.*

$$$$ 🏨 **The Homestead.** The Homestead in Hot Springs is to the luxury re-
★ sort what the Rolls-Royce is to the family wagon. Host to a prestigious clientele since 1761—Thomas Jefferson was the first of eight American presidents to visit—the Homestead has evolved from a country spa

famed for its mineral waters to a state-of-the-art resort and conference facility that spans 16,000 acres. From the glorious columns of the entry hall to the stunning views of the Appalachian Mountains, magnificence surrounds guests from first moment to last. Rooms in the older section of the hotel (which includes the tower and the south wing) have elegant Victorian decor and Chippendale-reproduction furnishings. The newer section features well-appointed duplexes with fireplaces and private bars. Four miles of streams stocked with rainbow trout, 100 mi of riding trails, skeet and trap shooting, 10 ski slopes, and three 18-hole golf courses are just a few of the sport and leisure facilities available. The natural mineral springs and spa offer up-to-the-minute treatment and weight-training equipment. An orchestra plays nightly in the formal dining room, which features such regional specialties as Virginia lamb in its six-course extravaganzas. ⊠ *Rte. 220, Hot Springs 24445,* ☎ *540/839–1766 or 800/838–1766,* FAX *540/839–7670. 521 rooms. 7 restaurants, 1 indoor and 2 outdoor pools, spa, 3 18-hole golf courses, 19 tennis courts, bowling, horseback riding, downhill skiing, cinema. AE, MC, V. Rates are MAP or European plan.*

$$$ ✶ 🏨 **Inn at Gristmill Square.** Occupying two of five restored buildings at the same site as the Waterwheel Restaurant, the rooms of this state historical landmark inn have a Colonial Virginia decor. Four units are in the original miller's house; the main building, formerly a country store, has a modern addition in period style. Near the inn and restaurant, a blacksmith shop and a hardware store have been combined and converted into a gift shop. ⊠ *Rte. 645, Box 359, Warm Springs 24484,* ☎ *540/839–2231,* FAX *540/839–5770. 10 rooms, 5 suites, 1 apartment. Restaurant, bar, pool, sauna, 3 tennis courts. D, MC, V.*

$$–$$$ 🏨 **Milton Hall.** This restored 1874 house, built as a country retreat by English nobility, is located on 44 acres adjacent to the George Washington National Forest. The location is good for hunting, fishing, hiking, and other outdoor activities, and the staff provides box lunches for guests who make arrangements in advance. ⊠ *Off I–64 (Exit 10) at Callaghan. 207 Thorny Lane, Covington 24426,* ☎ *540/965–0196. 5 rooms, 1 suite. MC, V. Full breakfast included.*

$ 🏨 **Roseloe Motel.** Some rooms in this modest, clean hostelry have a kitchenette; each has a refrigerator. The conventional decor differs from room to room—the larger rooms are in the addition—but a homelike atmosphere prevails throughout. The motel is halfway between Warm Springs and Hot Springs, and the fresh mountain air is bracing. ⊠ *Rte. 2 (Box 590), Hot Springs 24445,* ☎ *540/839–5373. 14 rooms. Kitchenettes, refrigerators. AE, D, MC, V.*

Nightlife and the Arts

Garth Newel Music Center (⊠ Hot Springs, ☎ 540/839–5018) has weekend chamber-music performances in summer; you can make reservations and plan to picnic on the grounds.

Outdoor Activities and Sports

GOLF

The **Homestead** has three excellent golf courses (⊠ Rte. 220, Hot Springs, ☎ 540/839–1766 or 800/838–1766, FAX 540/839–7670).

SKIING

Try cross-country, downhill, or night skiing at the **Homestead** (⊠ Rte. 220, Hot Springs, ☎ 540/839–1766 or 800/838–1766).

TENNIS

The **Homestead** (⊠ Rte. 39, Hot Springs, ☎ 540/839–1766 or 800/838–1766) has 12 tennis courts.

Roanoke

8 *49 mi south of Lexington (via I–81).*

The quiet and cheerful city of Roanoke is a hub for the railroad and the arts. In Market Square, at the heart of the city, a restored warehouse called **Center in the Square** (☎ 540/342–5700) contains the Mill Mountain Theatre (musicals, Shakespeare, contemporary drama) and three museums.

The **Science Museum of Western Virginia and Hopkins Planetarium** has displays on Virginia's natural history. Many exhibits are interactive and especially appealing to youngsters. Shows are given in the planetarium. ⊠ *Center in the Square,* ☎ *540/342–5710.* ⌨ *Combined museum and planetarium $6. Museum $5. Planetarium $2.60.* ☉ *Mon.–Sat. 10–5, Sun. 1–5.*

The **Roanoke Valley History Museum** displays a curious collection of regional artifacts, including relics of the local Native Americans, whose word for "shell wampum" forms the root of "Roanoke." A permanent exhibit explores the history of volunteer rescue units in America. ⊠ *Center in the Square,* ☎ *540/342–5770.* ⌨ *$2.* ☉ *Tues.–Fri. 10–4, Sat. 10–5, Sun. 1–5.*

The collection of the **Art Museum of Western Virginia** is strongest in regional works, particularly Appalachian folk art. The exhibition space extends into the Center on Church annex across the alley, which is linked by a second-floor gallery bridge; the gallery of 19th-century American art was tripled in size in 1990. ⊠ *Center in the Square,* ☎ *540/342–5760.* ⌨ *Free.* ☉ *Tues.–Sat. 10–5, Sun. 1–5.*

NEED A
BREAK?

Residents of Roanoke may steer you away from the **Texas Tavern** (⊠ 114 Church Ave., ☎ 540/342–4825), not because they are ashamed of it but because they want to keep it to themselves. A sign proclaims WE SERVE A THOUSAND, TEN AT A TIME—and there are just 10 stools. The tavern is often packed, especially late at night; chili is the specialty. This spot is not recommended for families.

Near Market Square, the **Virginia Museum of Transportation** is devoted almost exclusively to trains, for Roanoke got its start as a railroad town and is today the headquarters of the Norfolk and Western Railway (formerly the Norfolk Southern). The dozens of original train cars and engines, many built here in town, include a massive Nickel Plate locomotive—just one of the many holdings that constitute an unabashed display of civic pride peculiar to Roanoke. ⊠ *303 Norfolk Ave.,* ☎ *540/342–5670.* ⌨ *$5.* ☉ *Mon.–Sat. 10–5, Sun. noon–5. Closed Mon. Jan.–Feb.*

Dining and Lodging

$$$$ ✕ **The Library.** This quiet, elegant restaurant in the Piccadilly Square shopping center is decorated with shelves of books, and specializes in seafood dishes. ⊠ *3117 Franklin Rd. SW,* ☎ *540/985–0811. Reservations essential. AE, DC, MC, V. Closed Sun.*

$$$ ✕ **La Maison du Gourmet.** One by one, starting in 1978, the 12 rooms
★   of this brick Georgian Colonial house built in 1927 have been converted into dining rooms; one accommodates 50 people, another (a former bedroom) only 15. A second-floor terrace, used in warmer weather, overlooks the elaborate formal gardens that cover much of the 2-acre property—especially enjoyable during Sunday brunch. Dining rooms are variously distinguished by crystal chandeliers, fireplaces, slate floors, and bare wood floors. The tableside preparation of steak Diane is a sight: Filet mignon in bordelaise sauce is flambéed, then served with fresh mushrooms and scallions. The menu also offers a range of veal,

chicken, and lamb entrées. ⊠ *5732 Airport Rd.,* ☎ *540/366–2444. AE, D, DC, MC, V. No lunch. Closed Mon.*

$$ ✕ **The Homeplace.** Here's a prime restaurant for old-fashioned cooking served family-style, including fried chicken, mashed potatoes and gravy, green beans, pinto beans, baked apples, and hot biscuits. No alcohol is served. Try the Sunday brunch. ⊠ *I–81, Exit 141, Rte. 311 N, near Salem,* ☎ *540/384–7252. Reservations not accepted. MC, V. No lunch. Closed Mon.–Wed.*

$$$ 🏨 **Bernard's Landing.** A lakeside resort 45 minutes southeast of Roanoke, Bernard's offers one- to three-bedroom condominiums with water views, for periods of up to two weeks. As the condos are separately owned, decor varies widely, but all units have full kitchen facilities. Businesspeople schedule conferences here year-round, and summer vacationers come for the various sports facilities. ⊠ *775 Ashmeade Rd., Moneta 24121,* ☎ *540/721–8870 or 800/572–2048,* 🖷 *540/721–8383. 63 units. Restaurant, 2 pools, sauna, 6 tennis courts, exercise room, boating, fishing, playground. AE, D, MC, V.*

$$–$$$ 🏨 **Patrick Henry Hotel.** Strategically located at I–581 and Elm Avenue, this hotel is easy to reach and central to downtown attractions. The interior is attractively decorated, particularly the elegant lobby, and antiques in the restored rooms make each guest quarter unique. ⊠ *617 S. Jefferson St., 24011,* ☎ *540/345–8811 or 800/833–4567,* 🖷 *540/342–9908. 124 rooms. Restaurant, lobby lounge, kitchenettes. AE, MC, V.*

$$ 🏨 **Holiday Inn Civic Center.** The convenient downtown location—at I–581 and Williamson Road—of this 30-year-old facility helps to make it a popular accommodation with business travelers. The conventional two-story building is ringed by parking space; a pool surrounded by a courtyard with a pebble surface adds some privacy. The contemporary rooms have soundproofing and wood furniture, and the lobby is a model of modern Holiday Inn style, with sturdy but ordinary furnishings. ⊠ *501 Orange Ave., 24016,* ☎ *540/342–8961,* 🖷 *540/342– 3813. 152 rooms. Restaurant, lobby lounge, pool. AE, D, DC, MC, V.*

Nightlife and the Arts

DANCE

Throughout spring and fall, the **Roanoke Ballet Theatre** (☎ 540/345– 6099) attracts guest artists from around the world for performances at theaters around town and the Shenandoah Valley.

MUSIC

The Roanoke Symphony (☎ 540/343–9127) performs monthly in January, February, March, April, October, and November. In addition, there are picnic-with-the-pops performances in July and August, and holiday pops concerts in December.
Roanoke Valley Chamber Music Society (☎ 540/774–2899) hosts distinguished visiting performers from October to May at the Olin Theater on the campus of Roanoke College.

THEATER

Mill Mountain Theatre (⊠ Center in the Square, Roanoke, ☎ 540/342– 5740) offers year-round professional theater, plus a festival of new works.
Roanoke Comedy Club (⊠ Fiji Island Restaurant, 627 Townside Rd., ☎ 540/982–5693) combines dinner and laughs Thursday through Saturday nights, with headliners, feature acts, and amateur night.

Outdoor Activities and Sports

The Roanoke Valley Horse Show (⊠ Salem Civic Center, ☎ 540/389–7847), in June, is one of the top all-breed shows, attracting more than 1,000 entries each year.

OFF THE BEATEN PATH

DIXIE CAVERNS – Visitors to Dixie Caverns can wander inside a mountain and ascend into an enormous chamber called the Cathedral Room, and into smaller cavities with names such as Turkey Wing and Wedding Bell, all hung with beautiful stalactites and flows that look like taffy. There's also a mineral and fossil shop attached to the caverns. To get there from I–81, take Exit 132, which links up with Route 11/460. ⊠ *5753 W. Main St., Salem,* ☎ *540/380-2085.* ⌑ *$6.50.* ⊙ *Daily 9:30–6.*

BOOKER T. WASHINGTON'S BIRTHPLACE – This restored plantation 20 mi southeast of Roanoke is now a national monument and a museum of life under slavery. Washington, born in slavery, was a remarkable educator who went on to advise presidents McKinley, Roosevelt, and Taft and to take tea with Queen Victoria. More important, he started Tuskegee Institute in Alabama and inspired generations of African-Americans. Covering 224 acres, the farm presents restored buildings, tools, crops, animals, and, in summer, interpreters in period costume. The plantation is on Route 122, 5 mi east of Burnt Chimney (the junction of Routes 116 and 122). ⊠ *Rte. 122,* ☎ *540/721-2094.* ⌑ *Free.* ⊙ *Daily 9–5.*

MILL MOUNTAIN ZOO – Here you'll find 45 species of exotic and native animals, including a Siberian tiger, a snow leopard, and red pandas. ⊠ *Off the Blue Ridge Pkwy., Box 13484, Roanoke 24034,* ☎ *540/343-3241.* ⌑ *$4.* ⊙ *(Weather permitting) Memorial Day–Labor Day, daily 10–8 (gate closes at 7:30); rest of year, daily 10–5 (gate closes at 4:30).*

THE HIGHLANDS

The Highlands is the only region of the state where the atmosphere retains a residue of the frontier wilderness that enthralled adventurers such as Daniel Boone and provided a setting for their heroic exploits. The shortest route southwest through this rugged region is I–81; the scenic option is to continue south on the Blue Ridge Parkway to I–77, then take I–77 west to I–81.

Mabry Mill

❾ *70 mi southwest of Roanoke.*

Mabry Mill, north of Meadows of Dan and the Blue Ridge Parkway's junction with U.S. 58 at mile marker 176, is the parkway's point of greatest interest. Here are a sawmill and a restored water-powered gristmill, producing cornmeal and buckwheat flour (for sale). Regular demonstrations showcase blacksmithing and other trades. ☎ *540/952–2947.* ⌑ *Free.* ⊙ *May and Sept.–Oct., daily 8–6; June–Aug., daily 8–7.*

OFF THE BEATEN PATH

CHÂTEAU MORRISETTE WINERY INC. – The surrounding hills create a spectacular setting for this winery. Tours of the facilities are given, and tastings allow visitors to sample the dozen different wines produced on the premises. ⊠ *On Winery Rd., off Rte. 726, west of Blue Ridge Pkwy.,* ☎ *540/593-2865.* ⌑ *$1.* ⊙ *Mon.–Sat. 10–5, Sun. 11–5. Closed Thanksgiving, Dec. 25, Jan. 1.*

Newbern

🔟 *40 mi southwest of Roanoke (off I–81).*

The Wilderness Road Regional Museum in Newbern is a fascinating look at a past way of life. Settlers used to lodge here on their way west along the Wilderness Road, a route from Pennsylvania through the Cumberland Gap that had been used originally by Native Americans. The man who founded Newbern in 1810 built this house in the same year, and the structure has since served as a private home, a tavern, a post office, and a store. Today the house contains an eclectic collection: antique dolls, swords and rifles, an old loom, and other artifacts of everyday life. Museum guides will point out the several other 19th-century structures in town. ⊠ *I–81 (Exit 98),* ☎ *540/674–4835.* 🎟 *Free.* ☉ *Tues.–Sat. 10:30–4:30, Sun. 1:30–4:30.*

Dining and Lodging

$ ✕ **Valley Pike Inn.** Fried chicken, country-baked ham, roast beef, ★ homemade buttermilk biscuits, and old-fashioned fruit cobblers are served at this down-home family-owned restaurant. The building dates from 1830 and was originally an inn at a stagecoach stop. Wood walls and floors add to the farmhouse atmosphere. No liquor is served. ⊠ *Off I–81 (Exit 98),* ☎ *540/674–1810 or 540/980–6757. MC, V. Closed Jan.–Apr., Mon.–Thurs.; May–Dec., Mon.–Wed. No lunch.*

$$ 🏨 **Best Western Radford Inn.** Service and amenities (such as a bathroom phone) distinguish this facility from other highway motels of similar ambience and location. Rooms are decorated in Colonial Virginia style, and the views of the Blue Ridge Mountains are not utterly spoiled by the surrounding parking lot. ⊠ *1501 Tyler Ave. (Rte. 177), Radford 24141,* ☎ FAX *540/639–3000; 800/528–1234. 104 rooms. Restaurant, bar, indoor pool, sauna, exercise room. AE, D, DC, MC, V.*

$$ 🏨 **Boxwood Inn.** Between Roanoke and Abingdon, this 1835 home is surrounded by mountains and is within walking distance of crafts and antiques shops. A yard with English boxwoods adds to the 19th-century atmosphere. Breakfast is included in the room rate. ⊠ *460 E. Main St., Wytheville 24382,* ☎ *540/228–8911. 8 rooms. MC, V.*

Jefferson National Forest

Roughly parallel to I–81.

Distributed in scattered patches across southwestern Virginia, the 700,000 acres of campgrounds, picnic areas, and lakes of the Jefferson National Forest (now part of the George Washington and Jefferson National Forest system) provide a habitat for bobcats, black bears, and bald eagles. Here are more than 1,000 mi of hiking trails and hundreds of streams for fishing, with trout in abundance. The portion of Jefferson National Forest south of I–81 (and west of I–77) is the **Mount Rogers National Recreation Area** (⊠ Rte. 1, Box 303, Marion 24354, ☎ 540/783–5196), where Virginia's highest mountain, the 5,729-foot Mt. Rogers, is traversed by an extensive network of riding and hiking trails. The Appalachian Trail crosses the border into Tennessee here. Hunting and fishing are permitted in season; permits are available in most sporting goods stores. ⊠ *USDA Forest Supervisor, 5162 Valleypointe Pkwy., Roanoke 24019,* ☎ *540/265–5100.*

OFF THE
BEATEN PATH
CRAB ORCHARD MUSEUM AND PIONEER PARK – On the site of an archaeological dig just west of the town of Tazewell, these 110 acres were part of a hunting ground for the Shawnee and Cherokee nations,

and many of the traditional tools and pieces of furniture have been recovered. European settlement and the ensuing history are illustrated by displays of artifacts, and further exhibits show the social impact of farming and regional mining. Farm buildings and crafts shops nearby are fully accessible to the disabled. The park is west of Mt. Rogers, just off I–81. ⊠ *Rtes. 19/460, Tazewell,* ☏ *540/988-6755.* ⚏ *$5.* ☉ *Apr.–Oct., Mon.–Sat. 9–5, Sun. 1–5; Nov.–Mar., Mon.–Sat. 9–5.*

Abingdon

⑪ *80 mi southwest of Newbern; 135 mi southwest of Roanoke (via Rte. I–81).*

Abingdon, near the Tennessee border, is a cultural crossroads in the wilderness: The town of nearly 10,000 residents draws tens of thousands of visitors annually with a fine theater company (☞ *below*) and exuberant local celebrations. By far the most popular attraction here is the **Virginia Highlands Festival** during the first two weeks of August: 150,000 people come to hear live performances of music ranging from bluegrass to opera, to visit the exhibitions of mountain crafts, and to browse among the wares of more than 100 antiques dealers. This is followed by the **Burley Tobacco Festival,** held in September, where country-music stars perform and prize farm animals are proudly displayed. ⊠ *Abingdon Convention & Visitors Bureau, 335 Cummings St., 24210,* ☏ *540/676–2282.*

From April through the Christmas season, audiences flock to the prestigious **Barter Theatre** (⊠ 133 W. Main St., ☏ 540/628–3991 or 800/368–3240), America's longest-running professional repertory theater. Founded during the Depression by local actor Robert Porterfield, the theater got its name in the obvious way: Early patrons who could not afford the 40¢ tickets were offered admission for the equivalent in produce. Hume Cronyn, Ned Beatty, and Gregory Peck are among the many stars who began their careers at the Barter, which today presents the classics of Shakespeare as well as works by contemporary playwrights such as David Mamet. Although times have changed since Noël Coward was given a Virginia ham for his contributions, the official policy still permits you to barter for your seat. But don't just show up at the box office with a bag of arugula—all trades must be approved by advance notice.

Dining and Lodging

$$ ✕ **The Tavern.** This cozy restaurant—built in 1779 and standing as the oldest building in town—was a field hospital during the Civil War. Today, it has three small dining rooms and a cocktail lounge, all with fireplaces, stone walls, and brick floors. In warm weather you can dine outdoors on a balcony overlooking historic Court House Hill, or on a brick patio surrounded by trees and flowers. The menu features fresh seasonal seafood and rack of lamb. There is live music nightly. ⊠ *222 E. Main St.,* ☏ *540/628–1118. AE, MC, V.*

$$$–$$$$ ⛫ **Camberley's Martha Washington Inn.** Constructed as a private house in 1832, turned into a college dormitory in 1860, and used as a field hospital during the Civil War, the Martha Washington has been an inn since 1935; it's opposite the Barter Theatre, itself a historical landmark. The inn's rooms are furnished with antiques; some have fireplaces. The restaurant menu includes roasted rainbow trout with crayfish, loin of lamb with hominy cheese grits, and—for dessert—Martha's marbled strawberry shortcake. There is buffet dining Wednesday through Friday in Martha's Pantry, and complimentary afternoon tea

is offered Friday and Saturday on the porch of the inn. ⊠ *150 W. Main St., 24210,* ☎ *540/628–3161,* ℻ *540/628–8885. 50 rooms with bath, 11 suites. 2 restaurants, bar. AE, D, DC, MC, V.*

$ ⚟ **Alpine Motel.** The spacious, modern rooms of this clean motel have striking views of Virginia's highest mountain peaks: Mt. Rogers and Whitetop. The motel is set far back from the road and is therefore popular with families, as well as traveling salespeople. The renowned Barter Theatre is nearby. ⊠ *882 E. Main St., 24210,* ☎ *540/628–3178,* ℻ *540/628–4247. 19 rooms. AE, D, MC, V.*

<table>
<tr><td>OFF THE
BEATEN PATH</td><td>

BIG STONE GAP – About 60 mi west of Abingdon along Alternate U.S. Route 58, Big Stone Gap stands among the mountains that inspired the early 20th-century novel and later movie, *The Trail of the Lonesome Pine,* by John Fox, Jr. The tragic story of June Tolliver, mountain feuding, and vigilante law is retold every year during the summer months in an outdoor theater, where local performers have acted in this production for more than 30 years. The organization that sponsors the play also manages the 1880s June Tolliver House, where rooms are furnished from the period, and local arts and crafts, including coal carvings and quilts, are sold. ⊠ *Climpon Ave.,* ☎ *540/523-4707.* ⚟ *Free; donations accepted. Performance $7.* ⊙ *Performances: mid-June–Labor Day, Thurs.–Sat. 8:15* PM. *House: June–mid-Dec., Tues.–Sun. 12:30* PM–4:30 PM *and during theater intermission.*

SOUTHWEST VIRGINIA HISTORICAL MUSEUM – In a Victorian mansion built during the coal boom of 1888-93, you'll find the mine-manager's home furnishings and various other exhibits. ⊠ *Rte. 58, Big Stone Gap,* ☎ *540/523-1322.* ⚟ *$3.* ⊙ *Memorial Day–Labor Day, Mon.–Thurs. 10–4, Fri. 9–4, Sat. 10–5, Sun. 1–5; Labor Day Dec. 30 and Mar.–Memorial Day, Tues.–Fri. 10–4, Sat. 9–5, Sun. 1–5; closed Jan.–Feb. and major holidays.*

</td></tr>
</table>

Nightlife and the Arts

The renowned **Barter Theatre** (☞ *above*) has performances Wednesday–Sunday nights year-round. Plays change every four weeks.

SHENANDOAH VALLEY AND THE HIGHLANDS A TO Z

Arriving and Departing

By Bus

Greyhound Lines (☎ 800/231–2222) schedules several trips daily to and from Abingdon (⊠ 465 W. Main St., ☎ 540/628–4409) and Roanoke (⊠ 26 Salem Ave., ☎ 540/343–5436) on its transcontinental routes between major U.S. cities. Lexington (⊠ U.S. 11, north of bridge, ☎ 800/231–2222) and Staunton (⊠ 1143 Richmond Rd., ☎ 540/886–2424) have daily service to and from New York and points south.

By Car

I–81 and U.S. 11 run north–south the length of the Shenandoah Valley and continue south into Tennessee. I–66 west from Washington, DC, which is 90 mi to the east, passes through Front Royal to meet I–81 and U.S. 11 at the northern end of the valley. I–64 connects the same highways with Charlottesville, 30 mi to the east. Route 39 into Bath County connects with I–81 just north of Lexington. I–77 cuts off the southwest tip of the state, running north–south.

By Plane
Roanoke Regional Airport (☎ 540/362–1999) has flights by five major airlines and their regional affiliates, principally USAir (☎ 800/428–4322). **Tri-City Regional Airport** (☎ 423/325–6000), just across the state line in Blountville, Tennessee, is served by USAir and Delta.

By Train
Amtrak (☎ 800/872–7245) has service three days a week to Staunton, en route from New York and Chicago. The same train stops at Clifton Forge for the Homestead resort in Bath County. A complimentary shuttle bus on Sunday, Wednesday, and Friday connects Roanoke (Campbell Court and Roanoke Airport Sheraton) and Clifton Forge Rail Station.

Contacts and Resources

B&B Reservations Agencies
Accommodations in private homes and reconverted inns are available through **Blue Ridge Bed & Breakfast Reservation Service** (✉ Rte. 2, Box 3895, Berryville 22611, ☎ 540/955–1246 or 800/296–1246, FAX 540/955–4240).

Emergencies
Throughout the region, dial **911** for emergency assistance.

HOSPITALS
Roanoke: Carilion Roanoke Memorial Hospital (✉ Belleview Ave. and Jefferson St., ☎ 540/981–7000).
Fishersville: Augusta Medical Center (✉ 96 Medical Center Dr., ☎ 540/332–4000).

Guided Tours
The **Historic Staunton Foundation** (☎ 540/885–7676) offers free one-hour walking tours of Staunton Saturday morning at 10, Memorial Day through October, departing from the Woodrow Wilson Birthplace at 24 North Coalter Street. A brochure is available for a self-guided tour.

For $10, the **Lexington Horse-Drawn Carriage Company** (☎ 540/463–5647) will take visitors around town in a horse-drawn carriage for 45–50 minutes, from April through October. A walking-tour brochure is available at the Lexington Visitor Center (✉ 102 E. Washington St., ☎ 540/463–3777).

Visitor Information
Abingdon Convention & Visitors Bureau (✉ 335 Cummings St., Abingdon 24210, ☎ 540/676–2282).
Bath County Chamber of Commerce (✉ Rte. 220, Box 718, Hot Springs 24445, ☎ 540/839–5409).
Front Royal/Warren County Chamber of Commerce and Visitors Center (✉ 414 E. Main St., Front Royal 22630, ☎ 540/635–3185 or 800/338–2576).
Harrisonburg-Rockingham Convention and Visitors Bureau (✉ 800 Country Club Rd., Harrisonburg 22801, ☎ 540/434–2319 or 540/434–3862).
Lexington Visitor Center (✉ 102 E. Washington St., Lexington 24450, ☎ 540/463–3777).
Roanoke Valley Convention and Visitors Bureau (✉ 114 Market St., Roanoke 24011, ☎ 540/342–6025 or 800/635–5535).
Shenandoah Valley Travel Association (✉ Box 1040, New Market 22844, ☎ 540/740–3132).
Staunton/Augusta Travel Information Center (✉ 1303 Richmond Ave., Staunton 24401, ☎ 540/332-3972 or 800/332–3972).

4 Richmond and the Piedmont

Richmond, Virginia's capital, is rich with remnants of the past: In addition to numerous Civil War sites, the former capital of the Confederacy is also the proud parent of a gaslighted district full of 19th-century homes as well as the Thomas Jefferson–designed Virginia State Capitol. Charlottesville, the second most prominent city in the region, is the site of Monticello, the University of Virginia, Jefferson's Poplar Forest, and other sometime abodes and creations of the country's brilliant third president.

RICHMOND IS THE HEART OF VIRGINIA. Centered on the fall line of the James River, about 75 mi upriver from the Chesapeake Bay, Richmond completes the transition from Tidewater Virginia into the Piedmont, the central section of rolling plains that reaches toward the mountain barrier in the west. Not only is Richmond the capital of the commonwealth, it was also the capital of the Confederacy. As a result, the city is studded with historic sites.

Richmond has a long tradition as an industrial center, as well. It was, at the start of the Civil War, the most industrialized city in the South, and it remains home base to national industries such as Reynolds Metals and tobacco manufacturers. In recent years, Richmond has added high technology to traditional economic bases that include shipping and banking.

After years of urban decay, Richmond has transformed itself into a lively and sophisticated modern town. It's one of the South's preeminent art cities, flourishing with avant-garde painting and sculpture, in addition to the magnificent traditional works and artifacts such as Fabergé eggs exhibited in the Virginia Museum of Fine Arts. Drive beyond the historic downtown area and you'll find a fascinating array of charming and distinctive residential neighborhoods.

After Richmond, the most prominent city in this region is Charlottesville, 71 mi northwest of Richmond, at the core of what Virginians call Mr. Jefferson's country. While the influence of the third president of the United States is inescapable throughout the commonwealth (and far beyond its borders), in Albemarle and Orange counties Jefferson's presence is especially visible. Here are buildings and sites associated with him and the giants among his contemporaries. Here, too, are the locales of many crucial events in early American history.

Since 1819, when Jefferson founded the University of Virginia in Charlottesville, the area has been a cultural center. In recent years the countryside has been discovered by celebrities in search of privacy, among them the actresses Jessica Lange and Sissy Spacek. A growing community of writers and artists is making this affluent area a colony of the intelligentsia, the fashion-conscious, and others who appreciate a historic, out-of-the-way setting.

Exploring Richmond and the Piedmont

The capital of Virginia and former capital of the Confederacy, Richmond and its surroundings are bastions of American history. South of Richmond, in Petersburg, you can visit Petersburg National Battlefield and the Siege Museum. To the west, in Charlottesville, witness Thomas Jefferson's architectural accomplishments—Monticello and the University of Virginia. In the southwestern Piedmont, the restored Civil War–era village of Appomattox Court House takes visitors back in time.

RICHMOND

Numbers in the margin correspond to points of interest on the Richmond map.

①–**⑫** *104 mi south of Washington, DC (via I–95).*

Richmond's historic attractions lie north of the James River, which bisects the city with a sweeping curve. The heart of old Richmond is the Court End district, downtown. Running west from here is Main Street, which is lined with banks; stores are concentrated along Grace Street. Another east–west thoroughfare, Cary Street, becomes, between 12th and 15th streets, the cobblestoned center of Shockoe Slip, a fashionable shopping-and-entertainment zone converted from several blocks of warehouses. The downtown area gives way to residential neighborhoods as one moves farther west; Monument Avenue, 140 feet wide and divided by a verdant median, is lined with statues of Civil War heroes and the stately homes of some of the first families of Virginia. A block south, a series of streets fanning out southwesterly from Park Avenue creates the gaslighted Fan District, a treasury of restored turn-of-the-century town houses that has been the "hip" neighborhood for at least a decade.

Our tour begins in the Court End district, which contains seven National Historic Landmarks, three museums, and 11 more buildings on the National Register of Historic Places—all within eight blocks. At any one of the museums you will receive a self-guided walking tour with the purchase of a discount block ticket (🖼 $14), good for all admission fees.

❶ The **John Marshall House** was built in 1790 by the future chief justice of the United States, who also served as secretary of state and ambassador to France. The house, now fully restored and furnished, combines the Federal style with neoclassical motifs; it has wood paneling and wainscoting, arched narrow passageways, and a mix of period pieces and heirlooms ⬚ *9th and Marshall Sts.*, 🖼 *804/648–7998.* 🖼 *$3.* ⊙ *Apr.–Sept., Tues.–Sat. 10–5; Oct.–Dec., Tues.–Sat. 10–4:30.*

❷ The **Valentine Museum** impressively documents the life and history of Richmond. **Wickham House** (1812), a part of the Valentine, is more rightly called a mansion; it was designed by architect Alexander Parris, the creator of Boston's Faneuil Hall. John Wickham was Richmond's wealthiest citizen of the time, and Daniel Webster and Zachary Taylor were frequent guests at the house, which is stunning inside. Not all at the museum is opulence, however—the slave quarters, also meticulously restored, provide a chilling contrast to the mansion's splendor. ⬚ *1015 E. Clay St.*, 🖼 *804/649–0711.* 🖼 *$5.* ⊙ *Mon.–Sat. 10–5, Sun. noon–5.*

❸ The **Museum and White House of the Confederacy** are best seen in that order. The former offers elaborate permanent exhibitions on the Civil War era. The "world's largest collection of Confederate memorabilia" features such relics as the sword Robert E. Lee wore for his surrender at Appomattox. At the White House next door, preservationists have painstakingly re-created the interior as it was during the Civil War, when Jefferson Davis lived here. A brick house built in 1818, the building has been stuccoed to give the appearance of large stone blocks. Despite its name, it has always been painted gray. Group dinners with a Civil War theme are held here. ⬚ *1201 E. Clay St.*, 🖼 *804/649–1861.* 🖼 *One site $5; both sites $8.* ⊙ *Mon.–Sat. 10–5, Sun. noon–5.*

★ ❹ The **Virginia State Capitol** was designed by Thomas Jefferson in 1785, modeled on a Roman temple in the south of France. It contains a wealth of sculpture: busts of each of the eight presidents that Virginia has given the nation, and a famous life-size—and lifelike—statue of George Washington by Houdon. In the old Hall of the House of Delegates, Robert E. Lee accepted the command of the Confederate forces in Virginia (a bronze statue marks the spot where he stood). Elsewhere on the grounds, at the Old Bell Tower, you can get travel information for the entire state. ⬚ *Capitol Sq.*, 🖼 *804/786–4344.* 🖼 *Free.* ⊙ *Apr.–Nov., daily 9–5; Dec.–Mar., Mon.–Sat. 9–5, Sun. 1–5.*

Richmond

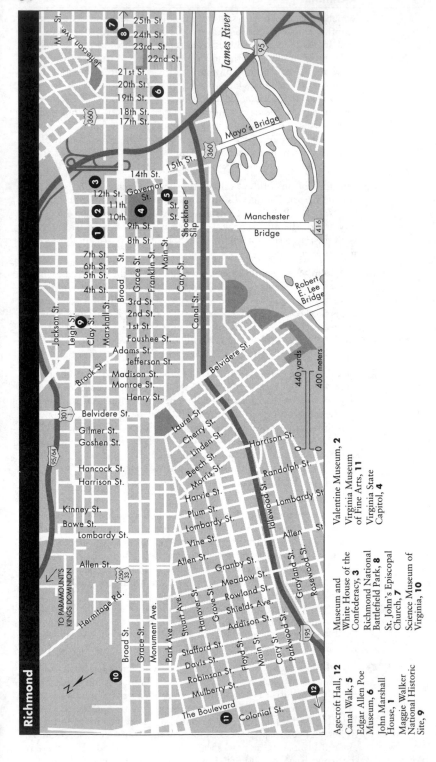

James River

95

Mayo's Bridge

360

Manchester
Bridge

416

Robert
E. Lee
Bridge

25th St.
24th St.
23rd. St.
22nd St.
21st St.
20th St.
19th St.
18th St.
17th St.

Jefferson Ave.

M. St.

360

15th St.

14th St.
12th St. Governor
11th St.
10th
9th St.
8th St.
7th St.
6th St.
5th St.
4th St.
3rd St.
2nd St.
1st St.
Foushee St.
Adams St.
Jefferson St.
Madison St.
Monroe St.
Henry St.

Broad St.
Grace St.
Franklin St.
Main St.
Cary St.
Canal St.

Shockhoe
Slip

Governor
St.

Jackson St.
Leigh St.
Clay St.
Marshall St.
Brook St.

301
1

95/64

Belvidere St.

Belvidere St.

Gilmer St.
Goshen St.

Laurel St.
Cherry St.
Linden St.
Beech St.
Morris St.

Harrison St.

440 yards

400 meters

Hancock St.
Harrison St.

Harvie St.
Plum St.
Lombardy St.
Vine St.

Randolph St.

Lombardy St.
Idlewood St.

Kinney St.
Bowe St.
Lombardy St.

Allen St.

Allen St.

Allen

Granby St.

Meadow St.
Rowland St.
Shields Ave.
Addison St.

Grayland St.
Rosewood St.

195

250
33

TO PARAMOUNT'S
KINGS DOMINION

Hermitage Rd.

Broad St.
Grace St.
Monument Ave.
Park Ave.
Stuart Ave.
Hanover St.
Grove St.

Cary St.
Parkwood St.

Stafford St.
Davis St.
Robinson St.
Mulberry St.

Floyd St.
Main St.

The Boulevard

Colonial St.

N

Agecroft Hall, **12**
Canal Walk, **5**
Edgar Allen Poe
Museum, **6**
John Marshall
House, **1**
Maggie Walker
National Historic
Site, **9**

Museum and
White House of the
Confederacy, **3**
Richmond National
Battlefield Park, **8**
St. John's Episcopal
Church, **7**
Science Museum of
Virginia, **10**

Valentine Museum, **2**
Virginia Museum
of Fine Arts, **11**
Virginia State
Capitol, **4**

⑤ **Canal Walk,** beginning south of the capitol at 12th and Main streets, follows the locks of the James River–Kanawha Canal proposed by George Washington to bring ships around the falls of the James River. Along the course of the walk, plaques note historic points of interest. At 12th and Byrd streets, a restored lock has been incorporated into Kanawha Park, where, under the archway, a free slide show (daily 9–5) recounts the history of the canal. The walk continues over a footbridge to Brown's Island, across from the ruins of the Tredegar Iron Foundry, a vital supplier of cannons throughout the Civil War. The island, terminus of the scenic walk, has a heliport and sculptures and hosts concerts in the warmer months.

⑥ The **Edgar Allan Poe Museum** in the Old Stone House—Richmond's oldest residence—is in the Church Hill Historic District just east of downtown Richmond. Poe grew up in Richmond, and, although he never lived in this structure of 1737, his disciples have made it a shrine, displaying some of the writer's possessions. The Raven Room is hung with illustrations inspired by his most famous poem. ⊠ *1914 E. Main St.,* ☎ *804/648–5523.* ☞ *$5.* ☉ *Tues.–Sat. 10–4, Sun.–Mon. noon–4.*

For security reasons, the rebellious Second Virginia Convention met
⑦ at **St. John's Episcopal Church** instead of at Williamsburg, and it was in this church on March 23, 1775, that Patrick Henry delivered the speech in which he demanded, "Give me liberty or give me death!" The speech is reenacted every summer Sunday at 2 PM. Those planning a Saturday visit should call ahead, especially in May and June; weddings often close the church to the public. ⊠ *2401 E. Broad St. at 24th St.,* ☎ *804/648–5015.* ☞ *$3.* ☉ *Mon.–Sat. 10–4, Sun. 1–4.*

⑧ The visitor center for **Richmond National Battlefield Park** is the launching point for tours of the Richmond battlefield and others nearby. Three campaigns were fought here: the Seven Days Battle (1862) and the Battle of Cold Harbor (1864), both Confederate victories, and the Battle of Fort Harrison (1864), a Union victory. Here you can see a movie about the city during the war and a slide show about the battlefields, then pick up a map for a self-guided tour. ⊠ *3215 E. Broad St.,* ☎ *804/226–1981.* ☞ *Free.* ☉ *Daily 9–5. Closed Jan. 1, Thanksgiving, Dec. 25.*

⑨ **Maggie Walker National Historical Site,** the home of a pioneering African-American businesswoman and educator, is now part of the battlefield-system tour administered by Battlefield Park personnel. Visitors may take a 30-minute tour of the furnished 22-room brick house where she lived from 1904 to 1934 and see a movie detailing her accomplishments. ⊠ *110½ E. Leigh St.,* ☎ *804/780–1380.* ☞ *Free.* ☉ *Wed.–Sun. 9–5.*

☚ ⑩ The **Science Museum of Virginia** is housed in the old train station, a massive domed building on the north side of the street. Aerospace and Crystal World are among the instructive exhibits here, many of which strongly appeal to children. The biggest spectacle is in the Universe Theater, also a planetarium, where an Omnimax screen draws the audience into the movie or the star show. ⊠ *2500 W. Broad St.,* ☎ *804/367–1080.* ☞ *Museum $4.75; museum, Omnimax, and planetarium $7.50.* ☉ *Mon.–Sat. 9:30–5, Sun. 1:30–5 (Fri. until 9 in summer).*

★ ⑪ The **Virginia Museum of Fine Arts** is in the Fan District, a fashionable neighborhood of restored turn-of-the-century town houses on Boulevard, south of Broad Street. The museum's most startling pieces are Duane Hanson's true-to-life wax figures; their everyday attire and provocative poses frequently lead visitors to think the figures are living persons. Among the more important works are paintings by Goya, Renoir, Monet, and van Gogh; African masks, Roman statuary, Oriental icons; and five Fabergé eggs. ⊠ *Boulevard and Grove Ave.,* ☎ *804/367–0844.* ☜ *$4 suggested.* ⊙ *Tues.–Sun. 11–5 (Thurs. until 8).*

⑫ **Agecroft Hall,** built in Lancashire, England, in the 15th century, was transported here in 1925. Set amid gardens, the country manor-house contains an extensive assortment of Tudor and early Stuart art and furniture (1485–1660) and a few priceless collector's items, such as a Ming vase. ⊠ *4305 Sulgrave Rd.,* ☎ *804/353–4241.* ☜ *$4.50.* ⊙ *Tues.–Sat. 10–4, Sun. 12:30–5.*

Dining and Lodging

$$$ ╳ **La Petite France.** The emerald green walls and tuxedoed waiters signal a formal and traditional dining atmosphere. Reproductions of 18th-century English landscapes and portraits hang on the walls. The diners seated at the 40 tables covered with white linen cloths are largely middle-aged and quiet; one dish they frequently order is lobster whiskey (lobster meat baked in a puff pastry with whiskey sauce). Among other specialties are Chateaubriand and Dover sole amandine. ⊠ *2108 Maywill St.,* ☎ *804/353–8729. AE, DC, MC, V. Closed Sun., Mon.*

$$ ╳ **Amici Ristorante.** Game specialties such as stuffed quail, buffalo with gorgonzola, and ostrich are regularly on the menu alongside authentic northern Italian dishes including calamari, fresh pasta, and veal dishes. A cozy atmosphere prevails on the first floor of the restaurant, where the walls around the booths are adorned with flowered tapestries and oil paintings of Italy. The second floor is more formally decorated, and the white walls are trimmed with stenciled grapes and vines. ⊠ *3343 W. Cary St.,* ☎ *804/353–4700. AE, MC, V.*

$ ╳ **Joe's Inn.** Spaghetti is the specialty—especially the Greek version, with feta and provolone cheese baked on top—and the sandwiches are distinguished for their generous proportions. Regular customers predominate at this local hangout in the Fan District, yet they make newcomers feel right at home. ⊠ *205 N. Shields Ave.,* ☎ *804/355–2282. AE, MC, V.*

$$$ ╳▦ **Mr. Patrick Henry's Inn.** Two houses circa 1858 were restored and
★   joined to create this restaurant and inn (three suites upstairs have kitchenette and fireplace). Antiques and fireplaces in the dining room contribute to the Colonial ambience, an English pub is in the basement, and there's a garden café. Especially popular dishes are the crisp roast duck with bing cherry sauce, and crab cakes (crabmeat and spices in a puff pastry). ⊠ *2300 E. Broad St.,* ☎ *804/644–1322. AE, D, DC, MC, V.*

$$$$ ▦ **Jefferson Hotel.** In the lobby of this famous downtown hotel, the
★   staircase of 36 steps was reputedly used as a model for a grand staircase in the movie *Gone with the Wind.* Built in 1895, the Jefferson is a National Historic Landmark. Yellow, blues, mauves, and dark woods are dominant in the relatively small rooms, which have reproduction 19th-century furnishings. ⊠ *Franklin and Adams Sts., 23220,* ☎ *804/788–8000 or 800/424–8014,* ℻ *804/225–0334. 275 rooms, 27 suites. 2 restaurants, bar, health club. AE, D, DC, MC, V.*

$$$$ ▦ **Omni Richmond.** This luxury hotel in the James Center Complex is conveniently located next door to Shockoe Slip. While the rooms are furnished in contemporary style, the impressive marble lobby calls to

mind a Venetian foyer with its green velvet chairs, equestrian statues, and Romanesque-style vases. ⊠ *100 S. 12th St., 23219,* ☎ *804/344–7000,* 𝔽𝔸𝕏 *804/648–6704. 363 rooms, 12 suites. 3 restaurants, bar, 1 indoor and 1 outdoor pool, sauna, exercise room, indoor track, racquetball, squash. AE, D, DC, MC, V.*

$$$ 🏨 **Radisson Hotel.** Guest rooms in this wedge-shape hotel in the business district have views of the Richmond skyline or the James River; triangular rooms at the point of the wedge have both views. The wallpaper is uniformly gray, carpeting is brown or pewter, and bedspreads have a paisley pattern whose colors match the carpeting. Guests get free covered parking and free transportation on request to area attractions and the airport. The three-story atrium lobby has an operating waterfall. Two concierge floors have additional amenities. ⊠ *555 E. Canal St., 23219,* ☎ *804/788–0900 or 800/333–3333,* 𝔽𝔸𝕏 *804/788–7087. 296 rooms, 10 suites. Restaurant, bar, indoor pool, saunas, health club, nightclub, airport shuttle, free parking. AE, D, DC, MC, V.*

$$$ 🏨 **Richmond Marriott.** The lobby of this luxury hotel near the 6th Street Marketplace has crystal chandeliers and marble flooring. Rooms are furnished in a contemporary style, and concierge service is available. A tanning salon keeps the beauty-conscious crowd content. ⊠ *500 E. Broad St., 23219,* ☎ *804/643–3400 or 800/228–9290,* 𝔽𝔸𝕏 *804/788–1230. 400 rooms. 2 restaurants, lounge, indoor pool, hot tub, health club. AE, D, DC, MC, V.*

$$ 🏨 **Days Inn North.** This three-story redbrick motel is 2 mi northwest of downtown in a neighborhood of government and private offices. Guest rooms renovated in 1990 have clunky but dependable hotel furniture and predominantly mauve fabrics. Rooms are entered directly from the parking lot. ⊠ *1600 Robin Hood Rd., 23220,* ☎ *804/353–1287 or 800/325–2525,* 𝔽𝔸𝕏 *804/355–2659. 87 rooms. Restaurant, bar, pool. AE, D, DC, MC, V.*

$ 🏨 **Massad House Hotel.** The four-story Massad House is not fancy, but it's clean and convenient and just five blocks from the capitol. On the north and south sides, rooms look out over alleyways and face other nearby buildings. A handful look out at undistinguished 4th Street, with a row of office buildings whose merit is silence after 6 PM. Guest rooms are small, with dressers doubling as writing desks by virtue of knee holes. ⊠ *11 N. 4th St., 23219,* ☎ *804/648–2893,* 𝔽𝔸𝕏 *804/780–0647. 64 rooms. Restaurant. AE, MC, V.*

Nightlife and the Arts

Bars with Music

Potter's Pub (⊠ 7007 Three Choppet Rd., Village Shopping Center, Richmond, ☎ 804/282–9999) encourages audience participation in its folk music fests.

Bogart's (⊠ 203 N. Lombardy St., Richmond, ☎ 804/353–9280) is a cozy club, with jazz on weekends.

Comedy

Skipjack Tavern and Comedy Club (⊠ 109 S. 12th St., Richmond, ☎ 804/643–5653) offers comedy on weekend nights. Reservations are required.

Dance

Concert Ballet of Virginia (⊠ Box 25501, Richmond 23260, ☎ 804/780–1279) performs modern and experimental works.

The Richmond Ballet (⊠ 614 N. Lombardy St., 23220, ☎ 804/359–0906) is the city's professional classical ballet company.

Music

The Richmond Symphony (☎ 804/788–1212), founded in 1957, often features internationally known soloists. The Richmond Symphony All-Star Pops hosts popular guest artists.

Theater

Barksdale Theatre (⊠ Hanover Tavern, about 15 mi north of Richmond on Rte. 301, Hanover, ☎ 804/537–5817), founded in 1953, was the first dinner theater in the country. Performances are given Thursday through Saturday evenings, and there are Sunday matinees.

Carpenter Center (⊠ Richmond, ☎ 804/782–3900), a restored 1928 motion picture palace, is now a performing-arts center, offering year-round opera, road shows, symphony, and ballet.

Richmond Landmark Theater (⊠ Main and Laurel Sts., ☎ 804/780–4213) hosts theater, dance, and classical and popular music. The ornate, Moorish-style auditorium is worth a visit even when no performances are scheduled.

Swift Creek Mill Playhouse (⊠ 17401 Jefferson Davis Hwy., Colonial Heights, ☎ 804/748–5203), a dinner theater, is housed in a 17th-century gristmill.

Theatre Virginia (⊠ Richmond, ☎ 804/353–6161), maintained by the Virginia Museum of Fine Arts, has a strong repertory.

Outdoor Activities and Sports

Golf

The **Crossings** (⊠ Jct. of I–95 and I–295, Glen Allen, ☎ 804/266–2254), 6 mi north of Richmond, has an 18-hole course open to the public.

Jogging

Joggers in Richmond use the running track in the park around the Randolph Pool (Idlewood Ave.) and the fitness track in Byrd Park, off the Boulevard.

Rafting

Richmond Raft (☎ 804/222–7238) offers guided white-water rafting through the heart of the city on the James River (class 3 and 4 rapids), as well as float trips upriver from March through November.

Spectator Sports

The **Richmond Coliseum** (☎ 804/780–4970) hosts ice shows, basketball, wrestling, and tennis tournaments; the coliseum seats 12,000.

AUTO RACING

In September and March, **auto races** (NASCAR Miller 400, Autolite Platinum, and Winston Cup) are held at the Richmond International Raceway (⊠ I–64 Laburnum Ave. Exit, ☎ 804/345–7223).

BASEBALL

The Richmond Braves, a Triple-A farm **baseball** team for Atlanta, play at the **Diamond** (⊠ 3001 N. Boulevard, ☎ 804/359–4444), a 12,500-seat stadium.

Basketball games at Randolph-Macon College, the University of Richmond, Virginia Commonwealth University, and Virginia Union University are listed in the *Times-Dispatch* and the *News Leader*.

Shopping

Shopping Districts

Sixth Street Marketplace has specialty shops, chain stores, and eating places.

Shockoe Slip, on East Cary Street between 12th and 15th streets in Richmond—a neighborhood of tobacco warehouses in the 18th and 19th centuries—is now full of boutiques and branches of upscale specialty stores.

Food Markets

The Farmers Market at 17th and Main streets makes fresh farm produce available directly to the consumer. Art galleries, boutiques, and antiques shops, many in converted warehouses and factories, are nearby.

OFF THE
BEATEN PATH

PARAMOUNT'S KINGS DOMINION – This entertainment complex in Doswell, 20 mi north of Richmond on I-95, is great for children, but parents will need to bring lots of money and patience; lines often begin forming an hour before the park opens. There are more than 100 rides, including a stand-up roller coaster, "The Hurler"—another scary coaster located in a section of the park whose theme is the parent company's popular *Wayne's World* movies—and, new in 1996, the "Xtreme Skyflyer," a variation on the bungee-jumping theme. ⊠ *I-95 (Doswell Exit),* ☎ *804/876-5000.* ☜ *$28.95. Parking $4.* ☉ *June, Sun.–Fri. 10–8, Sat. 10–10; July–Aug., daily 10–10; Apr.–May and Sept.–Oct., weekends 10–8.*

THE PIEDMONT

Numbers in the margin correspond to points of interest on the Piedmont map.

Virginia's Piedmont region was home to many Revolutionary War heroes, including Thomas Jefferson, James Monroe, James Madison, and Patrick Henry. It also figured prominently in the Civil War.

Petersburg

⓭ *20 mi south of Richmond (via I–95).*

Petersburg was the so-called last ditch of the Confederacy. A major railroad hub, the city was a crucial link in the supply chain for Lee's army. Grant laid siege to it for 10 months, and its capitulation in 1865 precipitated the evacuation of Richmond and the subsequent surrender at Appomattox.

With the exception of the Petersburg National Battlefield, all Petersburg attractions listed below are within the Old Towne and can be found easily by walking around or asking someone to direct you. Petersburg's visitor centers sell a variety of passes that offer reduced admission to Old Towne museums and attractions.

At the **Petersburg National Battlefield,** visitors can tread ground that absorbed the blood of more than 60,000 Union and Confederate soldiers. A pronounced depression in the ground is the eroded remnant of the Crater, the result of a 4-ton gunpowder explosion set off by Northern forces in one failed attack. The 1,500-acre park is laced with several miles of earthworks and includes two forts. In the visitor center, maps and models convey background information vital to the self-guided driving tour. Visitors park at specified spots on the tour road and proceed on foot to nearby points of interest. ⊠ *Rte. 36, Petersburg,* ☎

804/732–3531. ⊠ $4 car, $2 cyclist or pedestrian. ☉ Park: Mid-June–Labor Day, daily 8:30–dusk; Labor Day–mid-June, daily 8–5. Visitor center: daily 8:30–5:30.

In Old Towne Petersburg the Civil War is examined from a purely local perspective. Exhibits at the **Siege Museum** concentrate on details of ordinary civilian life in embattled Petersburg during the last year of the war. A short film narrated by the actor Joseph Cotten dramatizes the upheaval. ⊠ *15 W. Bank St.,* ☎ *804/733–2404.* ⊠ *$3.* ☉ *Daily 10–5.*

The **Trapezium House of 1817** is named for its geometric shape: four sides, none of them parallel. The construction is said to have followed a Caribbean superstition learned by the builder from one of his servants—that parallel lines and right angles harbor evil spirits. ⊠ *N. Market St.,* ☎ *804/733–2404.* ⊠ *$3.* ☉ *Apr.–Oct., daily 10–5; closed Nov.–Mar.*

The **Centre Hill Mansion** (1823) has been furnished with Victorian antiques, including a grand piano 3 yards long, in accord with the period of its last remodeling—in 1901. The house had previously been remodeled in the 1840s. ⊠ *Centre Hill Ct.,* ☎ *804/733–2401.* ⊠ *$3.* ☉ *Daily 10–5.*

The Federal-style brick **Farmers Bank** (1817), one of the oldest bank buildings in the nation, was restored by the Association for the Preservation of Virginia Antiquities. ⊠ *19 Bollingbrook St.,* ☎ *804/733–2400.* ⊠ *$3.* ☉ *Apr.–Oct., Fri.–Mon. 10–5; closed Nov.–Mar.*

Old Blanford Church is today a Confederate Shrine, surrounded by the graves of 30,000 Southern dead. The Memorial Day tradition is said to have begun in this cemetery. ⊠ *319 S. Crater Rd.,* ☎ *804/733–2396.* ⊠ *$3.* ☉ *Daily 10–5.*

☾ Petersburg's **Softball Hall of Fame Museum** features videos of great games and memorabilia of players inducted into the United States Slo-Pitch Softball Association Hall of Fame. ⊠ *3935 S. Crater Rd.,* ☎ *804/733–1005.* ⊠ *$2.* ☉ *Weekdays 9–4, Sat. 10–4, Sun. noon–4; closed holidays.*

OFF THE   **PAMPLIN PARK CIVIL WAR SITE** – Here, on the morning of April 2, 1865,
BEATEN PATH Union troops successfully attacked General Robert E. Lee's formerly impenetrable defense line, forcing Lee to abandon Petersburg. Today, you are greeted by the 300-foot-long facade of the interpretive center, a concrete representation of the Confederate battle lines. In addition to the interpretive center—which houses a museum, a fibre optics battle map, and interactive video programs—there's a 1.1-mi battle trail with 2,100 feet of 8-foot-high earthen fortifications, reconstructed soldier huts, and original picket posts. Also on the grounds is Tudor Hall, an 1812 plantation home that was commandeered in 1864 to serve as headquarters for Confederate General Samuel McGowan. Today it is furnished as it would have been both before and during its use by McGowan. Future plans include the construction of the National Museum of the Civil War Soldier, expected to be the best museum of its kind when it opens in 1999. ⊠ *6523 Duncan Rd., Petersburg,* ☎ *804/861–2408.* ⊠ *$3.* ☉ *Daily 9–5.*

Charlottesville

14 *71 mi northwest of Richmond (via I–64).*

Charlottesville is the epitome of Virginia's Piedmont area, and the major attraction in the Piedmont is nearby Monticello, the distinguished

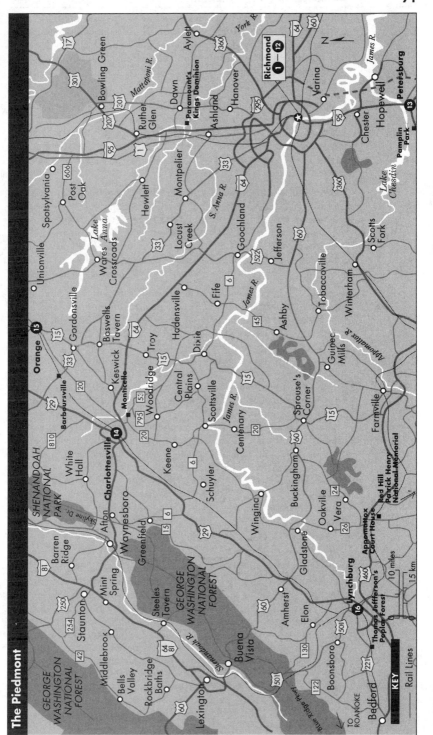

The Piedmont

71

home that Thomas Jefferson designed and built for himself. In Charlottesville, the visitors bureau on Route 20 distributes a walking-tour map of the downtown historic district, though there is little to see here. The downtown pedestrian shopping mall stretches along six blocks of Main Street, with fountains, outdoor restaurants, and restored buildings lining a brick-paved street.

Charlottesville is also the heart of Piedmont's verdant wine country. Contact the **Jeffersonian Wine Grape Growers Society** (⊠ Rte. 5, Box 429, Charlottesville 22901, ☎ 804/296–4188) for brochures about vineyards in the foothills around Charlottesville. The Virginia Department of Agriculture (☎ 800/828–4637) has a statewide guide to wineries and festivals.

At the **Monticello Visitors Center,** the exhibit "Thomas Jefferson at Monticello" provides extensive background information on both house and owner, and artifacts recovered during recent archaeological excavations are on display. A stop here is a must, either before or after visiting Monticello, since much of the history is not explained on the house tour. ⊠ *Rte. 20 S from Charlottesville (I–64 Monticello, Exit 121),* ☎ *804/977–1783.* ◷ *Mar.–Oct., daily 9–5:30; Nov.–Feb., daily 9–5.*

★ **Monticello,** the most famous of Jefferson's homes and his monument to himself, is a masterwork that was constructed over a period of 40 years, 1769–1809. Typical of no single architectural style, it is characteristic of Jefferson, who made a statement with every detail. The staircases are narrow and hidden because he considered them unsightly and a waste of space; and contrary to plantation tradition, his outbuildings are in the back, not on the east side, where his guests would arrive. In these respects and in its overall conception, Monticello was a revolutionary structure, a neoclassical repudiation of the prevalent English Georgian style and of the Colonial mentality behind it. As if to reflect this subversive aspect, a concave mirror in the entrance hall presents you with your own image, upside down. Throughout the house are Jefferson's inventions, including a seven-day clock and a "polygraph," a two-pen contraption that allowed him to make a copy of his correspondence as he wrote it. The Thomas Jefferson Center for Historic Plants includes interpretive gardens, exhibits, and a sales area. Tour guides are available to answer questions, but they must move visitors through the house quickly since other groups are always waiting. Don't plan on seeing everything in one visit. ⊠ *Rte. 53,* ☎ *804/984–9800.* ▨ *$8.* ◷ *Mar.–Oct., daily 8–5; Nov.–Feb., daily 9–4:30.*

Near Monticello, modest **Ash Lawn–Highland** is—like its grand neighbor—marked by the personality of the president who lived in it and who held more major national offices than any other man of his era. It is no longer the simple farmhouse built in 1799 for James Monroe, who lived in the L-shape single story at the rear; a later owner added the more prominent two-story section, though the furniture is mostly original, and it is not hard to imagine Monroe here at his retreat. Small rooms are crowded with gifts from notable persons and with souvenirs from his time as envoy to France. Such coziness befits the fifth U.S. president, the first to come from the middle class. Ash Lawn–Highland today is a working plantation, where spectacular peacocks roam the grounds. ⊠ *683 Thomas Jefferson Pkwy. (Rte. 795 southwest of Monticello),* ☎ *804/293–9539.* ▨ *$7.* ◷ *Mar.–Oct., daily 9–6; Nov.–Feb., daily 10–5.*

Its proximity to Monticello and Ash Lawn–Highland has made **Historic Michie Tavern** on Route 53 a popular attraction. Most of the complex was built 17 mi away at Earlysville, in 1784, and moved here piece by piece in 1927. Costumed hostesses lead visitors into a series of rooms, where they play recorded interpretations of the interiors. The restaurant's "Colonial" lunch is fried chicken. The old gristmill has been converted into a gift shop. ⊠ *Rte. 53,* ☎ *804/977–1234.* ⊡ *$6.* ⊙ *Daily 9–5.*

At the west end of town, the **University of Virginia,** one of the nation's most distinguished institutions of higher education, was founded and designed by Thomas Jefferson, who called himself its "father" in his own epitaph. A poll of experts at the time of the U.S. bicentennial designated this complex "the proudest achievement of American architecture in the past 200 years." Students vie for the rooms in the original pavilions that flank the lawn, a graduated expanse that flows down from the Rotunda, a half-scale replica of the Pantheon in Rome. Behind the pavilions, gardens and landscaping are laced with serpentine walls. Tours begin indoors in the Rotunda, whose entrance is on the lawn side, lower level. ☎ *804/924–1019.* ⊡ *Free; 30-min–1-hr historic tours daily at 10, 11, 2, 3, 4.* ⊙ *Rotunda: daily 9–4:45; closed during winter break.*

Ⓒ At Charlottesville's **Virginia Discovery Museum** children can step inside a giant kaleidoscope or observe bees in action in a working beehive. The hands-on exhibits are meant to interest children in science, history, and the humanities. The computer lab and make-it-and-take-it art studio (for ages 2–10) are big attractions. ⊠ *524 E. Main St.,* ☎ *804/977–1025.* ⊡ *$4.* ⊙ *Tues.–Sat. 10–5, Sun. 1–5.*

Jefferson Vineyards is home to Gabriele Rausse, the "guardian angel of Virginia vineyards." The vineyards are open daily for free tours and tastings. ⊠ *1399 Thomas Jefferson Pkwy.,* ☎ *804/977–3042.* ⊡ *Free.* ⊙ *Daily 11–5.*

Oakencroft Vineyard & Winery, with the Blue Ridge Mountains and a lake with Virginia water fowl as a backdrop, has produced award-winning chardonnays, cabernet sauvignons, and clarets. Free tours and tastings are offered during opening hours. ⊠ *1486 Oakencroft La.,* ☎ *804/296–4188.* ⊡ *Free.* ⊙ *Apr.–Nov., daily 11–5; March, weekends 11–5; Dec., daily noon–6.*

OFF THE
BEATEN PATH

AFTON MOUNTAIN VINEYARDS – Awarded in the past for its chenin blanc and gewürtztraminer, this winery also thrives on its stunning panoramic views of the Piedmont landscape and ridgelines. Tours and tastings are free. ⊠ *234 Vineyard La., Afton 22920,* ☎ *540/456–8667.* ⊡ *Free.* ⊙ *Wed.–Mon. 10–6 (until 5 in winter).*

Dining and Lodging

$$$$ ✕ **C&O Restaurant.** A boarded-up storefront hung with an illumi-
★ nated Pepsi sign conceals one of the best restaurants in town. The stark white formal dining room upstairs (seatings at 6:30 and 9:30) features fine regional French cuisine. Among the appetizers is a *terrine de campagne* (pâté of veal, venison, and pork); the entrées include coquilles St. Jacques. The wine list offers 300 varieties. A lively and less formal bistro downstairs serves pâtés, cheese, and light meals. ⊠ *515 E. Water St.,* ☎ *804/971–7044. MC, V. Closed Sun.; bistro open daily.*

$$$ ✕ **Eastern Standard.** Specialties in the formal dining room upstairs in-
★ clude pan-seared tuna topped with ginger-and-kumquat salsa; oysters in champagne-and-caviar sauce; and loin of lamb with mint pesto. Curries and stir-fry Asian dishes are also offered, giving truth to the restau-

rant's name. Escafé, the crowded and lively bistro downstairs, serves pastas and light fare to taped music, primarily jazz and rock. ☒ *Downtown Mall, ☎ 804/295–8668. AE, MC, V. No lunch.*

$$$ ✕ **Old Mill Room.** A fireplace, wrought-iron chandeliers, and prints and posters depicting the gristmill built here in 1834 set the mood in this dining room of the Boar's Head Inn, 1½ mi west of Charlottesville on Route 250 West. Waiters and waitresses in Colonial dress serve such offerings as bison carpaccio, cider-marinated pork loin, and rack of domestic lamb. Light fare is available in the Racquet's restaurant. ☒ *Boar's Head Inn, U.S. 250, ☎ 804/296–2181. AE, DC, MC, V.*

$$ ✕ **Crozet Pizza.** With up to 35 toppings to choose from, including sea-
★ sonal items such as snow peas and asparagus spears, this popular parlor 12 mi west of Charlottesville has some of Virginia's best pizza. On the weekend, takeout must be ordered hours in advance. Diners in the restaurant find hardwood floors and booths, portraits of the owners' forebears, and one wall covered with business cards from around the world. ☒ *Rte. 240, Crozet, ☎ 804/823–2132. No credit cards. Closed Sun., Mon.*

$$ ✕ **Hardware Store.** Deli sandwiches, burgers, salads, seafood, and ice cream from the soda fountain are today's merchandise in this former Victorian hardware store. Some of the original wood paneling and brick walls remain from 1890. Outdoor dining is popular in the warm-weather months. ☒ *316 E. Main St., ☎ 804/977–1518. AE, MC, V. Closed Sun.*

$$$$ ▥ **Boar's Head Inn.** A gristmill built in 1834 of brick and wood construction has been transformed into a luxurious resort with the character of a late Victorian English inn. Set on two small lakes, 2 mi west of Charlottesville on Route 250, the resort has simple but elegant rooms and suites furnished with reproduction Colonial-era antiques and art. Some suites have fireplaces, some are efficiencies; some rooms have king- or queen-size beds. In addition to swimming, golf, tennis, bicycling, and fishing, hot-air ballooning is available to guests through a nearby outfitter. ☒ *U.S. 250, Box 5307, Charlottesville 22905, ☎ 804/296–2181 or 800/476–1988, ℻ 804/972–6024. 173 rooms, 11 suites. 2 restaurants, 3 pools, spa, fitness center, 18-hole golf course, 20 tennis courts, fishing. AE, D, DC, MC, V.*

$$$$ ▥ **Omni Charlottesville.** This relatively new, attractive addition to the luxury chain looms over the Downtown Mall. The triangular rooms at the point of the wedge-shape building get light from windows on two sides. Blond wood and maroon fabrics, in a mixture of modern and Colonial styles, decorate the guest quarters, and potted plants soften the look of the bright seven-story atrium lobby. ☒ *235 W. Main St., 22902, ☎ 804/971–5500, ℻ 804/979–4456. 208 rooms, 3 suites. Restaurant, bar, 1 indoor and 1 outdoor pool, hot tub, sauna, exercise room. AE, DC, MC, V.*

$$$$ ▥ **Prospect Hill Plantation Inn.** This former plantation house was rebuilt in Victorian times, when columns and decorative cornice borders were added. Four furnished rooms and one suite are in the main house, where dinner (one sitting) is a leisurely production by the family of innkeepers and chefs. But the prize quarters are the eight refurbished rooms and suites in dependencies (outbuildings)—one is a cottage, one a carriage house, and several have Jacuzzis. The inn is 20 mi east of Monticello. ☒ *Rte. 3, Box 430, Trevilians 23093, ☎ 800/277–0844, ℻ 540/967–0102. 13 rooms. Restaurant, pool. D, MC, V. MAP rates.*

$$$$ ▥ **200 South Street Inn.** Two historic houses, one of them a former
★ brothel, have been combined and restored to create this old-fashioned inn in the historic district. Furnishings throughout are English and Belgian antiques. Several rooms come with a canopy bed, sitting room,

fireplace, and whirlpool, and all rooms have a private bath. ⊠ *200 South St., 22901,* ☎ *804/979–0200 or 800/964–7008,* ⅁ *804/979–4403. 17 rooms, 3 suites. AE, MC, V.*

$$$–$$$$ ⊡ **Silver Thatch Inn.** Four-poster beds and period antiques are just part
★ of the charm at this 18th-century white-clapboard Colonial farmhouse. The inn is 8 mi north of town, and the friendly hosts help guests arrange outdoor activities at nearby locations. The popular restaurant has an award-winning wine cellar: As visitors often discover to their chagrin that the dining room is booked solid, guests should reserve a table in advance to sample offerings such as roast quail, fresh fish, and rabbits and chickens locally raised on organic farms. ⊠ *3001 Hollymead Dr., Charlottesville 22911,* ☎ *804/978–4686,* ⅁ *804/973–6156. 7 rooms. Restaurant, pool. AE, DC, MC, V.*

$$$ ⊡ **High Meadows.** Two styles of architecture are joined by a hall in this bed-and-breakfast listed on the National Register of Historic Places and located 15 mi south of Monticello. Five rooms in the Victorian section, three rooms in the Federal section, and four rooms in the Queen Anne section have curtains and bed hangings of fabrics with a handcrafted look. The kitchen will prepare hot gourmet baskets (cassoulet is one option) to take away for evening meals Monday through Wednesday, and dinner is served in the dining room by reservation Thursday through Sunday. Hors d'oeuvres and samples of Virginia wines are offered nightly. Rates include breakfast. ⊠ *Rte. 4, Box 6, Scottsville 24590,* ☎ *804/286–2218 or 800/232–1832,* ⅁ *804/286–2124. 12 rooms, 4 suites, 1 cottage. AE, MC, V.*

$$$ ⊡ **Sheraton Charlottesville.** This modern Sheraton hotel on a hill 7 mi north of town, overlooks the Blue Ridge Mountains. Rooms have contemporary furnishings in muted tones, two restaurants feature Continental dining, and full conference facilities are available. ⊠ *2350 Seminole Trail (U.S. 29), Charlottesville 22901,* ☎ *804/973–2121,* ⅁ *804/978–7735. 240 rooms. 2 restaurants, bar, 1 indoor and 1 outdoor pool, 2 tennis courts. AE, D, DC, MC, V.*

$$ ⊡ **Best Western Cavalier Inn.** Guest rooms here were renovated with contemporary furnishings in 1995. The nearby grounds of the University of Virginia are delightful for strolling, and Monticello is within easy driving distance. Rates include Continental breakfast. ⊠ *105 Emmet St., 22905,* ☎ *804/296–8111,* ⅁ *804/296–3523. 118 rooms. Restaurant, bar, pool. AE, D, DC, MC, V.*

$$ ⊡ **English Inn.** A model treatment of the B&B theme on a large but comfortable scale, the English Inn has a three-story atrium lobby with cascading plants. A Continental breakfast is served in a 150-year-old Tudor-style dining room with fireplace. The suite accommodations have a sitting room, wet bar, king-size bed, and reproduction antiques; other rooms have modern furnishings. Rates include Continental breakfast. ⊠ *2000 Morton Dr., 22901,* ☎ *804/971–9900 or 800/338–9900,* ⅁ *804/973–6156. 67 rooms, 21 suites. Restaurant, bar, indoor pool, sauna, exercise room. AE, DC, MC, V.*

$ ⊡ **Econo Lodge.** Parents of University of Virginia students make up a large part of the clientele at this budget chain motel. It's handily located in the university neighborhood, across from the sports arena. Brown tones predominate the furnishings. ⊠ *400 Emmet St., 22903,* ☎ *804/296–2104. 60 rooms. Pool. AE, D, DC, MC, V.*

Nightlife and the Arts

For current information on cultural events, music, and movies, and a guide to restaurants, pick up a free copy of the *C-Ville Weekly,* an arts and entertainment newspaper available in restaurants and hotels throughout the city.

BARS AND CLUBS

Miller's (✉ 109 W. Main St., Downtown Mall, ☎ 804/971–8511), a large and comfortable bar, hosts blues and jazz musicians.

Trax (122 11th St. SW, ☎ 804/295–TRAX) is Charlottesville's main alternative music club, usually featuring national acts.

MUSIC AND THEATER

Dance, music, and theater performances take place all year long at the **University of Virginia** in Charlottesville; the *Cavalier Daily* usually has details.

McGuffey Art Center (✉ 201 2nd St. NW, ☎ 804/295–7973), housed in a converted school building, contains the Second Street Gallery, as well as the studios of painters and sculptors, and is the sight for many musical and theatrical performances.

Outdoor Activities and Sports

The **University of Virginia** is nationally or regionally ranked in several varsity sports. In season, you can watch the Cavaliers play first-rate ACC basketball in University Hall. There is also football at Scott Stadium, as well as baseball, soccer, and lacrosse. The *Cavalier Daily* has sports listings.

Shopping

Downtown Mall on Main Street is a six-block brick pedestrian mall with specialty stores, restaurants, and bars in restored 19th- and early 20th-century buildings.

En Route Between Charlottesville and Orange, the **Barboursville Vineyards** are the oldest vineyards in a state whose young wine industry is the eighth-largest in the United States. They were planted in 1976 by the sixth generation of an Italian viticulturalist dynasty on the former plantation of James Barbour, governor of the commonwealth from 1812 to 1814. The extensive ruins of his house, gutted by fire in 1884, afford a structural look at Jeffersonian architecture—the third president designed the building to resemble his own Monticello. During the first three weekends of August, "Shakespeare at the Ruins" presents outdoor performances of the Bard's classics amid this awesome setting; theatergoers may purchase a modest dinner here provided by a local caterer. The pastoral background of Route 20 as it winds its way to Orange makes the drive a pleasure in itself. ✉ *17655 Winery Rd. (near intersection of Rtes. 20 and 23), Barboursville,* ☎ *540/832–3824.* 🗌 *Tours and tastings free; theater performances $12.* ⊙ *Tastings: Mon.–Sat. 10–5; Sun. 11–5; tours: Sat. 11–4.*

Orange

⑮ *25 mi northeast of Charlottesville (via Rte. 20); 60 mi northwest of Richmond.*

St. Thomas's Episcopal Church (1833), the one surviving example of Jeffersonian church architecture, is a replica of Charlottesville's demolished Christ Church, which Jefferson designed. It is here that Robert E. Lee worshiped during the winter of 1863–64. The church's biggest decorative asset is its Tiffany window. ✉ *119 Caroline St.,* ☎ *540/672–3761.* 🗌 *Donation.* ⊙ *Tours by appointment.*

The **James Madison Museum** presents a comprehensive exhibition on the Founding Father most responsible for the Constitution. The collection includes some of the china and glassware recovered from the White House before the British torched it during the War of 1812. The fourth president's tiny Campeachy chair, an 18th-century recliner, reveals his small stature. ⊠ *129 Caroline St.,* ☎ *540/672–1776.* ☞ *$4.* ⊘ *Mar.–Nov., weekdays 9–4, weekends 1–4; Dec.–Feb., weekdays 9–4.*

OFF THE
BEATEN PATH
MONTPELIER – On Route 20, just west of Orange, is the residence of the fourth president of the United States, James Madison. Yet Montpelier in its present state has more to do with its 20th-century owners, the Du Pont family, who enlarged and redecorated it. This dual legacy poses a dilemma in the restoration, for today the house only vaguely resembles itself as it was in Madison's time. Markings on walls, floors, and ceilings, which show the locations of underlying door and window frames and other features, are guides to the restoration in progress. The process is slow, to the credit of the diligent preservationists of the National Trust. With a little imagination and attention to the guide's eloquent and evocative narration, one can appreciate the history of this mostly empty house. The building can be seen only on a guided tour of 1½ to two hours, which begins with a slide show on the history of the house, followed by a bus tour of the farm and paddock area, a tour of the mansion, and free time to wander the grounds, gardens, and the cemetery where James and his wife, Dolley, and other Madisons are buried. The annual Montpelier Hunt Races (steeplechase), which have been held since 1934, are run on the first Saturday in November, at which time the house tour does not run. Admission to the races is $5. ⊠ *Rte. 20, 4 mi south of Orange,* ☎ *540/672-2728.* ☞ *$6.* ⊘ *Jan.–Feb., weekends 10–4; Mar.–Dec., daily 10–4.*

Lodging

$$$$ ★
🏨 **Mayhurst.** A Victorian home built in 1859 by a grandnephew of James Madison makes a cozy and comfortable B&B surrounded by 36 acres of woods and hiking trails near Orange, about 30 mi northeast of Monticello. All rooms are decorated with early Victorian antiques. ⊠ *U.S. 15, Box 707, Orange 22960,* ☎ *540/672–5597. 6 rooms, 1 guest house. Fishing. MC, V.*

Lynchburg

⑯ *110 mi west of Richmond.*

Well to the south in the Piedmont is the city of Lynchburg. Although its founder, John Lynch, was a Quaker pacifist, the city's most prominent landmark is **Monument Terrace,** a war memorial: At the foot and head of the 139 limestone and granite steps that lead to the Old City Courthouse are statues honoring a World War I doughboy and a Confederate soldier. Visitors who hesitate to make the climb should at least catch the dramatic view from the bottom of Court House Hill, at Main and 9th streets. Self-guided walking tours designed by, and available from, the Lynchburg Visitors Information Center cover the historic Riverfront and Diamond Hill sections.

The **Confederate Cemetery** and garden of 60 roses (representing the history of the plant from 1565 to 1900) are next to the **Pest House Medical Museum,** which provides a brief but informative look into medical practices and instruments at the time of the Civil War and later. The 1840s frame building was the office of Dr. John Jay Terrell. ⊠ *4th and Taylor Sts.,* ☎ *804/847–1811 or 800/732–5821.* ☞ *$1.* ⊘ *Daily sunrise–sunset; tours by appointment.*

Northwest of Monument Terrace is **Point of Honor,** a mansion on Daniel's Hill that was built in 1815 on the site of a duel. Once part of a 900-acre estate, this redbrick house surrounded by lawns retains a commanding view of the James River. The facade is elegantly symmetrical, with two octagonal bays joined by a balustrade on each of the building's two stories. The interiors have been restored and furnished with pieces authentic to the early 19th-century Federal period, including wallpaper whose pattern is in the permanent collection of the Metropolitan Museum of Art in New York. ⊠ *112 Cabell St.,* ☎ *804/847–1459.* ⌫ *$3.* ☉ *Daily 1–4.*

OFF THE
BEATEN PATH

THOMAS JEFFERSON'S POPLAR FOREST – In Forest, less than 5 mi southwest of Lynchburg, Poplar Forest is an impressive piece of octagonal architecture. Conceived and built by Jefferson as his "occasional retreat" (he sometimes stayed here between 1806 and 1813), this Palladian hermitage exemplifies the architect's sublime sense of order that is so evident at Monticello. Erected on a slope, the front of the house is one story high, its rear elevation two stories. The octagon's center is a square, skylit dining room flanked by two smaller octagons. The attraction here is the economy of space throughout, never mind the unfinished state of the restoration. Every July 4th, a free celebration is held here. ⊠ *5 mi southwest of Lynchburg on Rte. 661, Forest,* ☎ *804/525–1806.* ⌫ *$5.* ☉ *Apr.–Nov., Wed.–Sun. and major holidays 10–4.*

APPOMATTOX COURT HOUSE – Twenty miles east of Lynchburg (via Route 24), the village of Appomattox Court House has been restored to its appearance of April 9, 1865, when General Lee surrendered the Army of Northern Virginia to General Grant. There are 27 structures in the national historical park; most can be entered. A highlight is the reconstructed McLean House, in whose parlor the articles of surrender were signed. The self-guided tour is well planned and introduced by exhibits and slide shows in the reconstructed courthouse. First-person interpreters cast as soldiers and villagers answer questions in the summer. ⊠ *3 mi north of Appomattox, on State Rte. 24,* ☎ *804/352–8987.* ⌫ *$2.* ☉ *June–Aug., daily 9–5:30; Sept.–May, daily 8:30–5.*

RED HILL–PATRICK HENRY NATIONAL MEMORIAL – In the town of Brookneal, 35 mi southeast of Lynchburg off Route 501, the Patrick Henry National Memorial was the final home of Revolutionary War patriot Patrick Henry, whose "Give me liberty or give me death" speech inspired a generation. The home has been restored near an original law office and contains numerous Henry-family furnishings. Other buildings, including a coachman's cabin and stable, stand near a garden and a boxwood maze. Henry's grave is on the property. ⊠ *35 mi southeast of Lynchburg, off Rte. 501, Brookneal,* ☎ *804/376-2044.* ⌫ *$3.* ☉ *Apr.–Oct., daily 9–5; Nov.–Mar., daily 9–4.*

RICHMOND AND THE PIEDMONT A TO Z

Arriving and Departing

By Bus
Greyhound Lines (☎ 800/231–2222) serves Charlottesville (⊠ 310 W. Main St., ☎ 804/295–5131) and Richmond (⊠ 2910 N. Blvd., ☎ 804/254–5910).

By Car
Richmond is at the intersection of Interstates 95 and 64, which run north–south and east–west, respectively. U.S. 1 also runs north–south by the city. Charlottesville is where U.S. 29 (north–south) meets I–64.

Lynchburg is the meeting point of U.S. 460 between Richmond and Roanoke and Route 29 south from Charlottesville.

By Plane

Richmond International Airport (☎ 804/226–3000), 10 mi east of the city, off I–64, has scheduled flights by nine airlines, including American (☎ 800/433–7300), Delta (☎ 800/221–1212), United (☎ 800/241–6522), and USAir (☎ 800/428–4322). A taxi ride downtown from the airport costs $18–$20.

Charlottesville-Albemarle Airport (☎ 804/973–8341), 8 mi north of Charlottesville on Route 29, is served principally by USAir Express, United Express, Colgan, and Comair via Delta Connection.

Lynchburg Regional Airport (☎ 804/582–1150) on Route 29 South is served by USAir Express and United Express.

By Train

Amtrak (☎ 800/872–7245) service between New York City and Newport News or Florida passes daily through Richmond Station (✉ 7519 Staples Mill Rd., Richmond, ☎ 804/553–2903).

Union Station (✉ 810 W. Main St., Charlottesville, ☎ 804/296–4559) is a stop on Amtrak's runs between Washington, DC and Chicago (three times a week) and between New York and New Orleans (daily).

Amtrak's *Crescent* runs between New York and New Orleans and stops daily at Lynchburg's Kemper Street Station.

Getting Around

By Bus

Greater Richmond Transit (☎ 804/358–4782) operates bus service in Richmond. Buses run daily, 5 AM–12:30 AM; fares are $1.25–$1.50 (exact change).

By Car

Having a car is advisable—though not necessary—in Richmond and indispensable for visiting Charlottesville and Lynchburg. I–64 is the main highway linking Richmond and Charlottesville.

By Taxi

Cabs are metered in Richmond; they charge $3 for the first mile and $1.50 for each additional mile.

Contacts and Resources

Bed-and-Breakfast Information

Guesthouses (✉ Box 5737, Charlottesville 22905, ☎ 804/979–7264) will arrange accommodations for you. For $1 you can get a brochure about local B&Bs.

Boat Tours

***Annabel Lee* Riverboat Cruises** (☎ 804/644–5700) ply the waters from April to December, with lunch, brunch, dinner, dancing, live riverboat show, and James River plantation cruises.

Emergencies

Throughout the region, dial **911** for emergency assistance.

Martha Jefferson Hospital (✉ 459 Locust Ave., Charlottesville, ☎ 804/982–7000), **Lynchburg General Hospital** (✉ 1901 Tate Springs Rd., ☎ 804/947–3000), and **Medical College of Virginia Hospital** (✉ 401 N. 12th St., Richmond, ☎ 804/828–9000) are open 24 hours.

CVS Pharmacy (✉ 2738 W. Broad St., Richmond, ☎ 804/359–2497) is open 24 hours.

Guided Tours

Historic Richmond Tours (☎ 804/780–0107) organizes tours on subjects such as women of Richmond, architecture, the canal system, the Civil War, the Revolution, homes and gardens, battlefields, and walking tours ($5). It also runs daily two- to four-hour driving tours of the city in air-conditioned vans, for $16–$22. Reservations are required. **Richmond Discoveries** (☎ 804/795–5781, FAX 804/795–1164) is a private company that offers an array of excursions in the Richmond area, including trips that highlight Civil War history, horseback tours, and customized rambles for large groups or small families.

Visitor Information

Charlottesville/Albemarle Convention and Visitors Bureau (✉ Rte. 20 S, Box 161, Charlottesville 22902, ☎ 804/977–1783).

Lynchburg Chamber of Commerce Visitors Center (✉ 216-12th St., Lynchburg 24504, ☎ 804/847–1811 or 800/732–5821).

Metro Richmond Convention and Visitors Bureau (✉ 1710 Robin Hood Rd., Exit 78 off I–95 and I–64, ☎ 804/358–5511; Bell Tower at Capitol Sq., 9th and Franklin Sts., ☎ 804/648–3146; Richmond International Airport, Exit 197 off I–64, ☎ 804/236–3260).

Petersburg Visitors Center/Department of Tourism. Write to the Department of Tourism (✉ 15 Bank St., Petersburg 23803, ☎ 804/733–2402), or stop by the Visitors Center (✉ 425 Cockade Alley, ☎ 804/733–2400 or 800/368–3595).

Virginia Division of Tourism (✉ 901 E. Byrd St., Richmond 23219, ☎ 800/932–5827) offers a state guide and map of Richmond.

5 Williamsburg, Jamestown, Yorktown

Even the most jaded travelers will be impressed by Colonial Williamsburg, one of the country's largest and most respected historical attractions. Despite the crowds—an estimated 1 million people annually—the village remains an unspoiled, accurate representation of life in the colonies. Nearby, Jamestown Island, the first permanent English settlement in North America, and Yorktown, site of the final major battle in the American War of Independence, illustrate two other essential epochs of American history.

VIRGINIA'S SINGLE LARGEST HISTORICAL attraction is the re-creation of an 18th-century American city—its buildings, trades, daily life, and even some of its citizens, portrayed by costumed interpreters. Colonial Williamsburg, a careful restoration of the former Virginia capital, gives visitors the chance to walk into another century and see how earlier Americans lived. The streets may be unrealistically clean for that era, and you'll find hundreds of visitors exploring the buildings with you, but the rich detail of the re-creation and the sheer size of the city could hold your attention for days. A ticket or pass (price is based on duration of visit) admits the holder to sites in the restored area, but it costs nothing just to walk around and absorb the atmosphere.

The 23-mi Colonial Parkway joins Williamsburg with two other significant historical sites on or near the peninsula bounded by the James and York rivers. Jamestown Island was the location of the first permanent English settlement in North America; Yorktown was the site of the final major battle in the American War of Independence. The sites themselves are maintained today by the National Park Service, which provides visitors with background information. Close by are the more purely entertaining Jamestown Settlement and the Yorktown Victory Center—both run by the Jamestown-Yorktown Foundation—which, like Colonial Williamsburg, re-create the buildings and activities of the 18th century, using interpreters in period dress.

EXPLORING WILLIAMSBURG, JAMESTOWN, AND YORKTOWN

Williamsburg, Virginia's first capital, is the state's largest and most-visited historical attraction. A few miles north of Williamsburg is Jamestown Island, site of the first permanent English settlement and now a living-history museum. The Yorktown Battlefield and Yorktown Victory Center are a few miles east in Yorktown, site of the battle that ended the war for independence from England. Several 18th- and 19th-century plantations lie west of Williamsburg.

Colonial Williamsburg

Numbers in the margin correspond to points of interest on the Colonial Williamsburg map.

★ ❶–⓱ *51 mi southeast of Richmond (via I–64).*

The most visited historic site in Virginia, Colonial Williamsburg is a convincing re-creation of the late-18th-century city. This was the capital of Virginia from 1699 to 1780, succeeding Jamestown and then succeeded by Richmond. Williamsburg has long ceased to be politically important, but now that it resembles itself in its era of glory, it ranks as a jewel of the commonwealth. The restoration project, begun in 1926, was inspired by a local pastor, W. A. R. Goodwin, and financed by John D. Rockefeller, Jr. Rockefeller died in 1960, but the work of the archaeologists and historians of the Colonial Williamsburg Foundation continues to this day, and the restored area of the city is operated by the foundation as a living-history museum.

In Colonial Williamsburg, 88 original 18th-century and early 19th-century structures have been meticulously restored, and another 40 have been reconstructed on their original sites. There are two architectural anomalies here: a 19th-century Federal house, privately owned and closed to the public, and a Victorian Carpenter's Gothic building, operated as a museum by the Association for the Preservation of Virginia Antiquities. In all, 225 period rooms have been furnished from the foundation's collection of more than 100,000 pieces of furniture, pottery, china, glass, silver, pewter, textiles, tools, and carpeting.

Period authenticity also governs the landscaping of the 90 acres of gardens and public greens. The restored area covers 173 acres—surrounded by another "greenbelt," it's controlled by the foundation, which guards against the encroachment of development that could destroy the illusion of the Colonial city.

Despite its huge scale, Williamsburg can seem almost cozy. One million visitors come here annually, and all year long hundreds of costumed interpreters, wearing bonnets or three-corner hats, rove and ride through the streets. Dozens of skilled craftspersons, also in costume, demonstrate and explain their trades inside their workshops. They include the shoemaker, the cooper, the gunsmith, the blacksmith, the musical instrument maker, the silversmith, and the wig maker. Their wares are for sale nearby. Four taverns serve food and drink that approximate the fare of 200 years ago.

Because of the sheer size of Williamsburg and the large numbers of visitors (especially in the warmer months), the best plan may be to begin a tour early in the day; it's a good idea to spend the night before in the area. The foundation claims that visitors must allow three or four days to do Williamsburg justice, but that will depend on one's own interest in the period—and one's interest often increases on arrival. Everyone should allow at least one full day to tour the city.

Visitors must tour the restored area on foot because all vehicular traffic is prohibited to preserve the Colonial atmosphere. Shuttle buses run continuously to and from the visitor center. Vans for people with disabilities are permitted by prior arrangement, and some structures have wheelchair ramps. Other services for visitors with disabilities are also available (☎ 757/220–7644).

❶ The **visitor center** is the logical first stop at Colonial Williamsburg. Here visitors can park free; buy their tickets; see a 35-minute introductory movie, *Williamsburg—the Story of a Patriot*; and pick up a *Visitors Companion* guide, with a list of regular events and special programs and a map of the Historic Area. ⊠ *I–64 (Exit 238),* ☎ *757/220–7645 or 800/447–8679.* ⊠ *Patriot's Pass ($33, price subject to change), good for 1 yr, admits bearer to every Colonial Williamsburg–run site, including Carter's Grove Plantation, the Governor's Palace, DeWitt Wallace Decorative Arts Gallery, and the Abby Aldrich Rockefeller Folk Art Center. A range of less expensive tickets allows more restricted visits. Tickets also sold at the Lumber House in historic area.* ☉ *Daily 9–5. Some sites close in winter on a rotating basis (Carter's Grove closed Jan.–mid-Mar. and Mon. year-round).*

The spine of Colonial Williamsburg's restored area is the broad, 1-mi-long **Duke of Gloucester Street.** On Saturday at noon, from March to October, the Junior Fife and Drum Corps marches the length of the street and performs a stirring drill. Along this artery alone, or just off it, are two dozen attractions.

❷ At the east end of Duke of Gloucester Street is the **capitol,** the building that made this town so important. It was here that the pre-Revolutionary House of Burgesses (dominated by the ascendant gentry) challenged the royally appointed council (an almost medieval body made up of the bigger landowners). The House eventually arrived at the resolutions that amounted to rebellion. An informative tour explains the development, stage by stage, of American democracy from its English parliamentary roots. In the courtroom a guide recites the harsh Georgian sentences that were meted out: For instance, theft of more than 12 shillings was a capital crime. Occasional reenactments, such as witch trials, dramatize the evolution of our jurisprudence.

What stands on the site today is in fact a reproduction of a structure of 1705 that burned down in 1747. Dark-wood wainscoting, pewter chandeliers, and towering ceilings contribute to a handsome impression. That an official building would have so ornate an interior was characteristic of aristocratic 18th-century Virginia. This was in telling contrast to the plain town meeting halls of Puritan New England, where other Founding Fathers were governing themselves at the same time.

Walking west on Duke of Gloucester Street from the capitol, visitors encounter a dozen 18th-century shops—including those of the apothecary, the wig maker, the silversmith, and the milliner.

❸ Raleigh Tavern, the scene of pre-Revolutionary revels and rallies that were often joined by Washington, Jefferson, and other major figures, is on Duke of Gloucester Street, just west of the capitol. The spare but elegant blue-and-white Apollo Room is said to have been the first meeting place of Phi Beta Kappa, the scholastic honorary society founded in 1776. The French general Marquis de Lafayette was feted here in 1824. In 1859 the original structure burned, and today's building is a reconstruction based on archaeological evidence and period descriptions and sketches of the building.

❹ Wetherburn's Tavern, which offered refreshment, entertainment, and lodging beginning in 1743, is on Duke of Gloucester Street, across the street from Raleigh Tavern. This is possibly the most accurately furnished building in Colonial Williamsburg, for the contents conform to a room-by-room inventory taken in 1760. Excavations at this site have yielded more than 200,000 artifacts. The outbuildings include the original dairy and a reconstructed kitchen. Vegetables are still grown in the small garden.

Between Botetourt and Colonial streets, on the south side of Duke of **❺** Gloucester Street, **James Anderson's Blacksmith Shop** is where smiths forge the nails, tools, and other iron hardware that are used in construction throughout the town. The shop itself was recently reconstructed by costumed carpenters using 18th-century tools and techniques—a project that was featured on public television.

West of Queen Street, on the south side of Duke of Gloucester Street, **❻** the original **Magazine** (1715), an octagonal brick warehouse, was used for storing arms and ammunition—at one time, 60,000 pounds of gunpowder and 3,000 muskets. It was used for this purpose by the British, then by the Continental army, and again by the Confederates during the Civil War. Today, 18th-century firearms are on display within the arsenal.

The magazine sits on the southern half of **Market Square,** an open green between Queen and Palace streets along Duke of Gloucester Street, and extending a block on either side. This was the outdoor site for the vending of cattle, seafood, dairy products, fruit, and vegetables. It was also the venue for slave auctions.

❼ The **Guardhouse,** on Duke of Gloucester Street near Queen Street, once served in the defense of the magazine's lethal inventory; now it con-

Colonial Williamsburg

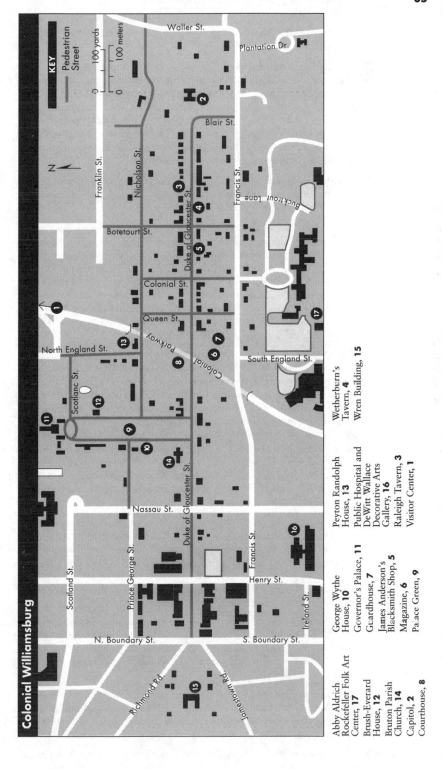

KEY

Pedestrian Street

Waller St.

Plantation Dr.

Blair St.

Nicholson St.

Franklin St.

Francis St.

Duke of Gloucester St.

Botetourt St.

Colonial St.

Queen St.

North England St.

Scotland St.

Nassau St.

Prince George St.

Scotland St.

Henry St.

Francis St.

Ireland St.

N. Boundary St.

S. Boundary St.

Richmond Rd.

Jamestown Rd.

South England St.

Bucktrout Lane

Colonial Parkway

Abby Aldrich
Rockefeller Folk Art
Center, **17**
Brush-Everard
House, **12**
Bruton Parish
Church, **14**
Capitol, **2**
Courthouse, **8**

George Wythe
House, **10**
Governor's Palace, **11**
Guardhouse, **7**
James Anderson's
Blacksmith Shop, **5**
Magazine, **6**
Palace Green, **9**

Peyton Randolph
House, **13**
Public Hospital and
DeWitt Wallace
Decorative Arts
Gallery, **16**
Raleigh Tavern, **3**
Visitor Center, **1**

Wetherburn's
Tavern, **4**
Wren Building, **15**

tains a replica fire engine (1750) that is seen on the town streets in the warmer months. Special interpretive programs about the military are scheduled here.

⑧ The original **Courthouse** of 1770 was used by municipal and county courts until 1932. Civil and minor criminal matters and cases involving slaves were adjudicated here; other trials were conducted at the capitol. Stocks, once used to punish misdemeanors, are located outside the building; modern-day visitors take perverse pleasure in photographing each other clapped in the stocks. The exterior of the courthouse has been restored to its original appearance. Visitors often participate in scheduled reenactments of court sessions.

⑨ The **Palace Green** runs north from Duke of Gloucester Street up the center of Palace Street, with the governor's palace at the far end and a notable historic house on each side of it.

⑩ On the west side of Palace Green is the **George Wythe House,** former residence of Thomas Jefferson's law professor. (Wythe was also a signer of the Declaration of Independence.) General Washington used the house as a headquarters just before his victory at Yorktown. The large brick structure, built in the mid-18th century, is conspicuously symmetrical: Each side has a chimney, and each floor has two rooms on either side of a center hallway. The garden in back is similarly divided. The outbuildings, including a smokehouse, kitchen, laundry, privies, and a chicken coop, have been reconstructed.

⑪ The **Governor's Palace,** built in 1720 by His Majesty's Governor Alexander Spotswood, sits at the northern end of Palace Green. Seven British viceroys, the last of them Lord Dunmore in 1775, lived in this appropriately showy mansion: Eight hundred guns and swords arrayed on the walls and ceilings of several rooms herald the power of the Crown. Some of the furnishings are original, and the rest are matched to an extraordinary inventory of 16,000 items. Lavishly appointed as it is, the palace is furnished to the time just before the Revolution. During the Revolution, it housed the commonwealth's first two governors, Patrick Henry and Thomas Jefferson. The original residence burned down in 1781, and today's reconstruction stands on the original foundation.

A costumed guide greets visitors at the door of the Governor's Palace and conducts them through the building, offering commentary and answering questions. Notable among the furnishings are several pieces made in Williamsburg and actually owned by Lord Dunmore, the last royal governor. Social events are described on the walk through the great formal ballroom. The supper room leads to the formal garden and the planted terraces beyond.

⑫ At Scotland Street and Palace Green, the **Brush-Everard House** was built in 1717 by John Brush, a gunsmith, and later owned by Thomas Everard, who was twice mayor of Williamsburg. The yellow wood-frame house contains remarkable ornate carving work but is open only for special-focus tours.

On the outskirts of the Historic Area, on N. England Street, **Robertson's Windmill** is where rural trades such as basket making, pit sawing, and coopering (barrel making) are demonstrated. The windmill operates only when the weather is willing.

⑬ The **Peyton Randolph House,** on Nicholson Street at N. England Street, was the home of a prominent colonist and revolutionary who served as attorney general under the British, then as Speaker of the House of Burgesses, and later as president of the first and second Continental

Congresses. The oak-paneled bedroom and Randolph family silver are remarkable, but unfortunately, this is another building open only for special tours.

East of the Peyton-Randolph House, on Nicholson Street, is the **military encampment.** During warm weather, "Join the Continental Army," an interactive theater performance, enables visitors to experience military life on the eve of the Revolution. Under the guidance of costumed militiamen, visitors drill and make camp in a 45-minute participatory program. If you want to join the ranks for a little while, you can volunteer at the site.

⑭ The brick Episcopal **Bruton Parish Church,** on Duke of Gloucester Street west of Palace Street, was built in 1715 and has served continuously as a house of worship. One of its 20th-century pastors, W. A. R. Goodwin, provided the impetus for Williamsburg's restoration. The church tower, topped by a beige wooden steeple, was added in 1769; during the Revolution its bell served as the local liberty bell. The white pews, tall and boxed in, are characteristic of the starkly graceful Colonial ecclesiastical architecture of the region. The stone baptismal font is believed to have come from an older Jamestown church. Many local eminences, including one royal governor, are interred in the graveyard. The church is open to the public; contributions are accepted.

NEED A
BREAK?

At the west end of Duke of Gloucester Street, for a block on both sides, **Merchant's Square** has more than 30 shops and restaurants, some serving fast food. Services include two banks.

⑮ The **Wren Building,** at the west end of Duke of Gloucester Street, is part of the College of William and Mary, founded in 1693 and the second-oldest college in the United States after Harvard University. The campus extends to the west; the Wren Building (1695) was based on the work of the celebrated London architect Sir Christopher Wren. Its redbrick outer walls are original, but the interiors were gutted by fire several times, and the present quarters are largely reconstructions of the 20th century. The faculty common room, with a table covered with green felt and an antique globe, suggests Oxford and Cambridge universities, the models for this New World institution. Jefferson studied and later taught law here to James Monroe and others. College undergraduates lead visitors on tours of the building, including the chapel where Peyton Randolph is buried.

Along with all the handsome public buildings, restored homes, reconstructed shops, and costumed interpreters of Colonial Williamsburg, museums bequeathed by three modern-day benefactors add another
⑯ cultural dimension that goes well beyond Colonial history. The **Public Hospital** on Francis Street is a reconstructed insane asylum of 1773 that provides a shocking glimpse of bedlamite squalor. It also serves as cover for an edifice of 1985 that houses very different exhibitions; visitors pass through the hospital lobby into the **DeWitt Wallace Decorative Arts Gallery.** Here English and American furniture, textiles, prints, metals, and ceramics of the 17th to the early 19th century are grouped by medium. Prizes among the 8,000 pieces in the collection are a full-length portrait of George Washington by Charles Willson Peale and a royally commissioned case clock surmounted by the detailed figure of a Native American.

⑰ The **Abby Aldrich Rockefeller Folk Art Center,** on S. England Street, is a showcase for American "decorative usefulware": toys, furniture, weather vanes, coffeepots, and quilts. There are also folk paintings, rustic sculptures, and needlepoint pictures. The exhibition spaces represent typical 19th-century domestic interiors. Since the 1920s, the 2,000-piece collection has grown from the original 400 pieces acquired by the wife of Colonial Williamsburg's first and principal benefactor.

OFF THE
BEATEN PATH

CARTER'S GROVE – Eight miles east of Colonial Williamsburg, the reconstructed Carter's Grove settlement examines 400 years of history, starting in 1619 with Wolstenholme Towne. The settlement has been reconstructed after extensive archaeological investigation and equipped with recorded narrative. Exhibits of the Winthrop Rockefeller Archaeology Museum, opened in 1991, provide further insight. The 18th century is represented by slave dwellings reconstructed on their original foundations, where costumed interpreters explain the crucial role African-Americans played on plantations. Finally, visitors may tour the mansion, built in 1755 by Carter Burwell, whose grandfather, "King" Carter, made the family fortune as one of Virginia's wealthiest landowners and greatest explorers. The mansion was extensively remodeled in 1919 to express its owner's fascination with the past, and additions were made in the 1930s. The interior is notable for the original wood paneling and elaborate carvings. A one-way scenic country road, used also for biking, leads from Carter's Grove through woods, meadows, marshes, and streams back to Williamsburg. Visitors also may return to the Historic Area on Route 60. ⊠ U.S. 60, ☎ 757/229-1000. ☞ $15 (included in $33 Patriot's pass from Williamsburg). ☉ Tues.–Sun. 9–5. Closed Jan.–mid-Mar.

BUSCH GARDENS WILLIAMSBURG – Three miles east of Williamsburg, this 360-acre amusement and theme park has more than 30 rides and nine re-creations of European and French Canadian hamlets. In addition to roller coasters, there are bumper cars and water adventures such as a "Rhine River" cruise and a "Roman Rapids" for rafting. Shows and rides are included in the admission price; food is additional. Costumed actors add character to the themed areas, and two covered trains circle the park while cable-car gondolas pass overhead. ⊠ U.S. 60, ☎ 757/253-3350. ☞ $29.95. ☉ Apr., Sat. 10–10, Sun. 10–7; mid-May–mid-June, Sun.–Fri. 10–7, Sat. 10–10; mid-June–July, daily 10–10; Aug., Sun.–Fri. 10–10, Sat. 10–midnight; Sept.–Oct. 31, Fri.–Tues. 10–7; Nov., weekends 10–7. Parking $2–$6.

Dining and Lodging

Dining rooms within walking distance of Colonial Williamsburg's restored area are often crowded, and reservations (☎ 800/447–8679) are necessary.

$$$$ ✕ **Regency Room.** This restaurant in the Williamsburg Inn is known for elegant decor, attentive service, and quality cuisine. In a setting of crystal chandeliers, Oriental silk-screen prints, and full silver service, diners sample chateaubriand carved tableside, as well as lobster bisque and rich ice-cream desserts. ⊠ Williamsburg Inn, 136 E. Francis St., ☎ 757/229–1000. Reservations essential. Jacket and tie at dinner and Sun. brunch. AE, D, MC, V.

$$$ ✕ **Aberdeen Barn.** Barn walls decorated with saws, pitchforks, oxen yokes, and the like surround lacquered wood tables set with linen napkins. The menu reflects more elaborate fare than typical country cooking. Specialties include slow-roasted prime ribs of beef; baby-back Danish pork ribs barbecued with a sauce of peach preserves and Southern Comfort; and shrimp Dijon. An ample but not esoteric wine list is dominated by Californian vintages. ⊠ 1601 Richmond Rd., ☎ 757/229–6661. AE, D, MC, V. No lunch.

$$$ ✕ **Berret's Restaurant and Raw Bar.** In addition to its choice location just behind Merchants Square, Berret's is popular for its outdoor raw

bar. Inside, a colorful tile wall and paintings by regional artists convey a nautical theme. Fish and shellfish dishes are best here—try the soft-shell crabs with peanut-bourbon butter. ⊠ *199 S. Boundry St.,* ☎ *757/253–1847. AE, D, MC, V.*

$$$ ✕ **Le Yaca.** A mall of small boutiques seems an unlikely setting for a convincingly country-French dining room with soft pastel colors, hardwood floors, candlelight, and a central open fireplace where a nightly spectacle is the specialty of the house: leg of lamb roasting on a spit. A rosemary-and-garlic sauce complements individual servings of the lamb. For dessert, the kitchen offers its square version of a chocolate truffle, *marquis au chocolat,* frozen and served atop crème anglaise. ⊠ *1915 Pocahontas Trail,* ☎ *757/220–3616. AE, DC, MC, V. Closed Sun., early Jan.*

$$$ ✕ **The Trellis.** Although the restaurant is in a Colonial building, its hardwood floors, ceramic tiles, and green plants evoke the atmosphere of a country inn in the Napa Valley. Executive chef Maurice Desaulniers has won national recognition for the imaginative menu, which changes with the seasons. Diners have a choice of five cozy dining rooms—in one, you can watch the mesquite fire—and 8,000 bottles of wine. The grilled seafood specialties are particularly good. ⊠ *Merchants Sq.,* ☎ *757/229–8610. AE, MC, V.*

★

$$$ ✕ **Yorkshire Inn Steak and Seafood House.** A cream color dominates the decor, with red carpeting in one dining room and gold in the other; brass chandeliers and candles light the rooms. The views of a motel swimming pool and a parking lot will not distract diners from the menu, which offers predominantly seafood. Recent entrées have included blackened tuna; trout stuffed with crab imperial; and traditional shish kebab—beef tenderloin, tomato, green pepper—as well as a seafood shish kebab variation, including lobster-tail meat, shrimp, and scallops. The wine cellar is highly diversified, with representatives of Germany and Greece among the customary French and Californian vintages. ⊠ *700 York St.,* ☎ *757/229–9790. AE, MC, V.*

$$ ✕ **Bray Dining Room.** From the dining room of this modern restaurant guests can watch the goings-on at the Kingsmill golf course through the picture windows that overlook the 18th green. This grill is atypical of its genre in that it features gourmet cuisine including steaks, beef, and seafood; the house specials are the grilled tuna and the swordfish. A piano player performs in the evening, and breakfast is served daily. ⊠ *Kingsmill Resort, 100 Golfclub Rd.,* ☎ *757/253–3900. AE, D, DC, MC, V. No dinner Mon.*

$$ ✕ **The Cascades.** Its location on the grounds of the visitor center means that this restaurant is full of tourists for breakfast and dinner; local residents come for Sunday brunch, when most of the visitors are off touring the restored area. Large windows look on to landscaped lawns and a waterfall, and at night the scene is illuminated. The all-American fare is a credit to its genre and features a broiled seafood platter with a distinctive baked crab imperial, which tastes like a lightly seasoned crab cake. The ample country chicken dinner begins with cheddar-cheese soup, includes sugar-cured ham with the fried chicken, and concludes with pecan pie. The daily Hunt Breakfast buffet includes fried chicken, oysters in season, and fruit waffles. ⊠ *Visitor-center area,* ☎ *757/229–1000. AE, DC, MC, V.*

$$ ✕ **The Lobster House.** A captain's wheel and other nautical paraphernalia adorn the wood-paneled walls of this restaurant, where diners select Maine lobsters from a tank and enjoy them boiled or stuffed with unadulterated crabmeat. Shrimp comes fried, sautéed, grilled, or steamed, along with the usual "turf" options of filet mignon or New York strip steak. ⊠ *1425 Richmond Rd.,* ☎ *757/229–7771. AE, MC, V. No lunch.*

$$$$ ⊞ **Liberty Rose.** On a hilltop-acre lot 1 mi from the restored area, this
★ slate-roof, white-clapboard house is surrounded by century-old beech,
oak, and poplar. The inn was constructed in the early 1920s and renovated in 1986; furnishings include European antiques and plenty of
silk and damask. Most remarkable is that every room has windows
on three sides. The large suite on the first floor has a unique bathroom
with a claw-foot tub, a red-marble shower, and antique mirrors. Breakfast, included in the room rate, is served on a sunporch. Smoking is
not permitted inside. ⊠ *1022 Jamestown Rd., 23185,* ☎ *757/253–
1260 or 800/545–1825. 4 rooms. AE, MC, V.*

$$$$ ⊞ **Williamsburg Hospitality House.** This four-story redbrick building,
constructed in 1973, faces the College of William and Mary; ask for
a room that looks onto the cobblestone courtyard with a fountain at
the center. Guest quarters have Chippendale reproduction furnishings
and matching decor. Its convenient location two blocks from Colonial
Williamsburg makes it a popular choice. ⊠ *415 Richmond Rd., 23185,*
☎ *757/229–4020 or 800/932–9192,* ℻ *757/220–1560. 300 rooms,
9 suites. Restaurant, bar, pool. AE, D, DC, MC, V.*

$$$$ ⊞ **Williamsburg Inn.** This award-winning grand hotel—built in 1937—
★ is owned and operated by Colonial Williamsburg. Rooms are individually
furnished in the English Regency style. For those who desire more ex-
clusive surroundings, a number of nearby Colonial houses and taverns
are furnished with period reproductions and serviced by the staff of
the inn. So is Providence Hall, which is adjacent to the inn but which
has a less formal atmosphere, with rooms in contemporary Oriental
decor overlooking tennis courts, a private pond, and a wooded area.
Together these structures have 235 rooms. ⊠ *136 E. Francis St. (Box
1776), 23187–1776,* ☎ *757/229–1000 or 800/447–8679,* ℻ *757/565–
8797. Restaurant, lobby lounge, pool, 18-hole golf course, tennis
court, hiking. AE, D, MC, V.*

$$$ ⊞ **Fort Magruder Inn.** Although this is primarily a convention facility,
it's a comfortable and convenient option for individuals and families,
too. The inn was built in 1975 on a Civil War battlefield, and some
rooms overlook the surviving fortifications. A neo-Colonial motif is
the decor for all rooms. ⊠ *6945 Pocahontas Trail, 23185,* ☎ *757/220–
2250 or 800/582–1010,* ℻ *757/220–3215. 303 rooms. Restaurant,
bar, 1 indoor and 1 outdoor pool, sauna, 2 tennis courts, exercise room,
playground. AE, DC, MC, V.*

$$$ ⊞ **Quality Suites.** This five-story, all-suites hotel, built in 1987, sits on
11 wooded acres next to a shopping center, less than 1 mi from the re-
stored area. Though there is no large meeting facility or restaurant to
attract conventioneers, the well-appointed hostelry offers a convenient
retreat from the bustle of Colonial Williamsburg. Guest rooms have a
mostly mauve, California-contemporary look. ⊠ *152 Kingsgate Pkwy.,
23185,* ☎ *757/229–6800 or 800/333–0924,* ℻ *757/220–3486. 169
suites. Indoor pool, sauna. AE, D, DC, MC, V.*

$$$ ⊞ **The Williamsburg Woodlands.** An official Colonial Williamsburg
hostelry, this motel was formerly the Motor House. Rooms are in a
variety of buildings, all set in a pine grove adjacent to the visitor-cen-
ter area. Furnishings are contemporary. ⊠ *102 Visitor Center Dr., 23185,*
☎ *757/229–1000 or 800/447–8679,* ℻ *757/565–8797. 315 rooms.
Restaurant, lobby lounge, 3 pools, miniature golf, putting green, ten-
nis court, horseshoes, Ping-Pong, shuffleboard, playground. AE, MC,
V.*

$$ ⊞ **Governor's Inn.** Here you'll find quality at a moderate rate. Although
it's only three blocks from the visitor center, shuttle-bus service is
available. Rooms are furnished with two double beds. ⊠ *506 N.*

Henry St., 23185, ☎ *757/229–1000,* FAX *757/220–7019. 200 rooms. Pool, video games. AE, D, MC, V.*

$$ 🏨 **Heritage Inn.** This comfortable three-story inn is decorated inside and out in Colonial style. Room furnishings include postered headboards, prints of Colonial Williamsburg, and an armoire concealing a TV. Some quarters open directly onto the parking lot, but this is an unusually quiet, leafy site, and the pool is set in a garden. ⊠ *1324 Richmond Rd., 23185,* ☎ *757/229–6220 or 800/782–3800,* FAX *757/229–2774. 54 rooms. Restaurant, pool. AE, DC, MC, V.*

$$ 🏨 **War Hill Inn.** Erected in 1970, the inn was designed by a Colonial Williamsburg architect to resemble a period structure: A two-story red-brick building at the center has two wood-frame wings. Inside, guests find appropriate antiques and reproductions. The setting is a 32-acre operating cattle farm, 4 mi from the Colonial Williamsburg information center. Those in search of privacy will want the two-room cottage or the first-floor suite (other rooms open onto a common hallway). All rooms have cable TV. ⊠ *4560 Long Hill Rd., 23188,* ☎ *757/565–0248. 5 rooms. MC, V.*

$ 🏨 **Bassett Motel.** Dogwood trees and many flower beds (azaleas and tulips in the spring, begonias in the fall) distinguish the site of this well-run, single-story brick property on the quieter east side of Williamsburg. Rooms are variously furnished, some with tables, some with desks, in a cream color scheme. ⊠ *800 York St. (U.S. 60), 23185,* ☎ *757/229–5175. 18 rooms. MC, V.*

$ 🏨 **Governor Spotswood Motel.** This one-story redbrick motel has been extended gradually, section by section, for more than 50 years, most recently in 1990. The decor reflects the influence of Colonial Williamsburg, but in classic motel design each room faces its parking space. There's lots of surrounding lawn and a sunken garden setting for the swimming pool. Seven cottages sleep four to seven people, and 14 of the rooms have kitchen units. ⊠ *1508 Richmond Rd., 23185,* ☎ *757/229–6444 or 800/368–1244,* FAX *757/253–2410. 78 rooms. Pool, shuffleboard, playground. AE, D, DC, MC, V.*

Nightlife and the Arts

BARS AND TAVERNS

Four taverns within Colonial Williamsburg serve Colonial-style foods in reconstructed Colonial settings. Smoking is not permitted in any of the taverns. Hours change according to season, so check by calling the reservations number (☎ 800/828–3767). Dress is casual and dinner reservations are recommended. All the taverns are moderately priced and accept American Express, MasterCard, and Visa.

✕ **Chownings Tavern** (⊠ Duke of Gloucester St.), a reconstructed 18th-century alehouse, serves light meals, including Brunswick stew, Welsh rarebit, oysters, and sandwiches—all complemented by Chowning's especially good bread and drink. It's open every night; in summer, guests may eat outside under the arbor.

✕ **Christiana Campbell's Tavern** (⊠ Waller St.) is almost as popular today as it was in the Colonial era. Seafood from the Chesapeake Bay is served in period (crab cakes) and nonperiod (spicy jambalaya) dishes.

✕ **Kings Arms** (⊠ Duke of Gloucester St.) is one of Williamsburg's most "genteel" establishments. The fare and the atmosphere mimic those experienced by Founding Fathers such as George Washington and Thomas Jefferson when they sat down to eat Virginia ham, game pie, and Sally Lunn bread over a political discussion. Weather permitting, guests may eat light meals in a garden behind the tavern.

✕ **Shields Tavern** (⊠ Duke of Gloucester St.), the newest member of the tavern foursome, recalls tavern-keeping in the early 18th century by a man named James Shields. Specialties include spit-roasted chicken and broiled beef tenderloin. Some outdoor seating is available.

MUSIC

Busch Gardens Williamsburg (⊠ U.S. 60, ☎ 757/253–3350) hosts a variety of popular song and dance shows (country, gospel, opera, German folk) in several theaters; the largest is the 5,000-seat Royal Palace, which features pop stars.

W&M Hall (☎ 757/221–3340) at the College of William and Mary, with 10,000 seats, holds concerts by well-known artists on tour.

Old Dominion Opry (⊠ 3012 Richmond Rd., ☎ 757/564–0200) offers family-oriented live country music and comedy. Shows run Tuesday through Saturday beginning at 8 PM.

THEATER

The Virginia Company (☎ 757/220–7645 or 800/447–8679) in Colonial Williamsburg presents rollicking 18th-century plays (mostly English) throughout the year. From June through August, performances are held in the open-air Playbooth Theater on the site of the first theater in the country. Colonial Williamsburg also offers a variety of plays, concerts, cultural events, and historical reenactments.

Student drama at the **College of William and Mary** (☎ 757/221–4000) takes place during the school year.

Outdoor Activities and Sports

BIKING

The pamphlet *Biking Through America's Historic Triangle,* available at bike shops, maps a 20-mi route.

Colonial Williamsburg ticket holders can rent bicycles at the **Williamsburg Lodge** on S. England Street.

Bikesmith (⊠ 515 York St., ☎ 757/229–9858) also rents bicycles.

GOLF

Colonial Williamsburg (☎ 757/220–7696 or 800/447–8679) operates three courses—the 18-hole Golden Horseshoe Course, rated one of the top 12 in the country; the 18-hole Golden Horseshoe Green; and the nine-hole Spotswood Course.

Kingsmill Resort (☎ 757/253–3906 or 800/832–5665), near Busch Gardens, has three 18-hole golf courses.

TENNIS

Colonial Williamsburg (☎ 757/220–7794 or 800/447–8679) has 10 tennis courts (six clay and two asphalt at the Williamsburg Inn and two asphalt at Williamsburg Woodlands).

Kingsmill (☎ 757/253–3945 or 800/832–5665) has 13 clay and two hard courts open to the public.

SPECTATOR SPORTS

The College of William and Mary fields varsity or club teams in football, basketball, baseball, track, wrestling, field hockey, soccer, swimming, tennis, and gymnastics. The listings in the weekly *Virginia Gazette* give specifics.

Shopping

CRAFTS

In the restored area of Colonial Williamsburg, nine stores and shops have been reconstructed to create the milieu of the Colonial merchant. Among the available wares typical of the 18th century are silver tea services, jewelry, pottery, pewter and brass items, ironwork, tobacco and herbs, candles, hats, baskets, books, maps and prints, and even baked goods. Two crafts houses sell approved reproductions of the antiques on display in the houses and museums. ✉ *Craft House, Merchant Sq.,* ☎ *757/220–7747; Craft House Inn, S. England St.,* ☎ *757/220–7749.*

OUTLETS

The **Williamsburg Pottery Factory** (✉ Rte. 60, ☎ 757/564–3326), less than 10 minutes west of Williamsburg, is an attraction in itself, and its parking area is usually crammed with tour buses. Covering 200 acres, the enormous outlet store sells luggage, clothing, furniture, food and wine, china, crystal, and pottery. It's the foremost among more than 100 outlet stores on the outskirts of Williamsburg.

Jamestown

Numbers in the margin correspond to points of interest on the Williamsburg and Environs map.

⑱ *9 mi northwest of Colonial Williamsburg (off Colonial Pkwy.).*

Jamestown Island, the site of the first permanent English settlement in North America (1607) and the capital of Virginia until 1699, is separated from the mainland by a narrow isthmus. That Jamestown is no longer inhabited makes its historical significance all the more stirring to the imagination. Redbrick foundation walls approximately delineate the settlement, and artists' conceptions of the original buildings can be seen at several locations. Audio stations narrate the evolving story of Jamestown. The only standing structure is the ruin of a church tower from the 1640s, now part of the Memorial Church built in 1907; the markers within indicate the original church's foundations. Other monuments around the site also date from the tercentenary celebration in 1907. Statues portray the founder of Jamestown, Captain John Smith, and his advocate, the Native American princess Pocahontas, whose pleas saved Smith from being beheaded. Ranger-guided tours of the site take place daily. Living-history programs are presented daily in summer and on weekends in spring and autumn. The museum in the visitor center contains one of the most extensive collections of 17th-century artifacts in the United States. A 5-mi nature drive that rings the island is posted with historically informative signs and paintings. On leaving the island, visitors can stop at the reconstructed **Glasshouse** to observe a demonstration of glassblowing, an unsuccessful business venture of the early colonists. The products of today are for sale in a gift shop. *Visitor Center* ☎ *757/229–1733.* ✉ *$8 car, $2 cyclist or pedestrian.* ◎ *Visitor center: daily 9–5 (gates close at 4:30); Island: daily 8:30–4:30.*

Adjacent to Jamestown Island, and not to be confused with it, is a living-history museum called **Jamestown Settlement.** A version of the early James Fort has been built here, and within it "colonists" cook, make armor, and describe their hard life living under thatched roofs and between walls of wattle and daub (stick framework covered with mud plaster). The largest structure in the complex is the church, where attendance was required twice a day. In the "Indian Village" you can enter a wigwam and see buckskin-costumed interpreters cultivate a garden and make baskets, tools, and pottery. This is one museum where everything may be handled—children especially enjoy this. Visitors may stroll to the pier and inspect large-scale reproductions of the ships in which the settlers arrived: *Godspeed, Discovery,* and *Susan Constant.* The *Godspeed* is a seaworthy vessel that retraced the original voyage in 1985. Visitors may climb aboard the *Susan Constant* and interrogate the sailor-interpreters. Jamestown Settlement's indoor museum has exhibits on

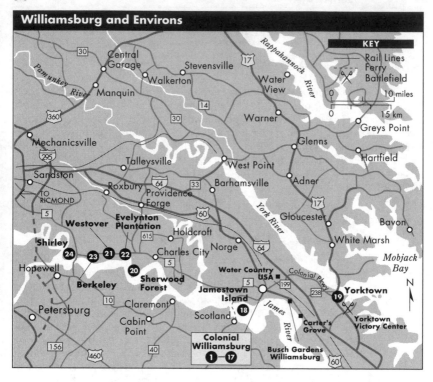

Williamsburg and Environs

the lives of the Powhatans and their English-born neighbors; permanent and changing exhibits explore their interaction and world conditions that encouraged colonization. There's also a 20-minute
docudrama, "Jamestown: The Beginning," as told from a Native American perspective. ✉ *Rte. 31 off Colonial Pkwy.,* ☎ *757/229–1607.* ✉
*$9. Combination ticket for Jamestown Settlement and Yorktown Vic-
tory Center: $12.50.* ☉ *Daily 9–5, except Dec. 25, Jan. 1.*

Yorktown

⑲ *14 mi northeast of Colonial Williamsburg (off Colonial Pkwy.).*

The combined American and French forces surrounded British troops
under Lord Cornwallis in 1781 at Yorktown, forcing an end to the American War of Independence. In Yorktown today, as at Jamestown, two
major attractions complement each other: Yorktown Battlefield, the
historical site, is operated by the National Park Service; and Yorktown
Victory Center, an informative entertainment, is operated by the state's
Jamestown-Yorktown Foundation. The town of Yorktown remains a
living community, albeit a small one. Route 238 leads into Yorktown,
whose Main Street is an array of preserved 18th-century buildings on
a bluff overlooking the York River. First settled in 1691, Yorktown had
become a thriving tobacco port and a prosperous community of several hundred houses by the time of the Revolution. Nine buildings from
that time still stand, not all of them open to visitors. **Moore House,**
where the terms of surrender were negotiated, and the elegant **Nelson
House,** the residence of a Virginia governor and a signer of the Declaration of Independence, are open for tours in summer. The **Swan Tav-**

ern, a reconstruction of a structure of 1722, now houses an antiques shop. On Church Street, **Grace Church,** built in 1697 and damaged in the War of 1812 and the Civil War, was rebuilt and remains an active Episcopal congregation; its walls are made of native marl (a mixture of clay, sand, and limestone containing fragments of seashells). On Main Street, the **Somerwell House,** built before 1707, and the **Sessions House** (before 1699)—the oldest houses in town—are privately owned and closed to the public. The latter was used as local headquarters by the Union forces during General George McClellan's Peninsula Campaign of the Civil War.

The museum in the visitor center at **Yorktown Battlefield** has on exhibit General George Washington's original field tent, pitched and furnished as it was during the fighting. Dioramas, illuminated maps, and a short movie about the battle make the sobering point that Washington's victory was hardly inevitable. A look around from the observation deck on the roof can help one to visualize better the events of the campaign. Guided by a taped audio tour rented ($2) from the gift shop, visitors may explore the battlefield by car, stopping at the site of Washington's headquarters, a couple of crucial redoubts (breastworks dug into the ground), and the field where surrender took place. ⊠ *Rte. 238 off Colonial Pkwy.,* ☎ *757/898–3400.* ☒ *Free.* ☉ *Visitor center: daily 8:30–5 (until 5:30 in summer).*

On the western edge of Yorktown Battlefield, at the **Yorktown Victory Center,** visitors follow the "Road to Revolution" walkway beginning at the orientation area: Textual and graphic displays cover the principal events and personalities of the period. The trail enters the main museum, where the story of Yorktown's critical role in the achievement of American independence is told, and where life-size tableaux feature six "witnesses," including an African-American patriot, a loyalist, a Quaker, two Continental Army soldiers, and the wife of a Virginia plantation owner. An action-packed, half-hour movie dramatization (more melodramatic than the one at the battlefield) is screened continuously. Outdoors, in a Continental Army encampment, interpreters costumed as soldiers and female auxiliaries reenact and discuss daily camp life, including the firing of muskets, drilling, the use of medical treatments, and cooking. In another outdoor area, costumed interpreters re-create 18th-century farm life and demonstrate the gardening of herbs, vegetables, flax, and tobacco. ⊠ *Rte. 238 off Colonial Pkwy.,* ☎ *757/887–1776.* ☒ *$6.75. Combination ticket for Yorktown Victory Center and Jamestown Settlement: $12.50.* ☉ *Daily 9–5. Closed Dec. 25, Jan. 1.*

Dining and Lodging

$$$ ✕ **Nick's Seafood Pavilion.** Fish and shellfish are prominent on a menu that includes seafood shish kebab, a buttery lobster pilaf, Chinese dishes, and baklava for dessert. ⊠ *At the foot of the bridge on Water St.,* ☎ *757/887–5269. AE, DC, MC, V.*

$–$$ ⌸ **Duke of York Motel.** All rooms in the two two-story buildings of the motel face the water and are only a few steps from a public beach. The motel also has a swimming pool and a restaurant that serves breakfast and lunch daily. ⊠ *508 Water St., 23690,* ☎ *757/898–3232,* ⅋ *757/898–5922. 57 rooms. Restaurant, pool. AE, D, DC, MC, V.*

Outdoor Activities and Sports

Along Water Street (Route 238) in Yorktown is a public beach for swimming and fishing. The public beach just over the bridge across the York

River, at Gloucester Point, has boat ramps. Beware of sea nettles (jellyfish) in July and August.

Charles City County

⓴–㉔ *35 mi northwest of Colonial Williamsburg (Rte. 5).*

Colonists founded Charles City County in 1616. Today, visitors can get a taste of those early days by following Route 5 on its scenic route, parallel to the James River, past nine plantations—some of which are now B&Bs.

⓴ **Sherwood Forest,** built in 1720 and said to be the longest wood-frame house in the United States at 300 feet, was the retirement home of John Tyler, 10th president of the United States. Tyler, who came into office when William Henry Harrison died a month after his inauguration, was a Whig who dissented from the party line on abolition in favor of the proslavery position of the Democrats. He died in 1862, having served briefly in the congress of the Confederate States of America. His house remains in the Tyler family and is furnished with heirloom antiques; it's surrounded by a dozen acres of grounds and the five outbuildings, including a tobacco barn. ⊠ *Rte. 5,* ☎ *804/829–5377.* ⊑ *Grounds $3. House tour $7.50.* ☉ *House and grounds: daily 9–5.*

㉑ **Westover** was built in 1735 by the flamboyant Colonel William Byrd II (1674–1744), an American aristocrat who spent much of his time and money in London. He was in Virginia frequently enough to serve in both the upper and lower houses of the Colonial legislature at Williamsburg and to write one of the first travel books about the region (as well as a notorious "secret diary," a frank and thorough account of plantation life and Colonial politics). He lived here with his library of 4,000 volumes. Westover's interior, celebrated for its moldings and carvings, is open to visitors only during Garden Week in late April. The grounds are arrayed with tulip poplars at least 100 years old, and gardens of roses and other flowers are well tended. Three wrought-iron gates, imported from England by the colonel, are mounted on posts topped by figures of eagles with spread wings. Byrd's grave is here, inscribed with the eloquent, immodest, and apt epitaph he composed for himself. ⊠ *Rte. 5, 7000 Westover Rd.,* ☎ *804/829–2882.* ⊑ *$2.* ☉ *Daily 9–5:30.*

㉒ **Evelynton Plantation** originally was part of Westover estate and is believed to have been part of the dowry of William Byrd II's eldest daughter, Evelyn. However, her father refused to allow her to wed her favorite suitor, and she never married. The plantation was purchased in 1846 by the Ruffin family, which had settled on the south shore of the James River in the 1650s. Edmund Ruffin, a celebrated agronomist prior to the Civil War, was a strident secessionist who fired the first shot at Fort Sumter. Evelynton was the scene of fierce skirmishing during the 1862 Peninsula Campaign; the manor house and outbuildings were destroyed during the war. The present Colonial Revival–style house on a hill at the end of a cedar-and-dogwood alley was built two generations later, using 250-year-old brick, under the direction of renowned architect Duncan Lee. The house is furnished with 18th-century English and American antiques and has handsomely landscaped lawn and gardens. Since it opened to the public in 1986, it has earned a reputation for artistic, abundant flower arrangements in every season. The house, gardens, and grounds are part of a 2,500-acre working plantation still operated by Ruffin descendants. Afternoon tea is held on the terrace during Historic Garden Week and the Christmas season. Flower arranging seminars are held three times a year; call for details.

⊠ *Rte. 5, 6701 John Tyler Hwy.,* ☎ *804/829–5075 or 800/473–5075.* ⊜ *$7.* ⊙ *Daily 9–5.*

㉓ Virginians say that the first Thanksgiving was celebrated at **Berkeley** on December 14, 1619, not in Massachusetts. This plantation was the birthplace of Benjamin Harrison, a signer of the Declaration of Independence, and of William Henry Harrison, who was briefly president in 1841. Throughout the Civil War, the Union general George McClellan used Berkeley as headquarters; during his tenure, his subordinate general Daniel Butterfield composed the melody "Taps" on the premises. The brick Georgian house, built in 1726, has been carefully restored following a period of disrepair after the Civil War. It is furnished not with original pieces but with period antiques. The gardens are in excellent condition, particularly the boxwood hedges. A restaurant has seating indoors and out. ⊠ *Rte. 5, then follow signs,* ☎ *804/829–6018.* ⊜ *$8.50.* ⊙ *Daily 8–5.*

㉔ **Shirley,** the oldest plantation in Virginia, has been occupied by a single family, the Carters, for 10 generations. Their claim to the land goes back to 1660, when it was settled by a relative, Edward Hill. Robert E. Lee's mother was born here, and the Carters seem to be related to every notable Virginia family from the Colonial and antebellum periods. The approach to the elegant 1723 Georgian manor is a dramatic one: The house stands at the end of a drive lined by towering Lombardy poplars. Inside, the hall staircase rises for three stories with no visible support. Family silver is on display, ancestral portraits are hung throughout, and rare books line the shelves. ⊠ *501 Shirley Plantation Rd.,* ☎ *804/829–5121.* ⊜ *$7.50.* ⊙ *Daily 9–4;30.*

Lodging

$$$$ ⛫ **Edgewood Plantation.** This Victorian wood house, built in 1849, stands out among its redbrick Colonial neighbors. Three stories high, it sits behind a porch on five largely wooded acres, ½ mi west of Berkeley Plantation and less than an hour from Williamsburg. The entire house is furnished with antiques and country crafts. Rooms have 18th- and 19th-century canopied king or queen beds and Oriental rugs, and period clothing is used as decoration. All rooms have private baths; four rooms have fireplaces. Two gazebos sit in the English garden, and a 1725 grist mill is in the process of being restored. Breakfast, included in the room rate, is served in the formal dining room. ⊠ *Rte. 5 (4800 John Tyler Memorial Hwy.), 23030,* ☎ *804/829–2962 or 800/296–3343,* ⅎⱮ *804/829–2962. 8 rooms. Pool. AE, MC, V.*

WILLIAMSBURG, JAMESTOWN, YORKTOWN A TO Z

Arriving and Departing

By Bus
Greyhound Lines (⊠ 468 N. Boundary St., Williamsburg, ☎ 757/229–1460 or 800/231–2222) has seven departures daily, both westbound (to Richmond) and eastbound (to Norfolk).

By Car
Williamsburg is west of I–64, 51 mi southeast of Richmond; the Colonial Parkway joins Williamsburg with Jamestown to the southwest and Yorktown to the southeast.

By Plane

Newport News/Williamsburg International Airport, in Newport News but close to Williamsburg, is served primarily by USAir (☏ 800/428–4322). **Norfolk International Airport** hosts American (☏ 800/433–7300), Delta (☏ 800/221–1212), United (☏ 800/241–6522), TWA (☏ 800/221–2000), and USAir (☏ 800/428–4322).

By Train

Amtrak (☏ 800/872–7245) trains stop at Williamsburg (✉ 468 N. Boundary St., ☏ 757/229–8750) on their way from New York, Washington, and Richmond to Newport News.

Contacts and Resources

B&B Reservation Agencies

Williamsburg Vacation Reservations (☏ 800/446–9244), representing more than 70 hostelries, provides free lodging reservation services year-round.

Emergencies

Throughout the region, dial **911** for emergency assistance.

In Williamsburg, **Williamsburg Community Hospital** (✉ 301 Monticello Ave., ☏ 757/259–6000; emergency room, ☏ 757/259–6005). **Riverside Regional Medical Center** (✉ 500 J. Clyde Morris Blvd., ☏ 757/594–2000; emergency room, ☏ 757/594–2050), in Newport News, is near many areas of York County.

Guided Tours

Interpreters well versed in Williamsburg and Colonial history are available to lead groups on tours of the Historic Area (☏ 800/228–8878).

Colonial Williamsburg's hour-long guided **walking tours** of the historic area depart from the Greenhow Lumber House (on Duke of Gloucester Street near Palace Green) daily from 9 to 5. Reservations should be made on the day of the tour at the Lumber House.

Colonial Williamsburg's **Lanthorn Tours** takes visitors on an evening walking tour of selected trade shops where jewelry and other products are made in 18th-century style. A separate ticket is required for this program and may be purchased at the visitor center or from the Greenhow Lumber House. **Carriage and wagon rides** are available daily, weather permitting. General ticket holders may purchase tickets on the day of the ride at the Lumber House.

Visitor Information

Williamsburg Area Convention and Visitors Bureau (✉ Drawer GB, 201 Penniman Rd., Williamsburg 23187, ☏ 757/253–0192 or 800/368–6511).
Colonial Williamsburg Visitor Center (✉ Box 1776, Williamsburg 23187–1776, ☏ 800/246–2099) has information on tours and special programs. To make dining and lodging reservations, call ☏ 800/447–8679.
Colonial National Historical Park (✉ Box 210, Yorktown 23690, ☏ 757/898–3400).

6 Hampton Roads Area and the Eastern Shore

The cities in southeast Virginia are defined by their proximity to the Chesapeake Bay and the rivers that empty into it: Witness Norfolk, a port with a strong shipbuilding industry; Virginia Beach, the state's most populous city and popular beach town; and Newport News, builder of the navy's biggest nuclear ships and point of embarkation during both world wars. Linked to the Hampton Roads area by the unusual Chesapeake Bay Bridge Tunnel is Virginia's "other coastline," the quiet, largely untrafficked Eastern Shore.

TIDEWATER, VIRGINIA, IS TECHNICALLY defined as the area east of the fall line of the rivers flowing into the Chesapeake Bay, although, in the popular imagination, the term "Tidewater" has also come to stand for a sort of aristocratic southern gentility. The eastern end of the Tidewater, however, around the mouth of the Chesapeake Bay along Virginia's brief stretch of Atlantic shoreline, cannot be so easily characterized. Norfolk is defined today by its role as a port, with a strong shipbuilding industry and military presence, while Virginia Beach thrives as the state's most populous city and chief beach town, complete with its own crowded boardwalk.

At the end of the Williamsburg peninsula, the enormous harbor of Hampton Roads—where the James, Elizabeth, and Nansemond rivers flow together and on into Chesapeake Bay—has played a crucial role in the discovery and settlement of the nation, the struggle for independence, and the conflict that nearly dissolved the Union. A history of violence and hardship provides a dramatic background for the prosperous present day in an area now dedicated to recreation and tourism.

Exploring the Hampton Roads Area and the Eastern Shore

The port of Hampton Roads extends from Virginia Beach on the Atlantic Ocean west to Williamsburg. The economy and many sights and activities are closely linked to the water. The Eastern Shore, a sliver of land that dangles from the portion of Maryland east of the Chesapeake Bay, can be reached by way of a 17½-mi bridge–tunnel. Here you'll find small towns and several islands—including Wallops Island, from which NASA launched many of its early rockets, and Assateague Island, a national wildlife refuge and beach.

HAMPTON ROADS AREA

Numbers in the margin correspond to points of interest on the Southeast Virginia map.

The Virginia Peninsula, extending southeast from the area of Williamsburg into the Chesapeake Bay, defines the port of Hampton Roads on the north and contains the cities of Newport News and Hampton. The southern side of Hampton Roads includes Norfolk, Suffolk, Portsmouth, Virginia Beach, and Chesapeake.

Newport News

❶ *23 mi southeast of Williamsburg.*

Newport News, on the James River, is said to have taken its name from a Captain Newport, whose return with supplies was "good news" to the early colonists. The world's largest privately owned shipyard is here.

A world history of seagoing vessels and the people who sailed them ★ occupies the **Mariners' Museum.** Many of the authentic scale models hand-carved by August Crabtree are so tiny that you must view them through magnifying glasses; they portray the world's shipbuilding accomplishments from ancient Egypt to 19th-century Britain. Among the more than 50 full-size craft on display are a Native American bark canoe, a sailing yacht, a speedboat, a gondola, a Coast Guard cutter, and a Chinese sampan. In one gallery visitors can often watch the progress of a boat under construction; in another are ornate and sometimes huge figureheads from the bows of sailing ships; in another, the watermen's culture of the Chesapeake Bay is explored. Examples of nautical gear—for example, trail boards, rudder heads, and paddle boxes—are on display, along with a selection of the intricate whale-tusk carvings called scrimshaw. Photographs and paintings recount naval history and the story of private-sector seafaring. A permanent "Age of Exploration" gallery opened in 1992. ⊠ *100 Museum Dr. (I-64 Exit 258A),* ☎ *757/595–0368.* ⊟ *$6.50.* ☉ *Daily 10–5.*

The **War Memorial Museum,** housing more than 60,000 of Virginia's artifacts from all over the world, including weapons, uniforms, wartime posters, photographs, and other memorabilia, traces military history from 1775 to Desert Storm and includes a history of African-Americans and women in the military. A **Vietnam War Memorial** is on the grounds of Huntington Park. An annual "Christmas in the Field" Civil War reenactment is performed the second weekend of December. ⊠ *9285 Warwick Blvd. (Rte. 60),* ☎ *757/247–8523.* ⊟ *$2.* ☉ *Mon.–Sat. 9–5, Sun. 1–5.*

The **U.S. Army Transportation Museum,** at Fort Eustis, traces the history of army transportation by land, sea, and air, beginning with the Revolutionary War era. More than 90 vehicles, including experimental craft, are on display. ⊠ *Besson Hall, Bldg. 300, I-64 (Exit 250A),* ☎ *757/878–1109.* ⊟ *Free.* ☉ *Tues.–Sun. 9–4:30.*

☺ **Peninsula SPCA** has a petting zoo with deer, donkeys, sheep, goats, turkeys, and wild animals, such as a caged jaguar, tiger, and leopard. ⊠ *523 J. Clyde Morris Blvd.,* ☎ *757/595–1399.* ⊟ *$2.* ☉ *Weekdays 10–5, Sat. 10–4:30, Sun. noon–5.*

☺ At the **Virginia Living Museum,** animals indigenous to the region live in wild or simulated wild lakefront habitats that allow visitors to observe their natural behavior. A trail leads to the water's edge, where otter and blue heron can be spotted, then upland past de-scented skunks, lame bald eagles (wounded by hunters), and cute but unpettable bobcats. A 40-foot-tall outdoor aviary puts visitors into a wetlands habitat. Indoors, the Planetarium offers more celestial sights; call for show times. ⊠ *524 J. Clyde Morris Blvd.,* ☎ *757/595–1900.* ⊟ *$5. Planetarium $2.50 (children under 4 not permitted in planetarium). Combination $6.* ☉ *Mid-June–Labor Day, Mon.–Sat. 9–9, Sun. 10–6; Sept.–mid-June, Mon.–Sat. 9–5, Sun. noon–5.*

Dining

$$ ✕ **Herman's Harbor House.** You may think you've gone off-course as
★ you drive through this residential neighborhood—just keep driving. Herman's, at the end of Deep Creek Road, serves the area's best crab cakes, accompanied by ample portions of vegetables. The diverse menu also includes other Tidewater-style seafood dishes as well as steak, veal, and pasta, and homemade desserts. On Friday and Saturday nights there's an all-you-can-eat seafood buffet. ⊠ *663 Deep Creek Rd. (I-64, Exit 258-A, to Warwick Blvd. to Deep Creek Rd.),* ☎ *757/930–1000. AE, D, MC, V.*

Outdoor Activities and Sports

BOATING AND CANOEING

Newport News Park (☎ 757/886–7911) has rentals available.
The Mariners' Museum (☎ 757/595–0368) rents boats for use on Lake Maury on museum grounds.

FISHING

James River Fishing Pier (☎ 757/247–0364) is open April through mid-Novemher.

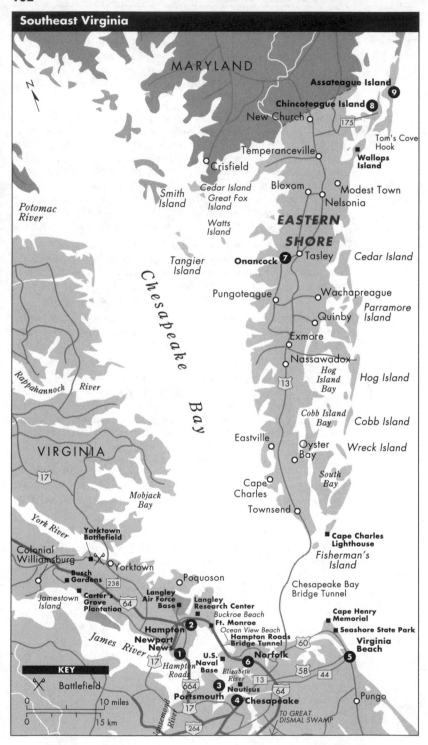

Southeast Virginia

MARYLAND

Assateague Island 9

Chincoteague Island 8

New Church

175

Temperanceville

Tom's Cove
Hook

Crisfield

**Wallops
Island**

*Cedar Island
Great Fox
Island*

Bloxom

Modest Town

*Smith
Island*

Nelsonia

*Watts
Island*

**EASTERN
SHORE**

*Potomac
River*

*Tangier
Island*

Onancock 7 Tasley

Cedar Island

Pungoteague

Wachapreague

Quinby

*Parramore
Island*

Exmore

Chesapeake Bay

Nassawadox

13

*Hog
Island
Bay*

Hog Island

Rappahannock River

*Cobb Island
Bay*

Cobb Island

Eastville

Oyster
Bay

Wreck Island

VIRGINIA

17

*South
Bay*

Cape
Charles

Townsend

*Mobjack
Bay*

■ **Cape Charles
Lighthouse**

York River

**Yorktown
Battlefield**

*Fisherman's
Island*

Colonial
Williamsburg

Yorktown

Poquoson

Chesapeake Bay
Bridge Tunnel

■ **Busch
Gardens**

238

**Carter's
Grove
Plantation**

64

*Jamestown
Island*

**Langley
Air Force
Base**

**Langley
Research Center**

Buckroe Beach

**Cape Henry
Memorial**

Hampton 2
Ft. Monroe

■ **Seashore State Park**

Ocean View Beach

**Virginia
Beach**

James River

**Newport
News** 1

**Hampton Roads
Bridge Tunnel**

60

Norfolk

5

17

*Hampton
Roads*

**U.S.
Naval
Base** 6

58 44

Portsmouth

3

*Elizabeth
River*

Nauticus

13

64

Pungo

264

4 **Chesapeake**

*TO GREAT
DISMAL SWAMP*

*Nansemond
River*

KEY

✕ Battlefield

0   10 miles

0   15 km

GOLF
Dell Run Golf Course Newport News Park (☎ 757/886–7925) has two 18-hole courses.

SPECTATOR SPORTS
Langley Speedway (☎ 757/865–1100) features late-model stock cars, grand stock, all-American stock, and ministock. Races are run from March to October.

Hampton

❷ *8 mi north of Newport News (via I–64); 16 mi northwest of Norfolk.*

Founded in 1610, Hampton is the oldest continuously existing English-speaking settlement in the United States. It is also home to the country's first aviation research facility, NASA Langley Research Center, established in 1917. The center was headquarters for the first manned space program in the United States. Astronauts for the *Mercury* and *Apollo* missions trained at this historic facility.

The **Virginia Air and Space Center,** on Hampton's downtown waterfront, traces the history of flight and space exploration. The nine-story, futuristic, $30-million center is the official repository of the NASA Langley Research Center and houses dramatic space artifacts, such as a 3-billion-year-old moon rock, the *Apollo 12* command capsule, and a lunar lander. The center also holds—among its imaginative novelties—a dozen full-size aircraft, Southeast Virginia's only IMAX theater, and hands-on exhibits that allow visitors to see themselves as an "astronaut-for-a-minute." ✉ *600 Settlers Landing Rd., I–64 (Exit 267),* ☎ *757/727–0800.* ☞ *Space Center $6. Space Center and 1 IMAX movie $9.* ☉ *Memorial Day–Labor Day, Mon.–Thurs. 10–5, Fri.–Sun. 10–7; rest of year, daily 10–5.*

Hampton was one of Virginia's principal Colonial cities. In 1718, Blackbeard, the pirate, was killed by Virginia sailors in a battle off North Carolina, and they brought his head back and mounted it on a pole at the entrance to the Hampton River. In subsequent years the city was partially destroyed three times: by the British during the Revolution and again during the War of 1812, then by Confederates preempting the Union invaders during the Civil War. The **Hampton Roads History Center,** in the Virginia Air and Space Center, depicts this colorful history through archaeological and audiovisual exhibitions that include partial reproductions of Colonial buildings, and what looks like a pirate's skeleton. Full-scale reproductions of the gun turret of the U.S.S. *Monitor* and a portion of the C.S.S. *Virginia* casemate show how the two ironclads changed the course of naval history in a famous Civil War battle in Hampton Roads.

Little of early Hampton has survived the shellings and conflagrations of the past. Yet the brick walls of **St. John's Church,** put up in 1728, have withstood the assaults of the British and the Confederates. Today, a stained-glass window honors Pocahontas, the Native American princess who is said to have saved the life of Captain John Smith in 1608. The communion silver on display, made in London in 1618, is the oldest such service in continuous use in this country. The parish, founded in the same year as the city, also claims to be the oldest in continuous service in America. Visitors may listen to a taped interpretation or take a guided tour (by arrangement) and visit a small museum in the parish house. ✉ *100 W. Queens Way,* ☎ *757/722–2567.* ☞ *Free.* ☉ *Weekdays 9–3:30, Sat. 9–noon.*

Hampton University was founded in 1868 as a freedmen's school. The alma mater of Booker T. Washington, it has had a distinguished history as an institution of higher education for African-Americans. The **Hampton University Museum,** on the waterfront campus, is most notable for its extensive and diverse collection of African art, which includes 2,000 pieces from 87 ethnic groups and cultures. Other valuable holdings include Harlem Renaissance paintings, Native American art and craft work, and art from Oceania. Another small exhibition tells the history of the university. ⊠ *I–64 (Exit 267),* ☎ *757/727–5308.* ▨ *Free.* ⊙ *Sept.–May, weekdays 8–5, weekends noon–4; June–Aug., weekdays 8–5.*

NEED A BREAK?	**Buckroe's Island Grill** (⊠ 1 Ivory Gull Crescent, ☎ 757/850-5757) has a double identity, making it a good place to stop for a drink or a bite any time of day. Both levels are open for lunch, dinner, and drinks, but the top level of this lighthouse-style building is more suited for the evening, when the bar loudly reverberates with voices of young adults and those who would like to be. There are a few tables, but there is also some seating outside on the porches. The more sedate ground-level dining room is a nice place for lunch, when a moderately priced—but limited—menu is offered.

In a downtown waterfront park near the Virginia Air and Space Center, the **Hampton Carousel** is an operating antique: Its prancing steeds and bright-color chariots carry visitors round and round to the tunes of carnival music. The 1920 carousel, a fixture at the former Buckroe Beach Amusement Park in the city for 60 years, has been meticulously restored by expert artisans. ⊠ *Off Settlers Landing Rd.,* ☎ *757/727– 6381.* ▨ *50¢.* ⊙ *Apr.–Sept. 15, Mon.–Sat. 10–8, Sun. noon–6; Sept. 16–Dec., Mon.–Sat. 10–6, Sun. noon–6; times may vary, depending on weather.*

OFF THE BEATEN PATH	**FORT MONROE** – The channel between Chesapeake Bay and Hampton Roads is the "mouth" of Hampton Roads. On the north side of this passage, Hampton's Fort Monroe, built in stages between 1819 and 1834, is the largest stone fort in the country and the only one on active duty that is enclosed by a moat. Robert E. Lee and Edgar Allan Poe served here in the antebellum years, and it remained a Union stronghold in Confederate territory throughout the Civil War. Afterward, Confederate president Jefferson Davis was imprisoned for a time in one of the fort's casemates (a chamber in the wall); his cell and adjacent casemates now house the Casemate Museum. Exhibits of weapons, uniforms, models, drawings, and extensive Civil War relics retell the fort's history, depict coastal artillery activities, and describe military lifestyle through the Civil War years. ⊠ *Rte. 258 (Mercury Blvd.) in Ft. Monroe,* ☎ *757/727– 3391.* ▨ *Free.* ⊙ *Daily 10:30–4:30. Closed Thanksgiving, Dec. 25, and Jan. 1.*

Dining and Lodging

$$–$$$ ✕ **Victor's.** The Radisson Hotel Hampton, in which this establish-
★ ment is housed, offers restaurants with a variety of settings and fares, but Victor's is its top-of-the-line eatery. Its mauve-and-green decor gives the dining room a contemporary look, and high windows overlook an adjacent marina and river. The menu has a good selection of seafood, but it also has a creditable list of steak, chicken, and pasta dishes. A typical three-course meal might include oysters or clams on the half shell, shrimp and sea scallops sautéed in lime-and-ginger sauce, and chocolate fettuccine. Possible entrée substitutes include Virginia crab cakes, filet mignon, and sautéed medallions of veal. During the sum-

mer, the outdoor under-the-awning Oyster Alley serves a shorter and lighter menu that includes salads, sandwiches, and desserts from noon to 9. Its marina-side setting keeps the restaurant from all traffic except that which passes on the river or boardwalk. ⊠ *Radisson Hotel Hampton, 700 Settlers Landing Rd.,* ☎ *757/727–9700. AE, D, DC, MC, V.*

$$ ✕ **Captain George's.** One in a chain of six, this smorgasbord restaurant has a nautical motif. A Chesapeake Bay mural dominates the largest of four dining rooms, with polyurethane tabletops embedded with seashells, sections of rope, and small brass boat fixtures. Although there is an ample à la carte menu, the main attraction is the all-you-can-eat buffet of fried, steamed, and broiled seafood. Highlights of the 70-item buffet are steamed Alaskan crab legs, steamed shrimp with Old Bay seasoning (a locally made favorite), broiled flounder, steamed mussels, and she-crab soup. Among the 15 desserts are baklava and five fruit cobblers. ⊠ *2710 W. Mercury Blvd.,* ☎ *757/826–1435. AE, MC, V. Lunch Sun. only.*

$$ ✕ **Fisherman's Wharf.** Decorated with ship figureheads and other seagoing paraphernalia, this restaurant occupies the top floor of a waterfront building constructed several decades ago when the lobsters inexplicably moved southward along the Atlantic Coast. A seafood-dominated buffet of up to 75 items, including Dungeness or snow crab legs, mussels, cherrystone clams, fish, and prime rib, is set up nightly and is popular locally. The regular menu also emphasizes seafood—the tasty Hampton-style crab cake consists of back-fin crabmeat flecked with bits of peas and carrots—but has a few other specialties, such as fried chicken strips in honey sauce. ⊠ *14 Ivy Home Rd.,* ☎ *757/723–3113. AE, D, DC, MC, V.*

$$ ✕ **The Grate Steak.** Farm implements and unfinished pine walls decorate the four windowless dining rooms where tables are draped with vinyl cloths printed in a blue floral calico pattern. Consistent with this rusticity, diners may step up to a common barbecue pit and grill for themselves the steak, shrimp, or chicken of their choosing. The menu also includes fried shrimp, grilled tuna, and baby-back pork ribs. Make-it-yourself salad bars feature baked potatoes, among other selections. Prime rib, served on the bone (as often it is not in this region), is slowly roasted by a professional chef. ⊠ *1934 Coliseum Dr.,* ☎ *757/827–1886. AE, D, DC, MC, V. No lunch.*

$$$ ▥ **Radisson Hotel Hampton.** The nine-story Radisson has the premier location in town, right at a marina and a block away from the Virginia Air and Space Center. Guests cross the lobby's white-marble floors to Victor's Restaurant (☞ *above*) or Signals Sports Grill. Upstairs, most rooms look over the harbor or the handsome plaza in front of the Virginia Air and Space Center. ⊠ *700 Settlers Landing Rd., 23669,* ☎ *757/727–9700 or 800/333–3333,* ℻ *757/722–4557. 172 rooms. Restaurant, bar, café, pool, exercise room, racquetball. AE, D, DC, MC, V.*

$$–$$$ ▥ **Holiday Inn Hampton.** Halfway between Colonial Williamsburg and Virginia Beach, this complex of buildings stands on 13 beautifully landscaped acres. A four-story atrium with plants, fountains, and conference facilities are recent additions. About half the rooms have a pink-and-green color scheme; others have a darker look, with cherry-wood dressers and tables. Sofas convert into extra beds in many rooms. Some rooms overlook the indoor pool in the atrium; others have doors that open, motel-style, directly onto the parking lot. ⊠ *1815 W. Mercury Blvd., 23666,* ☎ *757/838–0200 or 800/842–9370,* ℻ *757/838–4964. 320 rooms. Restaurant, bar, 1 indoor and 1 outdoor pool, sauna, exercise room. AE, D, DC, MC, V.*

Nightlife and the Arts

MUSIC

Hampton Coliseum (✉ 1000 Coliseum Dr., ☎ 757/838–4203) holds country, rap, rhythm-and-blues, and rock concerts.

Ogden Hall, at Hampton University (☎ 757/727–5359 or 757/727–5308), hosts performances on a regular basis by recognized artists.

Outdoor Activities and Sports

BEACHES

Buckroe Beach has adequate parking and a nearby park.

FISHING

Chesapeake Charter Service (✉ 519 Bridge St., ☎ 757/723–0998) offers charter trips.

Charters are offered from April to October by **Al Hartz Poquoson Charter Boats** (✉ E. River Rd., Poquoson, ☎ 757/868–6821).

GOLF AND TENNIS

Hampton Golf and Tennis (☎ 757/727–1195) has an 18-hole course.

Portsmouth

❸ *6 mi southwest of Norfolk (via I–264).*

Across the Elizabeth River from Norfolk is the town of Portsmouth, with its well-maintained Olde Towne buildings. The **Portsmouth Naval Shipyard Museum,** on the waterfront, can be reached conveniently by the pedestrian ferry—a diverting experience in itself—from the Waterside in Norfolk. The museum's exhibits of naval history include models of 18th-century warships, and visitors can board the retired coast guard lightship (a floating lighthouse) whose quarters below deck have been furnished authentically. ✉ *2 High St.,* ☎ *757/393–8591.* 🎟 *$1.* ☉ *Tues.–Sat. 10–5, Sun. 1–5.*

Portsmouth Children's Museum has rooms where children can learn engineering and scientific principles by playing with bubbles and blocks. ✉ *221 High St.,* ☎ *757/393–8393.* 🎟 *$4, good also for Art Center Gallery, Lightship, and Portsmouth Naval Shipyard Museum.* ☉ *June 10–Labor Day, Mon.–Sat. 10–7, Sun. 1–5; rest of year, Tues.–Fri. 10–5, Sat. 10–7, Sun. 1–5.*

Lodging

$$ 🏨 **Holiday Inn on the Waterfront.** With the Portsmouth waterfront just out the door, and Olde Towne's attractions so nearby, this hotel is very well situated. The undistinguished appearance of the building hides a pleasant atmosphere: Public and guest rooms vary in size, but all have a modern look, and some private guest rooms share water views. The restaurant overlooks the Elizabeth River and Norfolk's downtown skyline on the opposite shore. ✉ *8 Crawford Pkwy., 23704,* ☎ *757/393–2573 or 800/465–4329,* 🖷 *757/399–1248. 264 rooms, 6 suites. Restaurant, lobby lounge, pool, exercise room, free parking, convention center. AE, D, DC, MC, V.*

Nightlife and the Arts

Portsmouth applauds the restoration of the art deco atmosphere in the **Commodore Theatre** (✉ 421 High St., ☎ 757/393–6962), built in 1945. Crystal chandeliers and wall murals provide a handsome setting for light dinner fare with first-run movies. There are tables on the main floor and traditional theater seating in the balcony.

Chesapeake

❹ *19 mi southeast of Portsmouth (I–64); 16 mi south of Norfolk.*

The principal attraction of Chesapeake (established 1963) is its entrance to the **Great Dismal Swamp.** That forbidding name was assigned to the area by William Byrd on one of his early 18th-century surveying expeditions. Today the swamp is a 106,000-acre National Wildlife Refuge that harbors bobcat, black bear, and more than 150 varieties of birds. A remarkably shallow lake—3,000 acres, 6 feet deep—is surrounded by skinny cypress trees that lend the scene a primeval quality. Several cleared and marked nature trails make this a spectacular contrast to nearby downtown Norfolk. ⊠ *Great Dismal Swamp National Wildlife Refuge, Rte. 32 and follow signs, Box 349, Suffolk 23434,* ☎ *757/986–3705.* ☉ *Apr.–Sept., daily 6:30–8; Oct.–Mar., daily 6:30–5.*

Virginia Beach

❺ *24 mi northeast of Chesapeake; 18 mi east of Norfolk (via I–64 to Rte. 44).*

The heart of Virginia Beach—a stretch of the ocean shore from Cape Henry south to Rudee Inlet, consisting of 6 mi of crowded public beach and a busy 40-block boardwalk—has been a popular summertime gathering place for many years. Recently renovated, the Boardwalk and Atlantic Avenue have unique lighting, teak benches, oceanfront park, and a 2-mi resort bike trail. Yet never in living memory has this been a place for peaceful communion with nature. In the surf and at the amusements on land, the crowds generate a certain excitement that should appeal most strongly to young people. One advantage of the commercial concentration here is the easy access to sailing, surfing, and scuba equipment rentals. The farther north visitors go on Virginia Beach, the more beach they will find in proportion to bars, T-shirt parlors, and video arcades. There's free entertainment from April through Labor Day weekend, nightly, at the 24th Street stage or 24th Street Park on the Boardwalk.

Along the oceanfront, the **Old Coast Guard Station** (formerly called the Lifesaving Museum of Virginia), set in a 1903 Seatack Lifesaving Station, contains photographic exhibits, lifesaving equipment on shipwrecks, and a gallery that depicts German U-boat acitivity off the coast during World War II. ⊠ *24th St. and Atlantic Ave.,* ☎ *757/422–1587.* ⊠ *$2.50.* ☉ *Mon.–Sat. 10–5, Sun. 12–5. Closed Mon. Oct.–Memorial Day.*

OFF THE
BEATEN PATH

ASSOCIATION FOR RESEARCH AND ENLIGHTENMENT – Matters of the spirit and the flesh are on the agenda at this research institution founded by the psychic Edgar Cayce. Cayce was known for his ability to diagnose the causes of illness by "reading" a case history; his writings on history, philosophy, and other topics have been collected in the library here. Following a brief slide show on Cayce, visitors may have their ESP quotient determined by an electronic apparatus. A meditation garden features a pond stocked with goldfish, and a meditation room overlooks the ocean. Lectures and movies are scheduled in the afternoon. ⊠ *67th St. and Atlantic Ave., Virginia Beach,* ☎ *757/428-3588.* ⊠ *Free.* ☉ *Mon.–Sat. 9–8, Sun. 11–8.*

Inland from the bay shore is a late 17th-century attraction, the **Adam Thoroughgood House,** named for the prosperous plantation owner who held a land grant of 5,350 acres and who died in 1640. This little (45- by 22-foot) brick house, probably constructed by a Thoroughgood grandson, recalls the English cottage architecture of the period, with a protruding chimney and a steeply pitched roof. The four-room early plantation home has a typical 17th-century garden with characteristic hedges. ⊠ *1636 Parish Rd.,* ☎ *757/622–2787.* ⌨ *$2. Combination ticket with Moses Myers House and Willoughby-Baylor House: $4 for all three sites.* ⊙ *Jan.–Mar., Tues.–Sat. noon–5; Apr.–Dec., Tues.–Sat. 10–5, Sun. noon–5.*

The sea is the subject at the **Virginia Marine Science Museum** on General Booth Boulevard, almost 2 mi inland from Rudee Inlet at the southern end of Virginia Beach. A massive facility with more than 200 exhibits, and a very popular state attraction, this is no place for passive museum goers; many exhibits require participation. Visitors use computers to predict the weather and solve the pollution crisis, watch the birds in the salt marsh through telescopes on a deck, handle horseshoe crabs, take a simulated journey to the bottom of the sea in a submarine, and study fish up close in tanks that re-create various underwater environments. ⊠ *717 General Booth Blvd.,* ☎ *757/425–3474.* ⌨ *$4.75.* ⊙ *Daily 9–5 (until 9 Mon.–Sat., mid-June–Labor Day).*

<table>
<tr>
<td>OFF THE
BEATEN PATH</td>
<td>

OLD CAPE HENRY LIGHTHOUSE – At the northeastern tip of Virginia Beach, on the cape where the mouth of the bay meets the ocean, the historic Old Cape Henry Lighthouse marks the site where the English landed on their way to Jamestown in 1607. You can still climb to the top of the old lighthouse in summer; a new, working lighthouse is closed to visitors. ☎ *757/422-9421.* ⌨ *$2.* ⊙ *Mid-Mar.–Oct., daily 10-5.*

SEASHORE STATE PARK – Inland from the Cape Henry lighthouses and the army installation at Fort Story, and south of U.S. 60, botanists will have a field day at Seashore State Park. Spanish moss grows no farther north than here, and blue spruce appears no farther south. The park is also a haven for red and gray fox, raccoon, opossum, water snake, and other denizens of swamp and dune. Boardwalks built just above the water level let you get close to flora and fauna while keeping your feet dry, and there are campgrounds, picnic areas, and guided tours. ☎ *757/481-4836.* ⌨ *Apr.–Oct., $2 per car weekdays, $3 weekends; Nov.–Mar., $1 per car.* ⊙ *Daily 8 AM–sundown. Visitor center, daily 9-6.*

</td>
</tr>
</table>

Dining and Lodging

$$$ ✕ **Coastal Grill.** Though it's in a mall, this place has a warm, even el-
★ egant look, with a big open bar and artful lighting. But food is the reason to come here: Chef-owner Jerry Bryan prepares American classics with an innovative, irresistible twist. Spinach salad is paired with sautéed chicken liver and balsamic vinaigrette; New York strip steak comes with melted onions and horseradish cream; and the fresh seafood dishes—including seasonal oysters on the half shell—are sublime. The moderately priced wine list is user-friendly, complete with suggestions for wine-and-food pairings. Come early and expect a wait. ⊠ *1427 Great Neck Rd.,* ☎ *804/496-3348. Reservations not accepted. AE, D, DC, MC, V. No lunch.*

$$$ ✕ **The Lighthouse.** All tables in the six dining rooms overlook the ocean or the inlet (most overlook both) through picture windows. The bare lacquered wood tables are set with candles, fresh flowers, and linen napkins; the floors are red clay tile; the walls have dark wood paneling. Nevertheless, the main attraction here is the seafood. If you can't decide whether you want Maine lobster, chicken, shrimp, or crab cakes, you can try their mixed grill, where you can mix and match any two items. The Sunday brunch menu includes a mimosa and side

dishes of apples, cheese, and sautéed mushrooms. ⊠ *1st St. and Atlantic Ave.,* ☏ *757/428–7974. AE, D, DC, MC, V.*

$$–$$$ ✕ **501 City Grill.** The bar here packs in young locals on the make, and the big boisterous dining room, with its raised booths and ceiling fans, often fills to capacity. The open kitchen adds to the lively atmosphere, as do the whimsical menu and chalkboard "additions." Try tobacco onion rings for starters, then move on to grilled 1-pound Angus steak with cabernet sauce or jumbo prawns stuffed with lump crab. Oenophiles will appreciate the enormous selection of affordable, quality wines, as well as the exposed cellar. ⊠ *501 N. Birdneck,* ☏ *757/425–7195. AE, DC, MC, V. No lunch.*

$$ ✕ **Duck Inn.** Just east of the Lynnhaven Bridge, off Shore Drive, this family seafood restaurant is near the water and within sight of the bridge-tunnel. Pine paneling sets the scene for indoor dining; the warm months allow dining on an outdoor deck, or appetizers and drinks in the gazebo. The specialty of the house, a milk-based fisherman's chowder, contains shrimp, crabmeat, and mushrooms. Crab cakes are popular here, as is the nightly buffet. ⊠ *3324 Shore Dr.,* ☏ *757/481–0201. Reservations not accepted. AE, D, DC, MC, V.*

$ ✕ **Charlie's Seafood Restaurant.** A funky family restaurant on the south side of Shore Drive near Lynnhaven Inlet, Charlie's is usually full of people sitting at vinyl-top tables eating some of the best seafood on the Eastern Shore. Enjoy the relaxed ambience while biting into light, crispy, tasty crabs that are beyond comparison. Or, if you are in a hurry, you can buy a quart of she-crab soup to go (packed in ice). ⊠ *3139 Shore Dr.,* ☏ *757/481–9863. Reservations not accepted. AE, MC, V.*

$$$$ ▥ **Cavalier Hotels.** In the quieter north end of town, this 18-acre resort complex combines the original Cavalier Hotel of 1927, a seven-story redbrick building on a hill, with an oceanfront high-rise that was built across the street in 1973. The clientele is about evenly divided between conventioneers and families. F. Scott and Zelda Fitzgerald were regular visitors to the older section, which has been lavishly refurbished. Guests in the hilltop facility can see the water—and get to it easily by shuttle van or with the help of push-button crossing lights. The newer building overlooks 600 feet of private beach. There is a fee for tennis, but the other extensive athletic facilities are free. ⊠ *Atlantic Ave. and 42nd St., 23451,* ☏ *757/425–8555 or 800/446–8199,* ℻ *757/428–7957. 400 rooms in summer; 262 rooms and 10 suites in winter. 3 restaurants, 1 indoor and 1 outdoor pool, wading pool, putting green, 4 tennis courts, croquet, volleyball, beach, baby-sitting, children's programs, playground. AE, D, DC, MC, V.*

$$$$ ▥ **Ramada Plaza Resort Oceanfront.** In 1985 this five-story hotel added a 17-story tower, becoming the tallest hotel in the city. In 1986 the rooms in the older section were all renovated. Rooms that do not face the ocean directly have either a sideways view or overlook the swimming pool. ⊠ *57th St. and Oceanfront, 23451,* ☏ *757/428–7025 or 800/365–3032,* ℻ *757/428–2921. 215 rooms. Restaurant, bar, indoor-outdoor pool, sauna. AE, D, DC, MC, V.*

$$ ▥ **Idlewhyle Motel.** This motel on the beach and boardwalk usually caters to families, who choose between rooms and efficiencies. The walls are a drab beige vinyl, and the furniture, of recent vintage, is serviceable. Rooms that do not face the ocean look onto the pool in the glass-roofed courtyard. ⊠ *2705 Atlantic Ave., 23451,* ☏ *757/428–9341 or 800/348–7263,* ℻ *757/425–5355. 23 rooms, 23 efficiencies. Coffee shop, indoor pool. AE, D, MC, V.*

Outdoor Activities and Sports

BOATING AND CANOEING

For canoeing and fishing boat rentals, try **Munden Point Park** (☎ 757/426–5296).

GOLF

Cypress Point (☎ 757/490–8822), Owl's Creek (☎ 757/428–2800), Hell's Point (☎ 757/721–3400), and Honey Bee (☎ 757/471–2768) have 18-hole courses.

WATER SPORTS

Chick's Beach Sailing Center (☎ 757/460–2238) offers Hobie Cat and Windsurfer rentals and lessons. **Scuba Ventures** (☎ 757/473–0847) offers scuba lessons, gear, and trips. Also try **Lynnhaven Dive Center** (☎ 757/481–7949).

Shopping

The **Great American Outlet Mall** (⊠ 3750 Virginia Beach Blvd., ☎ 757/463–8665) contains more than 40 off-price and manufacturers' outlets, including Fieldcrest, Cannon, and Van Heusen.

NORFOLK

❻ *16 mi south of Hampton.*

South of Hampton Roads, Norfolk is reached from the peninsula by the Hampton Roads Bridge-Tunnel. There's plenty to see in this old navy town, but the sites are rather spread out so you'll probably want to drive or take bus tours.

The springtime Azalea Festival is held at the 175-acre **Norfolk Botanical Gardens,** near the airport, on the eastern edge of the city. Here is an abundance of azaleas, rhododendrons, and camellias, and a special feature: a fragrance garden for the blind, which also has identification labels in braille. A delicately landscaped Japanese garden has trees native to that country, including unusual strains of cherry and maple. From mid-March to October, boats and trackless trains carry visitors along routes to view seasonal plants and flowers, including 4,000 varieties of roses on 3½ acres. Year-round, visitors can stroll 12 mi of paths. Eleven marble statues of famous artists, carved in the late-19th century by Moses Ezekiel, enhance the natural beauty of the gardens. Lakeside is ideal for picnics. ⊠ *Azalea Garden Rd.,* ☎ *757/441–5831.* ⊠ *$3. Boat and train tours $2.50.* ☉ *Daily 9–7.*

Occupying a 16th-century English Tudor–style house that was reproduced by a textile tycoon at the turn of the century, the **Hermitage Foundation Museum** contains the largest privately owned collection of Oriental art in the United States—including ivory and jade carvings, ancient bronzes, and a 1,400-year-old marble Buddha from China. The decorative-art collections include Tiffany glass, Persian rugs, and furniture from the Middle East, India, Europe, and America. Visitors may picnic on the 12 acres of grounds along the Lafayette River. ⊠ *7637 North Shore Rd.,* ☎ *757/423–2052.* ⊠ *$4.* ☉ *Mon.–Sat. 10–5, Sun. 1–5.*

★ By any standard the **Chrysler Museum** downtown qualifies as one of America's major art museums, and the *Wall Street Journal* called it one of the 20 best. The permanent collection includes works by Rubens, Gainsborough, Renoir, Picasso, and Pollock—a list that suggests the breadth you'll find here. The classical and pre-Columbian civilizations are also represented; the decorative-arts collection includes exquisite English porcelain, and the Institute of Glass shows artifacts from ancient Rome as well as Tiffany pieces. Comfortably arranged exhibition spaces make a visit a particularly agreeable experience. ⊠ *245 W. Olney Rd.,* ☎ *757/664–6200.* 🖭 *Free; $3 donation suggested.* ☉ *Tues.–Sat. 10–4, Sun. 1–5.*

The Federal-style redbrick **Moses Myers House,** built by its namesake in 1792, is exceptional, and not just for its elegance. In the long Adam-style dining room, a wood secretary displays under glass a collection of fine china—and a set of silver kiddush cups, for Moses Myers was Norfolk's first permanent Jewish resident. A transplanted New Yorker, Myers made his fortune in Norfolk in shipping, then served as a diplomat and a customshouse officer. His grandson married James Madison's grandniece, his great-grandson served as mayor, and the family kept the house for five generations. The furnishings, 70% of them original, include family portraits by Gilbert Stuart and Thomas Sully. ⊠ *331 Bank St.,* ☎ *757/622–2787.* 🖭 *$2. Combination ticket with Willoughby-Baylor House and/or Adam Thoroughgood House in Virginia Beach: $4 for all three sites.* ☉ *Jan.–Mar., Tues.–Sat. noon–5; Apr.–Dec., Tues.–Sat. 10–5, Sun. noon–5.*

The **Douglas MacArthur Memorial** is the burial place of the controversial war hero. An "army brat" with no hometown, the general designated this navy town as the site for a monument to himself because it was his mother's birthplace—and perhaps because no one as well known as he had a monument nearby (MacArthur had a formidable ego). In the rotunda of the old City Hall, converted according to MacArthur's design, is the mausoleum; 11 adjoining galleries house mementos of MacArthur's career, such as his signature corncob pipe and the Japanese instruments of surrender that concluded World War II. Next door the general's staff car is on display and a 24-minute biography is screened continuously. ⊠ *Bank St. and City Hall Ave.,* ☎ *757/441–2965.* 🖭 *Free.* ☉ *Mon.–Sat. 10–5, Sun. 11–5.*

St. Paul's Church, constructed in 1739, was the only building to survive the bombardment and conflagration inflicted by Lord Dunmore, the last royal governor, on New Year's Day, 1776; a cannonball remains embedded in the southeastern wall. An earlier church on this site had been built in 1641, and today the churchyard contains graves dating from the 17th century. The interior was restored to the Colonial style in 1912, following Victorian alterations in the last century. ⊠ *St. Paul's Blvd. and City Hall Ave.,* ☎ *757/627–4353.* 🖭 *Donation.* ☉ *Tues.–Fri. 10–4.*

Built in 1794, the **Willoughby-Baylor House** downtown is a redbrick town house that combines the Federal and Georgian styles. The authentic period antiques are not original to the house, but they follow an inventory made in 1800 on the death of Captain William Willoughby, who built the house. The herb-and-flower garden is also in keeping with the era. ⊠ *601 E. Freemason St.,* ☎ *757/622–1211.* 🖭 *$2. Combination ticket with Moses Myers House and/or Adam Thoroughgood House in Virginia Beach: $4 for all three sites.* ☉ *By appointment only, within these hrs: Jan.–Mar., Tues.–Sat. noon–5; Apr.–Dec., Tues.–Sat. 10–5, Sun. noon–5.*

The Waterside, a shopping center on the harbor with a nautical motif, bills itself as Tidewater's festival marketplace. Like other developments of the Rouse Company (Harborplace in Baltimore, the 6th Street Marketplace in Richmond), the Waterside has spurred the economic revival of the downtown area. Musical performances and temporary art exhibitions take place in the public spaces, and there are plenty of places to eat and shop. The Tidewater Regional Transit

(TRT) kiosk (☎ 757/623–3222) is a source of visitor information and the launching point for all sorts of tours. ✉ *333 Waterside Dr.* ☉ *Tours depart hourly late May–Labor Day, Mon.–Sat. 10–10, Sun. noon–8; Labor Day–late May, Mon.–Sat. 10–9, Sun. noon–6.*

NEED A
BREAK?

Doumar's (✉ 20th St. and Monticello Ave., ☎ 757/627–4163) is a Norfolk institution. This drive-in restaurant, founded in 1934 by Abe Doumar—inventor of the ice-cream cone—is still operated by his family. Here, veteran waitresses carry to your car the specialties of the house: barbecue, natural limeade, and ice cream in fresh waffle cones made according to an original recipe.

★ The **Norfolk Naval Base,** on the northern edge of the city, is an impressive sight and home to more than 115 ships of the Second Fleet. Among the boarders is the USS *Theodore Roosevelt,* a nuclear-powered carrier with a crew of 6,300, said to be one of the largest warships in the world. The submarine piers and the heliport are also memorable sights. Visitors pass by but may not enter the windowless, top-secret Fleet Anti-Submarine Warfare Training Center building. Tour buses operate year-round, departing from the TRT kiosk at the Waterside and from the naval-base tour office. ✉ *Hampton Blvd.,* ☎ *757/444–7955 or 757/444–1577 (naval base visitors office).* ▣ *Tour $5.* ☉ *Tour hrs vary seasonally. Naval base: daily 8–4.*

The newest addition to Norfolk's much-redeveloped waterfront is **Nauticus,** the National Maritime Center, which opened mid-1994 and has already become one of the area's busiest attractions. With more than 70 high-tech exhibits on three "decks," the site displays concepts as ancient as shipbuilding right next to interactive displays that encompass the modern naval world. Weather satellites, underwater archaeology, and the Loch Ness Monster all come together here in a stimulating and informative environment. There are additional fees for the AEGIS Theater and Virtual Adventures. ✉ *1 Waterside Dr.,* ☎ *757/664-1000.* ▣ *$10.95.* ☉ *Memorial Day–Labor Day, daily 10–7; Labor Day–Memorial Day, Tues.–Sun. 10–5.*

☙ **Virginia Zoological Park** in Norfolk is the largest in the state, with more than 100 species living on 55 acres—including rhinos and ostriches as well as such domesticated animals as sheep. With the assistance of docents, children may handle some animals. Elephant demonstrations are regularly scheduled during summer months. Next door, Lafayette Park has picnic shelters and facilities for tennis, basketball, football, and softball. ✉ *3500 Granby St.,* ☎ *757/441–2706.* ▣ *$2; free after 4 on Sun. and Mon.* ☉ *Daily 10–5.*

Dining and Lodging

$$$ ✕ **La Galleria.** In just a few years this restaurant has earned a reputa-
★   tion as one of the best in Norfolk. The decor, which is not done in the usual homey southern style, may appear cold to some, but it is impressively Roman. Decorations include large urns imported from Italy, Corinthian columns, and a long, sculpted wall adorned with frames and half frames: The interior design may explain the restaurant's name. A pianist entertains with soft music. Menu choices include *vongole al casino* (baked clams sprinkled with herbs, garlic, and bread crumbs) as one of the appetizers, and a variety of excellent pastas and main courses, such as *salmone La Galleria* (salmon sautéed in herbs, garlic, and white wine). A predinner visit can be made to the d'Art Center (☞ *Shopping, below*) across the street, a working community for the visual arts. ✉ *120 College Pl.,* ☎ *757/623–3939. AE, MC, V.*

$$$ ✕ **The Riverwalk.** Through picture windows, and in good weather from the veranda, guests can watch passersby on the boardwalk and along the Elizabeth River while they dine. Start your meal with grilled barbecue shrimp quesadillas or an organic baby lettuce salad, then try the grilled tuna-and-filet mignon combination, or the crawfish-and-shrimp pasta. ⊠ *Omni Riverside Hotel, 777 Waterside Dr.,* ☎ *757/622–6664. AE, D, DC, MC, V.*

$$$ ✕ **The Ship's Cabin.** This often-mentioned restaurant is best known for
★ its seafood but has good steaks as well. For an appetizer try the Oysters Bingo—Eastern Shore salt oysters lightly rolled in batter, sautéed in butter, and served hot in the shell with bits of scallions and parsley in white wine. Follow that with a New York strip steak. Bread is served with the meal and is baked fresh daily on site; the blueberry bread is almost a dessert in itself. Window-side booths in one room look across tufted sand dunes to the Chesapeake Bay and the lights of the Chesapeake Bay Bridge-Tunnel; the other dining rooms, lighted by fireplace and candles, provide even cozier settings. ⊠ *4110 E. Ocean View Ave.,* ☎ *757/362–4659. AE, D, DC, MC, V.*

$$ ✕ **Freemason Abbey Restaurant and Tavern.** A Victorian atmosphere
★ prevails in this former church building. Standing for more than 120 years, the building has 40-foot-high cathedral ceilings and large windows that look onto the old-style business district. The upstairs, the reconstructed steel mezzanine of the former church, offers intimate dining, while downstairs you can get lighter fare or sit at the bar and lounge. On Wednesday Freemason Abbey features a lobster special, and on Thursday prime rib heads the menu. For an appetizer try the artichoke dip. ⊠ *209 W. Freemason St.,* ☎ *757/622–3966. AE, D, MC, V.*

$$ ✕ **Il Porto.** Plenteous portions of pasta, seafood, and veal are served in a dining room with a river view, and on the terrace during warm weather. The bar is bright and spacious, and a piano player entertains most nights. ⊠ *The Waterside, 333 Waterside Dr.,* ☎ *757/627–4400. AE, D, DC, MC, V.*

$ ✕ **Kelley's.** The TV set in the small dining room lends Kelley's an Irish-tavern ambience, and the cuisine follows suit. The large cheeseburger is the most popular item, but the rich soups (she-crab, clam, broccoli, and a daily special) are also in demand. Food is served on the patio when weather permits, even on warm winter days. ⊠ *1408 Colley Ave.,* ☎ *757/623–3216. Reservations not accepted. AE, D, MC, V.*

$$$$ 🏨 **Norfolk Waterside Marriott.** This 1991 addition to the redeveloped downtown area of Norfolk is connected to the Waterside shopping area by a ramp and is close to Town Point Park, site of many festivals. The handsome lobby, with wood paneling, a central staircase, silk tapestries, and Federal-style furniture, sets a high standard that continues throughout the hotel. Rooms are somewhat small, but each has everything the business traveler could ask for—including two telephones, voice mail, and a modem hook-up. ⊠ *235 E. Main St., 23510,* ☎ *757/627–4200 or 800/228–9290,* 𝔽𝔸𝕏 *757/628–6466. 396 rooms, 8 suites. 2 restaurants, lobby lounge, indoor pool, parking (fee). AE, D, DC, MC, V.*

$$$ 🏨 **Hilton Airport.** Don't let the gray cement exterior scare you away; the interior of this six-story highway-side Hilton is neither drab nor harsh. The hotel has an atrium, a concierge floor, some king-size beds, and a free shuttle to the airport. ⊠ *1500 N. Military Hwy., 23502,* ☎ *757/466–8000 or 800/422–7474,* 𝔽𝔸𝕏 *757/466–8000. 246 rooms, 4 suites. 3 restaurants, 2 bars, coffee shop, pool, tennis court, health club, airport shuttle. AE, D, DC, MC, V.*

$$$ ⊞ **Omni Waterside Hotel.** Modern is the word for the decor, from the bright, spacious lobby to the ample rooms and large suites—but services follow more traditional lines. A ground-floor bar with dramatic 30-foot windows overlooks the river. Many rooms have a beautiful view over the Elizabeth River and the city's working harbor. The nightclub presents live dance bands on weekends. This property is convenient to the Waterside shopping area. ⊠ *777 Waterside Dr., 23510.* ☎ *757/622–6664,* FAX *757/625–8271. 426 rooms, 20 suites. Restaurant, pool, nightclub, parking (fee). AE, D, DC, MC, V.*

$$ ⊞ **Old Dominion Inn.** This motel, family owned and operated, has touches suggestive of a country inn. Guest rooms are entered not from the parking area but from interior hallways. The three-story building, completed in 1989, with Colonial Williamsburg decor, has late-18th-century antiques in the lobby and reproductions in guest rooms. Ceilings have crown moldings along the perimeter and an anachronistic fan in the center. The inn is across from Old Dominion University on busy Hampton Boulevard, but the guest rooms are set back from the road, out of range of most traffic noise. Rates include Continental breakfast. ⊠ *4111 Hampton Blvd., 23508,* ☎ *757/440–5100. 60 rooms. AE, D, DC, MC, V.*

$ ⊞ **YMCA of Tidewater.** The rooms at this Y have daily maid service,
★ private bath, and no curfew for guests—who are of all ages, both genders, and all faiths. Even though rooms have no phone or (with a few exceptions) TV, this is one of the all-time American hotel bargains. The six-story building is in a historic, largely residential neighborhood, 2½ blocks from the Chrysler Museum. Yet the Y's biggest asset is the extraordinary sports facility on the premises, free for the use of all guests. ⊠ *312 W. Bute St., 23510,* ☎ *757/622–6328 or 757/622–9622. 76 rooms. Indoor pool, indoor track, racquetball. MC, V.*

Nightlife and the Arts

DANCING

The **Spirit of Norfolk** (⊠ 333 Waterside Dr., Norfolk, ☎ 757/627–7771) offers the area's only dinner-dance cruises with live music and entertainment. Lunch and brunch cruises are also available.

Fifth National Banque (⊠ 1849 E. Little Creek Rd., ☎ 757/480–3600) offers authentic country-western entertainment and dancing, and free dance lessons.

MUSIC

The **Virginia Opera** (☎ 757/623–1223), performing in and around Virginia, has a widely acclaimed company joined by major guest artists; the season (October to March) often sees American and world premieres.

Scope Center (⊠ 1 Scope Plaza, ☎ 757/664–6464) is a venue for country, rap, rhythm-and-blues, and rock concerts.

THEATER

The **Virginia Stage Company** (⊠ Box 3770, 23514, ☎ 757/627–1234 or 757/627–6988) performs at the Wells Theatre (⊠ 118 Tazewell St., ☎ 757/441–2764).

Broadway shows on tour appear at **Chrysler Hall** (⊠ 1 Scope Plaza, ☎ 757/441–2161).

Outdoor Activities and Sports

BEACHES

Ocean View Beaches, 14 mi of beach along the Chesapeake Bay, have waters that are much calmer than those of the ocean—and safer for children. Sea trout and flounder make good fishing here.

FISHING

Charters and pier fishing are offered in season at **Harrison Boat House** (⊠ 414 W. Ocean View Ave., ☎ 757/588–9968). **Willoughby Bay Marina** (1651 Bayville St., ☎ 757/588–2663) also has charters.

GOLF

Lake Wright (6282 N. Hampton Blv., ☎ 757/459–2255) has an 18-hole course.

HOCKEY

The **Hampton Roads Admirals** of the East Coast Hockey League play at Norfolk's Scope (⊠ 201 E. Brambleton Ave., ☎ 757/640–1212).

Shopping

Ghent (⊠ Colley Ave. and 21st St.) is a picturesque neighborhood with an eclectic mix of chic shops.

The d'Art Center (⊠ 125 College Pl., ☎ 757/625–4211) allows you to watch painters, sculptors, glass workers, quilters, and other artists at work in their studios; the creations are for sale in two galleries on the premises.

Rowena's Jam and Jelly Factory (⊠ 758 W. 22nd St., ☎ 757/627–8699) offers tours of the factory Monday through Wednesday, but you must make arrangements in advance. For sale in the shop are home-made jams, cooking sauces, fruit curds, and cookies. This tour is accessible to the disabled.

EASTERN SHORE

U.S. 13 runs north from Virginia Beach via an engineering marvel: the 17½-mi Chesapeake Bay Bridge-Tunnel (toll, $10), which gives travelers the rare experience of being surrounded by the sea while never leaving their cars. An observation pier and a restaurant are located 4 mi from the southern end. The northern end is Virginia's Eastern Shore, where the wildlife, the sea, and the sun are abundant, and human beings—except on popular Chincoteague—are not.

Driving north on U.S. 13, travelers encounter historic towns that preserve period structures in especially secluded environs. You will have to leave the main highway to experience the quaint towns and fishing villages that still carry an aura of simpler times. Nineteenth-century **Cape Charles,** once the southern terminus of the new railroad and the largest and busiest city on the Eastern Shore in Virginia, today is less energetic, but its residential areas still maintain their charm. Eighteenth-century **Eastville,** 15 mi above the bridge-tunnel and bisected by Route 13, has been the county seat since 1677; here you can see historic structures such as the old courthouse, erected in 1732, and a debtor's prison, raised in 1814.

Onancock

❼ *65 mi north of Virginia Beach; 70 mi northeast of Norfolk (via Rte. 13).*

This 300-year-old port began as a settlement of four or five Indian families, and today it is one of the loveliest towns on the Eastern Shore of Virginia. Here you can visit a general store that dates from 1842 or walk down to the wharf and imagine yourself waiting for a steamer to Baltimore. At day's end look west across Chesapeake Bay and you can see the sun set over water—a rare sight for East Coast residents.

Dining and Lodging

$$ ✕ **Trawler Restaurant and Lounge.** This inland restaurant maintains a nautical attitude in both decor and menu. "Rick and Steve" is a delicious combination of scallops, shrimp, and crabmeat sautéed in butter with fresh garlic and mushrooms. The menu also includes she-crab soup and crab cakes. Meals are accompanied by sweet-potato biscuits, which have achieved a widespread reputation (and whose recipe is a guarded secret, despite requests from national magazines), and a salad bar. Three dining areas are decorated with wildlife drawings and hand-carved duck decoys, mostly by local artists. (The Eastern Shore is widely known for its decoy carvers.) ⊠ *Rte. 13, Exmore,* ☎ *757/442–2092. D, MC, V.*

$$–$$$ ✕⛨ **The Garden and the Sea Inn.** The restaurant part of this five-room bed-and-breakfast specializes in fresh local seafood and vegetables prepared French-style. The menu is not extensive, but it is select, and it changes frequently. Specialties include pasta enlivened by Louisiana shrimp, local scallops, oysters, tomatoes, and mushrooms; and Chicken Virginia (chicken breast and Smithfield ham prepared with apple brandy, cream, and local apples). The structure was built in 1802 as Bloxom's Tavern and enlarged before the end of the century. ⊠ *Turn west off Rte. 13 at Rte. 710 (First Virginia Bank) and go ¼ mi, Box 275, New Church 23415,* ☎ *757/824–0672. Restaurant. AE, D, MC, V. Closed Dec.–Feb.*

$$ ⛨ **Colonial Manor Inn.** This large, 1882 three-story wood-frame house has an enclosed front porch with rocking chairs, and a candlelit gazebo in the back yard. None of the rooms has a telephone, but all have queen-size beds and TV; some have private baths. The harbor is five blocks away, and several restaurants are nearby. Full breakfast is complimentary, as is use of the inn's bicycles. Kids are welcome, but smoking is not. ⊠ *84 Market St., 23417,* ☎ *757/787–3521. 14 rooms. Bicycles. MC, V.*

$$ ⛨ **Pickett's Harbor.** At the southern tip of the Eastern Shore sits this putty-color clapboard house with redbrick ends and siding. Built in 1976 according to a Colonial design, the home has 200-year-old floors, doors, and cupboards from several James River farms that were installed to ensure authenticity. Suitable antiques and reproductions furnish the rooms, two of which have private bath. All the guest quarters overlook small sand dunes and the bay beyond, and the backyard has 17 acres of private beach; this is very much a retreat. Rates include a full breakfast. ⊠ *Rte. 600, Box 96, Townsend 23443,* ☎ *757/331–2212. 6 rooms. No credit cards.*

Nightlife and the Arts

The **Trawler Dinner Theater** (⊠ Rte. 13, Lankford Hwy., Exmore, ☎ 757/442–2092) offers three or four productions a year.

Chincoteague Island

❽ *30 mi northeast of Onancock; 100 mi northeast of Norfolk.*

Many know the name of Chincoteague Island from Marguerite Henry's book for children, *Misty of Chincoteague,* first published in the 1940s. Chincoteague, smaller and closer to shore than Assateague, makes a sobering contrast to its neighbor. The dozens of billboards along Route 175, on the drive from the mainland, suggest the overdevelopment that is spoiling the place as substandard accommodations proliferate in the scramble for tourist dollars. An annual custom recalls a simpler time: On the last Thursday in July the ponies from Assateague are driven across the channel to Chincoteague, where they are placed at auction; those that remain unsold swim back home. During the rest of the year, the proximity to fine beaches and natural beauty justifies a sojourn here.

In addition to the horse auction, there are a few other seasonal events to look for in Chincoteague. The Seafood Festival and the Harvest Festival (held the first Wednesdays of May and October, respectively) attract local gourmands. Tickets, which are usually sold out months in advance, can be purchased from the Chamber of Commerce (☎ 757/787–2460). But by far the most important food fair is the **Oyster Festival** on Columbus Day weekend. In this celebration of a major local industry, oysters are served in every conceivable form, from stew to fritters. Tickets to the festival, limited to 2,000, must be purchased well in advance from the Chamber of Commerce (☎ 757/336–6161).

The **Oyster and Maritime Museum** tells the history of oyster farming and other local lore. ⊠ *Maddox Blvd.,* ☎ *757/336–6117.* ☞ *$2.* ☺ *June–Oct., daily 10–5; call ahead for winter hrs.*

Dining and Lodging

$$–$$$ ✕ **Landmark Crab House.** Ask for a table by the window at this beachside restaurant, for although the cavernous dining hall is not much to look at in itself, there are wide views of the water from three sides. The servings are as generous as the vista. Whole loaves of fresh white bread precede the meal, and every entrée allows a visit with a large plate to the conventional salad bar. A creamy crab imperial, baked in a terrine, is touted as the specialty; the crab cakes are a slightly drier alternative. Beef dishes, well represented on the regular menu, often appear as specials. A children's menu that includes hamburgers makes this a spot for family dining rather than for couples in search of a romantic evening out. ⊠ *N. Main St.,* ☎ *757/336–5552. AE, D, DC, MC, V.*

$$$–$$$$ ◩ **Channel Bass Inn.** Built in the 1870s and expanded 50 years later,
★ this three-story, beige clapboard house was renovated in 1978; today it's an inn of impeccable luxury. The soundproof rooms are individually decorated with four-poster beds and Erté prints. A full breakfast and a traditional English afternoon tea are included in the room rate. Smoking is not permitted. ⊠ *6228 Church St., 23336,* ☎ *757/336–6148. 10 rooms. D, MC, V. Closed Jan.–Feb.*

$$–$$$$ ◩ **Miss Molly's.** In 1886, a prosperous clammer built this bay-side Victorian inn named after his daughter, Molly, who was born in the house in 1887 and lived there until 1971. The American Empire antiques correspond to the period in which the house was constructed (though the building was gutted and renovated in 1982). The sunny master bedroom, where Marguerite Henry wrote the novel *Misty of Chincoteague,* is the only room with a private bath. Breakfast is included in the rates; weather permitting, it's served in a gazebo attached to a corner of the screened back porch. There is also afternoon tea. ⊠ *4141 N. Main St., 23336,* ☎ *757/336–6686. 7 rooms. D, MC, V. Closed Jan.–Feb.*

$$ ◩ **Island Motor Inn.** On the Intracoastal Waterway, this three-story motel offers ocean and bay views from every room. Guests can relax on their private balconies and watch the passersby on the boardwalk or simply gaze at the beautiful sunset. All rooms have refrigerators. Despite a popular location, this laid-back motel has managed to maintain its homeyness. ⊠ *4391 N. Main St., 23336,* ☎ *757/336–3141,* 𝔽𝔸𝕏 *757/336–1483. 60 rooms. Café, refrigerators, room service, 1 indoor and 1 outdoor pool, 2 exercise rooms, coin laundry. AE, D, DC, MC, V.*

Outdoor Activities and Sports

Bait and tackle are available from **Barnacle Bill's** (✉ 3691 Main St., ☎ 757/336–5188). Rent boats from **Captain Bob's** (✉ 2477 S. Main St., ☎ 757/336–6654). Boats can also be rented at **R&R Boats** (✉ 4183 Main St., ☎ 757/336–5465).

OFF THE   **WALLOPS ISLAND** – NASA's Wallops Flight Facility was the site of early
BEATEN PATH   rocket launchings. Today, although satellites are sent up occasionally, at-
                mospheric research is the main activity. Visitors can see a collection of
                spacecraft as well as exhibits and videos on the space program. ✉ 20
                mi southwest of Chincoteague, ☎ 757/824–2298 or 757/824–1344.
                ▦ Free. ☉ July–Aug., daily 10–4; Sept.–June, Thurs.–Mon. 10–4.

Assateague Island

★ ❾   *105 mi northeast of Chincoteague Island (via bridge); 100 mi north-
         east of Norfolk.*

Assateague Island is a 37-mi-long national wildlife refuge and national seashore that extends north into Eastern Maryland (☞ Chapter 10). The ocean beaches and the hiking and biking trails here are
extensive and unsullied. In addition to the pristine scenery, as many as
300 species of birds can be seen here, including migrant geese and swans.
The island's best-known residents are wild ponies, originally brought
to the island by settlers trying to avoid taxes and the expense of fences
on the mainland. Remember that these are wild animals, so you should-
n't get too close. Swimming, biking, hiking, surf fishing, and picnicking are permitted, but there is no camping in the Virginia portion of
Assateague Island. Visitors should bring their own food and drink; island facilities are limited to bathhouses and water fountains. ✉ *Rte.
13 to Hwy 175 East, ☎ 757/336–6577. ▦ $4 car, $2 per person for
cyclists and pedestrians. ☉ Visitor center: daily 9–5; park: Apr.–Oct.
daily 5 AM–10 PM, Oct.–Apr. daily 6 AM–8 PM. Wildlife drive closed to
cars before 3 PM.*

Outdoor Activities and Sports

On the southern end of Assateague Island at Tom's Cove Hook are 5
mi of well-maintained beach, with bathhouses and picnic areas. Just
to the north are 12 mi of pristine beach.

HAMPTON ROADS AREA
AND THE EASTERN SHORE A TO Z

Arriving and Departing

By Bus

Greyhound Lines (✉ 2 W. Pembrook, Hampton, ☎ 757/722–9861;
701 Monticello Ave., Norfolk, ☎ 757/625–7500; 1017 Laskin Rd.,
Virginia Beach, ☎ 757/422–2998; 1562 Holland Rd., Suffolk, ☎
757/539–8101) typically has half a dozen departures daily, both north
and south, from each city.

By Car

The I–664 road creates a circular beltway through the Hampton Roads
area. I–664 connects Newport News and Norfolk, via Suffolk. I–64
runs northwest through Norfolk to intersect with I–664 in Hampton
and I–95 at Richmond. U.S. 58 and Route 44 (toll road) connect I–64
to Virginia Beach.

By Plane

Newport News/Williamsburg International Airport (☎ 757/877–0221), formerly Patrick Henry International, in Newport News, served primarily by USAir, opened a new terminal in 1992.

Norfolk International Airport (☎ 757/857–3351), between Norfolk and Virginia Beach, is served by American, Continental, Delta, Northwest, TWA, United, USAir, Midway, and several regional carriers. Limousine service is available.

By Train

Amtrak (☎ 800/872–7245) provides service between Boston (and intervening points) and Newport News (✉ 9304 Warwick Blvd., ☎ 757/245–3589), with one train daily in each direction. At Newport News, a shuttle bus connects to Norfolk.

Getting Around

By Boat

The **Elizabeth River Ferry** conveys pedestrians from Waterside, in Norfolk, to Portsmouth, whose Olde Towne is dense with 18th- and 19th-century houses. The five-minute ferry trip is more fun than driving through the tunnel; it departs Norfolk every 30 minutes, on the quarter hour. ☎ 757/640–6300. ✉ *Fare: 75¢.* ☉ *Operates daily 7:15 AM–11:45 PM.*

By Car

The area is well served with expressways and interstate highways, but you'll have to share these routes with a lot of local drivers as well. Because the ragged coastline is constantly interrupted by water, driving from one town to another usually means going through a tunnel or over a bridge, either one of which may create a traffic bottleneck. The entrance to the tunnel between Hampton and Norfolk can get very congested, especially on weekends, so listen to your car radio for updated traffic reports. In congested periods, use the less-traveled I–664. The 17½-mi Chesapeake Bay Bridge-Tunnel is the only connection between Virginia Beach and the Eastern Shore; U.S. 13 is the main route up the spine of the Eastern Shore peninsula into Maryland.

Contacts and Resources

B&B Reservations

Virginia Beach Reservations (☎ 800/213–7645).

Emergencies

Chesapeake General Hospital (✉ 736 Battlefield Blvd. N, Chesapeake, ☎ 757/482–6128).
Newport News General Hospital (✉ 5100 Marshall Ave., Newport News, ☎ 757/247–7357).
Northampton-Accomack Memorial Hospital (✉ 9507 Hospital Ave., Nassawadox, ☎ 757/442–8777).
Sentara Bayside Hospital (✉ 800 Independence Blvd., Virginia Beach, ☎ 757/363–6137).
Sentara Norfolk General Hospital (✉ 600 Gresham Dr., ☎ 757/668–3551).

Guided Tours

The **Hampton Circle Tour** (☎ 757/727–1102) is a self-guided driving trip that passes all of Hampton's attractions. Maps are available from the Tourist Information Center.

The **Norfolk Trolley**'s guided tour of the historic downtown area allows you to get on and off as you please. Tickets are available at the

TRT kiosk at the Waterside. ☎ 757/640–6300. ✉ Fare $3.50. ⊙ Operates May–Sept.

Portsmouth's **Olde Towne Trolley Tour** gives you the inside story of major historical events since 1752. It departs from the Portside Information Center. ✉ 6 Crawford Pkwy., Portside, ☎ 757/393–5111. ✉ $3.50. ⊙ Late May–early Sept., daily 11–3:30.

The **Virginia Beach Tour** (☎ 800/822–3224 or 757/473–4888) is a self-guided driving trip past both beach and historic points. Maps are available at the visitor center, but signs mark the route.

Wharton's Tours (✉ Newport News, ☎ 757/245–1533) offers a cruise of the harbor. Also available are special voyages on the James River and a short segment of the Intracoastal Waterway, a series of canals that extends from Boston, Massachusetts to Brownsville, Texas.

BOAT TOURS

American Rover Sailing Tours (☎ 757/627–7245), which operates a striking 135-foot topsail schooner, cruises Hampton Roads's nautical historical landmarks and the Norfolk naval base.

The **Carrie B** (☎ 757/393–4735), a scaled-down reproduction of a Mississippi riverboat, cruises Hampton Roads to give visitors a look at the naval shipyard and the site of the encounter of the *Monitor* and the *Merrimack* during the Civil War.

The **Miss Hampton II** (☎ 757/727–1102) sails down Hampton River, passing the site where Blackbeard's head hung on a stake, and Hampton University's handsome campus. The boat then sails across Hampton Roads, past the Norfolk Naval Base. The trip includes a stop at Fort Wool, situated on an artificial island off Hampton, where remnants of fortifications dating from the early 19th century to World War II may be explored.

Discovery Cruise (☎ 757/422–2900) features a handsome luxury yacht that explores Virginia Beach's Broad Bay.

Visitor Information

Chincoteague Chamber of Commerce (✉ Box 258, Chincoteague 23336, ☎ 757/336–6161).
Eastern Shore of Virginia Chamber of Commerce and Tourism Commission (✉ Box 460, Melfa 23410, ☎ 757/787–2460).
Hampton Convention and Visitors Bureau (✉ 710 Settlers Landing Rd., Hampton 23669, ☎ 757/727–1102).
Newport News Tourism and Conference Bureau (✉ 2400 Washington Ave., Newport News 23607, ☎ 757/928–6843).
Norfolk Convention and Visitors Bureau (end of 4th View St., 23503, ☎ 757/441–1852 or 800/368–3097).
Portsmouth Convention and Visitors Bureau (✉ 505 Crawford St., Suite 2, Portsmouth 23704, ☎ 757/393–5327 or 800/767–8782).
Virginia Beach Visitor Information Center (✉ 2100 Parks Ave., Virginia Beach 23451, ☎ 757/437–4888 or 800/446–8038).

7 Baltimore

Harborplace and the Inner Harbor, Oriole Park at Camden Yards, the Maryland Science Center, the National Aquarium, the American Visionary Art Museum—these and other attractions have transformed Baltimore in the past 30 years. Equally lively are the historic neighborhoods including Federal Hill, named in 1788 to commemorate Maryland's ratification of the U.S. Constitution, and Fells Point, the center of Baltimore's thriving shipbuilding industry in the 18th and 19th centuries.

BEFORE THE 1970S IT WAS A JOKE TO SPEAK of Baltimore as a tourist destination. Middle-class residents had been steadily fleeing for the suburbs since World War II, and there had been a corresponding decline in the quality of entertainment and accommodations, not to mention the level of public safety, in the downtown areas. The city's only glory lay in its past.

In 1980 the christening of two shopping pavilions called Harborplace symbolized the revival of Baltimore's formerly decaying Inner Harbor and surrounding neighborhoods. Hotels, office buildings, and attractions such as the Maryland Science Center and the huge National Aquarium were built around Inner Harbor; restaurants and shops proliferated; and the city's historic structures and neighborhoods received unprecedented numbers of visitors. Today, a second renaissance is exploding across Inner Harbor and downtown Baltimore: A $27-million children's museum called Port Discovery is expected to open by early 1998, along with the Columbus Center Hall of Exploration, a multimillion-dollar science museum expected to open in late 1996. Among Baltimore's newest attractions is the American Visionary Art Museum, which exhibits the creative works of everyday men and women. Other major attractions such as Harborplace and the Baltimore Convention Center are in the midst of major renovations.

At the same time, Baltimore's image has received a boost from the arrival of a new professional football franchise, the Baltimore Ravens, formerly the Cleveland Browns. Drawing on the city's brief but memorable association with Edgar Allan Poe, the Ravens will begin the 1996 season at Memorial Stadium, former home of the Colts and the Orioles, until a new stadium is completed near Oriole Park at Camden Yards. The city's fascination with baseball and the success of the new stadium, Oriole Park at Camden Yards, has spurred the building of a Baseball Center in the adjacent Camden Station Passenger Terminal building, slated to open in late spring 1997. Historical exhibits, interactive displays, and a baseball-themed restaurant are planned.

In a sense, the city has come full circle since its early, prosperous days. The town was established by the Colonial government in 1729, at the end of the broad Patapsco River that empties into the Chesapeake Bay. Named for George Calvert, First Lord Baltimore, the founder of Maryland, the town grew as a port and shipbuilding center and enjoyed booming business during the War of Independence. A quantum leap came at the turn of the 19th century: From 6,700 in 1776, the population reached 45,000 by 1810. During the War of 1812, because it was the home port for a significant portion of U.S. navy vessels and for privateers (many of them the compact and swift Baltimore Clippers) that preyed on British shipping, the city was a natural target for the enemy. After capturing and torching Washington, DC, the British fleet sailed up the Patapsco River and bombarded Baltimore's Ft. McHenry, but in vain. The 30-foot by 42-foot, 15-star, 15-stripe flag was still flying "by the dawn's early light," a spectacle that inspired Francis Scott Key to write "The Star-Spangled Banner."

After the War of 1812, Baltimore prospered as a slave market, and during the Civil War the population's sympathies were divided between North and South, provoking riots. The first bloodshed of the Civil War occurred in Baltimore when the Sixth Massachusetts Regiment was stoned by an angry group of Baltimoreans. (This is a town whose regional identity has always been, and remains, ambiguous.) President Lincoln, mistrusting the loyalty of certain city officials, had these particular government authorities summarily detained—an act that was no doubt strategically effective but was probably unconstitutional.

In the postbellum period, Baltimore became a manufacturing center, notably of iron, steel, chemical fertilizer, and textiles. It also became the oyster capital of the world, packing more of those tasty mollusks than any other place in 1880. After a 1904 fire destroyed 1,500 structures, Baltimore rebuilt valiantly and rode the economic roller coaster over two world wars and the Great Depression. The city's manufacturing base became a liability in the 1950s and '60s as U.S. competitiveness in that sector faltered. But the massive revitalization efforts of the '80s helped the city get back on its feet.

Today, Baltimore's Inner Harbor serves as the pulse of not only a vibrant, growing metropolis but of the city's environs as well. The downtown renaissance at Charles Center and Inner Harbor spurred a growth in tourism, making it a $1-billion-a-year industry by the mid-1980s. Historic neighborhoods such as Bolton Hill, Federal Hill, Fells Point, Otterbein, and Roland Park (developed by Frederick L. Olmsted, designer of New York City's Central Park) are home to businesspeople and families who only a few years ago might have lived in the suburbs.

Baltimore is a great city from which to plan day trips. Within 2 hours by car are historic Annapolis; Washington, DC; Pennsylvania Dutch Country; Hershey; Gettysburg; Civil War battlefields; Michener's Chesapeake Country; the Brandywine Valley; and the colony's original settlement at St. Mary's City.

EXPLORING BALTIMORE

The city of Baltimore fans out northward from Inner Harbor, with newer attractions such as the National Aquarium and Orioles Park at Camden Yards concentrated at the center, and more historic neighborhoods and sites out toward the edges. Downtown streets are laid out in a grid, although it is by no means regular. From Pratt Street, which runs east along Inner Harbor, the major northbound artery is Charles Street. Cross streets' addresses are marked "East" or "West" according to which side of Charles Street they are on; similarly, Baltimore Street marks the dividing line between north and south. It's easy to explore Inner Harbor by foot, but beyond this a car is by far the most efficient means of transportation.

Charles Street and Mount Vernon

Historic churches and 19th-century brownstones are interspersed with modern office buildings and stores in this gentrified neighborhood. Charles Street, north of Inner Harbor, provides an ideal setting for a leisurely afternoon stroll, with stops at some of Baltimore's notable 19th-century landmarks. The area also abounds with distinguished art galleries that exhibit (and hope to sell) the work of a diverse group of artists and craftspeople, including some locals. Gallery admission is usually free, and most venues are open Monday to Saturday 10–5. Galleries generally have a new show every month.

The blocks north of Charles between Saratoga and Chase streets—a stretch of more than ½ mi—are known as Restaurant Row, with eating options to please every palate and price range. At Charles and Mount Vernon Place lies the city's famed Mount Vernon Square, site of one of the nation's oldest monuments to George Washington.

A Good Tour

Numbers in the text correspond to numbers in the margin and on the Baltimore map.

This tour is best accomplished with a car, though you may want to park somewhere around Charles Street and walk to the first seven attractions. Begin at the intersection of Charles and Baltimore streets at Charles Center and head north, walking uphill. At Saratoga Street, you'll pass one of the many historic churches in Baltimore, St. Paul's Episcopal Church, begun in 1854 and dedicated for St. Paul's Parish in 1732. The **Basilica of the Assumption** ①, the nation's oldest Catholic cathedral, is one block west of Charles Street on Mulberry Street. West of the Basilica is the **Enoch Pratt Free Library** ②, which abounds with works by Edgar Allan Poe and H. L. Mencken. Returning to Charles Street, notice the First Unitarian Church, at Franklin Street, one block up: Designed by Maximilian Godefroy in 1819, the church is famous because its founder, Dr. Channing, gave the definitive sermon for the church here. About two blocks north is the **Walters Art Gallery** ③, an impressive museum with more than 30,000 paintings, sculpture, and other art works. A block north of the art gallery is **Mount Vernon Square** ④, four lovely parks dominated by the **Washington Monument** ⑤. At the base of the monument is Mount Vernon Methodist Church (Mount Vernon Pl. and Washington Pl.), built in the mid-1850s on the site of Francis Scott Key's home and place of death. The Peabody Conservatory of Music and the **Peabody Library** ⑥ are on the south side of Mount Vernon Square. Then head west on Mount Vernon Place, which turns into Monument Street, to visit the **Maryland Historical Society** ⑦ for an intriguing look at the past.

Drive north on Charles Street 1½ mi to the **Baltimore Museum of Art** ⑧, where an excellent art collection is housed in a John Russell Pope–designed building. The art museum is contiguous to the Homewood campus of **Johns Hopkins University** ⑨, where the historic house of John Carroll, Jr., is open to the public.

From Johns Hopkins University, turn left on Charles Street and drive several blocks north to Stratford. Turn right on Stratford and drive to where it intersects with Greenway to reach **Sherwood Gardens** ⑩, where tulips and azaleas abound. Backtrack one block to St. Paul Street, which then curves northwest to meet Charles Street; two blocks north of that intersection, at Charles Street and Cold Spring Lane, stands the grand **Evergreen House** ⑪, where guided tours will give you a sense of the lives of the rich and famous at the turn of the century.

Timing

The many historic sights along Charles Street and Mount Vernon merit at least an entire morning. Save the afternoon for the Baltimore Museum of Art and the Homewood campus of Johns Hopkins University.

Sights To See

⑧ **Baltimore Museum of Art.** Works by Matisse, Picasso, Cézanne, Gauguin, van Gogh, and Monet are among the 100,000 paintings, sculptures, and decorative arts on exhibit at this impressive museum, near Johns Hopkins University. Particular strengths include an encyclopedic collection of postimpressionist paintings donated to the museum by the Cone sisters, Baltimore natives who were pioneers in the collection of early 20th-century art; the world's second largest collection of Andy Warhol pieces, with an entire gallery devoted to his work; and a wide variety of 18th- and 19th-century American painting and decorative arts. The museum building was designed by John Russell Pope, who was also the architect of the National Gallery in Washington. From the museum restaurant you can look out at 20th-century sculpture displayed in two landscaped gardens. A modern wing is the site of visiting exhibitions and other temporary shows. ⊠ *10 Art Museum Dr.,* ☎ *410/396–7101.* ⊠ *$5.50; free Thurs.* ⊙ *Wed.–Fri. 10–4, weekends 11–6.*

OFF THE
BEATEN PATH

BALTIMORE STREETCAR MUSEUM – This often overlooked museum lets visitors travel back to an era when streetcars dominated city thoroughfares. A free film traces the vehicle's evolution. Best of all, visitors can actually take a ride on a restored streetcar. ⊠ *1901 Falls Rd.,* ☎ *410/547–0264.* ⊠ *$4.* ⊙ *Weekends noon–5.*

❶ Basilica of the Assumption. Completed in 1821, the Basilica of the Assumption is the oldest Catholic cathedral in the United States. Designed by Benjamin Latrobe, the architect of the U.S. Capitol, it stands as a paragon of neoclassicism, with a grand portico fronted by six Corinthian columns suggesting an ancient Greek temple. Two towers are surmounted by cupolas. Inside, the sanctuary fills with light through nine stained-glass windows. Bells ring the Angelus daily at 6 AM, noon, and 6 PM. A basement-level gift shop sells religious goods. ⊠ *Mulberry St. at Cathedral St.,* ☎ *410/727–3564.* ⊙ *Daily 7:30–5.*

❷ Enoch Pratt Free Library. One of the country's largest libraries, the Enoch Pratt has room devoted to the works and lives of two prominent writers associated with Baltimore, Edgar Allan Poe and H. L. Mencken. This is the main branch of the city's public library system and it was here that Mencken's seven typescript volumes of autobiographical writings were locked up in a vault for 35 years until early 1991. ⊠ *400 Cathedral St.,* ☎ *410/396–5500).* ⊙ *Tues.–Wed. 10–8, Thurs. and Sat. 10–5.*

⓫ Evergreen House. Built in the 1850s, this 48-room Italianate mansion was the home of the 19th-century diplomat and collector John Work Garrett, whose father was president of the Baltimore and Ohio Railroad (the Garrett family continued to live here until the 1950s). Today the yellow-brick building with its Corinthian columns and large collections of books, prints, paintings, and porcelain is the property of Johns Hopkins University. A tour of the mansion provides a fascinating look at the luxury that surrounded a rich American family at the turn of the century. ⊠ *4545 N. Charles St.,* ☎ *410/516–0895.* ⊠ *$5.* ⊙ *Weekdays 10–4, weekends 1–4.*

❾ Johns Hopkins University. The 140-acre Homewood campus is the heart of Johns Hopkins University. All of this land was once the estate of Charles Carroll, Jr., son of Charles Carroll of Carrollton, a signer of the Declaration of Independence (you can visit his residence at the City Life Museums, ☞ *below*). Homewood, the house of the younger Carroll, has been restored to its appearance of 1800. Also on campus is the Lacrosse Hall of Fame, the only national museum dedicated to the sport. ⊠ *Charles and 34th Sts.,* ☎ *410/516–5589.* ⊠ *$5.* ⊙ *Tues.–Sat. 11–4, Sun. 12–4.*

OFF THE
BEATEN PATH

THE BALTIMORE ZOO – The 150 acres of the Baltimore Zoo—the third-oldest zoo in the country—make a natural stomping ground for little ones who enjoy the spectacle of elephants, lions, giraffes, hippos, and penguins, among the 1,200 animals that make this their home. Favorite sights include a new chimpanzee house and leopard lair; river otters in an outdoor pond; a petting zoo with a re-created barnyard; and a Maryland Wilderness exhibit with animals native to the state. A ride on "Zoo-Choo" provides further diversion. ⊠ *Druid Hill Park, Druid Hill*

Baltimore

Broadway

Chase St.

Madison Square

Eager St.

Harford Ave.

Biddle St.

Johnston Square

Greenmount Ave.

State Penitentiary

Baltimore Streetcar Museum

Chase St.

TO AMTRAK PENN STATION

Guilford St.

Calvert St.

Read St.

Saint Paul St.

Eager St.

Charles St.

Cathedral St.

Read St.

Biddle St.

Hoffman St.

Madison St.

Monument St.

Maryland General Hospital

Martin Luther King, Jr. Blvd.

Baltimore Zoo

Madison St.

Monument St.

Washington Pl.

Centre St.

Franklin St.

Park Ave.

Howard St.

Eutaw St.

Mulberry St.

Saratoga St.

Liberty St.

Greyhound Bus Terminal

Fayette St.

Johns Hopkins Hospital

Church Home Hospital

Fairmount Ave.

Central Ave.

Monument St.

Old Town Mall

McElderry St.

Aisquith St.

Orleans St.

Ensor St.

Front St.

Hillen St.

Gay St.

Fallsway

Main Post Office

Fayette St.

Baltimore St.

Gay St.

Holliday St.

Davis St.

Sun Papers Building

Pleasant St.

Mercy Hospital

Saint Paul Pl.

Saint Paul St.

Charles St.

83

147

45

40

1 2 3 4 5 6 7 8 9 10 11 23 24 25 26

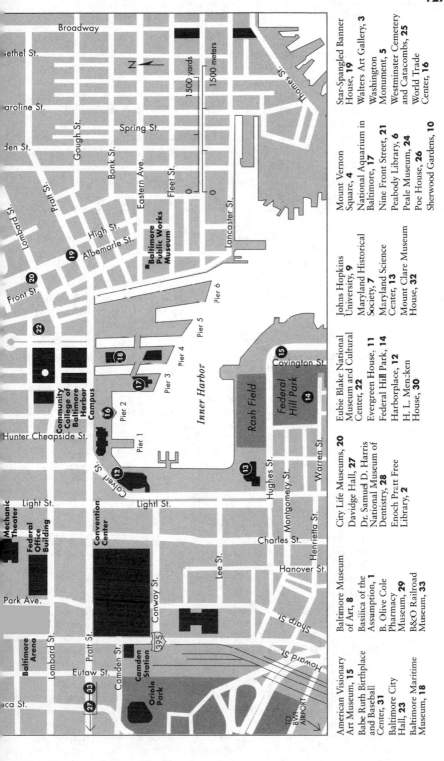

Broadway

ethel St.

aroline St.

den St.

Spring St.

Gough St.

Bank St.

Eastern Ave.

High St.

Albemarle St.

Fleet St.

N

1500 yards

1500 meters

0

0

Thames St.

Lancaster St.

Pier 6

Baltimore Public Works Museum

Pratt St.

Lombard St.

Front St.

19

20

22

18

17

16

15

13

12

Pier 5

Pier 4

Pier 3

Pier 2

Pier 1

Covington St.

Community College of Baltimore Harbor Campus

Inner Harbor

Rash Field

Federal Hill Park

14

Hunter Cheapside St.

Calvert St.

Hughes St.

Warren Ave.

Montgomery St.

Mechanic Theater

Light St.

Lightl St.

Federal Office Building

Convention Center

Charles St.

Hanover St.

Park Ave.

Lee St.

Henrietta St.

Conway St.

Sharp St.

395

Baltimore Arena

Lombard St.

Eutaw St.

Camden St.

Pratt St.

Camden Station

Oriole Park

Howard St.

TO BWI AIRPORT

ca St.

33

27

American Visionary
Art Museum, **15**

Babe Ruth Birthplace
and Baseball
Center, **31**

Baltimore City
Hall, **23**

Baltimore Maritime
Museum, **18**

Baltimore Museum
of Art, **8**

Basilica of the
Assumption, **1**

B. Olive Cole
Pharmacy
Museum, **29**

B&O Railroad
Museum, **33**

City Life Museums, **20**
Davidge Hall, **27**

Dr. Samuel D. Harris
National Museum of
Dentistry, **28**

Enoch Pratt Free
Library, **2**

Eubie Blake National
Museum and Cultural
Center, **22**

Evergreen House, **11**

Federal Hill Park, **14**

Harborplace, **12**

H. L. Mencken
House, **30**

Johns Hopkins
University, **9**

Maryland Historical
Society, **7**

Maryland Science
Center, **13**

Mount Clare Museum
House, **32**

Mount Vernon
Square, **4**

National Aquarium in
Baltimore, **17**

Nine Front Street, **21**

Peabody Library, **6**

Peale Museum, **24**

Poe House, **26**

Sherwood Gardens, **10**

Star-Spangled Banner
House, **19**

Walters Art Gallery, **3**

Washington
Monument, **5**

Westminster Cemetery
and Catacombs, **25**

World Trade
Center, **16**

Lake Dr., ☎ *410/366–5466.* ▭ *$7.50.* ⊙ *Daily 10–4 (till 5:30 in summer).*

Lovely Lane Methodist Church. Built in 1882, Lovely Lane Methodist Church is honored with the title "The Mother Church of American Methodism." Stanford White designed the interior with wood—almost entirely black birch—and the stained-glass windows are excellent examples of Italian mosaics. The buildings to the north that resemble the church are the original campus of Goucher College. Dr. Goucher, the college's founder, was a pastor at Lovely Lane Church. ⊠ *2200 St. Paul St.,* ☎ *410/889–1512. Tours of church and Methodist Historical Society available by appointment.*

❼ Maryland Historical Society. Maryland's heritage of fine living and of the Chesapeake Bay are depicted in displays of period furnishings and the Radcliffe Maritime Collection. Featured are portraits by the Peale family and Joshua Johnson, America's first black portrait artist. Two major attractions are the original manuscript of "The Star-Spangled Banner" and the world's largest collection of 19th-century American silver. ⊠ *201 W. Monument St.,* ☎ *410/685–3750.* ▭ *$3.50.* ⊙ *Year-round, Tues.–Fri. 10–5, Sat. 9–5; Oct.–Apr., also Sun. 1–5.*

Mother Seton House. This modest brick house was the Baltimore home of Elizabeth Ann Seton, first American-born saint, who later moved to Emmitsburg and established the nation's first parochial school. ⊠ *600 N. Paca St.,* ☎ *410/523–3443.* ⊙ *Sun. 1–4 and by appointment.*

❹ Mount Vernon Square. Surrounding Washington Monument is Mount Vernon Square, once the heart of Baltimore's most fashionable neighborhood. The picturesque square is flanked by four parks, each a block in length, arranged east and west along the median of Mount Vernon Place and north and south along Washington Place. The sculptures in the parks deserve a close look; of special note is a bronze lion by Barye in the middle of West Mount Vernon Place. Take a moment to admire the brownstones along the north side of East Mount Vernon Place, inviolate in their 19th-century elegance. This neighborhood was a setting for the 1986 movie *The Bedroom Window.*

❻ Peabody Library. Adjacent to the Peabody Conservatory of Music, the Peabody Library is a fine example of neo-Renaissance architecture. Its stunning reading room reflects the scholarly interests of the 19th century, with more than a quarter of a million books lining the shelves. Most impressive, though, are the cast-iron balconies towering above the black-and-white marble floor. A skylight, 61 feet above, brightens the room. ⊠ *17 E. Mount Vernon Pl.,* ☎ *410/659–8179.* ▭ *Free.* ⊙ *Weekdays 9–3; call for Sat. schedule.*

❿ Sherwood Gardens. A popular spring destination for Baltimore families is Sherwood Gardens, a lovely 6-acre park where more than 80,000 tulips bloom in late April. Azaleas peak in late April and the first half of May. The gardens are usually at their best around Mother's Day. ⊠ *Stratford Rd. and Greenway, east of St. Paul St.,* ☎ *410/366–2572.* ▭ *Free.* ⊙ *Dawn–dusk.*

★ **❸ Walters Art Gallery.** In historic Mount Vernon, the Walters Art Gallery contains more than 30,000 artworks spanning 5,000 years. The older wing was built in 1904 and contains Renaissance and Baroque paintings, as well as a sculpture court that befits this Italianate palace. The newer structure (1974) has displays of ancient, medieval, Oriental, Islamic, and Byzantine art, and many 19th-century paintings. Also on display are medieval armor and artifacts, jewelry, and decorative works; Egyptology exhibits, which children love; and a wonderful gift

In case you want to be welcomed there.

We're here to see that you're always welcomed at establishments everywhere. That's why millions of people carry the American Express® Card – for peace of mind, confidence, and security, around the world or just around the corner.

do more

AMERICAN EXPRESS

Cards

In case you're running low.

We're here to help with more than 118,000 Express Cash locations around the world. In order to enroll, just call American Express before you start your vacation.

do more

Express Cash

And just in case.

We're here with American Express® Travelers Cheques and Cheques *for Two*.® They're the safest way to carry money on your vacation and the surest way to get a refund, practically anywhere, anytime.
Another way we help you...

do more

Travelers
Cheques

shop filled with moderately priced souvenirs and keepsakes. ✉ *600 N. Charles St.,* ☎ *410/547–9000.* ☞ *$4. Free entry Sat. 11–noon.* ☉ *Tues.–Sun. 11–5.*

⑤ **Washington Monument.** Erected in 1829, the marble Doric column that towers above Mount Vernon Place is the oldest formal monument to the Father of this Country. (A more humble structure, made of stones and built in the shape of a mason jar, stands atop South Mountain in Western Maryland; it was constructed about the same time). The 178-foot monument, surmounted by a 16-foot white marble statue of the nation's first chief executive, was designed by Robert Mills, who was also responsible for the more famous Washington Monument in the nation's capital. Built on land donated to the city by John Eager Howard, the monument—representing Washington resigning his commission—was built far from the center of the city so that it would not harm any buildings were it to fall. Visitors can climb the 228 steps to the top of the monument for a bird's-eye view of the city. ✉ *600 N. Charles St.,* ☎ *410/396-0929.* ☞ *Donation $1.*

Inner Harbor and Environs

At the southern edge of downtown Baltimore, the basin of the northwest branch of the Patapsco River is an almost landlocked body of water with six piers jutting into it from the north side. This is Baltimore's Inner Harbor, one of the city's liveliest neighborhoods, with shops, restaurants, and major cultural attractions. It's also a working port, with rental craft, water taxis, and battery-operated paddle boats (available at the foot of the World Trade Center) for those who want to enjoy a river perspective of the waterside architecture.

A Good Walk

You can spend the whole day strolling along the brick promenades that surround Baltimore's harbor; if you are feeling ambitious, you can cover Inner Harbor in the morning, then spend the afternoon visiting Museum Row and the attractions around it. Begin at the northwest corner of Inner Harbor, at **Harborplace** ⑫, where two glass-enclosed shopping malls invite you to while away the hours. Walk down to the southwest corner of Inner Harbor, to the **Maryland Science Center** ⑬, where an IMAX movie theater and hundreds of hands-on exhibits attract children and adults. From there it's just a short walk to **Federal Hill Park** ⑭ and the adjacent **American Visionary Art Museum** ⑮, one of Baltimore's newest, and most unusual, major attractions.

Return to Harborplace and walk east along the northern edge of Inner Harbor to Pier Two: Here, at the **World Trade Center** ⑯, you can enjoy a panoramic view of Baltimore from the 27th floor. At Piers Three and Four is the **National Aquarium in Baltimore** ⑰, with its thousands of fish, sharks, dolphins, jellyfish, reptiles, and amphibians. Docked just to the east, at Pier Four, is the **Baltimore Maritime Museum** ⑱, whose three vessels include the USS *Torsk,* a submarine credited with sinking the last two Japanese warships during World War II.

If you're ready for more, walk to Pier Six at the northeast corner of Inner Harbor, and head east on Pratt Street to Albemarle Street. Here is the **Star-Spangled Banner House** ⑲, where the original American flag was sewn. Two blocks to the north, the **City Life Museums** ⑳, at Lombard Street between Front and Albermarle Streets, include the Morton K. Blaustein City Life Exhibition Center, the Center for Urban Archaeology, the 1840 House, and Carroll Mansion. Another two blocks north, at Baltimore Street, **Nine Front Street** ㉑ is a visitor information center housed inside a circa-1790 town house.

If your energy still hasn't flagged, head south to the **Eubie Blake National Museum and Cultural Center** ㉒, where exhibits depict the famous jazz musician's life and works. Two blocks north and one block west is the **Baltimore City Hall** ㉓—and, farther north on Holliday Street, the **Peale Museum** ㉔, the oldest museum in the country.

Timing

Allow plenty of time to visit Inner Harbor, by far Baltimore's busiest area. Arrive early at the National Aquarium to ensure admission, which is by timed intervals; by noon, the wait is often two or three hours.

Sights To See

★ ⑮ **American Visionary Art Museum.** A national museum dedicated to the self-taught or "outsider" artist, the American Visionary Art Museum opened in 1995. The seven galleries of the 35,000-square-foot building exhibit the unusual creations of farmers, homemakers, mechanics, the homeless, and the disabled—including paintings, sculptures, reliefs, and other media. Carved roots, embroidered rags, tattoos, toothpicks, and household wares are among the unconventional materials used. The Joy American Cafe (☞ *below*) has a view of Baltimore Harbor and an exuberant menu to match its playful name. ⊠ *800 Key Hwy.,* ☎ *410/244-1900.* ⊡ *$6.* ◷ *Tues.–Thurs., Sun. 10–6, Fri.–Sat. 10–8.*

㉓ **Baltimore City Hall.** Built in 1875, Baltimore City Hall consists of mansard roofs and a gilt dome over a 110-foot rotunda, all supported by ironwork. In addition to grand architecture, City Hall offers visitors exhibits on Baltimore's history and tours of the chambers. Directly across the street is **City Hall Plaza,** on what was originally the site of the Holliday Street Theatre. The Theatre was owned and operated by the Ford Brothers; they also operated Ford's Theatre in Washington, DC, where President Lincoln was assassinated. "The Star-Spangled Banner" was first publicly sung here. ⊠ *City Hall: 100 N. Holliday St.,* ☎ *410/396–4900.* ◷ *Weekdays 8–4:30.*

🖐 ⑱ **Baltimore Maritime Museum.** Consisting of three docked vessels, this museum gives visitors a good sense of Baltimore's maritime heritage. On the west side of the pier, the submarine **USS Torsk,** the "Galloping Ghost of the Japanese Coast," is credited with sinking the last two Japanese warships in World War II. The lightship *Chesapeake,* built as a floating Chesapeake Bay lighthouse in 1930 and now out of commission, remains fully operational. The *Taney* is a Coast Guard cutter that saw action at Pearl Harbor. ⊠ *Pier Four,* ☎ *410/396–3453.* ⊡ *$4.50.* ◷ *Daily 10–4; weekends 10–5. Extended summer hrs.*

OFF THE
BEATEN PATH

FELLS POINT – If you can't get enough of the maritime theme, take the water taxi to Fells Point, the center of Baltimore's thriving shipbuilding industry in the late 18th and early 19th centuries. (The USF *Constellation,* now being restored, was one of many distinguished craft built here.) The neighborhood today is one of cobblestone streets and more than 350 historic houses, many of them brick structures dating from the early 1700s that now serve as shops, galleries, and restaurants. Seafood dining rooms and lively taverns make this a popular social area at night. The **Robert Long House,** built by a merchant in 1765, is the city's oldest dwelling. ⊠ *S. Ann and Thames Sts.,* ☎ *410/675-6750.* ⊡ *$1.* ◷ *Tours daily 10 AM, 1 PM, and 3 PM and by appointment.*

⑳ **City Life Museums.** This complex of museums, centered around a single courtyard and sharing the same admission policies and hours, was recently given new life with the addition of the $8.5-million **Morton**

K. Blaustein City Life Exhibition Center. Here, everyday objects such as white vinyl reclining chairs from the 1950s and black gas stoves from the 1930s provide a fascinating glimpse at Baltimore's urban and cultural history. Look for Nipper, the 1,700-pound fiberglass dog, the famous mascot of the RCA Record Co., which once stood atop a downtown building.

The other City Life Museums are more traditional. The **1840 House** (⊠ 50 Albermarle St., ☎ 410/396–3279) is the reconstructed row house of a wheelwright and his family, portrayed today by costumed interpreters. An aristocratic complement to the 1840 House, the **Carroll Mansion** (⊠ 800 E. Lombard St., ☎ 410/396–3524) was the home of Charles Carroll of Carrollton, who was the last surviving signer of the Declaration of Independence. The elegant house, built in 1808, has been fully restored and furnished in the Empire style, as it was at the time of Carroll's death in 1832. The **Center for Urban Archaeology** displays 18th- and 19th-century ceramics and glassware discovered around Baltimore. Visitors can observe archaeologists examining the artifacts. The **Shot Tower**—one of the few remaining buildings of its kind—was built in 1829 from a million bricks and was used in the manufacture of lead shot ammunition. Standing 234 feet high, the tower tapers toward the top and is capped with pseudomedieval battlements. On one nearly forgotten day in late March many years ago, an ad appeared in a Baltimore newspaper announcing that a Baltimorean would "fly" from the top of the Shot Tower . . a hoax perpetuated by Baltimore's Edgar Allan Poe. ⊠ 800 E. Lombard St., ☎ 410/396-3523. ☜ *$6 for all museums. Admission free on Sat.* ☉ *Apr.–Sept., Tues.–Sat. 10–5, Sun. noon–5; Oct.–Mar., Tues.–Sat. 10–4, Sun. noon–4.*

OFF THE **BALTIMORE PUBLIC WORKS MUSEUM** – The oldest of its kind in the coun-
BEATEN PATH try, the Baltimore Public Works Museum consists of an unusual collection of artifacts displayed in an unusual location: the 80-year-old Eastern Avenue Sewage Pumping Station. Here you can examine several generations of water pipe, including wood piping nearly 200 years old; other exhibits tell the history of city services such as trash removal. Outdoors, a life-size model reveals what lies underneath Baltimore streets ⊠ *751 Eastern Ave.,* ☎ *410/396–5565.* ☜ *$2.50.* ☉ *Wed.–Sun. 10–4. Extended summer hrs.*

㉒ **Eubie Blake National Museum and Cultural Center.** A tribute to the native Baltimorean and renowned composer of jazz and show tunes best known for "I'm Just Wild About Harry," this is also a place for musicians, dancers, and actors to study and perform. Exhibits depict Blake's life and career; additional exhibits are by local artists. ⊠ *34 Market Pl.,* ☎ *410/396–8128.* ☜ *Free.* ☉ *Weekdays noon–5.*

⑭ **Federal Hill Park.** On the south side of Inner Harbor, Federal Hill Park was named in 1788 to commemorate Maryland's ratification of the U.S. Constitution. Later it was the site of Civil War fortifications, built by less-than-welcome Union troops under the command of Major General Benjamin "Spoonie" Butler. Until the early 1900s, a signal tower atop Federal Hill displayed the "house" flags of local shipping companies, notifying them of the arrival of their vessels. The summit provides an excellent view of Rash Field, of Inner Harbor beyond, and of the downtown skyline. The best vantage point for photographing Baltimore, it is also a favorite spot for watching holiday fireworks. ⊠ *Battery St. and Key Hwy.*

OFF THE **BALTIMORE MUSEUM OF INDUSTRY** – Housed in an 1865 oyster cannery,
BEATEN PATH about a ½-mi walk south of Inner Harbor along Key Highway, the Balti-

more Museum of Industry is a fascinating glimpse at the city's industrial and labor history. Here, you can watch and help operate the functional re-creations of a machine shop circa 1900, a print shop, and a garment workroom. A restored steam-driven tugboat that plied the waterfront for the first half of this century is docked outside. ⊠ *1415 Key Hwy.,* ☎ *410/727–4808.* ☜ *$3.50.* ◷ *Memorial Day–Labor Day, Tues.–Fri. noon–5, Sat. 10–5, Sun. noon–5; Sept.–May, Wed. 7–9 PM, Thurs.–Fri. noon–5, Sat. 10–5, Sun. noon–5.*

★ ◐ **Ft. McHenry.** At the end of the peninsula that bounds the northwest branch of the Patapsco is Ft. McHenry, a star-shape brick-and-earthen structure built in 1803 that has also been used as a prison and a hospital. It is most famous for its role in the War of 1812, which is immortalized in the national anthem. In September 1814 a Maryland lawyer named Francis Scott Key was detained aboard a ship of truce after having obtained the release of a friend, Dr. William Beanes. The British bombardment of Ft. McHenry was about to begin, and Key knew too much about the attack plan to be released. During the 25-hour battle that ensued, Key often witnessed his country's flag drifting in and out of view through the smoke and haze. "By the dawn's early light" of September 14, 1814, he saw the 30-foot by 42-foot "Star-Spangled Banner" still waving and was inspired to pen the words to a poem. The poem was set, ironically, to the tune of an old English drinking song, "To Anacreon in Heaven." The flag that Key saw had 15 stars, 15 stripes, and was hand-sewn for the fort by Mary Pickersgill, a Baltimore resident whose house in the city is also open to visitors (☞ Star-Spangled Banner House, *below*). A visit to the fort includes a 16-minute history film. The National Park Service has begun a $3-million renovation of the fort's deteriorating walls. ⊠ *Fort Ave. (from Light St., take Key Hwy. for 1½ mi and follow signs),* ☎ *410/962–4299.* ☜ *$2.* ◷ *Sept.–May, daily 8–5; mid-June–Labor Day, daily 8–8.*

⑫ **Harborplace.** Like Boston's Quincy Market and New York's South Street Seaport, this was a development of the Rouse Company. Here, two glass-enclosed shopping malls house more than 100 specialty shops, restaurants, and gourmet markets. Street entertainers frequently perform at an outdoor amphitheater between the two buildings. The Light Street pavilion has a food court; a skywalk across Pratt Street leads to **The Gallery,** a five-story shopping mall with another 70 shops, and about a dozen restaurants.

At the corner of the Inner Harbor between the two pavilions is the **Ceremonial Landing** used for the skipjack *Minnie V,* a turn-of-the-century oyster boat that has been restored and is now used for short informational cruises. ⊠ *100 Pratt St.,* ☎ *410/332–4191.* ◷ *Mon.–Sat. 10–9, Sun. 10–6. (Light Street Pavilion has extended summer hrs; some restaurants open earlier for breakfast, and most close very late.)*

Lloyd Street Synagogue. Built in 1845, this was the first synagogue in Maryland and the third in the United States. It has been restored and now serves as a museum. ⊠ *Lloyd St.,* ☎ *410/732-6400.* ☜ *$2.* ◷ *Tues.–Thurs., Sun., noon–4.*

◐ ⑬ **Maryland Science Center.** Originally known as the Maryland Academy of Sciences, this 200-year-old institution, one of the oldest scientific institutions in the United States, is housed in a contemporary building whose unusual design includes a red neon strip wrapped around the perimeter. In addition to a planetarium and hundreds of hands-on exhibits on the Chesapeake Bay, energy resources, and other subjects, the center has an IMAX movie theater: Across a screen five stories high are thrilling scenes shot from hang gliders and roller coasters. ⊠ *601*

Light St., ☎ *410/685–5225.* 🎫 *$9.* 🕐 *July–Labor Day, Mon.–Thurs.*
10–6, Fri.–Sun. 10–8; Sept.–June, weekdays 10–5, weekends 10–6.

★ ⑰ **National Aquarium in Baltimore.** The exhibit "Jellies: Phantoms of the
Deep," is the newest attraction at the National Aquarium, the most
visited tourist site in Maryland. In addition to jellyfish, the aquarium
is home to 5,000 fish, sharks, dolphins, reptiles, birds, amphibians, in-
vertebrates, and plants that dwell in, or around, its 2 million gallons
of water. In the main building, spectators roam through seven levels
joined by escalators. A rooftop glass pyramid 64 feet high encloses a
rain forest: a climate controlled re-creation of an entire neotropical
ecosystem that harbors two-toed sloths in the calabash trees, parrots
in the palms, iguanas on the ground, and red-bellied piranhas in a pool.
In the Marine Mammal Pavilion, seven Atlantic bottlenose dolphins
live in a 1.2-million-gallon pool surrounded by a 1,300-seat amphitheater; entertaining presentations highlighting the natural agility
and intelligence of these mammals take place several times a day. The
aquarium's famed Shark Tank and Atlantic Coral Reef exhibit recently reopened after multimillion-dollar refurbishings. Children may
handle such docile sea creatures as horseshoe crabs and starfish, under
the supervision of volunteer guides. ✉ *Pier Three,* ☎ *410/576–3810.*
🎫 *$11.95.* 🕐 *Open daily. Closed Thanksgiving and Dec. 25.*

㉑ **Nine Front Street.** This cute two-story brick town house, built in 1790,
was once the home of Mayor Thorowgood Smith. The Women's Civic
League restored it and maintains it as a visitor information center. ✉
9 Front St., ☎ *410/837–5424.* 🕐 *Tues.–Fri. 9:30–2:30.*

Old Otterbein United Methodist Church. In the shadow of the Baltimore
Convention Center is the oldest ecclesiastical building in Baltimore, the
Old Otterbein United Methodist Church, built in 1785. ✉ *112 W. Con-*
way St., ☎ *410/685-4703.* 🕐 *Sun. after services.*

㉔ **Peale Museum.** The oldest museum building in the United States, the
Peale Museum was built in 1814 by Rembrandt Peale to honor his father,
Charles Willson Peale. Today its attractions are temporary shows from
the museum collection and a permanent exhibition on Baltimore cultural and architectural history. The museum's prize possessions, 29 paintings by members of the Peale family, are displayed on the third floor.
✉ *225 Holliday St.,* ☎ *410/396–1149.* 🎫 *$2.* 🕐 *Daily 10–5.*

⑲ **Star-Spangled Banner House.** Built in 1793, this Federal-style home
was where Mary Pickersgill hand-sewed the 15-star, 15-stripe flag that
survived the British bombardment of Ft. McHenry in 1814 and inspired
Francis Scott Key. The house contains Federal furniture and American
art of the period. Outdoors, a map of the United States has been made
of stones from the various states. A museum connected to the house
tells the history of the War of 1812. ✉ *844 E. Pratt St.,* ☎ *410/837–*
1793. 🎫 *$4.* 🕐 *Tues.–Sat. 10–4.*

★ ⑯ **World Trade Center.** With 32 stories, this is the world's tallest pentag-
onal building. The 27th-floor observation deck (Top of the World) allows an unobstructed view of Baltimore and environs. Indoor exhibits
focus on local economic growth and on Baltimore's sister cities in other
nations. ✉ *401 E. Pratt St.,* ☎ *410/837–4515.* 🎫 *$2.50.* 🕐 *Mon.–Sat.*
10–5, Sun. noon–5. Extended hrs in summer.

Zion Lutheran Church. Site of the first Lutheran congregation in Baltimore (1755), this church near the Peale Museum offers some services
in German. ✉ *Holliday and Lexington Sts.,* ☎ *410/727-3939.*

West Baltimore

Despite their proximity to Inner Harbor, the neighborhoods farther west are often overlooked by first-time visitors to Baltimore. Yet some of the city's most colorful residents have lived in these working-class areas, where museums commemorate them today. Babe Ruth was born in a house that still stands as a museum to one of baseball's greatest; it's just a few blocks from Oriole Park at Camden Yards. Nearby are the former homes (now museums) of Baltimore's literary son, Edgar Allan Poe, and H. L. Mencken, the city's most famous journalist.

A Good Drive

Start this tour at Fayette and Greene streets, where the **Westminster Cemetery and Catacombs** ㉕ hold the remains of Edgar Allan Poe—perhaps Baltimore's most renowned literary figure. Less than a mile away—follow Greene Street north, turn left on Saratoga Street, and follow it just a few blocks to Amity Street—you'll find the **Poe House** ㉖, where Edgar Allan Poe wrote his first horror story.

Next, venture farther into the outskirts of town, toward the University of Maryland Hospital complex. Those of a medical bent will appreciate **Davidge Hall** ㉗, the oldest building in the Western Hemisphere used continuously for teaching medicine, and the adjacent **Dr. Samuel D. Harris National Museum of Dentistry** ㉘—a block away—the **B. Olive Cole Pharmacy Museum** ㉙, which recounts the history of pharmacies.

About a mile west of the Inner Harbor on Lombard Street, turn right (north) onto Stricker Street, go one block and turn left (west) onto Hollins Street, and go to the middle of the block to the **H. L. Mencken House** ㉚, home of the Baltimore journalist who ruled American letters from the 1920s to the 1940s, and one of Baltimore's leading cultural institutions.

Just south of Pratt Street, on Emory Street, is the **Babe Ruth Birthplace and Baseball Center** ㉛—only three blocks from Oriole Park. From there, drive west on Pratt Street to Martin Luther King Boulevard, turn left and go two blocks, then turn right onto Washington Boulevard. At the eighth traffic light, turn into Carroll Park on the right. At the top of the hill you'll find the **Mount Clare Museum House** ㉜, which once belonged to Charles Carroll–The Barrister, a member of the Continental Congress. Drive east along Pratt Street to the **B&O Railroad Museum** ㉝, the birthplace of railroading in America.

Timing

Several hours should suffice to cover all the sights on this tour. Reserve an extra hour around lunchtime to stroll among the food stands at Lexington Market. The tour is best done by car, as the sights are dispersed and the neighborhood is less safe than downtown Baltimore.

Sights To See

🤚 ㉛ **Babe Ruth Birthplace and Baseball Center.** This modest brick row house, just three blocks from Oriole Park at Camden Yards, was the birthplace of "The Bambino." Although Ruth was born here in 1895, his family never lived in the home; they lived in a nearby apartment, above a tavern run by Ruth's father. The row house has been furnished in a turn-of-the-century style, and the adjoining buildings make up a museum devoted to Ruth's life and to the local Orioles baseball club. Film clips, rare photos of Ruth, and many other artifacts can be found here. Orioles memorabilia, including bats and collectors items associated with shortstop Cal Ripken, will be moved to the Baseball Center near Camden Yards, a 28,000-square-foot, interactive museum slated to open by mid-1997. ✉ *216 Emory St.,* ☎ *410/727–1539.* ⌨ *$5.* ☺

Apr.–Oct., daily 10–5; Nov.–Mar., daily 10–4; until 7 on the days of Orioles home games.

③ ㉝ B&O Railroad Museum. The birthplace of the famous Baltimore and Ohio Railroad, this museum contains more than 120 full-size locomotives and a great collection of railroad memorabilia. The 1884 roundhouse (240 feet in diameter and 120 feet high) adjoins the world's first railroad station. From this station, the legendary race between the *Tom Thumb* (a working replica is inside) and the gray horse took place: Reportedly, the horse won when the *Tom Thumb* lost a fan belt. Samuel Morse's first transmission of Morse code, WHAT HATH GOD WROUGHT?, in 1844, passed through wires here, en route from Washington to the B&O Pratt Street Station. Train rides are available on weekends. ⊠ *901 W. Pratt St.,* ☎ *410/752–2490.* ⊠ *$6.* ⊙ *Daily 10–5.*

㉙ B. Olive Cole Pharmacy Museum. This endearing little museum contains a replica of an early 19th-century pharmacy and paintings that recount the history of pharmacies. ⊠ *650 W. Lombard St.,* ☎ *410/727–0746.* ⊠ *Free.* ⊙ *Weekdays by appointment.*

㉗ Davidge Hall. Built in 1812 for the sum total of $35,000, this green-domed structure has been used for teaching medicine for more than a century. Part of the downtown campus of the University of Maryland at Baltimore, Davidge Hall is undergoing partial restoration. The construction of a three-story Health Sciences Hall will link Davidge Hall to the new Samuel D. Harris National Museum of Dentistry, which opened in June, 1997. ⊠ *522 W. Lombard St.,* ☎ *410/706–7454.* ⊠ *Free.* ⊙ *Weekdays 8:30–4:45.*

㉘ Dr. Samuel D. Harris National Museum of Dentistry. Appropriately, this unusual museum, which displays George Washington's wooden dentures, is on the campus of the University of Maryland, the world's first dental school. Housed in a Roman Renaissance Revival–style building, the museum has exhibits on the anatomy and physiology of human and animal teeth and the history of dentistry. One popular exhibit displays the dental instruments used in treating Queen Victoria in the mid-19th century. ⊠ *31 Greene St.,* ☎ *410/706–0600.* ⊠ *$4.50.* ⊠ *Wed.–Sat. 10–4, Sun. 1–4.*

㉚ H. L. Mencken House. Baltimore's most famous journalist lived in this modest row house, about a mile west of the Inner Harbor. Known as the Sage of Baltimore, Mencken ruled American letters from the 1920s to the 1940s as author, editor, and columnist; at the height of his career he stood at the pinnacle of American culture. One of Baltimore's leading cultural institutions, the Mencken house is still full of Victorian flavor and is furnished with many of Mencken's favorite possessions, including his grand piano. One of the remaining life masks of Beethoven also can be found here. Of particular interest is Mencken's beloved garden—an English row-house garden restored to the pundit's own taste. ⊠ *1524 Hollins St.,* ☎ *410/396–7997.* ⊠ *$2.* ⊙ *Sat. 10–5, Sun. noon–5.*

㉜ Mount Clare Museum House. One of the oldest residences in Baltimore, this elegant Georgian mansion predates the American Revolution. The home was owned by Charles Carroll–The Barrister, formerly one of the major landowners in the state, author of the Maryland Declaration of Independence, and member of the Continental Congress. Begun in 1754, the state's first historic museum house has been carefully restored to its Georgian elegance; there are many original 18th-century furnishings, including rare pieces of Chippendale and Hepplewhite silver, crystal, and Chinese export porcelain. Washington, Lafayette, and John Adams are among the mansion's past guests. The greenhouses here are famous in their own right: They provided rare trees and plants for Washington's Mount Vernon. ⊠ *21230 Carroll Park,* ☎ *410/837–3262.* ☜ *$5.* ☉ *Tues.–Fri. 11–3, Sat.–Sun. 1–3.*

㉖ **Poe House.** Though the "Master of Macabre" only lived in this tiny row house three years, he wrote his first horror story, "Berenice," in the tiny garret chamber that's now furnished in an early 19th-century period style. Besides visiting this room, you can view changing exhibits and a video presentation about Poe's short, tempestuous life. The house was undergoing renovation in late 1996. ⊠ *203 N. Amity St.,* ☎ *410/396–7932.* ☜ *$3.* ☉ *Wed.–Sat. noon–3:45 p.m.*

㉕ **Westminster Cemetery and Catacombs.** The city's oldest cemetery is the final resting place of Edgar Allan Poe and other famous Marylanders, including 15 generals from the American Revolution and the War of 1812. Originally dating from 1786, the cemetery was known as the Old Western Burying Grounds. In the early 1850s a city ordinance demanded that burying grounds be part of a church. So, the building was constructed on arches above the cemetery, creating catacombs beneath the church. Poe's monument was donated from pennies collected by Baltimore schoolchildren in the 1930s. ⊠ *W. Fayette and Greene Sts.,* ☎ *410/706–2072.* ☉ *Daily dawn–dusk.*

NEED A
BREAK?

Lexington Market (⊠ Lexington and Eutaw Sts., ☎ 410/685–6169), founded in 1782, is the oldest, largest, and most famous of six city-owned markets. More than 130 vendors operate out of stalls, selling fresh meat, produce, seafood, baked goods, delicatessen items, poultry, and food products from around the world.

DINING

In 1859 Oliver Wendell Holmes, Sr., called Baltimore "the gastronomic metropolis of the Union." Although other cities' culinary reputations have eclipsed Baltimore's since then, this is certainly a city where it's easy to eat well. Baltimore's restaurants offer the cosmopolitan dining advantages that one commonly finds in major cities: dining rooms that stay open later (many kitchens operate until 10 PM, especially on weekends), a large number of restaurants within a compact central area, and a variety of ethnic cuisine, in some cases at very moderate prices.

If you're interested in local flavor, drive or take a taxi east from the Inner Harbor along Pratt Street to reach Little Italy, where there's a tempting concentration of authentic Italian restaurants near the intersection of Pratt and High streets.

American

$$$$ ✕ **McCafferty's.** Named for former Baltimore Colts coach Don McCafferty, this is a haven for fans of both pigskin and beef. The house specialty is aged prime beef; locals and visitors alike rave about its preparation. Other popular selections include lamb and salmon dishes, but what really draws attention is the restaurant's decor: Football helmets, signed baseballs, and jerseys are all on display. ⊠ *1501 Sulgrave Ave.,* ☎ *410/664–2200. AE, D, DC, MC, V. No lunch weekends.*

$$$$ ✕ **The Prime Rib.** Bustling and crowded, this dark dining room is just
★   north of Mount Vernon Square and only five minutes from Inner Harbor. Tables are set close together under a low ceiling, creating an intimate atmosphere well suited to bankers and lawyers, as well as couples on expensive dates. Consistently ranked among the city's best restaurants, the Prime Rib has a traditional menu headed by a sterling prime rib and an even better filet mignon; jumbo lump crab cakes are also

great here. The wine list is surprisingly short and predominantly Californian. ✉ *1101 N. Calvert St.,* ☎ *410/539–1804. Reservations essential. Jacket and tie. AE, D, DC, MC, V.*

$$$ ✗ **Joy America Cafe.** Chef Peter Zimmer presides over Baltimore's most
★ creative kitchen, which overlooks the harbor from the unusual American Visionary Art Museum. In a spare, open dining room of contemporary design, Zimmer offers museumgoers an appropriately unconventional seasonal menu that draws on the flavors of many countries, including dishes such as tropical fruit–barbecued halibut served with fresh peaches, bitter chocolate, and tomato-and-watermelon salsa. ✉ *American Visionary Art Museum, 800 Key Hwy,* ☎ *410/244–6500. AE, DC, MC, V.*

$$$ ✗ **Windows.** Picture windows allow diners to watch, from five floors up, the comings and goings in and around Inner Harbor. Less spectacular than the view, the dining room is tasteful and understated, and its tables are set far enough apart to ensure privacy at every meal. The contemporary American cuisine includes such seafood staples as salmon, swordfish, and crab cakes; a tortellini and shrimp scampi stir-fry is a favorite. Desserts are made fresh in the hotel. The wine list is heavily American—mostly Californian, with even a Maryland vintage—but France, Italy, and Germany are represented. ✉ *Renaissance Harborplace Hotel, 202 E. Pratt St.,* ☎ *410/547–1200. Reservations essential. AE, D, DC, MC, V.*

$ ✗ **Burke's Cafe and Comedy Club.** This Baltimore institution, situated at Light and Lombard streets, is famous for large, frosty mugs of beer and soda. Burke's gigantic burgers, homemade soups, oyster stew, sandwiches, salads, and the city's best onion rings make this a popular lunch spot, as well as a busy post-theater and post–baseball game retreat. It's open until the wee hours. ✉ *36 Light St., at Lombard St.,* ☎ *410/752–4189. AE, MC, V.*

$ ✗ **The Buttery.** On Mount Vernon Square, around the corner from the Walters Art Gallery and looking out at the Washington Monument, this 24-hour diner is a beloved institution in a neighborhood of artists and young professionals. At the counter, or in one of two rooms of booths, diners can order from the full menu at any time of day. Pancakes are the most dependable breakfast item, and are served with eggs, bacon, sausage, or ham. The triple-decker roast beef, turkey, and ham sandwiches are generously endowed. Coffee is always fresh, as is (notably in such a place) the seasonal fruit. Ice-cream sundaes and homemade pies are the most popular choices for dessert. ✉ *1 E. Centre St.,* ☎ *410/837–2494. No credit cards.*

Cajun

$ ✗ **Midtown Yacht Club.** Peanut shells litter the floor of this one-room saloon on Mount Vernon Square, which resounds every night until 2 AM with juke box music. Dartboards, pool tables, and video games offer entertaining alternatives to conversation. The menu, available until midnight, stands out from typical bar fare with its strong Cajun influence: Jambalaya, a rice dish with clams and mussels; and seafood gumbo, a crab-and-shrimp stew, are among the spicy New Orleans–style selections. For less daring palates, there are crab cakes, steamed shrimp, and burgers. Fifty brands of premium beer are available in bottles, and nine are on tap. ✉ *15 E. Centre St.,* ☎ *410/837–1300. AE, MC, V.*

Continental

$$$$ ✗ **Hamptons.** A panoramic view of Inner Harbor and the distinctive
★ National Aquarium building compete with the restaurant's elegant interior: Sheraton-style tables, set with bowls of dahlias, are spaced generously in a dining room styled after an English country house. Roasted rack of lamb with vegetable gratin, and breast of duck seared and served

with dauphinoise potato, are among recent additions to the menu. Seasonal choices include venison marinated and braised with endive, fennel, and basil oil. The major attraction on Sunday is the champagne brunch. Hamptons was named among the top 40 restaurants in the United States by *Condé Nast Traveler* magazine in 1995. ⊠ *Harbor Court Hotel, 550 Light St.,* ☎ *410/234–0550. Reservations essential. Jacket and tie. AE, D, DC, MC, V. Closed Mon.*

$$$ ✕ **Polo Grill.** Near the Johns Hopkins University campus, this place
★ has an appropriately masculine, dark decor with lots of wood and brass fittings; but it's still a warm and comfortable place for dinner. Hosts Leonard and Gail Kaplan live up to their strong reputation with popular dishes such as grilled veal chops in Madeira sauce, with mixed wild mushrooms and creamy polenta; and the Oriental-style barbecued salmon on warm spinach leaves and shiitake mushrooms. Fried lobster tail is the specialty. ⊠ *Inn at the Colonnade, 4 W. University Pkwy.,* ☎ *410/235–8200. Reservations essential. AE, D, DC, MC, V.*

French

$$$ ✕ **M. Gettier.** Chef-owner Michael Gettier, formerly the executive chef
★ at the well-known Conservatory Restaurant of the Peabody Court Hotel, has accomplished great things here. The decor is French provincial, the food sophisticated and decadent. You might find crown rack of lamb with green peppercorn sauce or fillet of rockfish with white alba truffle butter on the menu—if so, order them. Conclude your meal with bread pudding, considered among the best in Baltimore, or liqueur-laced strawberries Romanoff. ⊠ *505 S. Broadway,* ☎ *410/732-1151. Reservations essential. AE, DC, MC, V. Closed Sun.*

German

$$ ✕ **Haussner's.** Since its opening in 1926 this restaurant has been one
★ of Baltimore's favorite special-occasion spots: If you have but one meal in this city, it should be here. The restaurant doubles as a gallery, with walls adorned with works of art by Van Dyck, Whistler, Bierstadt, Rembrandt, Elsley, and Gainsborough, to name but a few. Sculpture, statuary, ceramics, silver, and crystal fill the cabinets that border the rooms. But Haussner's fine food and reasonable prices are the real drawing card. More than 80 freshly prepared items appear on the menu, and there are dozens of vegetables to choose from. While German specialties and wild game are featured, there is something to satisfy anyone's taste, especially at dessert time. Haussner's strawberry pie is an all-time favorite; and the pastries you'll see as you enter will tempt you before you've even ordered your meal. Many of the waitresses, clad in their fresh white attire, are as much an institution as the restaurant—some have worked here for 40 years or more. ⊠ *3244 Eastern Ave.,* ☎ *410/327–8365. Reservations not accepted. AE, D, DC, MC, V. Closed Sun. and Mon.*

Greek

$$ ✕ **Acropolis.** Greektown, 15 minutes by cab from the major hotels, has
★ ethnic restaurants that cost less than those in Little Italy to the west. In this festive, informal restaurant, you'll find murals and music of Greece, and a clientele composed largely of families. Portions are generous, with rockfish and red snapper leading the fresh seafood menu. Try shrimp oregano—jumbo shrimp sautéed in white wine and served over rice pilaf; or Lamb Giouvetsi—baby lamb braised in olive oil and baked with orzo, with a sauce of tomatoes, green peppers, and onions. ⊠ *4718 Eastern Ave.,* ☎ *410/675–3384. AE, D, DC, MC, V.*

Indian

$$ ✕ **Akbar.** A few steps below street level on the business-and-retail Charles Street corridor, this small restaurant is usually crowded and always filled with pungent aromas and the sounds of Indian music. Among the vegetarian dishes, *alu gobi masala,* a potato-and-cauliflower creation, is prepared with onions, tomatoes, and spices. Tandoori chicken is marinated in yogurt, herbs, and strong spices, then barbecued in a charcoal clay oven. ✉ *823 N. Charles St.,* ☎ *410/539–0944. AE, D, DC, MC, V.*

Italian

$$$$ ✕ **Da Mimmo.** From Inner Harbor, it's a five-minute cab ride east to Little Italy, whose neighborhood restaurants are more expensive than the quaint location might suggest. Da Mimmo is the most worthwhile, even though the dining room can be noisy and the tables are too close together. Diners keep the reservations book filled for the cuisine alone, although there is nightly piano music and live entertainment. The seafood entrées are led by shrimp and red snapper. Veal is prepared with rosemary and sage, and portions are large. Like the menu, the list of Italian wines is the best in the neighborhood. ✉ *217 S. High St.,* ☎ *410/727–6876. Reservations essential. AE, DC, MC, V.*

$$$ ✕ **The Brass Elephant.** The rooms of this grand pre–Civil War house
★ on Charles Street are filled with classical music and the chatter of diners (the Teak Room is the quietest, the Oak Room the noisiest). An atrium meant to suggest a Venetian café has moss painted on pink walls, and the rest of the decor, including the elephant sconces, is just as remarkable. So is the northern Italian menu. Veal Valdostano, a favorite of the owner and chef, is a cutlet sautéed with butter, shallots, mushrooms, cream, white wine, and Fontina cheese. Hot antipasto is an unusual treat. ✉ *924 N. Charles St.,* ☎ *410/547–8480. Reservations essential. AE, DC, MC, V.*

Japanese

$$ ✕ **Kawasaki.** Amid art galleries and shops, this lively dining room is a good setting for a convivial dinner. Though the menu offers the familiar teriyaki and tempura dishes, the standouts are sushi and sashimi, whose preparation can be watched at the sushi bar in the front dining room; some people say it's the best sushi in town. ✉ *413 N. Charles St.,* ☎ *410/659–7600. AE, DC, MC, V. Closed Sun.*

Mexican

$$ ✕ **Lista's.** Owners Kathy and Ruben Evangelista have struck the right chord with their "new Mexican" restaurant, whose popularity has certainly been helped along by its dockside location. The water taxi that runs between the Inner Harbor and nearby Fells Point shuttles patrons to the door. Once you've settled in with a margarita and chosen from the variety of fish, chicken, and more traditional Mexican dishes (all rated for spiciness with one to four chili peppers), you can scan the displays of southwestern arts and crafts, which are available for sale. ✉ *1637 Thames St.,* ☎ *410/327–0040. AE, D, DC, MC, V.*

Seafood

$$ ✕ **Bertha's.** All over the region, visitors who see the bumper sticker "Eat Bertha's Mussels"—come here to find out why that curious slogan is so enthusiastically displayed. This family-run establishment on Fells Point, first opened as a bar in 1972, has gradually expanded into two cozy but spacious dining rooms. The unusual menu partially reflects the Caledonian heritage of one of the married proprietors: Scottish afternoon tea, offered every day but Sunday, is a rich array of Scotch eggs (hard-boiled eggs deep-fried with a sausage coating); sausages baked

Baltimore Dining and Lodging

141

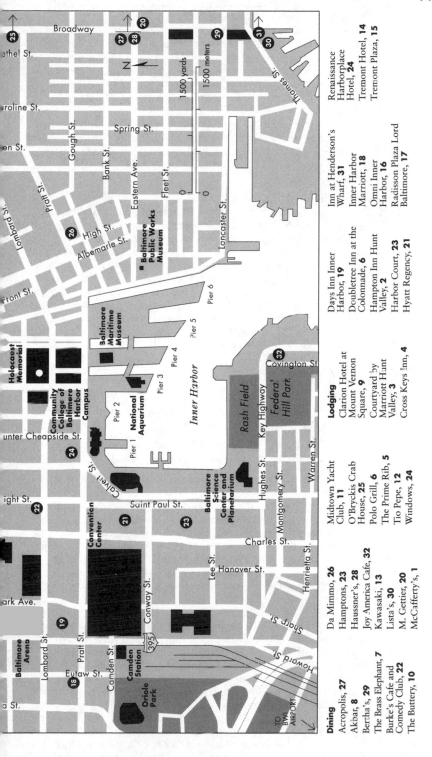

Dining

Acropolis, **27**
Akbar, **8**
Bertha's, **29**
The Brass Elephant, **7**
Burke's Cafe and Comedy Club, **22**
The Buttery, **10**
Da Mimmo, **26**
Hamptons, **23**
Haussner's, **28**
Joy America Cafe, **32**
Kawasaki, **13**
Lista's, **30**
M. Gettier, **20**
McCafferty's, **1**
Midtown Yacht Club, **11**
O'Bryckis Crab House, **25**
Polo Grill, **6**
The Prime Rib, **5**
Tio Pepe, **12**
Windows, **24**

Lodging

Clarion Hotel at Mount Vernon Square, **9**
Courtyard by Marriott Hunt Valley, **3**
Cross Keys Inn, **4**
Days Inn Inner Harbor, **19**
Doubletree Inn at the Colonnade, **6**
Hampton Inn Hunt Valley, **2**
Harbor Court, **23**
Hyatt Regency, **21**
Inn at Henderson's Wharf, **31**
Inner Harbor Marriott, **18**
Omni Inner Harbor, **16**
Radisson Plaza Lord Baltimore, **17**
Renaissance Harborplace Hotel, **24**
Tremont Hotel, **14**
Tremont Plaza, **15**

in dough blankets; cheese-tomato pasties; fresh-baked scones with lemon, jam, and butter; and various dessert pastries. On the main menu, the ballyhooed mussels are the outstanding item. They come steamed, with a choice of eight butter-based sauces such as a garlic sauce with capers, or—in late summer through fall—a basil-pesto sauce made with homegrown basil. ⊠ *734 S. Broadway,* ☎ *410/327–5795. Reservations essential for tea, not accepted at other times. MC, V.*

$$ ✕ **O'Bryckis Crab House.** Here, pictures of early 1900s Baltimore cover the walls, which are painted to give the illusion of pealing plaster and exposed brick. For 50 years this has been Baltimore's crab house of choice; once you taste the steamed crabs and crab cakes you'll understand why. ⊠ *1727 E. Pratt St.,* ☎ *410/732–6399. AE, D, DC, MC, V.*

Spanish

$$$$ ✕ **Tio Pepe.** Candles illuminate the whitewashed walls of these cellar
★   dining rooms, which are usually hopping (the Shawl Room is quietest), and the menu represents all regions of Spain. The staple is paella à la Valenciana (chicken, sausage, shrimp, clams, and mussels with saffron rice); a less well-known Basque recipe for red snapper includes clams, mussels, asparagus, and boiled egg. For appetizers, be certain to sample the mushrooms from the caves of Segovia, and the shrimp scampi. The short but diverse wine list has many Spanish vintages, and there is a more expensive reserve list. Make reservations well in advance. ⊠ *10 E. Franklin St.,* ☎ *410/539–4675. Reservations essential. Jacket and tie at dinner. AE, DC, MC, V.*

LODGING

All hotels listed are within a short drive or a half-hour's walk of Inner Harbor. Lodging reservations must be made well in advance for Preakness weekend, the third weekend in May.

Prices are for a standard double room, excluding service charge. (☞ The Baltimore price chart *in* How to Use This Book.)

$$$$ 🏨 **Harbor Court.** In spite of its less central location on the west side of
★   Inner Harbor, this well-managed, eight-story, redbrick tower built in 1986 has become the most prestigious transient address in Baltimore. The decor is ersatz English country house à la Ralph Lauren. Guests enter the hotel through a brick courtyard. A grand, curving staircase dominates the lobby; a ground-floor "library" stocked with collectors' editions and dominated by a Chinese lacquer screen is the domain of a concierge who personifies an obliging staff. The luxurious guest rooms are adorned with 18th-century English landscapes and portraits; bathrooms have marble floors. The staterooms (business-class accommodations) are distinguished by canopied four-posters. Suites have wood parquet floors. The most desirable (and most expensive) rooms have a harbor view. Courtyard rooms are quietest. ⊠ *550 Light St., 21202,* ☎ *410/234–0550 or 800/824–0076,* 📠 *410/659–5925. 195 rooms, 8 suites. 2 restaurants, bar, indoor pool, sauna, tennis court, exercise room, racquetball. AE, D, DC, MC, V.*

$$$$ 🏨 **Inner Harbor Marriott.** This 10-story hotel, one of the city's largest, has nondescript contemporary public areas that are surprisingly quiet. Many of the rooms are decorated with black-and-white nature photographs and make prominent use of the color jade. The best views are from those that face the Inner Harbor and Camden Yards, which is just a few blocks away. Guests on the 10th floor enjoy concierge-level privileges such as bathrobe and shoeshine. ⊠ *Pratt and Eutaw Sts., 21201,* ☎ *410/962–0202 or 800/228–9290,* 📠 *410/962–8585.*

525 rooms, 14 suites. Restaurant, bar, indoor pool, sauna, exercise room. AE, D, DC, MC, V.

$$$$ 🏨 **Renaissance Harborplace Hotel.** The most conveniently located of Baltimore hotels—across the street from the shopping pavilions, where the Inner Harbor area renaissance began—the Renaissance Harborplace meets the needs of tourists, business travelers, and conventioneers alike. While the guest-room decor is light and cheerful, the furnishings—oversize pieces of stained mahogany veneer accented with brass—take up an inordinate amount of space. Rooms with a harbor view are the most popular. Guests on the 12th-floor concierge level, accessible only by card-key, enjoy free breakfast and snacks (and cocktails at a charge) in a staffed club room. ⊠ *202 E. Pratt St., 21202,* ☎ *410/547–1200 or 800/468–3571,* 🖷 *410/539–5780. 622 rooms, 60 suites. Restaurant, bar, indoor pool, sauna, exercise room. AE, D, DC, MC, V.*

$$$ 🏨 **Clarion Hotel at Mount Vernon Square.** Formerly the Latham Hotel, this 13-story building, built as an apartment house in 1924, faces the Washington Monument in Mount Vernon Square, with churches, museums, restaurants, and the Peabody Conservatory of Music in the immediate neighborhood. The hotel has undergone renovation under new ownership, including the building of a mezzanine-level food court to replaced the Citronelle restaurant—but the original distinguished lobby and dark wood paneled library remain. Business travelers will be at home here, since rooms have desks and office supplies, and a lobby business center has a fax machine, copier, and computer station. Rooms with park views are the best choice. ⊠ *612 Cathedral St., 21201,* ☎ *410/727–7101,* 🖷 *410/789–3312. 103 rooms. AE, D, DC, MC, V.*

$$$ 🏨 **Doubletree Inn at the Colonnade.** Directly across the street from Johns Hopkins University, within walking distance of the Baltimore Museum of Art, and just 10 minutes north of downtown, this suburban inn couldn't be more centrally located. Rooms are welcoming, with rich, warm furnishings, and there are extras such as an indoor swimming pool, whirlpools, and complimentary transportation to center-city destinations. ⊠ *4 W. University Pkwy., 21218,* ☎ *410/235–5400,* 🖷 *410/235–5572. 125 rooms and suites. Restaurant, lobby lounge, indoor pool, business services, meeting rooms. AE, DC, MC, V.*

$$$ 🏨 **Hyatt Regency.** This stretch of Light Street is practically a highway, but the unenclosed skyways allow ready pedestrian access to the Harborplace mall and the convention center. Despite its downtown location, the Hyatt resembles nothing more than an airport hotel; the reserved, though polite, staff does little to dispel the somewhat desolate atmosphere. Over the past few years the public areas have lost some of their original shine and glitz, but the lobby still has glass elevators and the chain's trademark atrium. Guest rooms have basic furnishings and desks. Room views are of the harbor or the city. The 12th floor is the club level, with free Continental breakfast and hors d'oeuvres available. ⊠ *300 Light St., 21202,* ☎ *410/528–1234 or 800/233–1234,* 🖷 *410/685–3362. 487 rooms, 9 suites. 2 restaurants, bar, pool, sauna, 3 tennis courts, exercise room. AE, D, DC, MC, V.*

$$$ 🏨 **Inn at Henderson's Wharf.** Built in the mid-1800s as a B&O Railroad tobacco warehouse, this is a richly decorated, warmly inviting bed-and-breakfast–style accommodation with waterfront or garden views from all of its 38 rooms. It is situated at the water's edge in historic Fells Point, less than a mile from Baltimore's Inner Harbor and linked by water taxi. A complimentary European breakfast is offered, and the entire inn is pleasantly smoke free. Adjacent to the inn is the Fells Point Marina, with slips to 150 feet; all possible amenities are available to visiting yachtsmen. Plenty of nightlife is also nearby. ⊠ *1000 Fell St., Fells Point 21231,* ☎ *410/522–7777 or 800/522–2088,* 🖷 *410/522–*

7087. *38 rooms. Exercise room, concierge, meeting rooms. AE, DC, MC, V.*

$$$ 🏨 **Omni Inner Harbor.** Baltimore's largest accommodation, with more than 700 rooms in twin towers, also houses the largest ballroom in the city, making the hotel especially popular with conventioneers. More than its rooms, the Omni is known for its fine restaurants. A $15-million renovation in 1991 brought wining and dining to the fore with the Corner Bar, which offers light dining and a Library of Liquors (complete with ladder for the top shelf). At Jackie's you can get light fare all day, including eggs and designer pizza. The Baltimore Grille, which draws crowds for its Sunday-brunch buffet, is a classic steak house featuring grilled seafood, steak, poultry, and wild game, all served with 22 condiments from a tableside cart. In 1991 the restaurant received the *Wine Spectator* magazine award for its extensive collection of wines—more than 220 vintages are available, many by the glass. ✉ *101 W. Fayette St., 21201,* ☎ *410/752–1100,* 📠 *410/752–0832. 707 rooms, 6 suites. 2 restaurants, bar, pool, exercise room. AE, D, DC, MC, V.*

$$$ 🏨 **Radisson Plaza Lord Baltimore.** Built in 1928, this 23-story hotel is distinguished by its cavernous Art Deco lobby, whose dark green walls, set off by elaborately carved brown-and-gold moldings, are dimly lit by frosted-glass sconces. The Jazz Age elegance does not extend to the guest rooms, which are somewhat cramped. Rooms on the south side have the best view, and from the top three floors you can see the water. Rooms on the east side, with views of a wall and an alley, are the least desirable. The hotel is quiet, clean, and comfortable, and its location is central. A restaurant serves three meals a day; the lobby bar hosts ethnic happy hours (Mexican on Wednesday, Italian on Thursday, etc.). ✉ *20 W. Baltimore St., 21202,* ☎ *410/539–8400,* 📠 *410/625– 1060. 416 rooms, 4 suites. 2 restaurants, bar, sauna, exercise room. AE, D, DC, MC, V.*

$$$ 🏨 **Tremont Hotel.** Built in the 1960s as an apartment house on a quiet
★   downtown block, the 13-story Tremont was renovated in 1983 to become a small European-style hostelry with an elegant home-away-from-home ambience. The lobby and the hotel's 8 East restaurant are intimate and private—qualities that attract guests who might be easily recognized. Like the Tremont Plaza, which is owned by the same company, the hotel has only suites; they come in two sizes, all with kitchen, microwave, toaster oven, and coffeemaker. A view to the north, which includes the Washington Monument, is more impressive than the view of shady Pleasant Street. The level of service is unsurpassed by that of any other hotel in town: The concierge will arrange local transportation, in most cases free of charge. Staff will also do guests' personal shopping (groceries, clothing). Room phones have conference and speaker functions. ✉ *8 E. Pleasant St., 21202,* ☎ *410/576–1200,* 📠 *410/244–1154. 60 suites. Restaurant, bar, kitchenettes. AE, D, DC, MC, V.*

$$ 🏨 **Cross Keys Inn.** In a quiet, wooded part of the village of Cross Keys, about 10 minutes north of downtown, this inn is a respite from the bustle of the city. Accommodations are steps from shops, boutiques, and restaurants. The Sunday Champagne Brunch offered at the Crossroads Restaurant is legendary: Arrive early, as folks line up well in advance. Dinners at Crossroads are also good. The inn offers complimentary van service within a 15-minute radius, which hits most of Baltimore's main attractions. There's free parking and a secluded pool. ✉ *5100 Falls Rd., Cross Keys 21210,* ☎ *410/532–6900,* 📠 *410/532–2403. 148 rooms. Restaurant, lobby lounge, pool, meeting rooms. AE, DC, MC, V.*

$ ⊡ **Courtyard by Marriott Hunt Valley.** About 15 minutes from downtown, in an affluent suburb that is a growing corporate center, this motel provides comfortable and affordable chain lodging. The simple guest rooms are as standardized as Courtyard's signature white-stucco exterior; a coffee service, including cups and hot water, is the only unusual touch in the rooms. The neighbors are office buildings, which means that all rooms enjoy quiet nights but uninteresting views. ⊠ *221 International Circle, Hunt Valley 21030,* ☎ *410/584–7070,* FAX *410/584–8151. 146 rooms, 12 suites. Restaurant, bar, indoor pool, hot tub, exercise room. AE, D, DC, MC, V.*

$ ⊡ **Days Inn Inner Harbor.** Less than three blocks from the Inner Harbor and the baseball stadium, this nine-story redbrick building, built in 1984, provides reliable and relatively economical accommodations in the center of town. The mostly lavender guest rooms are sparsely furnished, but each has a small desk, a television (some with remote control), and a refrigerator. Rooms on the west side have views of the stadium. ⊠ *100 Hopkins Pl., 21201,* ☎ *410/576–1000,* FAX *410/576–9437. 250 rooms, 8 suites. Restaurant, bar, refrigerators, pool. AE, D, DC, MC, V.*

$ ⊡ **Hampton Inn Hunt Valley.** Built in 1986, this seven-story building stands across the road from a farmer's market and is next door to a restaurant, about a 15-minute drive from downtown. The guest rooms are simply and brightly decorated, with mauve carpets and bedspreads. Furniture is basic: The only extra is a small refrigerator. Free coffee is served, and on Tuesday and Thursday from 5:30 to 7 there are free cocktails. Rates include Continental breakfast. ⊠ *11200 York Rd., Hunt Valley 21031,* ☎ *410/527–1500,* FAX *410/771–0819. 126 rooms. Refrigerators. AE, D, DC, MC, V.*

$ ⊡ **Tremont Plaza.** In 1984 this 37-story apartment building in the
★   densest part of the business district was converted into a hotel. The building's plain gray facade and the minuscule brass-and-marble lobby belie the tasteful guest rooms decorated in earthtones. Like its sister property, the Tremont Hotel one block north, this is a suite hotel; all units—there are six sizes to choose from—have kitchens with a microwave, toaster oven, and coffeemaker. The best views, of the city and the small park in the center of St. Paul Place, are from rooms numbered 06. The concierge floors (30 and above) have larger rooms, and their guests receive free breakfast and cocktails. The restaurant Tugs has a nautical theme and a menu rich in seafood, but the hotel's major culinary distinction is its gourmet delicatessen, judged the best in town by readers of *Baltimore* magazine. ⊠ *222 St. Paul Pl., 21202,* ☎ *410/727–2222,* FAX *410/685–4215. 253 suites. Restaurant, bar, kitchenettes, pool, sauna, exercise room. AE, D, DC, MC, V.*

NIGHTLIFE AND THE ARTS

Events listings appear in the "Maryland Live" Thursday supplement to the *Baltimore Sun*; the monthly *Baltimore* magazine; and the *City Paper,* a free weekly distributed in shops and street-corner machines.

Bars and Lounges

"Pub crawling" is a popular pastime in Fells Point, where the young professionals who call the neighborhood home mingle with visitors from throughout the city and surrounding areas. Many of the bars have outdoor or rooftop tables and serve domestic and local brews. Most also have notable bar food, often including a seafood specialty. Entertainment runs the musical gamut from rock and reggae to jazz and blues.

In the **Explorer's Lounge,** at the Harbor Court Hotel (⊠ 550 Light St., ☎ 410/234–0550), the most remarkable sights are the elephants and monkeys in the murals, and the eclectic furnishings include elephant tusks and leopard-skin chairs that might have been collected by a 19th-century great white hunter. A pianist performs every night, and on Friday and Saturday nights there's a full jazz band.

COMEDY

Slapstix Comedy Club (⊠ 34 Market Pl., ☎ 410/659–7527) is one of the best. Also try **Shamrock Pub and Comedy Club** (⊠ 102 Water St., ☎ 410/576–8558).

BLUES

8x10 (⊠ 8 E. Cross St., ☎ 410/625–2000) emphasizes the blues, yet rock and occasional jazz can be heard here as well.

SPORTS BARS

At **Balls** (⊠ 200 W. Pratt St., ☎ 410/659–5844), fans banter about trivia, dispute scores, and commiserate over cheating scandals while watching sports programming on the telescreen.

Film

The **Baltimore Museum of Art** (⊠ Art Museum Dr., ☎ 410/396–7100) screens themed repertory programs. The **Enoch Pratt Free Library** (⊠ 400 Cathedral St., ☎ 410/396–5430) is another venue for specialty films.

Music

Meyerhoff Symphony Hall (⊠ 1212 Cathedral St., ☎ 410/783–8000) is the city's principal concert hall and the home of the Baltimore Symphony Orchestra, led by maestro David Zinman.

Theater

Center Stage (⊠ 700 N. Calvert St., ☎ 410/685–3200), the state theater of Maryland, has performed works by Shakespeare and Samuel Beckett.

Fells Point Corner Theater (⊠ 251 S. Ann St., ☎ 410/276–7837), a center for acting and directing workshops, stages eight off-Broadway productions a year, with performances on weekends.

Lyric Theater (⊠ 140 W. Mt. Royal Ave., ☎ 410/685–5086) hosts plays and musicals in addition to opera productions.

Morris A. Mechanic Theatre (⊠ Baltimore and Charles Sts., ☎ 410/625–4230) houses road shows of Broadway hits and serves as a testing ground for Broadway-bound productions.

Friedberg Hall (⊠ E. Mount Vernon Pl. and Charles St., ☎ 410/659–8124), part of the Peabody Conservatory of Music, is the scene of recitals, concerts, and opera performances by students, faculty, and distinguished guests.

Pier Six Concert Pavilion (⊠ Pier Six at Pratt St., ☎ 410/752-8632) began more than 10 years ago as a temporary summer-entertainment venue, but was rebuilt in 1991. It is now open May–September.

Spotlighters Theater (⊠ 817 St. Paul St., ☎ 410/752–1225) stages a variety of works ranging from Shakespeare to musicals; there is one production a month, with performances on weekends.

Vagabond Players (⊠ 806 S. Broadway, ☎ 410/563–9135) perform recent Broadway hits throughout the year, on Friday, Saturday, and Sunday.

OUTDOOR ACTIVITIES AND SPORTS

Participant Sports

Bicycling

Best Bike Routes in Maryland is a series of 10 well-documented maps of on-road and off-road touring routes throughout Maryland. The color-coded, waterproof, and tearproof maps are available, for $9.95 each or $29.95 for the set, at area bookstores, bicycle shops, and by mail order (⊠ Box 16388, Baltimore, MD 21210, ☎ 410/685–3626).

Baltimore and Annapolis Trail Park (⊠ Rte. 50 in Arnold to Dorsey Rd., ☎ 410/222–6244) includes 13.3 mi of paved trails, open space, bridges, and woodlands.

Northern Central Railroad Hike and Bike Trail is a 21-mi trail that extends along the old railroad to the Maryland–Pennsylvania line, beginning at Ashland Road, just east of York Road, and heading north 20 mi to the Pennsylvania border. Parking is available at seven points along the way. It was on this line that President Lincoln rode to deliver the Gettysburg Address and on which—after his assassination—his body was carried to Gettysburg and on to Illinois, his home state. For more information and a map, write or call Gunpowder Falls State Park (⊠ Box 480, Kingsville, MD 21087, ☎ 410/592–2897).

Canoeing

Springriver Corp. (⊠ 6434 Baltimore National Pike, ☎ 410/788–3377) offers daily canoe and kayak rentals for use on bay tributaries and lakes in the region.

Fishing

Annual licenses ($7–$12) are available at many sporting-goods stores or from the **Maryland Department of Natural Resources** (⊠ 580 Taylor Ave., Annapolis 21404, ☎ 410/974–3211).

The Fishin' Shop (⊠ 9026C Pulaski Hwy., ☎ 410/391-0101) and **Tochterman's** (⊠ 1925 Eastern Ave., ☎ 410/327–6942) are bait-and-tackle shops that can also provide personal guides for fly-fishing and other fishing.

Golf

Carroll Park (⊠ Monroe St. and Washington Blvd., ☎ 410/685–8344) has 12 holes. The following courses all have 18 holes: **Clifton Park** (⊠ Harford Rd. and St. Lo Dr., ☎ 410/243–3500); **Forest Park** (⊠ 2900 Hillsdale Rd., ☎ 410/448–4653); **Mount Pleasant** (6101 Hillen Rd., ☎ 410/254–5100); **Pine Ridge** (⊠ Dulaney Valley Rd., ☎ 410/252–1408).

Health and Fitness Clubs

A few clubs offer temporary membership to transients. Your hotel may provide this as a courtesy, so ask the concierge. Of hotels, the **Harbor Court** has by far the best athletic facilities.

At the **Downtown Athletic Club** (⊠ 210 E. Centre St., ☎ 410/332–0906), guests of area hotels pay an $18 daily fee to play squash and racquetball and to use the indoor pool and exercise equipment.

Jogging

One conveniently located, scenic area is **Rash Field,** on the south side of Inner Harbor, adjacent to the Science Center and Federal Hill Park. Many conventioneers jog around the promenade at Baltimore's Inner Harbor, or on the path at the water's edge at Ft. McHenry.

Tennis

Though there are several city maintained courts around town, serious tennis players will be better off using the various hotel courts (☞ Lodging, *above*). **Carroll Park** (⊠ Monroe St. and Washington Blvd., ☎ 410/396–5828) has six courts. **Clifton Park** (⊠ Harford Rd. and St. Lo Dr., ☎ 410/396–6101) has nine courts. **Druid Hill Park** (⊠ Druid Hill Lake Dr., ☎ 410/396–6106) has 24 courts. **Patterson Park** (⊠ Eastern Ave., ☎ 410/396–3774) has 10 courts.

Water Sports

Springriver Corp. (⊠ 6434 Baltimore National Pike, ☎ 410/788–3377) has sea kayaks and white-water kayaks, in addition to rafts and canoes for hire.

Trident Electric Boats (⊠ Aquarium Dock, Harborplace, ☎ 410/539–1837) rents eight-foot, two- or three-passenger electric-powered craft for cruising the Inner Harbor waters.

Spectator Sports

The **USAir Arena** (☎ 410/792–7490), less than an hour away from Baltimore, in Landover, is the home of the Washington Bullets (basketball) and the Washington Capitals (hockey).

Baseball

The **Orioles** (☎ 410/685–9800), a sometime contender in the American League East division, play their home games at Oriole Park at Camden Yards, from early April until early October.

Lacrosse

The **Thunder** (☎ 410/347–2090) are members of the Major Indoor Lacrosse League, competing from January to March in the Baltimore Arena (⊠ 201 W. Baltimore St., ☎ 410/347–2020).

Outdoor high school and college lacrosse are very popular and fiercely played in spring. The **Johns Hopkins University team** is a perennial favorite; their games are played at the Homewood Field (⊠ Charles St. and University Pkwy.). Another hometown favorite is the **Loyola Greyhounds,** whose games are played at the Loyola campus (⊠ Charles St. and Cold Spring La.).

Soccer

The **Spirit** (☎ 410/625–2320), a team in the Eastern Division of the Major Soccer League, plays from October to April at the Baltimore Arena.

SHOPPING

Shopping Districts

The Pratt Street and Light Street pavilions of **Harborplace** (☎ 410/332–4191), together with The Gallery, just across Pratt Street, contain almost 200 specialty shops that sell everything from business attire to children's toys; markets for gourmet food, wine, and flowers; and 60 eating places ranging from fast-food stalls to expensive restaurants.

Owings Mills Town Center (☎ 410/363–1234), at the Owings Mills exit from I–795, includes Macy's and Hecht's; smaller specialty clothing stores; and shoe, toy, and book stores. Both fast-food and formal restaurants are among the mall's numerous eating places. The mall is near the northern end of the metro.

Towson Town Center (⊠ Dulaney Valley Rd. and Fairmount Ave., in Towson, ½ mi south of I–695 at Exit 27A, ☎ 410/494–8800) has nearly

200 specialty shops within a one-million-square-foot shopping space, making it one of the mid-Atlantic region's largest malls. Hecht's and Nordstrom are the center's main department stores.

Village of Cross Keys (✉ 5100 Falls Rd., ☎ 410/323–1000), about 6 mi from downtown off I–83, has an eclectic collection of 30 boutiques and stores ranging from women's, men's, and children's clothing shops to a flower store, and restaurants. The open-air court offers an alternative to fluorescent-lighted, enclosed shopping malls and is often visited by families on weekends and—during the week—by businesspeople staying at the Cross Keys Inn (☎ 410/532–6900). Occasional outdoor spring and summer concerts and promotional events are held in the courtyard.

Department Stores

Hecht's: Golden Ring Mall (☎ 410/574–1600), Marley Station (☎ 410/766–2055), Owings Mills Town Center (☎ 410/363–7700), Towson Town Center (☎ 410/337–3600), White Marsh Mall (☎ 410/931–2000).

Macy's: Marley Station (☎ 410/760–2100), Owings Mills Town Center (☎ 410/363–7400), White Marsh Mall (☎ 410/931–7000).

Nordstroms: Towson Town Center (☎ 410/494-9111), Annapolis Mall (☎ 410/573-1121).

Food Markets

All year long the following indoor food markets, which are all at least 100 years old, accommodate vendors of fresh fish, fowl, meat, and produce: **Belair Market** (✉ Gay and Fayette Sts.), **Broadway Market** (✉ Broadway and Fleet St.), **Cross Street Market** (✉ Light and Cross Sts.), **Hollins Market** (✉ Hollins and Arlington Sts.), **Lexington Market** (✉ Lexington and Eutaw Sts.), and **Northeast Market** (✉ Monument and Chester Sts.). Lexington Market is the largest and most famous, but all feature fresh, taste-tempting foods for on-premise consumption.

Specialty Stores

Antiques

Gaines McHale Antiques and Home (✉ 836 Leadenhall St., ☎ 410/625–1900) brings new meaning to the word "recycling." Owners Jean and Mike McHale build new pieces with old wood. Among their specialties is turning antique armoires into entertainment centers, wet bars, computer desks, and other furniture that fits the needs of the '90s.

Books

Bibelot (✉ Festival at Woodholme Center, 1819 Reisterstown Rd., ☎ 410/653-6933), with more than 100,000 books, manages to retain a welcoming atmosphere. Besides books, the 25,000-square-foot store has a large selection of magazines, newspapers, and compact discs and cassettes. Authors regularly show up to read from their works. There's an Italian coffee bar within the store.

Kelmscott Bookshop (✉ 32–34 W. 25th St., ☎ 410/235–6810) is known internationally for its enormous, well-preserved stock of old and rare volumes in every major category, especially art, architecture, American and English literature, and travel. The books are clearly organized in 12 rooms on two floors of two converted town houses. The shop also provides a diligent search service for out-of-print titles.

Gifts

Crafts Concepts (✉ Greenspring Station, Falls and Joppa Rds., ☎ 410/823–2533) is a good place to find unusual birthday, wedding, or house-warming gifts. Of particular note are the handmade ceramic vases and plates, and the unique hand-woven and hand-painted women's clothing and handmade jewelry.

The Store Ltd. (✉ Village of Cross Keys, ☎ 410/323–2350) is actually a retail museum of top-quality (and pricey) collections, including handcrafted jewelry designs by local artist Betty Cook, reproduction calendars, stationery, and women's sportswear. You'll also find state-of-the-art kitchen gadgets, coffee-table books, hats, whimsical lawn items, and lifelike stuffed animals.

Jewelry

Marley Gallery of Contemporary Jewelry, Inc. (✉ Festival at Woodholme Gallery, 1809 Reisterstown Rd., Pikesville, ☎ 410/486–6686) offers a unique selection of fine designer jewelry from leading contemporary artists, and original designs by Marley Simon. All work is done in-house.

Men's Clothing

Jos. A. Bank's Clothiers (✉ 100 E. Pratt St., ☎ 410/547-1700) is a nearly century-old Baltimore institution that features men's tailored clothing and casual ware.

Women's Clothing

Bare Necessities (✉ 10751 Falls Road, ☎ 410/583–1383) received the "Baltimore's Best" award for its tasteful selection of women's lingerie and accessories in 1995, and it's still going strong.

Ruth Shaw (☎ 410/532–7886), **Octavia** (☎ 410/323–1652), and **Jones and Jones** (☎ 410/532–9645), all in the Village of Cross Keys, carry women's clothing on a par—in both style and price—with New York's 5th Avenue boutiques. Among the three you'll find such genres as cruise wear, formal evening attire, and casual dress sold by stylish sales people.

The White House, Inc. (✉ Pratt St. Pavilion at Harborplace (☎ 410/659–0283; Owings Mills Town Center, ☎ 410/363–0036) began in 1985 at Harborplace and now has about 40 stores throughout the country. The boutique carries white—and only white—clothing, lingerie, and accessories for women, as well as pearl and crystal jewelry and other gift items.

SIDE TRIPS FROM BALTIMORE

Not far from Baltimore, Maryland's landscape is dotted with well-preserved 18th- and 19th-century towns. In Harford County, Havre de Grace, at the top of the bay, and nearby Aberdeen, with its legacy of military history, make for an ideal day trip.

Havre de Grace

Less than 40 mi northeast of Baltimore, on the site of one of Maryland's oldest settlements, is the neatly laid-out town Havre de Grace, reputedly named by the Marquis de Lafayette. Because this "harbor of mercy" on the Chesapeake Bay at the mouth of the Susquehanna River was shelled and torched by the British in the War of 1812, almost none of its structures dates from before the 19th century.

One of the few 18th-century structures in Havre de Grace—and the town's most historically significant building—is the **Rodgers House** (✉ 226 N. Washington St.), a two-story redbrick Georgian town house topped by a dormered attic. This was the home of Admiral John Rodgers, who fired the first shot in the War of 1812; like most of the historic houses of Havre de Grace, it is closed to the public at present, but it's worth a drive past.

The **Havre de Grace Decoy Museum,** housed in a converted power plant, has 1,500 facsimiles of duck, goose, and swan made from wood, iron, cork, papier-mâché, or plastic. Three classes of decoy—decorative, decorative floater, and working decoys—are represented. Exhibits change periodically. A permanent exhibit of six human figures portrays 20th-century carvers, including the prolific R. Madison Mitchell, and a recorded narration covers the lore of the craft. On weekends, decoy carvers demonstrate their art in the museum basement. A festival during the first full weekend in May includes carving contests and demonstrations by retrievers. ⊠ *Giles and Market Sts.,* ☎ *410/939–3739.* 🎫 *$2.* ⊙ *Daily 11–4. Closed major holidays.*

The **Susquehanna Museum,** at the southern terminal of the defunct Susquehanna and Tidewater Canal, tells the history of the canal and the people who lived and worked there. From 1839 until 1890 the canal ran 45 mi north to Wrightsville, Pennsylvania, a thoroughfare for mule-drawn barges loaded with iron ore, coal, and crops. The museum, in the lock tender's cottage built in 1840, is partially furnished with modest midcentury antiques that recall its period of service. Outdoors, a pivot bridge across the lock has been restored and the original wooden gates have been dragged up onto land. There are demonstrations of a reconstructed lock, with vessels passing up this small segment of the canal. A 10-minute video explains the operation of the canal. ⊠ *Erie and Conesto Sts.,* ☎ *410/939–5780.* 🎫 *Free.* ⊙ *Apr.–Dec., Sat.–Sun. 1–5, candlelight tour 2nd Sun. in Dec.*

The **Concord Point Lighthouse** has served as a beacon for sailors and boaters in the Upper Chesapeake Bay for more than 160 years, making it the oldest continuously operated Chesapeake Bay lighthouse remaining on its original site. Built in 1827, it was restored in 1980. Visitors can climb 30 feet for views of the bay, the river, and the town. Unlike many screw-pile lighthouses, the Concord Point Lighthouse has the classic conical design and is too small for anyone to live in. ⊠ *Concord and Lafayette Sts. at the Susquehanna River,* ☎ *410/939–9040.* 🎫 *Free.* ⊙ *May–Oct., Sun. 1–5.*

Susquehanna State Park, 6 mi upriver from Havre de Grace, sits on 2,500 acres where visitors can fish, bird-watch, hike, bike, and camp. A covered stone pavilion by the river is ideal for picnics. ⊠ *Rte. 155,* ☎ *410/836-6735.* ⊙ *Daily 10–sunset.*

The **Steppingstone Museum** is a 10-acre complex of seven restored turn-of-the-century farm buildings plus a replica of a canning house. Among the 12,000-plus artifacts in the collection are a horse-drawn tractor and an early gas-powered version, manual seeders and planters, and horse-drawn plows. A blacksmith, a weaver, a wood-carver, a cooper, a dairymaid, and a decoy artisan regularly demonstrate their respective crafts in the workshops. ⊠ *461 Quaker Bottom Rd.,* ☎ *410/939-2299.* 🎫 *$2.* ⊙ *May–Oct., weekends 1–5.*

Ladew Topiary Gardens consists of 15 flower gardens planned and designed by the late Harvey Smith Ladew. They include a formal rose garden, cottage garden, water garden, berry garden, and America's finest sculpted topiary trees and shrubs, which together cover 22 acres. In summer, there are special events such as concerts and polo matches. The house is filled with English antiques, paintings, photographs, and fox-hunting memorabilia. The standout room is the Oval Library, considered one of the most beautiful rooms in America. ⊠ *3535 Jarrettsville Pike, Monkton,* ☎ *410/557–9466.* ⊡ *House and gardens $6.* ⊙ *Mid-Apr.–late Oct., Tues.–Fri. 10–4, weekends 12–5.*

Aberdeen

A site for artillery testing since 1917, Aberdeen celebrates its heritage every year on Armed Forces Day (the third Saturday in May), with tank parades and firing demonstrations.

The **Aberdeen Proving Ground** is a 75,000-acre U.S. Army installation on the Chesapeake Bay, about 30 mi northeast of Baltimore's Inner Harbor.

The **U.S. Army Ordnance Museum** maintains one of the largest collections of armored fighting vehicles in the country—225 at last count. Some are one-of-a-kind inventions: "The Christie" was designed in the United States in 1934 to run at a speed of 60 mph when its competition could go no faster than 8 mph. The 3-ton Ford tank of 1919, from the first line of American tanks, is the only one in existence with its original Model T twin engines. General John Pershing's World War I staff car is here, and so is a 1916 Dodge used by Lieutenant George Patton in the first mechanized raid across the Mexican border. A huge 16-inch American gun from World War I is on display, as well as the first surface-to-air missile, devised by the Germans in 1945. The collection of small arms includes a 15th-century matchlock—a musket whose powder ignites from a slow-burning wick. ⊠ *Exit 85 off I–95.* ⊡ *Free.* ⊙ *10–4:45 daily.*

Dining and Lodging

$$$ ✕ **Crazy Swede.** A nautical theme prevails in this restaurant on the
★   first floor of a former hotel on a tree-lined avenue. Windows and mirrors on all sides keep the dining room well lighted whether or not the sailboat lanterns at the tables are burning. In winter the tables are covered with cloths in the blue-and-maroon scheme; in summer the wooden tables are bare except for straw mats. Anything on the diverse surf-and-turf menu can be ordered Cajun-style, prepared with the moderately spicy house seasoning. One popular choice for this treatment is shrimp scampi with garlic on a bed of rice. Veal Havre de Grace, served with a savory cream sauce and crab, is another specialty. ⊠ *400 N. Union Ave.,* ☎ *410/939–5440. AE, MC, V.*

$$$ ✕ **Josef's Country Inn.** This tidy, European-style restaurant is much like what you'd expect to find in the Bavarian countryside—and is very unassuming from the outside. In addition to German specialties, seafood and American continental cuisine are served. ⊠ *2410 Pleasantville Rd.,* ☎ *410/877–7800. AE, D, DC, MC, V.*

$$$ ✕ **MacGregor's.** Behind the original redbrick facade of a bank built in 1928, MacGregor's occupies two dining rooms on two levels, with glass walls on three sides looking onto Chesapeake Bay. The interior is adorned with carved duck decoys, mounted guns, and antique prints of the town; there's also an outdoor deck with a gazebo. Seafood is the specialty, and the kitchen claims to have the best crab cakes on the bay. ⊠ *331 St. John's St.,* ☎ *410/939–3003. AE, D, DC, MC, V.*

$$$ ✕ **Vandiver Inn.** Of this inn's three elegant dining rooms, one is a glassed-in sunporch; the other two have stained-glass windows and photographs of the town in 1866, the year the building was constructed. In all three, chairs and tables—the latter draped with white linen cloths—are solid mahogany antiques. Candles at tables and a crystal chandelier in one room illuminate dinner. The prix-fixe menu changes with the chef's fancy, but beautifully prepared local seafood dishes are

a standard. A Chambord cheesecake with a black-chocolate crust is made with fresh raspberries and raspberry liqueur. The Vandiver also has four warm, Victorian-style guest rooms with antiques and comfortable furnishings (☞ *below*). ✉ *410 S. Union Ave.,* ☎ *410/939–5200. Reservations essential. AE, D, MC, V. Closed Sun.–Thurs. No lunch.*

$ ✕ **Fortunato Brothers.** This bustling Italian eatery occupies the first floor of a two-story redbrick building in Havre de Grace's historic district; within, a maroon-and-white tile floor and bare wooden tables strike a casual chord. All the pastas come with a small dinner salad and garlic bread, making this an exceptional bargain. Homemade meat lasagna, served in large portions, is the biggest hit. Fortunato Salad is an alternative meal in itself, including ham, turkey, and mozzarella. A conspicuous omission at a restaurant in this waterside town is seafood. ✉ *103 N. Washington St.,* ☎ *410/939–1401. No credit cards.*

$ ▦ **Spencer-Silver Mansion.** This house was built in 1886 of gray gran-
★   ite quarried at Port Deposit, 5 mi up the Susquehanna—the same kind of granite that was used in the Brooklyn Bridge and the United Nations building. Characteristic Victorian features include stained-glass windows, a wraparound porch, and a turret. One guest room is a round turret room; another has a queen-size brass bed and a view of the garden. All rooms are furnished with period antiques supplemented by select reproductions. The formal parlor has a brass chandelier with ornate glass globes. A full breakfast is included in the rates. ✉ *200 S. Union Ave., 21078,* ☎ *410/939–1097. 4 rooms. No credit cards.*

$ ▦ **Vandiver Inn.** This three-story wood house, built in 1886 and listed on the National Register of Historic Places, sits on a 1-acre property 1½ blocks from the bay. Green with a dark green trim on the outside, the inn has a Victorian look, with antique beds and other period pieces. The O'Neil and the Rodgers suites have their own porches. Another porch extends the width of the house front, and the gazebo in the backyard is as old as the house itself. A full breakfast is included in the rates, and for dinner, the restaurant is among the best in the area. ✉ *410 S. Union St., 21078,* ☎ *410/939–5200 or 800/245-1655. 8 rooms, 2 suites. Restaurant. AE, D, MC, V.*

Havre de Grace A to Z

ARRIVING AND DEPARTING
Havre de Grace is about a 40-minute drive from downtown Baltimore. From downtown, take I-395 to I-95; pick up I-95 east to New York and follow it to Harford County and Havre de Grace. Route 155 off Exit 89 leads to downtown Havre de Grace.

BALTIMORE A TO Z

Arriving and Departing

By Bus
Greyhound Lines (✉ 210 W. Fayette St., ☎ 800/231–2222) has scheduled daily service to and from major cities in the United States and Canada.

By Car
From the north, I–83, also called the Jones Falls Expressway, winds through Baltimore and ends at the Inner Harbor. I–395 serves as the primary access to downtown from I–95. From the west, I–70 merges with the Baltimore Beltway, I–695. Drivers headed downtown should use I–395.

By Plane

Baltimore-Washington International Airport (☎ 410/859–7111 for information and paging), is 10 mi south of Baltimore off Route 295 (Baltimore-Washington Pkwy.). It has scheduled daily flights by most major airlines, including Air Aruba (☎ 800/882–7822), Air Jamaica (☎ 800/523–5585), Air Canada (☎ 800/776–3000), American (☎ 800/433–7300), America West (☎ 800/235–9292), British Airways (☎ 800/247–9297), Business Express (☎ 800/345–3400), Continental (☎ 800/525–0280), Delta (☎ 800/638–7333), El Al (☎ 800/223–6700), Icelandair (☎ 800/223–5500), Laker Airways (☎ 800/545–1300), Northwest (☎ 800/225–2525), Southwest (☎ 800/435–9792), TWA (☎ 800/221–2000), United (☎ 800/241–6522), and USAir (☎ 800/428–4322).

BETWEEN THE AIRPORT AND DOWNTOWN

By Bus: BWI Super Shuttle (☎ 410/724-0009) provides van service between the airport and downtown hotels, every half hour, 6 AM–11 PM. Travel time is about 30 minutes; the fare, $10. Hotel vans, which are operated independently of the hotels, take 30 minutes on average. Some hotels may provide complimentary limousine service.

By Limousine: Carey Limousines (☎ 410/880–0999 or 800/336–4646) should be reserved 24 hours in advance.

By Taxi: Airport Taxis (☎ 410/859–1100) stand by to meet arriving flights. The ride into town on I–295 takes 20 minutes; the fare between the airport and downtown is about $17.

By Train: There are 25 trains a day between the airport and Baltimore's downtown Penn Station. Continuous free shuttle-bus service links the rail station with the airport terminal less than 10 minutes away. **Amtrak** (☎ 800/872–7245) service between the BWI Airport rail station (☎ 410/672–6167) and Penn Station (✉ Charles St. and Mt. Royal Ave.) is available daily at irregular intervals, so call ahead. The ride takes 10 to 15 minutes and costs $5. **Maryland Area Rail Commuter** (MARC, ☎ 800/325–7245) trains travel between the BWI Airport and Penn Station in about 20 minutes, weekdays 7 AM–10 PM, at a fare of $3.25.

By Train

Amtrak's (☎ 800/872–7245) trains on the northeast corridor service between Boston and Washington all stop at Baltimore's Penn Station (☎ 410/291-4261).

Getting Around

The majority of Baltimore's attractions are within walking distance or a short cab ride from Inner Harbor. Beyond that area a car would be useful, for the clean and speedy metro line is somewhat limited and riding public buses can involve a number of transfers. Parking rates downtown are about $12 a day. Inner Harbor sites and other downtown attractions are best reached on foot, by water taxi, or by trolley.

By Bus

Buses provide an easy, inexpensive means to see much of Baltimore. The Mass Transit Administration (MTA, ☎ 410/539–5000) has more than 70 bus routes; the fare is $1.35. All-day passes are $3 and can be used with light rail or metro travel. There is also MTA bus service between Baltimore and Annapolis. Some routes have service 24 hours daily.

By Light Rail

Light rail is an easy, comfortable way to reach downtown from the northern and southern suburbs. Stops near downtown include Oriole Park at Camden Yards, Howard Street, and Centre Street near Mount Vernon. The city's cultural center can be reached by the Cathedral Street stop. Light rail service is expected to connect Hunt Valley and BWI Airport by spring 1997. The fare is $1.35. For schedules, call MTA (☎ 410/539–5000).

By Subway

The Baltimore metro serves visitors coming into the city from the suburban northwest. Stops include Charles Center and Lexington Market, both within walking distance of the Inner Harbor. The single line runs from Owings Mills to Johns Hopkins Hospital, east of downtown; the fare is $1.35. Trains run weekdays 5 AM–midnight, Saturday 8 AM–midnight, and Sundays during Orioles games. For more information, call MTA (☎ 410/539–5000).

By Taxi

Yellow Cab (☎ 410/685–1212) provides computer-dispatched cars.

Contacts and Resources

Emergencies

For police, ambulance, and fire, dial **911.**

HOSPITALS

Johns Hopkins Hospital (✉ 600 N. Wolfe St., ☎ 410/955–2280).
Maryland General Hospital (✉ 827 Linden Ave., ☎ 410/225–8100).

Guided Tours

ORIENTATION TOURS

Baltimore Trolley Tours (☎ 410/724-0077) are lively driver-guided tours through Baltimore's major attractions. The route is an endless loop (20 stops, including downtown hotels), so passengers can get on and off as they choose, with unlimited reboarding. The continuous tour operates Saturday and Sunday, 10 AM–4 PM, every 30 minutes and costs $12. This is a good orientation tour because you can see as much or as little as you choose, in detail or in overview. Maps and brochures are available at major hotels and most tourist offices.

PERSONAL GUIDES

Group and custom tours are provided by **About Town Tours** (☎ 410/592–7770), **Baltimore Rent-A-Tour** (☎ 410/653–2998), and **Diversions** (☎ 410/486–3604).

SPECIAL-INTEREST

Bill Rohrbaugh's Charter Service (✉ 3395 Main St., Manchester, ☎ 410/239-8000) offers customized itineraries—inside and outside of Baltimore—for professional groups, parties, and individuals.
Diversions, Inc. (☎ 410/486–3604) customizes an itinerary to the client's interests, inside or outside of Baltimore.

WALKING

Zippy Larson's Shoe Leather Safaris (☎ 410/817-4141) conducts neighborhood, literary, and ethnic expeditions that are popular with local residents as well as visitors because of their witty and well-researched narration. Zippy is a local woman who thoroughly researches her material.

WATER TOURS

There are numerous opportunities to explore the harbor and the nearby Chesapeake Bay by water. Most cruise and tour boats depart from docks in the Inner Harbor. **Clipper City** (☎ 410/575–7930) offers excursions around the harbor aboard a 158-foot replica of an 1850s topsail schooner. **Harbor Cruises, Ltd.** (☎ 800/695–2628 or 410/727–3113) presents lunch, dinner, and evening cruises around the harbor aboard the *Bay Lady* or *Lady Baltimore*. **Maryland Tours, Inc.** (☎ 410/685–4288) offers a variety of sightseeing tours of the harbor and excursions to Ft. McHenry. **Schooner Nighthawk Cruises** (✉ Thames St., Fells Point, ☎ 410/327–7245) offers cruises aboard a 19th-century two-masted schooner.

Visitor Information

Baltimore Area Convention and Visitors Association (✉ 100 Light St., 21202, ☎ 410/659–7300).

Baltimore Area Visitors Center (✉ 301 E. Pratt St., 21202, ☎ 410/837-4636 or 800/282-6632).

Baltimore County Promotion and Tourism (✉ 400 Washington Ave., Towson, 21204, ☎ 410/887–8040).

Baltimore Office of Promotion (✉ 200 W. Lombard St., 21201, ☎ 410/752–8632).

Harford County Office of Tourism (✉ 220 S. Main St., Bel Air 21014, ☎ 410/638–3339).

8 Frederick and Western Maryland

Mountains, forests, and unspoiled rivers checker the westernmost portion of Maryland, whose fertile valleys were first farmed in the 1700s. The 250-year-old town of Frederick has a 33-block historic district and was the site of repeated clashes between Confederate and Union troops. Also in the vicinity are Antietam National Battlefield, where Union and Confederate troops fought on the bloodiest single day of the Civil War, and Cumberland, a onetime transportation hub where you can still see remnants of the historic Chesapeake & Ohio Canal.

THE MARYLAND MOUNTAINSIDE IS THE STATE'S best-kept secret. Stretching from the rolling farmland of the state's Piedmont region to the remote mountaintops of Garrett County and the heights of the Appalachians, the region is full of historic towns, Civil War battlefields, and miles of hardwood forests where white-tail deer, wild turkey, and even black bear roam among vast stretches of oaks, hickories, and maples. The nation's first pioneers crossed these worn, majestic mountains as they made their way westward on the National Pike. Today, campers, hikers, hunters, and visitors seeking an escape from Baltimore, Washington, and the suburbs head to these hills.

In the early 1700s, Germans and other immigrants came to farm the fertile valleys of Frederick and Washington counties, where large dairy farms still dot the pastoral landscape. The Irish and Scots arrived in the first half of the 19th century to help build railroads, the nation's first federal highway (called the National Pike), and the magnificent Chesapeake and Ohio Canal. This nearly 185-mi-long waterway paralleled the meandering Potomac River from Washington's Georgetown to Cumberland. Remnants of it remain, and today the canal towpath is a popular hiking and biking trail.

Because of its proximity to Baltimore and Washington, Frederick, the region's largest city, became a staging area for many important events in American history. Ben Franklin helped plan aspects of the French and Indian War from Braddock Heights, a mountain on Frederick's western edge. Meriwether Lewis stopped by before meeting up with William Clark on their trek westward. During the Civil War, Confederate and Union troops clashed on the streets of Frederick, on their way to the battles of South Mountain and Antietam.

A surprising number of American presidents have visited Frederick. George Washington slept here. Abraham Lincoln passed through after the Battle of Antietam, which was fought on the other side of the green mountains that border Frederick on the western horizon. Franklin Roosevelt stopped here with British Prime Minister Winston Churchill. George and Barbara Bush even purchased some of their Christmas gifts at a Frederick mall just a few years ago.

The region's other big towns, Hagerstown and Cumberland, were transportation hubs in earlier centuries. Though the railroad plays a less important role in both cities today, both Hagerstown and Cumberland are promoting their rich transportation past to lure tourists. Hagerstown is known for its Roundhouse Museum, which has an extensive collection of railroad memorabilia, history books, and a miniature railroad layout. Cumberland, the western terminus of the Chesapeake & Ohio (C&O) Canal, hopes to attract visitors with a multimillion-dollar effort to restore a stretch of the canal. The city's Victorian-era train station has already been restored and is the starting point of a popular tourist excursion up the mountains.

The region's mountains, forests, and world-famous rivers are an equally important draw. Kayakers and white-water rafters rave about the rapids on the Savage River and the north-flowing Youghiogheny River, while hikers, bicyclists, and campers flock to state parks throughout the region. Deep Creek Lake, the state's largest, is popular with boaters and fishermen.

Disagreement lingers on just where Western Maryland begins. For Baltimoreans, more familiar with the Eastern Shore and Ocean City, anything west of the city's beltway is Western Maryland. Washingtonians, on the other hand, tend to lump Frederick and points west together as a distinct region. For the people who live in the hills of Allegany and Garrett counties, Western Maryland begins just west of a man-made cut in a mountain called Sideling Hill. This unusual geological formation has become a popular tourist attraction among motorists tooling along Interstate 68, the new National Highway. Past rock formations several million years old, the highway opens to sweeping views of mountain ridges, shaded blue in the fading sunset. These are the Alleghenies, Maryland's mountainside.

Exploring Frederick and Western Maryland

Frederick, Maryland's third largest city, is surrounded by rolling farmlands and rugged mountains where outdoor activities beckon. In Washington County, northwest of Frederick, Hagerstown is the county seat and a great base for excursions to the C&O Canal, various state parks, and the Appalachian Trail. Further west, the rugged mountains of Allegany County are traversed by the Old National Highway: Today the site of a scenic railroad excursion, this is the very route that westward pioneers traveled in covered wagons. Maryland's westernmost county, Garrett County, was once the vacation destination of railroad barons and Washington's high society; today it's a big destination for boaters, fishermen, and outdoor enthusiasts from nearby metropolitan areas.

FREDERICK

Numbers in the margin correspond to points of interest on the Frederick map.

Frederick, which recently celebrated its 250th anniversary, has one of the best-preserved historic districts in Maryland, perhaps second only to Annapolis. Within the 33-block district, tree-lined streets are lined with buildings from the 18th and 19th centuries, and brick walks connect lovely courtyards. Eclectic shops, antiques stores, and fine restaurants attract crowds of weekend visitors.

★ ❶ Frederick's most popular attraction is the **Barbara Fritchie House and Museum.** After visiting this modest brick cottage, a replica of the original, it's easy to imagine Dame Fritchie sticking her white-capped head out of a second-floor window and waving a flag at Confederate troops. Poet John Greenleaf Whittier made her famous; his poem, "Barbara Fritchie," appeared in the *Atlantic Monthly* a year after Confederate troops passed through Frederick. His stirring account of Fritchie defiantly waving the flag at the invading Confederates stirred patriotism and made the 95-year-old woman a heroine. Fritchie was interesting in her own right. At age 40, she married a man 14 years her junior. She was an outspoken woman and a stout patriot. Her story, at least as told by Whittier, has fascinated history enthusiasts around the world. Even British Prime Minister Winston Churchill visited the house; on his way to Camp David with President Franklin Roosevelt, he stood outside and recited Whittier's poem, "Shoot if you must, this old gray head, but spare your country's flag. . . ." A prized tea set Fritchie used to serve George Washington is on display. ✉ *154 W. Patrick St.,* ☎ *301/698–0630.* ⏱ *Apr.–Sept., Mon. and Thurs.–Sat. 10–4; Oct.–Nov., Sat. 10–4, Sun. 1–4. Closed Dec.–Mar.*

❷ Often overlooked by visitors, the two-story Federal-style **Roger Brooke Taney House** contains a museum dedicated to Taney's brother-in-law, Francis Scott Key, author of the "Star-Spangled Banner." History remembers Supreme Court Justice Taney as the author of the Dred Scott

Frederick

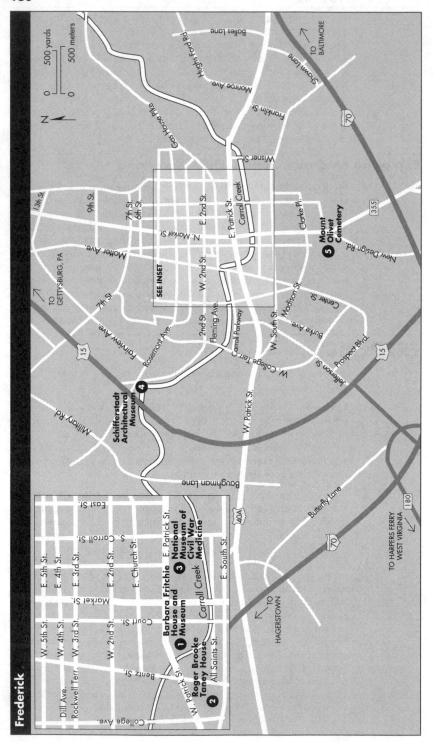

500 yards
500 meters

N

TO GETTYSBURG, PA

TO BALTIMORE

Bolles Lane
Hughs Ford Rd.
Shawn Lane
Monroe Ave.
Franklin St.
Wisner St.

Gas House Pike
13th St.
9th St.
7th St.
6th St.
N. Market St.
E. 2nd St.
E. Patrick St.
Carroll Creek
Clarke Pl.

70

355

5 Mount Olivet Cemetery

New Design Rd.

SEE INSET

W. 2nd St.
Motter Ave.
4th St.
Fairview Ave.
Rosemont Ave.
2nd St.
Fleming Ave.
Carroll Parkway
W. College Terr.
W. South St.
Madison St.
Center St.
Burke Ave.
Jefferson St.
Prospect Blvd.

15

15

Military Rd.

Schifferstadt Architectural Museum 4

W. Patrick St.

Baughman Lane

Butterfly Lane

180

70

TO HARPERS FERRY WEST VIRGINIA

College Ave.
Dill Ave.
Rockwell Terr.
W. 5th St.
W. 4th St.
W. 3rd St.
W. 2nd St.
Bentz St.
Court St.
W. Patrick St.
All Saints St.

E. 5th St.
E. 4th St.
E. 3rd St.
E. 2nd St.
E. Church St.
East St.
S. Carroll St.
Market St.

1 Barbara Fritchie House and Museum

2 Roger Brooke Taney House

3 National Museum of Civil War Medicine

E. Patrick St.
Carroll Creek
E. South St.

40A

TO HAGERSTOWN

Use your MCI Card® for the easy way to call when traveling.

MCI Calling Card

415 555 1234 2244
J.D. SMITH

Convenience on the road

- Your MCI Card® number is your home number, guaranteed.
- Pre-programmed to speed dial to your home.
- Call from any phone in the U.S.

MCI™

1 - 8 0 0 - 7 5 4 - 8 9 4 1

http://www.mci.com

Decision, which stated that blacks had no constitutional rights. Taney and Key practiced law together in Frederick; their office still stands across from City Hall. Personal belongings of both men are on display at the Taney house. Behind the home is the former slave quarters, one of the few such surviving structures in the region. ⊠ *121 S. Bentz St.,* ☎ *301/663–8687.* ☉ *By appointment.*

❸ The **National Museum of Civil War Medicine** tells the medical story of the Civil War, in which more than 600,000 Americans lost their lives. More than 3,000 medical artifacts are on display—including the only known surviving Civil War surgeon's tent, as well as a Civil War ambulance. A multimedia exhibit uses photographs, artifacts, and videos to explain the complicated story of medicine during the Civil War. Coincidentally, the building housing the museum was used to embalm the dead after the Battle of Antietam. The museum is the starting point of a walking tour of the city's Civil War history. ⊠ *48 E. Patrick St.,* ☎ *301/695–1864.* ▣ *Charge anticipated.* ☉ *Tues.–Fri. 10–5, Sat.–Sun. noon–5.*

❹ Frederick's most unusual structure is the **Schifferstadt Architectural Museum,** a stone house built in 1756 by German immigrants. Spared from the wrecking ball just two decades ago by preservation-minded citizens, the house is considered one of the finest examples of German architecture in Colonial America. Its barren rooms allow visitors to observe structural details such as the sandstone walls, which are 2½ feet thick. ⊠ *1110 Rosemont Ave.,* ☎ *301/663–3885.* ▣ *Donation.* ☉ *Apr.–mid-Dec., Tues.–Sat. 10–4, Sun. noon–4.*

❺ **Mount Olivet Cemetery** is the resting place of some of Frederick's most famous sons and daughters, including Francis Scott Key and Barbara Fritchie. The cemetery also shelters the graves of more than 800 Confederate and Union soldiers killed during the battles of Antietam and Monocacy. ⊠ *515 S. Market St.,* ☎ *301/662–1164.* ☉ *Daily.*

Dining and Lodging

$$$ ✕ **Brown Pelican.** Though you won't find many pelicans at this restaurant many miles from the Chesapeake Bay, you will find some of the finest dining in the Frederick area. Although it's below street level, the restaurant succeeds in creating a romantic atmosphere, with white-linen tablecloths and candlelight. A standout on the American nouveau menu is Veal Brown Pelican, savory veal cutlets sautéed with ham, mushrooms, and cream. Seafood, beef, and duckling are also excellent choices. ⊠ *5 E. Church St.,* ☎ *301/695–5833. AE, DC, MC, V.*

$$$ ✕ **Di Francesco's Restaurant.** This popular Italian restaurant has one of the few outdoor cafés in Frederick, along one of the city's busiest streets. Inside, the four spacious dining rooms are semiformal, with exposed beams, plants, and hanging lights. Try the homemade *agnolotti,* triangular pasta pillows stuffed with ricotta cheese and spinach, or the *scampi alla di Francesco,* shrimp sautéed in olive oil with whole cloves of garlic and white wine. An antipasto bar is popular. ⊠ *26 N. Market St.,* ☎ *301/695–5499. D, DC, MC, V. No lunch Mon.*

$$–$$$ ✕ **Tauraso's.** Its rectangular bar and wood-oven-baked pizza make this a popular choice, especially with young crowds. Pizza selections include lighter choices such as *pizza verdure,* white pizza with artichoke hearts, spinach, and fresh tomato. The regular menu includes such popular entrees as rigatoni chicken, steaks, and seafood; Tauraso's own seafood sausage is a favorite appetizer. Wood paneling, white tablecloths, and black-and-white chairs add simple elegance to a separate dining room, and a garden patio is open in the warm months. Tauraso's has won

Wine Spectator's Excellence Award four years in a row. ⊠ *6 East St.,* ☎ *301/663–6600. AE, D, MC, V.*

$$$$ ✕⊡ **Stone Manor.** Part of a 114-acre working farm, this 18th- century
★ stone home (with additions from later centuries) is secluded among the
rolling farmland of Frederick County; deer and wildfowl can frequently be spotted on the grounds. The majestic house, with 10 working fireplaces, has five suites individually decorated with floral-print
armchairs and sofas, antique reproductions, and canopy or carved poster
beds. A popular choice is the Thistle Suite, which has a cathedral ceiling, skylights, and a whirlpool. Breakfast is served in one of the three
lovely dining rooms or in the suites—but dinner is the main event. Herbs
from the chef's garden figure prominently in all the dishes, from wild
game and fowl to seafood and beef. Diners choose from a four- or five-
course menu, which might include braised pheasant on a savory
turnover with blueberry ginger, followed by lemon-thyme roasted
breast of duck or pan-seared Virginia trout. Desserts are exquisite. Plan
to linger. ⊠ *5820 Carroll Boyer Rd., Middletown 21769,* ☎ *301/473–*
5454, 𝔽𝔸𝕏 *301/371–5622. 5 suites. AE, MC, V. 3 dining rooms (no lunch).*

$$$ ✕⊡ **Turning Point Inn.** Once the home of a prominent doctor, this Ed-
wardian-era home is now a bed-and-breakfast inn where some of the
guest rooms have been converted from a dairy barn and carriage house.
Flowering trees, lilacs, and rhododendrons line the long driveway, set-
ting the stage for a relaxing weekend getaway. In the main house, all
five rooms are painted in rose, gray, and white, and furnished with an-
tique reproductions. Bowls of fruit add a nice touch to each room. A
country breakfast is served in one of the dining rooms; in addition, the
inn has an excellent restaurant with an enclosed garden patio overlooking
well-manicured wildflower and rose gardens. The menu includes Chesa-
peake Bay seafood, roast duckling, and beef; almost everything is pre-
pared with local produce and herbs. ⊠ *8406 Urbana Pike, Urbana*
21704, ☎ *301/874–2421,* 𝔽𝔸𝕏 *301/831–8092. 5 rooms, 2 guest houses.*
Restaurant, 2 dining rooms (no lunch Mon. and Sat.). D, MC, V.

$$$ ⊡ **Tyler-Spite House.** The only inn in Frederick's historic district, this early
19th-century house was built to spite city officials who planned to build
a road through the owner's property. He laid the foundation overnight,
thwarting the roadway—hence the house's name. The three-story Federal-style mansion has 13-foot-high ceilings, wide-plank Georgia pine floors,
a curving stairway, and antique furniture. Eight rooms have working fireplaces, including the dining, living, and music rooms, and the owner proudly
claims that the gas lights here were the first to be installed in America.
There's high tea on weekends and a daily breakfast of Belgian waffles,
breads, and homemade jams, served in the formal dining room or on the
garden patio in the warm months. ⊠ *112 W. Church St., Frederick*
21701, ☎ *301/831–4455. 9 rooms. Dining room, pool. AE, MC, V.*

Outdoor Activities and Sports

Five miles southeast of Frederick, **Holly Hills Country Club** (⊠ 5502
Mussetter Rd., Ijamsville, ☎ 301/694–8322) has 18 holes.

Nightlife and the Arts

The **Frederick Coffee Co. and Café** (⊠ 100 East St., ☎ 301/698–0039)
is inside a renovated garage whose bays have been converted into windows overlooking Everedy Square & Shab Row. Folk and jazz musicians perform during the week; poets recite their works on weekends.

The **Weinberg Center for the Arts** (⊠ 20 W. Patrick St., ☎ 301/694–8585) was a silent movie house in the '20s. Now it's an Art Deco theater offering plays, musicals, and concerts throughout the year.

Shopping

In downtown Frederick, **Everedy Square & Shab Row** was once a complex of buildings that manufactured kitchen utensils and wares; now it's a center for retail shops, restaurants, and boutiques. At **The Candy Kitchen** (⊠ 52 N. Market St., ☎ 301/698–0442), you can get chocolates hand-dipped by a family of second- and third-generation Greek immigrants.

The Trail House (⊠ 17 S. Market St., ☎ 301/694–8448) sells and rents hiking, backpacking, camping, and cross-country skiing equipment, and arranges outdoor excursions. **Wonder Book & Video** (⊠ 1306 W. Patrick St., ☎ 301/694–5955) wows visitors with its inventory of more than 600,000 new and used books, videos, and compact discs.

Francis Scott Key Mall (⊠ 5500 Buckeystown Pike, ☎ 301/662–5151), just a few miles south of downtown, has three department stores and many smaller retail stores and restaurants.

SIDE TRIPS FROM FREDERICK

Numbers in the margin correspond to points of interest on the Side Trips from Frederick map.

Not only is Frederick within easy driving distance of Baltimore and Washington, it's also surrounded by other areas of interest, including historic towns, scenic parks, and national battlefields.

Monocacy National Battlefield

❻ *2 mi south of Frederick (via Rte. 355).*

Monocacy National Battlefield was the site of a little-known confrontation between 18,000 Confederates and 5,800 Union troops on July 9, 1864; many historians believe the Union victory thwarted a Confederate invasion of Washington. The farmland surrounding the battlefield remains largely unchanged. An electronic map in the visitor center explains the battle. ⊠ *4801 Urbana Pike,* ☎ *301/662–3515.* ⊠ *Free.* ☉ *Wed.–Sun. 8–4:30.*

New Market

❼ *8 mi east of Frederick (via Rte. 355).*

The self-proclaimed antiques capital of Maryland, New Market is a 200-year-old village tucked among rolling farmland. Not much has changed here over the past two centuries, except for the throngs of tourists who walk Main Street in search of antiques.

Dining

$$$ ✕ **Mealey's.** Once a store and hotel on the National Pike, Mealey's today is a busy restaurant in the heart of New Market, appropriately decorated with antiques. A large stone fireplace dominates the spacious main dining room, which is often filled to capacity on weekend evenings and Sunday afternoons; smaller dining rooms offer more privacy. Every meal is accompanied by a relish tray of cottage cheese, apple butter, cole slaw, and pickled beets. Desserts are worth saving room for—especially the bread pudding, which is served with a bourbon vanilla sauce. ⊠ *8 Main St.,* ☎ *301/865–5488. AE, D, MC, V.*

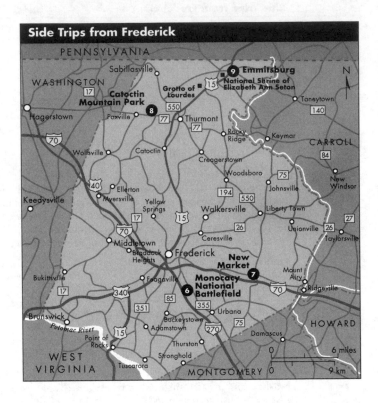

Side Trips from Frederick

Outdoor Activities and Sports

WestWinds Golf & Country Club (⊠ 11411 Gas House Pike, New Market, ☎ 301/831–3832) has an 18-hole golf course, a pool, and fitness facilities.

Catoctin Mountain Park

8 *15 mi north of Frederick (Rte. 15).*

Hidden within this park is Camp David, the presidential retreat that was the site of the famous peace accords between Egypt and Israel. You won't find the camp, which has been used by presidents since Franklin D. Roosevelt, and if you even come close, you'll run into security officers. What you will find are 6,000 acres of rocky outcrops and thick forests traversed by miles of moderate to strenuous hiking trails. A small visitor center has exhibits on the area's wildlife. Across Route 77 is **Cunningham Falls State Park,** the site of a cascading 78-foot waterfall and a man-made lake. Both parks have camping facilities. ⊠ *Rte. 77, west of Rte. 15, Thurmont,* ☎ *301/663–9330.* ☞ *Free.* ☉ *Visitor center: Mon.–Fri. 10–4:30, Sat.–Sun. 8:30–5; Park: Daily dawn–dusk.*

Emmitsburg

9 *24 mi north of Frederick (Rte. 15).*

Nestled among the foothills of the Catoctin Mountains, Emmitsburg, founded in 1757, was the site of the first parochial school in the United States and the final home of the first American saint. Its Main Street remains a showcase of fine examples of Federal, Georgian, and Victorian architecture, and many of the buildings are still in use as homes and businesses.

The **Grotto of Lourdes** is a replica of the famous grotto in France where a peasant girl saw visions of the Virgin Mary. The grotto, tucked into a mountain overlooking Mount Saint Mary's College, draws more than one million visitors a year, and a sunrise Easter service attracts a crowd. Beautifully landscaped paths lead to the grotto and a small chapel. ⊠ *U.S. Rte. 15, Emmitsburg, ☎ 301/447–5318. ☉ Daily dawn–dusk.*

The **National Shrine of St. Elizabeth Ann Seton** contains the home of the first American-born saint, who came to the Maryland mountains to establish the nation's first parochial school and the Sisters of Charity. A classroom contains authentic furnishings. A short film and exhibits tell St. Elizabeth Ann Seton's story. She is buried in a small graveyard on the well-maintained and shaded grounds. Pope John Paul II designated the chapel of her shrine a minor basilica in 1991. ⊠ *333 S. Seton Ave., Emmitsburg, ☎ 301/447–6606. ☉ Daily 10– 4:30. Closed last 2 wks in Jan., Mondays in Dec.*

WESTERN MARYLAND

Numbers in the margin correspond to points of interest on the Western Maryland map.

The South Mountains that divide Frederick and Washington counties once sheltered Confederates, who formed a defensive line against advancing Union soldiers just before the Battle of Antietam. Only a few monuments and road signs mark this lesser known battle today. But the South Mountains still offer shelter for hikers and cyclists, who come to travel the Appalachian Trail and marvel at panoramic views of the Potomac River or the pleasant valley that surrounds Hagerstown to the west.

Hagerstown

⑩ *25 mi west of Frederick; 75 mi west of Baltimore (via I–70).*

Once a prosperous railroad hub and manufacturing center, Hagerstown today is struggling to redefine itself, as millions of dollars are spent to refurbish downtown buildings for offices and retail stores. Among the new tenants is the nation's largest Civil War battlefield preservation group, the Association for the Preservation of Civil War Battlefields, which also spent thousands of dollars to help preserve land at the nearby Antietam National Battlefield in Sharpsburg.

Hagerstown may have lesser ties to the Civil War than Frederick, but these pages of the city's past are being tapped as a tourism magnet— and there's some justification. Two significant battles were fought just outside Hagerstown, the Battle of Antietam and the lesser known Battle of South Mountain. Confederates occasionally came through town, most noticeably in 1864 when they threatened to burn the city; the Rebels relented after city officials paid a $20,000 ransom.

Washington County Museum of Fine Arts. This impressive collection of American paintings, drawings, prints, and sculpture from the 18th century to the present includes the work of James Abbott McNeill Whistler; Benjamin West, of the Peale family dynasty; and Norman Rockwell. Two portraits by Joshua Johnson, believed to be the first African-American portrait artist, were recent acquisitions. A recently completed $3.2-million addition expanded permanent exhibit space. The museum is tucked into Hagerstown's beautiful City Park, a 27-acre wooded and landscaped haven with two small, man-made lakes that swarm with ducks, geese, and swans during the spring and fall. ⊠ *91 Key St.,* ☎ *301/739–5727.* ⊠ *Free.* ⊙ *Tues.–Sat. 10–5, Sun. 1–6.*

The **Hager House and Museum** is the original home of the founder of Hagerstown, Jonathan Hager, who built the home in 1739 over two springs to give his family a protected water supply and an indoor spring house. Built of uncut fieldstones, the house has 22-inch thick walls and 18th-century furnishings. Colonial-style flower and herb gardens surround it. A small museum next to the house contains an extensive collection of 18th- and 19th-century coins, bone forks and combs, pottery, buttons, and ironwork, excavated when the house was restored in 1953. ⊠ *110 Key St., Hagerstown,* ☎ *301/739–8393.* ⊠ *$3.* ⊙ *Tues.–Sat. 10–4, Sun. 2–5. Closed Jan.–Mar.*

Lodging

$$ ⊞ **Sheraton Inn Hagerstown.** Blue and mauve color schemes and touches of wood in these recently renovated rooms create a surprisingly warm atmosphere for business travelers. Business suites have Murphy beds and conference tables. The hotel attracts non-business travelers as well. ⊠ *1910 Dual Hwy., Hagerstown 21740,* ☎ *301/790–3010,* FAX *301/733–4550. 108 rooms. Restaurant, bar, pool, exercise room, meeting rooms. AE, D, DC, MC, V.*

⊞ **Venice Inn Best Western.** This well-kept motel has standard rooms with double or king-size beds. The decor is contemporary. ⊠ *431 Dual Hwy., Hagerstown 21740,* ☎ *301/733–0830,* FAX *301/733–4978. 222 rooms. Restaurant, bar, pool, exercise room. AE, D, DC, MC.*

Nightlife and the Arts

Maryland Theatre. Just off Hagerstown's main square, this restored early 20th-century neoclassical theater is the home of the Maryland Symphony Orchestra; it also stages shows, concerts, and film screenings. You may recognize the theater from the film *Guarding Tess.* ⊠ *21 S. Potomac St.,* ☎ *301/790–2000.*

Outdoor Activities and Sports

Appalachian Valley Bicycle Touring (⊠ 31 E. Fort Ave., Baltimore, ☎ 410/837–8068) offers organized, guided tours of Civil War battlefields and other areas in Western Maryland.

River and Trail Outfitters (⊠ 604 Valley Rd., Knoxville 21758, ☎ 301/695–5177), offers guided raft, canoe, kayaking, and fishing trips along the Potomac River.

Sharpsburg

⑪   *10 mi south of Hagerstown (via Rte. 65); 20 mi west of Frederick (via Alt. Rte. 40 to Rte. 34).*

★   Among the corn fields and woods that surround Sharpsburg is the **Antietam National Battlefield,** where Union and Confederate troops clashed on September 17, 1862, the bloodiest single day of the war: More than 23,000 men were killed or wounded. Landmarks on the largely undisturbed battlefield include the Burnside Bridge, Dunkard Church, and Bloody Lane. The Union's victory at Sharpsburg gave President Abraham Lincoln the opportunity to issue the Emancipation Proclamation, which freed all slaves in Rebel states and infused the North's cause with moral power. A visitor center offers Civil War artifacts, a short film about the battle, and rental cassettes with narrated driving tours. An overlook provides a panoramic view of the battlefield and the countryside. ⊠ *Rte. 65, Sharpsburg Pike, Sharpsburg,* ☎ *301/432–5124.* ⊠ *$2.* ⊙ *Visitor Center: daily 8:30–5; Battlefield: daily dawn–dusk.*

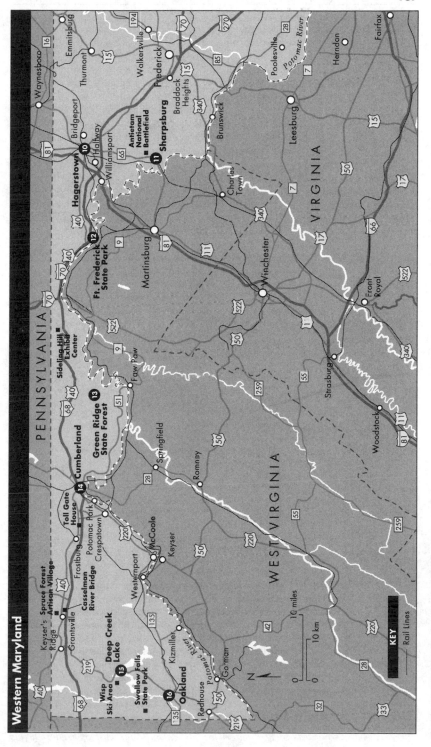

Western Maryland

Dining and Lodging

$$$ ✕ **South Mountain Inn.** Built in 1732, the South Mountain Inn was a trading post in its early days, then a stagecoach stop, then a summer home. Now a restaurant, the 18th-century stone structure is perched atop South Mountain along the National Pike (now Route 40), near a pair of scenic state parks: the Washington Monument State Park, which claims to have the oldest monument to the nation's first president; and Greenbrier State Park, popular with hikers and swimmers. In addition to an indoor dining room, seating options include an enclosed garden patio with white wicker furniture, plants, and natural light and a garden patio for dining alfresco. The Continental menu specializes in prime rib, seafood, and beef Wellington. Many guests rave about a horseradish-crusted salmon fillet that's served on a bed of garlic mashed potatoes with a chive-oil sauce. The dessert crepes are also best-sellers. The restaurant has a fine selection of California wines. ⊠ *6132 Old National Pike, Boonsboro 21713,* ☎ *301/432–6155,* ℻ *301/432–2211. AE, DC, MC, V. Closed Mon.*

$$ ⛺ **Ground Squirrel Holler.** On the main road leading to the Antietam National Battlefield, this eclectic bed-and-breakfast inn is surrounded by tall shade trees and flower gardens. The owner's vast hat collection is displayed on the main floor, along with other unusual items such as "ruby slippers"—copies of the famous shoes worn by Dorothy in the *Wizard of Oz,* attached to a pair of striped legs sticking out from beneath a sofa. Rooms have a country feel, with wood floors, rag rugs, down mattresses, and fresh-cut flowers. When weather permits, guests eat breakfast on a deck overlooking a field where llamas graze. The innkeepers offer llama hikes on the towpath of the nearby C&O Canal, with catered lunches included ($50). ⊠ *6735 Sharpsburg Pike, Sharpsburg 21782,* ☎ *301/432–8288. 3 rooms. No credit cards.*

Ft. Frederick State Park

⑫ *17 mi west of Hagerstown; 40 mi west of Frederick (via I–70).*

Here stands one of the few surviving stone forts from the French and Indian War. Barracks were reconstructed in the 1930s by the Civilian Conservation Corps, to whom a small museum on the grounds is dedicated. A visitor center displays artifacts from the French and Indian War and the Colonial era. ⊠ *11100 Ft. Frederick Rd., Big Pool,* ☎ *301/842–2155.* ▨ *Future charge anticipated.* ◯ *Visitor center: daily 8–4; call ahead Nov.–Mar., when staffing is lighter. Park: daily dawn–dusk.*

En Route Interstate 68 cuts through Sideling Hill—the mountain that separates Washington and Allegany counties—thus exposing nearly 850 vertical feet of sedimentary rock that was formed 350 million years ago. At the top of the mountain is the **Sideling Hill Exhibit Center,** where one of the best rock exposures in the northeastern United States is explained. In addition, the four-story visitor center has interpretive exhibits of animals native to Western Maryland; there's also an orientation program. Picnic areas overlook the stunning valleys. ⊠ *11100 Ft. Frederick Rd., Big Pool,* ☎ *301/842–2155.* ▨ *Free.* ◯ *Daily 9–5.*

Green Ridge State Forest

⑬ *23 mi west of Ft. Frederick State Park; 62 mi west of Frederick (via I–70 to I–68).*

Maryland's second largest forest—nearly 40,000 acres—stretches across most of eastern Allegany County; its vast stands of oaks, maples, hickories, and pine attracts Baltimore residents, who come here to hunt, bike, and camp in the fall and spring. Beneath the forest growth, decaying tombstones and crumbling stone foundations are remnants of the lives of the immigrants who once lived here while working on the C&O Canal and the railroad. Within the forest is a Potomac River overlook where Union soldiers once stood sentinel for Confederate saboteurs; several years ago, Union reenactors came to the same spot, known as Point Lookout, to film the opening scenes of the movie, *Gettysburg*. A *Baltimore Sun* columnist called one of the park's overlooks, just off the interstate, "the best deck in Maryland" because of its phenomenal view of heavily wooded mountains. ⊠ *Box 50, I–68, Flintstone,* ☎ *301/478–3124.* ⊑ *Free.* ☉ *Daily dawn–dusk.*

Cumberland

⓮ *89 mi west of Frederick; 142 mi west of Baltimore (via I–70 to I–68).*

Cradled in the picturesque Allegheny Mountains, Cumberland was once a young America's gateway to the west. Pioneers, and later trains and motorists, took advantage of 1-mi-long natural pass in the mountains—the Narrows—to make their way west. The National Pike, the first federally funded highway; the Chesapeake and Ohio Canal; and the Baltimore and Ohio Railroad all converged here in the mid-19th century. The B&O Railroad beat the canal to Cumberland, dooming the waterway as the future transportation route.

Today, Cumberland is returning to its transportation heritage to rejuvenate its economy and attract tourists. A two-lane highway and an excursion train now cross through the 900-foot-deep Narrows, whose exposed red shale and sandstone cliffs above make for a scenic ride. In addition, millions of dollars are being spent to restore a stretch of the canal and offer mule-drawn barge rides to visitors. Just outside of Cumberland, a $54-million hotel and conference center are being built at Rocky Gap State Park, the site of an annual country music festival.

In the mid- to late-19th century, Cumberland's leading politicians, doctors, lawyers, and businessmen lived in the **Washington Street Historic District,** which stretches along Washington Street from Wills Creek to Allegany Street and from Greene Street to Fayette Street. The six-block district, named to the National Register of Historic Places, still reflects the architecture of the period, with prominent Federal, Greek Revival, Italianate, Queen Anne, and Georgian Revival homes. Of particular interest is the **Emmanuel Episcopal Church and Parish Hall,** (⊠ 16 Washington St.) built in 1849-50, on the site of the former Ft. Cumberland, a frontier outpost during the French and Indian War. The Gothic Revival cross-shape church was built of native sandstone.

George Washington's Headquarters (⊠ Washington and Greene Sts.) during the French and Indian War and the Whiskey Rebellion stands at the corner of Washington Street, at Prospect Square in Riverside Park. Only a small portion of the original log structure remains.

The Second Empire–style **History House** was built in 1867 by Josiah Gordon, president of the C&O Canal, in Cumberland's then-fashionable Washington Street. Today it's the home of the Allegany County Historical Society, and a repository for hundreds of items of local and national significance, including furniture, clothing, hats, accessories, and toys. ⊠ *218 Washington St.,* ☎ *301/777–8678.* ⊑ *$3.* ☉ *May–Oct., Tues.–Sat. 11–3, Sun. 1:30–4.*

The **Western Maryland Scenic Railroad** allows riders to relive the glory days of trains in Cumberland. A 1916 Baldwin locomotive, once used in Michigan's Upper Peninsula, carries visitors through the Narrows and up scenic mountains on a 32-mi round-trip to Frostburg, the summer camp of the Washington Redskins. A 90-minute layover in Frostburg allows time for lunch at the Old Train Depot or at one of the many restaurants on the city's main street, just up the hill. Also in Frostburg, the **Thrasher Carriage Collection Museum** contains almost every style of horse-drawn vehicle, including carriages, milk wagons, sleighs, and funeral wagons. The trip back to Cumberland is all downhill. ⊠ *13 Canal St.,* ☎ *301/759–4400 or 800/872–4650.* ⌨ *Train fare: $14.75 May–Sept and Nov.–Dec., $16.75 Oct.* ☉ *May–Sept., Tues.–Sun. 11:30., Oct., Tues.–Sun. 11:00 and 4:00, Nov.–Dec., weekends 11:30.*

Dining and Lodging

$$$ ✕ **Au Petit Paris.** A re-created Paris street scene serves as the entrance to this well-regarded French restaurant in Frostburg. Inside the three intimate dining rooms, pictures of Paris and France give guests the feel of a French bistro. Duckling, lamb, veal, and seafood are the specialties here: Try Lamb Noisettes Madeira, lamb tenderloins in a Madeira wine sauce; or tournedos *au xeres,* two petite fillets in a cream-and-sherry sauce. Desserts include bananas Foster and cherry jubilee. The extensive wine list includes Californian and European selections. ⊠ *86 E. Main St., Frostburg,* ☎ *301/689–8946. Reservations essential. AE, D, DC, MC, V. Closed Sun. and Mon.*

$$–$$$ ✕ **Oxford House.** Tucked away in the basement of the Inn at Walnut Bottom, the Oxford Inn is cozy but elegant, with oak chairs and white lace tablecloths. Noteworthy among the Swedish and Italian dishes are pork tenderloins, fresh Norwegian salmon, and Swedish Princess Torte—an angel-food cake with custard, strawberries, and whipped cream. ⊠ *118 Greene St.,* ☎ *301/777–7101. AE, D, MC, V.*

$$ ✕ **J. B.'s Steak Cellar.** A blazing fireplace, dark paneling, and cushioned chairs create a warm atmosphere in this basement-level restaurant, where skiers returning home from the Wisp Ski Area in neighboring Garrett County gather in the winter months. Cuts of beef and fresh seafood are displayed in a glass case in one of the two small dining rooms, and steaks are grilled in front of guests: Try the 20-ounce T-bone steak or prime rib. The crab soup is exceptional. ⊠ *Exit 46, I–68, 1 mi east of Cumberland,* ☎ *301/722–6155. AE, D, MC, V.*

$$ ✕ **L'Osteria.** Diners are treated like house guests at this family-owned trattoria outside Cumberland, overlooking Interstate 68. In the three Victorian-style dining rooms, lace and floral patterns abound. Veal and pasta are specialties: Try veal piccata, veal served with mushrooms and a light lemon-butter sauce—or any of the fresh seafood dishes. ⊠ *Exit 46, I–68, 1 mi east of Cumberland,* ☎ *301/777–3553. AE, D, DC, MC, V. Closed Sun.*

$$–$$$ ⌂ **The Castle.** In the old coal mining town of Mount Savage, this Gothic Revival stone house was built in 1840 to entice Dr. Alexander Thompson, the first town doctor, to the then-thriving frontier community. Dr. Thompson remained in the home until his death in the 1880s. A second owner doubled the house's size in 1890 and built a 12- to 15-foot stone wall that still surrounds the 2-acre estate. Modeled after a castle in Scotland, the 5,800-square-foot house has 21 rooms, two bathrooms with original clawfoot tubs and ceramic sinks, and a second-floor library where bookshelves line the walls from floor to ceiling. Guests are invited to enjoy the rose garden or the herb garden, where a pond is stocked with fish. Guests are served breakfast in the formal dining room; among the specialties are peach pancakes. ⊠ *Rte. 36, Mount*

Savage 21545, 9 mi northwest of Cumberland, ☎ *301/264–4645. 21 rooms. Dining room. AE, D, MC, V.*

$$–$$$ 🖭 **Inn at Walnut Bottom.** Within two 19th-century row houses connected by a modern addition, this charming country inn is near Cumberland's historic district. Antiques and reproductions of 19th-century country furniture are standard in each of the guest rooms. Lemonade, apple cider, and homemade sweets are served every afternoon in an upstairs sitting room, filled with games, puzzles, books and magazines. Breakfast is served in the Oxford House, a restaurant on the basement level (☞ *above*). Guests may rent bicycles for a ride along the flat towpath of the C&O Canal. ⊠ *120 E. Greene St., Cumberland 21502,* ☎ *301/777–0003 or 800/286–9718,* ℻ *301/777–8288. 12 rooms. Restaurant, bicycles. AE, D, MC, V.*

$–$$ 🖭 **The Braddock Best Western.** Along the Old National Highway, this atypical Best Western motel has a southwestern motif—a teal, aqua, and mauve color scheme, and plenty of plants. The motel is popular with business travelers. ⊠ *1268 National Hwy., LaVale 21502, 4 mi west of Cumberland,* ☎ *301/729–3300 or 800/296–6006,* ℻ *301/729–3300. 96 rooms, 12 suites. Restaurant, bar, pool, hot tub, sauna, exercise room.*

OFF THE
BEATEN PATH

SPRUCE FOREST ARTISAN VILLAGE AND PENN ALPS – The history and craftsmanship of Upper Appalachia are exhibited at this rustic museum village in Grantsville, where spinners, weavers, potters, stained-glass workers, wood sculptors, and bird carvers demonstrate their skills. Within the village, the Winterberg House, a log stagecoach stop, is the last remaining log tavern along the Old National Pike. It is now used as a crafts store and restaurant. ⊠ *Rte. 40, Grantsville, 21 mi west of Cumberland,* ☎ *301/895-3332.* ☉ *Memorial Day–Oct., Mon.–Sat. 10–5.*

CASSELMAN RIVER BRIDGE – Near Spruce Forest Artisan Village and Penn Alps is Casselman River Bridge, where America's largest single-span stone arch (when it was built in 1813), stands near the Spruce Artisan Village and Penn Alps. Though the bridge is no longer in use, it serves as the backdrop of a small state park and picnic area.

En Route   Along the Old National Highway out of Cumberland, now known as Route 40, stands the only remaining toll house on the National Pike in Maryland. Built in 1836, **Toll Gate House** is a four-room building that housed the gatekeeper, who collected tolls along the road until the 1900s. ⊠ *Old National Hwy. (Rte. 40), LaVale,* ☎ *301/729–3047.* ☉ *May–Aug., Sat.–Sun. 1:30–4:30.*

Deep Creek Lake State Park

⑮   *45 mi west of Cumberland; 135 mi west of Frederick.*

Garrett County's greatest asset, the 3,900-acre Deep Creek Lake was created in the 1920s as a water source for a hydroelectric plant on the Youghiogheny River—a favorite among kayakers and white-water rafters. Though much of the lake's 65-mi shoreline is inaccessible to the public, the lake is visible from Route 219 and from many restaurants and motels, many with private docks. Deep Creek Lake State Park offers a small public beach, camping, and interpretive programs.

Near Deep Creek Lake is Maryland's only alpine ski resort, the **Wisp Ski Area,** atop the 3,080-foot Marsh Mountain. Called "the Wisp" by locals, the mountain has a humble history: Its eastern face was once a cow pasture. Today it's one of Western Maryland's most popular destinations.

Dining and Lodging

$$–$$$ ✕ **McClives.** Overlooking Deep Creek Lake and the Wisp Ski Area, Mc-Clives is one of the region's busiest restaurants. One of the dining rooms has a Mediterranean feel; the other is designed like a ski chalet. Cathedral ceilings dominate both rooms, and the walls are decorated with painting of local scenery and landmarks. Specialties on the largely Continental menu include crab cakes, blackened prime rib, and chicken marsala. Be sure to try one of the homemade apple dumplings. ⊠ *1375 Deep Creek Dr., McHenry,* ☎ *301/387–6172. AE, D, DC, MC, V.*

$$–$$$ 🏠 **Lake Point Inn.** One of the area's newest properties, this restored 1890 stone farmhouse sits on a cove just 13 feet from Deep Creek Lake. A stone fireplace dominates the inn's Great Room, where guests can relax by a blazing fire. A wraparound porch has rocking chairs where you can pass the afternoon gazing out at the lake. The floor and paneling on the first floor are original chestnut. All rooms have lake views, and some overlook the ski slopes. Hors d'oeuvres are served in the Great Room in the evenings. ⊠ *174 Lake Pointe Dr., McHenry 21541,* ☎ *301/387–0111 or 800/523–5253,* FAX *301/387–0190. 9 rooms. D, MC, V.*

$$ 🏠 **Wisp Resort Hotel and Conference Center.** At the base of the ski slopes that crisscross Marsh Mountain, this seven-story hotel is a local landmark. Many rooms have views of the slopes or the hotel's 18-hole golf course. The lobby is homey and welcoming, with game boards, a comfortable sofa, and chairs and tables that invite guests to linger. Most of the rooms are suite-style, with contemporary furniture. Rooms here are simple but clean. ⊠ *290 Marsh Hill Rd., McHenry 21541,* ☎ *301/387–5581,* FAX *301/387–4127. 169 rooms. 2 restaurants, 2 bars, pool, 18-hole golf course, 2 tennis courts, mountain bikes, rollerblading, downhill skiing, ski shop. AE, D, DC, MC, V.*

Outdoor Activities and Sports

BICYCLING

High Mountain Sports (⊠ Rte. 219, McHenry, ☎ 301/387–4199) rents mountain bikes.

Rudy's (⊠ 290 Marsh Hill Rd., McHenry, ☎ 301/387–4640), at the Wisp ski resort, rents mountain bikes for nearby trails.

FISHING

Deep Creek Outfitters (⊠ 1899 Deep Creek Dr., McHenry, ☎ 301/387–6977) rents pontoon boats, fishing boats, and ski boats.

GOLF

Golf Club at Wisp (⊠ 290 Marsh Hill Rd., McHenry, ☎ 301/387–4911), an 18-hole course, is ranked one of the top 10 in Maryland by *Golf Digest Magazine.*

SKIING

Wisp Ski Area (⊠ 290 Marsh Hill Rd., McHenry, ☎ 301/387–4911) has 23 slopes and 80 acres of trails ranging from beginner to difficult; most are open for night skiing. Facilities include a ski shop, restaurants, bars, and a hotel (☞ *above*).

Oakland

⑯ *11 mi southwest of Deep Creek Lake State Park; 146 mi west of Frederick.*

Though it's the Garrett County seat, the town of Oakland keeps a low profile. Tucked away in Maryland's extreme southwestern corner, the town sits atop a mountain plateau, 2,650 feet above sea level. Oakland prospered during the last half of the 19th century, when the famous Baltimore and Ohio Railroad reached town, bringing summer vacationers. Trains no longer bring tourists, but Oakland survives as the government and commercial center of the county.

At **Swallow Falls State Park,** in the extreme southwestern corner of Maryland, paths wind along the Youghiogheny River, past shaded rocky gorges and rippling rapids, to a 63-foot waterfall. The park is also known for its stand of 300-year-old hemlocks and for its excellent camping, hiking, and fishing facilities. ⊠ *222 Herrington Ln., off Rte. 219, Oakland,* ☎ *301/334–9180.* ⊡ *$2 Memorial Day–Labor Day; free Labor Day–Memorial Day.* ⊙ *Daily dawn–dusk.*

Dining and Lodging

$$ ✕ **Four Seasons Dining Room.** Natural wood and local stone add to the natural grandeur of the Four Seasons Dining Room, which overlooks Deep Creek Lake; beige tablecloths and burgundy napkins set a subdued tone. The seasonal menu makes use of regionally grown produce in dishes such as Flounder Four Seasons—a flounder fillet sautéed with shrimp and served with a rich cream-and-Vermouth sauce. An Austrian pastry chef creates delectable desserts: Meringue shells with fresh fruit are popular in the summer. ⊠ *20160 Garrett Hwy., Oakland,* ☎ *301/387–5503, ext. 2201. AE, D, DC, MC, V.*

$$–$$$ ⛺ **Will O'the Wisp.** Although it's a condominium complex, the Will O'the Wisp rents 47 units to overnight guests. The units vary from one- to three-bedrooms, depending on availability. All of them overlook Deep Creek Lake, and many have fireplaces. ⊠ *20160 Garrett Hwy., Oakland 21550,* ☎ *301/387–5503. 47 units. Restaurant, pool, sauna, exercise room, beach. AE, D, MC, V.*

$$ ⛺ **The Oak and Apple Bed and Breakfast.** A 10-column front porch greets visitors to this three-story Colonial Revival house, built in 1915. Within, early-20th-century antiques add to the historic but livable mood. A "gathering room" on the second floor is filled with games, books, and a television; and a refrigerator is kept stocked with soft drinks. Three guest rooms have private baths; the other two share a hallway bathroom. Breakfast is served in an enclosed sunporch; baked oatmeal and homemade granola are typical morning fare. ⊠ *208 N. 2nd St., Oakland 21550,* ☎ *301/334–9265. 5 rooms. MC, V.*

Outdoor Activities and Sports

Upper Yough Expeditions (⊠ Macadam Rd., Friendsville, ☎ 301/746–5808 or 800/248–1893) provides guided white-water rafting trips on the Upper Youghiogheny and Savage rivers.

Precision Rafting (⊠ Main St., Friendsville, ☎ 800/477–3723) offers kayaking instruction and rafting trips on the Youghiogheny River.

FREDERICK AND WESTERN MARYLAND A TO Z

Arriving and Departing

Greyhound Lines (☎ 800/231–1607) makes several runs daily to Frederick from Baltimore and Washington, DC

By Bus

Greyhound Bus Lines (☎ 301/663–3311) provides daily transportation to Frederick, Hagerstown, Cumberland, and Keysers Ridge in Garrett County, from Baltimore; Washington, DC; and Pittsburgh, Pennsylvania.

By Car

I–70 connects Baltimore to Frederick and Hagerstown. About 30 mi west of Hagerstown is the start of I–68, which passes through Cumberland and Garrett County. I–270 connects Washington, DC, to Frederick and I–70.

By Plane

Frederick, Hagerstown, and Cumberland are all served by regional airports. Hagerstown has commuter flights to the Baltimore-Washington International Airport (BWI).

By Train

The Maryland Rail Commuter (MARC) line runs from Baltimore to Washington, DC, and to Brunswick and Point of Rocks in Frederick County. Amtrak service is available from Washington, DC, to Cumberland.

Getting Around

By Bus

Greyhound Bus Lines (✉ E. All Saints St., Frederick, ☎ 301/663–3311) has daily runs to Hagerstown, Cumberland, Frostburg, and Keysers Ridge. Frederick, Hagerstown, and Cumberland all operate municipal bus lines. Fares vary.

Frederick Transit provides bus service within Frederick and to outlying towns, including Thurmont, Emmitsburg, Jefferson, and Walkersville. Shuttle buses transport commuters to the Washington Metro at Shady Grove and Maryland's commuter train at Point of Rocks. The fare is $1.

By Car

The best way to see Western Maryland is by car. I–70 links Frederick to Hagerstown and intersects with Route 15 and I–270, the main highway to Washington, DC. West of Hagerstown, I–68—the main road through Western Maryland—passes through some of the most scenic stretches of the state. Follow Route 219 off I–68 to reach Deep Creek Lake and the more remote areas of Garrett County.

Contacts and Resources

Car Rentals

Allegany Rent-A-Car (✉ Cumberland Regional Airport, Rte. 1, Box 99, Wiley Ford, WV, ☎ 304/738–0002). **Avis Rent-A-Car** (✉ Washington County Regional Airport, 18434 Showalter Rd., Hagerstown, ☎ 800/831–2847).

Enterprise Leasing and Rent-A-Car (✉ 5728 Buckeystown Pike, Frederick, ☎ 301/831–4626).

Emergencies

For police, fire, and medical emergencies, dial 911.

HOSPITALS

Frederick Memorial Hospital (✉ 400 W. 7th St., Frederick, ☎ 301/698–3300). **Garrett County Memorial Hospital** (✉ 251 N. 4th St., Oakland, ☎ 301/334–2155). **Memorial Hospital and Medical Center** (✉ Memorial Ave., Cumberland, ☎ 301/777–4000). **Sacred Heart Hospital** (✉ 900 Seton Dr., Cumberland, ☎ 301/759–4200).

Guided Tours

Costumed guides lead walking tours, focusing on Frederick's 250 years of history. Tours start at the visitor center.

Heritage Koaches (✉ Box 26, Cumberland, 21501, ☎ 301/777–0714) provides horse-drawn trolley, carriage, and stagecoach tours of Cumberland.

Westmar Tours (✉ Box 26, Cumberland 21501, ☎ 301/777–7823) provides costumed theme tours of the Allegheny Mountain region.

Shircliffe Express Tours (✉ Box 624, Cumberland 21501, ☎ 301/759–0510 or 800/459–0510) offers guided bus tours of historic sites in Allegany and Garrett counties, as well as horse-drawn trolley rides.

Visitor Information

Washington County Convention and Visitor's Bureau (✉ 16 Public Sq., Hagerstown 21740, ☎ 301/791–3246) offers brochures on Hagerstown and county tourist attractions.

Allegany County Visitor's Bureau (✉ Mechanic and Harrison Sts., Cumberland 21502, ☎ 301/777–5905) publishes brochures on Allegany County and Cumberland historical and recreational sites.

Garrett County Promotion Council (✉ 200 S. 3rd St., Oakland 21550, ☎ 301/334–1948) annually publishes a glossy booklet about Garrett County and promotes a variety of outdoor activities, including hiking, biking, and camping trips at nearby state parks.

The Tourism Council of Frederick County (✉ 19 E. Church St., Frederick 21701, ☎ 301/663–8687), in the heart of the historic district, provides brochures that outline a self-guided tour in addition to guided walking tours.

9 Annapolis and Southern Maryland

The presence of more than 50 pre-Revolution buildings lends Annapolis an appropriate dignity. But Maryland's capital also has an unstoppable liveliness: City Dock draws pleasure seekers with outdoor dining and concerts, and sailboat and powerboat shows receive national coverage. South of Annapolis is the tobacco land of Calvert and St. Mary's counties, each dotted with small seaside towns. In the vicinity, ancient 100-foot trees shade a cypress swamp sanctuary, and 40- to 100-foot-tall clay cliffs tower over Calvert Cliffs State Park.

MARYLAND'S PAST IS NEVER FAR FROM the present among the scenic towns and villages that dot the coves, rivers, and creeks of the Chesapeake Bay's western shore. Colonial Maryland thrives in the 20th century in the port city of Annapolis. Outside Annapolis, southern Maryland's gentle landscape, sandy beaches, and bay breezes encourage visitors to linger. Tobacco fields blanket the countryside farther south along the peninsula to St. Mary's County, the mainland's southernmost point.

Exploring Annapolis and Southern Maryland

Annapolis and Southern Maryland encompass the western shore of the Chesapeake Bay, an area within easy driving distance of both Baltimore and Washington, DC. Annapolis, situated on a peninsula bounded by the Severn and South rivers and the Chesapeake Bay, is Maryland's sailing capital and the gateway to Southern Maryland, where tobacco fields are lingering reminders of another era. Neighboring Calvert County, less than an hour's drive south of Annapolis, offers compelling bayside scenery that includes the imposing Calvert Cliffs and several miles of bay beaches. Beyond the Patuxent River, across the 1½-mi Thomas Johnson Bridge, lies St. Mary's County, a peninsula that protrudes farther into the Chesapeake, with the Patuxent and the Potomac rivers on either side of it.

ANNAPOLIS

Numbers in the margin correspond to points of interest on the Annapolis map.

Annapolis, capital of Maryland, contains one of the highest concentrations of 18th-century architecture in the United States, including more than 50 pre-Revolutionary buildings. This considerable Colonial and early republican heritage is largely intact and, because it's all within walking distance, highly accessible; a visitor can do Annapolis justice in a single well planned day.

Puritan settlers relocating from Virginia in 1649 established the town of Providence at the mouth of the Severn River, a tributary of Chesapeake Bay. Lord Baltimore, who held the Maryland Royal charter, named the area around the town Anne Arundel County, after his wife. Anne Arundel Town was established in 1684 on the south side of the Severn, across from Providence, and in 1694 this town became Annapolis, the colonial capital city. From 1783 to 1784 Annapolis served as the nation's capital as well—the first peacetime capital of the United States.

Throughout the 18th century Annapolis was a major port, important in the tobacco trade. Today Baltimore is the principal Chesapeake port, but Annapolis remains a favored destination of oystermen and yachtsmen, and on warm days City Dock is thronged with sails billowing against a background of redbrick waterfront shops and restaurants. The sailboat and powerboat shows in October are events of national importance, and the nautical atmosphere of the town is accentuated by the regular presence on city streets of the strikingly uniformed midshipmen of the United States Naval Academy.

A good place to begin a tour of Annapolis is the visitor center that operates May–September at **City Dock** on the waterfront. Boats dozens of feet long, under motor and sail power, moor right at the edges of Dock Street and Market Square (also called Market Space), an open dockside area roughly the size of four city blocks, ringed with restaurants with outdoor seating. The Markethouse pavilion at the center of the square offers gourmet refreshments. The **Kunta Kinte Plaque,** on the sidewalk at the head of the dock, commemorates the 1767 arrival of the African slave immortalized in Alex Haley's *Roots.* On some summer evenings Market Square is the site of a band concert.

② The **Historic Annapolis Foundation Museum Store and Welcome Center,** on Main Street just off Market Square, occupies the site of a Continental army storehouse during the War of Independence, when Annapolis was a vital link in the chain of supply. Exhibits on the history of maritime commerce include a diorama of the city's waterfront in the 18th century and artifacts of Colonial-era trade. Walking tours of Annapolis narrated by Walter Cronkite can be rented here. ⊠ *77 Main St.,* ☎ *410/268–5576.* 🎫 *Free.* ☉ *Sun.–Mon. 10–5, Sat. 10–8.*

③ Main Street leads uphill to Church Circle, where the Episcopal **St. Anne's Church** (1858), the third church of that name on this site, incorporates some of the structure of an earlier church. The parish was founded in 1692, with the Protestant king of England William III donating the communion silver, which is still in service. In the churchyard is the grave of the last Colonial governor, Sir Robert Eden. ⊠ *Church Circle,* ☎ *410/267–9333.* ☉ *Daily 8–5.*

④ On Franklin Street, a block west of Church Circle, an ivy-covered redbrick former church houses the **Banneker-Douglass Museum of Afro-American Life,** the first African Methodist Episcopal Church of Annapolis, founded in 1803. Changing exhibits, lectures, and films present a picture of African-American life in Maryland. ⊠ *84 Franklin St.,* ☎ *410/974–2893.* 🎫 *Free.* ☉ *Tues.–Fri. 10–3, Sat. noon–4.*

★ **⑤** At State Circle, the domed **Maryland State House** of 1780 is the oldest state capitol in continuous legislative use and the only one that has housed the U.S. Congress—and its dome is the largest wooden dome in the country built without nails. When Congress convened here in 1783–84, it accepted the resignation of George Washington as commander-in-chief of the Continental army and ratified the Treaty of Paris, which concluded the War of Independence. Both proceedings took place in the Old Senate Chamber, whose intricate woodwork—featuring the ubiquitous tobacco motif—is attributed to William Buckland. Here, too, is the Charles Willson Peale painting, *Washington at the Battle of Yorktown.* The Maryland House and Senate meet in other chambers in the building. On the grounds is the oldest public edifice in Maryland, the minuscule redbrick **Treasury** of 1735. ⊠ *State Circle,* ☎ *410/974–3400.* ☉ *Daily 9–5.*

NEED A BREAK?   Deli sandwiches, milk shakes, and other ice-cream concoctions are the bill of fare at **Chick and Ruth's** (⊠ 165 Main St.), a longtime local counter-and-table institution with friendly waitresses, where the person on the next stool eating the Reuben sandwich may be a state legislator.

⑥ On College Street is **St. John's College.** The most famous alumnus of St. John's is Francis Scott Key, who wrote the verses of the "Star-Spangled Banner," but since 1937 the college has been best known for a Great Books curriculum that is structured on reading the works of more than 100 classic authors, from Homer to Freud, in seminars.

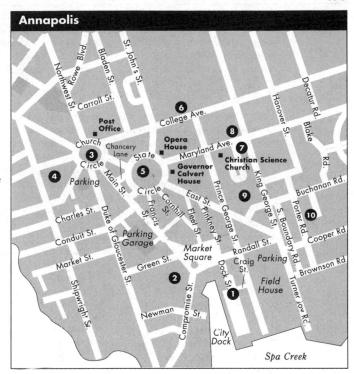

McDowell Hall, approached from College Avenue by a long brick path up a gradual slope, is a grand sight under its golden cupola. Begun in 1742 to serve as the governor's residence, it was never used for that purpose and took half a century to complete. This is the third-oldest academic building in the country, just as St. John's— founded as King William's School in 1696—is the third-oldest college in the country after Harvard and William and Mary. Here colonists and Native Americans concluded treaties in the 17th century, revolutionaries rallied in the 18th, and Union troops encamped in the 19th. The Liberty Tree, still standing on campus, is a 400-year-old tulip tree that served as a rallying point for meetings of the Sons of Liberty prior to the Revolutionary War. College commencement takes place here in spring.

The **Carroll-Barrister House** (☏ 410/263–2371), now the college admissions office, was built in 1722 at Main and Conduit streets and moved to the campus in 1957. It was the birthplace of Charles Carroll, who helped draft Maryland's Declaration of Rights.

7 On Maryland Avenue, the three-story, redbrick **Hammond-Harwood House** (1774) is the only verified full-scale example of the work of William Buckland, Colonial America's most prominent architect at his death in 1774. Buckland was famous for his woodwork, including that of the Chase-Lloyd House across the street and George Mason's Gunston Hall (near Mount Vernon). The Hammond-Harwood is distinguished by exquisite moldings, cornices, and other carvings, including garlands of roses above the front doorway. These refinements were garnishes on a manorial wedding present from Matthias Hammond, a lawyer and revolutionary, to a fiancée who jilted him before it was finished. After this disappointment, Hammond never married and he never lived in this elegant home. The Harwood family inhabited the house in the second half of the 19th century and during the first quarter of this century. The house is known for its fine collection of 18th-century and early 19th-century furniture and paintings, including the works of Charles Willson Peale. ⊠ *19 Maryland Ave.,* ☎ *410/269– 1714.* ⌑ *$4.* ⊙ *Mon.–Sat. 10–4, Sun. noon–4.*

To appease the tobacco planter Edward Lloyd IV, Matthias Hammond extended octagonal wings from his house rather than build to a height
⑧ that would block Lloyd's view of the harbor from the **Chase-Lloyd House** across the street—so the story goes. Work on the grand Georgian house actually began in 1769 for Samuel Chase, a U.S. Supreme Court Justice and signer of the Declaration of Independence. Lloyd finished the home in 1773; since then it has been in continuous use. (His daughter, Mary Taylor Lloyd, even married Francis Scott Key here in 1802.) The redbrick house has a massive but graceful facade with a central section that juts out dramatically from beneath a pediment. The interior is William Buckland's handiwork, including a parlor mantelpiece decorated with tobacco leaves (the source of the wealth that made the house possible, and a carved motif that can often be found throughout many early Maryland homes) carved in marble. The staircase parts dramatically around a Palladian window (a triple window whose center segment is taller than its flanks and arched). For most of this century the house has served as a home for elderly Episcopalian women. The boxwoods behind the home remain from the original gardens. ⊠ *22 Maryland Ave.,* ☎ *410/263–2723.* ⌑ *$2.* ⊙ *Mar.–Dec., Mon.–Wed., Fri.–Sat. 2–4.*

⑨ The 37-room redbrick **William Paca House and Gardens** mansion looms over Prince George Street, its raised portico and dormer windows (windows that emerge from the roof) lending it a strikingly steep aspect. The five-part house, built in 1765, and the gardens, originally finished in 1772 and restored in the present century, are what remain of the estate of William Paca, a signer of the Declaration of Independence and a governor of Maryland. Its furnishings are authentic period pieces, many of them from England, and its pine floors and front door are original. The adjacent 2-acre garden permits a longer perspective of the house from the rear, plus attractions of its own: a Chinese Chippendale bridge, a pond, a wilderness area, and beautiful formal arrangements. ⊠ *186 Prince George St.,* ☎ *410/263–5553.* ⌑ *$4 house, $3 gardens, $6 both.* ⊙ *Jan.–Feb., Fri.–Sat. 10–4, Sun. noon–4; Mar.–Dec., Mon.–Sat. 10–4, Sun. noon–4.*

⑩ At the **United States Naval Academy,** visitors can join a one-hour guided tour or set out on an independent expedition from the visitor center at Ricketts Hall, by the gate at Randall and King George streets. The academy, founded in 1845 on the site of a U.S. army fort, occupies 329 riverside acres. The most prominent structure on campus is the bronze dome of the interdenominational **U.S. Naval Chapel;** the building contains the crypt of the Revolutionary War hero John Paul Jones ("I have not yet begun to fight!"). A museum in **Preble Hall** tells the story of the U.S. Navy with displays of miniature ships and flags from the original vessels. There are periodic full-dress parades of midshipmen and, in the warmer months, noontime musters. Yet the most remarkable sight may be the representative student quarters—considerably neater than the typical college dorm room. ⊠ *52 King George St.,* ☎ *410/263–6933.* ⌑ *Free. Tours $5.* ⊙ *Daily 9–5. Tours depart Mar.–Dec., Mon.–Sat. 11 AM and 1 PM; Sun. 12:30 PM and 2:30 PM.*

Dining and Lodging

Dinner reservations in Annapolis are recommended throughout the summer and at times of Naval Academy events. Hotel reservations are necessary, even a year in advance, during the sailboat and powerboat shows in the spring and fall and Naval Academy commencement in May. Summer weekends are busy throughout the region.

$$$ ✕ **The Corinthian.** One of the most formal dining rooms in Annapolis, the Corinthian has the elegant feel of an old Maryland home, with padded armchairs, oil lamps, and a view of the six-story atrium that it overlooks. Corinthian Crab Cakes, made with angel-hair pasta as binders, and seared honey-hazelnut encrusted salmon are delectable seafood choices. All beef is dry-aged three weeks, including the New York strip steak and the filet mignon. This is also the place for an elegant breakfast any morning of the week. ⊠ *Loews Annapolis Hotel, 126 West St.,* ☎ *410/263–1299. AE, DC, MC, V.*

$$$ ✕ **Harry Browne's.** Sitting quietly across from Maryland's statehouse, this elegant dining room is a popular place for entertaining special guests and friends. Attentive service and quality Continental cuisine pack in a crowd, especially during the legislative session (mid-January–late March) and during June Week at the Naval Academy. The seasonal menu emphasizes seafood, though rack of lamb is also a specialty. In the lounge, there's entertainment ('70s and '80s music) Friday–Saturday, and Irish music on Monday nights. ⊠ *66 State Circle,* ☎ *410/263–4332. Reservations essential. MC, V.*

$$$ ✕ **Middleton's Tavern.** Since 1750, this waterfront building has served as a tavern. The present chef, a 40-year veteran, long ago perfected his own rich version of crab imperial, called crab Middleton; and his heavy Cuban black-bean soup is a rare treat in this neighborhood. The mood is warm and inviting: Wooden tables bear blue-and-white-check tablecloths at night, and in winter, fireplaces blaze in all four dining rooms. In the warmer months, three dozen tables out front allow diners to watch the lively stream of pedestrian traffic at City Dock. Acoustic pop music is performed nightly in the Oyster Bar lounge, where the famous Oyster Shooter—raw oysters served in a shot glass with vodka and cocktail sauce and washed down with beer—supposedly originated. Live entertainment is on hand upstairs on Friday and Saturday. ⊠ *2 Market Space,* ☎ *410/263–3323. AE, D, MC, V.*

$$–$$$ ✕ **Café Normandie.** Wood-beamed ceilings and rough-plastered walls make this a romantic retreat. A large fireplace dominates the dining room, where guests can sit at either wooden tables or wooden booths. The eclectic menu includes Continental as well as French cuisine, and a variety of entrée and dessert crepes that changes nightly. A local favorite is crepes Annapolis, shrimp and scallops served with a lobster sauce. The extensive wine list is mostly French. ⊠ *185 Main St.,* ☎ *410/263–3382. AE, MC, V.*

$$ ✕ **McGarvey's Saloon and Oyster Bar.** This casual spot just a block from the Annapolis dock offers excellent East Coast seafood, steaks, burgers, and finger food. The full menu is available daily until 1 AM. ⊠ *8 Market Space,* ☎ *410/263–5700. AE, MC, V.*

$$$$ ▥ **Annapolis Marriott Waterfront.** A recent renovation of this luxury waterfront hotel resulted in a new pastel-and-floral theme in the rooms. In addition, the restaurant—now called Pusser's Landing—now has a Caribbean-British flair, offering English fish-and-chips, British ales, and Jamaican-style finger foods. The best rooms offers guests vantage points for enjoying the bustle of City Dock, but even the less expensive rooms look out on the water or over the Annapolis historic district. Most guests are business travelers and conventioneers, and hotel services are oriented to them, with exercise equipment reserved for occupants of concierge-level (top-floor) rooms. The lively outdoor bar at the water's edge is especially popular on summer nights. ⊠ *80 Compromise St., 21401,* ☎ *410/268–7555,* FAX *410/269–5864. 150 rooms. Restaurant, 2 bars, business services, meeting rooms. AE, D, DC, MC, V.*

$$$$ 🖬 **Governor Calvert House.** The original brick structure was built in
★ 1727 on property owned by Charles Calvert, second governor of Maryland. It was expanded in the 19th century to become the mayor's residence, then more extensively in 1986 to serve as a full-service, intermediate-size hotel—large for an inn, small for the well-equipped conference center it is. The Colonial and Victorian era rooms are furnished in period antiques, the modern additions with quality reproductions. Some of the rooms are in historical buildings; others are in new additions. Governor Calvert House also serves as the registration desk for three other neighboring properties of Historic Inns of Annapolis: Robert Johnson House, with 30 rooms; State House Inn, with nine rooms, three of them "Jacuzzi suites"; and Maryland Inn, with 44 rooms, a restaurant, a tavern, and a wine bar. ⊠ *58 State Circle, 21401,* ☎ *410/263–2641 or 800/847–8882,* FAX *410/268–3813. 51 rooms. AE, DC, MC, V.*

$$$$ 🖬 **Loews Annapolis Hotel.** Just six blocks from City Dock, this luxu-
★ rious hotel offers a panorama of downtown and the water from rooms (with balconies) on the top two floors. Guest quarters come in more than a dozen sizes and shapes, at various prices, but all have desks, bathroom phones, and bright, flowery wallpaper. A Starbucks Coffee bar is open in the morning in the lobby. The hotel's conference center—in a converted railroad powerhouse next door—and fitness facilities are provided with the business traveler in mind. ⊠ *126 West St., 21401,* ☎ *410/263–7777 or 800/223–0888,* FAX *410/263–0084. 220 rooms. 2 restaurants, bar, exercise room, concierge, convention center. AE, DC, MC, V.*

$$ 🖬 **Gibson's Lodgings.** Three detached houses stand together on the other side of a fence from the United States Naval Academy (offering guests occasional glimpses of Navy enlistees sneaking in and out of the academy). Although one formal dining room here is equipped for gatherings of up to 50, the inn's character is predominantly that of bed-and-breakfast intimacy. Furnishings of the guest rooms and common rooms in each of the three houses reflect a harmoniously eclectic taste, with brass and wood beds suited to their respective rooms. A hallway lined with mirrors is a striking feature in one of the houses. Even more unusual is the first-floor room designed for disabled access, with a specially equipped bathroom and a small private porch. Six other rooms have private bath, TV, and phone. Free parking in the courtyard is a big advantage in the heart of a small city with heavy traffic. Room rates include Continental breakfast, served in the formal dining room of the 200-year-old Patterson House. ⊠ *110–114 Prince George St., 21401,* ☎ *410/268–5555. 20 rooms; 2 suites. Dining room. Free parking. AE, MC, V.*

$$ 🖬 **Prince George Inn.** This three-story brick Italianate Victorian town
★ house was built in 1884. The rooms, two with baths, are decorated with antiques of the period. One room is distinguished by a bay window. All rooms face the street, with views of either Prince George Street or—beyond neighboring yards—Maryland Avenue, but traffic noise is minimal at night. Breakfast is served in an enclosed sunporch, which overlooks a flower garden and fountain. ⊠ *232 Prince George St., 21401,* ☎ *410/263–6418. 4 rooms. MC, V. Rates include breakfast.*

$$ ⊞ **William Page Inn.** Built in 1908, this dark brown, cedar-shingle, wood-frame structure was the local Democratic party clubhouse for 50 years. Today its wraparound porch is furnished with Adirondack chairs, and among the period antiques indoors are appropriate Victorian reproductions. All rooms have a queen-size bed and no phone; only the sloped-ceiling third-floor suite with dormer windows and an Italian-marble bathroom with Jacuzzi has a TV. Guests in two rooms walk out into the hall to reach a bathroom. Breakfast (included in the rate) is served in the common room. ⊠ *8 Martin St., 21401,* ☎ *410/626–1506. 4 rooms; 1 suite. AE, MC, V.*

Nightlife and the Arts

Bars with Entertainment

King of France Tavern (⊠ 16 Church Circle, ☎ 410/263–2641) sees bands jam from 9 PM on Monday. There are folk performances from 9 PM Thursday.

Marmaduke's Pub (⊠ 3rd and Severn Sts., Eastport, ☎ 410/269–5420) has a sing-along in its upstairs pub on Friday and Saturday nights.

Middleton Tavern (⊠ City Dock, ☎ 410/263–3323) has live acoustical music nightly at the upstairs bar; on Sunday nights from 7 to 10 you can join the Sunday Blues.

Theater

The Colonial Players (⊠ 108 East St., ☎ 410/268–7373) is the city's principal theater troupe.

Annapolis Summer Garden Theater (⊠ Compromise and Main Sts., ☎ 410/268–0809) stages a mix of musicals and plays, including occasional works by local authors.

Outdoor Activities and Sports

Participant Sports

BEACHES

Anne Arundel County has **Sandy Point State Park** (⊠ Rte. 50, 12 mi east of Annapolis, ☎ 410/974–2149), with a mile of beach for fishing and swimming, 22 launching ramps for boats, rock jetties extending into the bay, and a fishing pier.

BICYCLING

Ten different waterproof and tearproof maps of the "Best Bike Routes in Maryland" are available for $9.95 each, or $29.95 for the set (⊠ Box 16388, Baltimore 21210, ☎ 800/394–3626), or from most bike shops.

The Baltimore & Annapolis Trail (⊠ Earleigh Heights Rd., Severna Park, ☎ 410/222–6244) runs through 13 mi of farmland and forests as well as urban and suburban neighborhoods, from Annapolis to Glen Burnie. It follows the old Baltimore & Annapolis Railroad and is open sunrise to sunset to hikers, bikers, runners, and rollerbladers.

Pedal Pushers Bike Shop (⊠ 546 Baltimore and Annapolis Blvd., Severna Park, ☎ 410/544–2323) rents bikes for the B&A Trail.

FISHING

Anglers (⊠ 1456 Whitehall Rd., ☎ 410/974–4013) sells and rents fishing equipment.

Chesapeake Bay Adventures (⊠ 1934 Lincoln Dr., Suite B, 21401, ☎ 410/268–4298) offers sportfishing trips, customized yacht charters (power or sail), and Chesapeake Bay excursions. Charters can be designed for any size group.

"Samuel Middleton" Fishing Charters (⊠ 2 Market Space, 21401, ☎ 410/263–3323) charters a vintage Chesapeake Bay fishing boat for a day (or half-day) jaunt on the bay. Later, you can have your catch prepared at the Middleton Tavern, which overlooks the harbor.

GOLF

Eisenhower Golf Course (⊠ Generals Hwy., Crownsville, ☎ 410/222–7922) is 3 mi northwest of Annapolis.

HEALTH AND FITNESS CLUBS

Merritt Athletic Club (⊠ 1981 Moreland Pkwy., ☎ 410/263–5400) offers a three-visit membership for $5 to guests at any Annapolis hotel. Facilities include Nautilus and StairMaster equipment, stationary bicycles, racquetball and squash courts, and whirlpools.

SAILING

Annapolis Sailing School (⊠ 601 6th St., ☎ 410/267–7205) is "America's oldest and largest sailing school," where the inexperienced can take a two-hour basic lesson. In addition, live-aboard, cruising, and advanced-sailing programs are available, as are boat rentals. **Womanship** (⊠ Boathouse, 410 Severn Ave., ☎ 410/267–6661 or 800/342–9295) is a sailing program *by* women, *for* women, at all levels of experience.

SWIMMING

Arundel Olympic Swim Center is an outstanding facility that includes an indoor 50-meter swimming pool, large spa, wading pool, and two 1-meter diving boards. Facilities are disabled-accessible. ⊠ *2690 Riva Rd.,* ☎ *410/222–7933.* ◌ *Daily. Call for hrs.*

TENNIS

The **Annapolis Department of Parks and Recreation** (☎ 410/263–7958) maintains six lighted courts at Truxton Park (⊠ Forest Dr. and Hilltop La.) and 10 lighted courts at Annapolis High School (Riva Rd.).

WATER SPORTS

Paradise Bay Yacht Charters (⊠ 410 Severn Ave., ☎ 410/268–9330 or 800/877–9330) has well-maintained sail and power yachts. Captained and bareboat charters are available for a day, weekend, week, or longer.

Spectator Sports

The **United States Naval Academy Athletic Association (NAAA)** (ticket office, ☎ 410/268–6060) offers 33 varsity sports, most notably football. The team plays home games in the fall at the Navy–Marine Corps Stadium on Rowe Boulevard in Annapolis.

BOAT RACES

Annapolis Yacht Club (☎ 410/263–9279) sponsors sailboat races at 6:30 PM each Wednesday in July and August in Annapolis Harbor, starting at the Eastport bridge.

JOUSTING

The **Amateur Jousting Club of Maryland** (⊠ Box 367, Glen Arm 21057, ☎ 410/592–5952) can provide details on about 48 jousting tournaments and events that take place from April through November. The longest-running tournament of the state sport is held the last Saturday in August at Christ Episcopal Church in Port Republic.

Shopping

In **downtown Annapolis** you'll find arts and crafts, funky and foolish fashion, home decor, whimsical junk, outdoor apparel, clothing and necessities for salts and would-be sailors, and, of course, souvenirs.

Annapolis Mall (⌂ 109 Annapolis Mall, Annapolis 21401, ☎ 410/841–6111) presents more than 125 clothing and shoe stores, home design and appliance centers, audio and video outlets, boutiques, general merchandise department stores, and restaurants.

Antiques

Annapolis Antique Gallery (⌂ 2009 West St., Annapolis, ☎ 410/266–0635) is a consortium of 20 dealers with an inventory that ranges from Victorian to Art Deco.

Ron Snyder Antiques (⌂ 2011 West St., Annapolis, ☎ 410/266–5452) specializes in 18th- and 19th-century American furniture displayed in seven tastefully decorated rooms.

En Route Eight miles south of Annapolis, at Edgewater on the South River, the **Londontowne Publick House** is an 18th-century inn and terminus to a ferry route to Annapolis. It's the only remaining building of a once thriving community and is furnished as it might have looked during that period. There are more than 10 acres of landscaped and wooded gardens, in addition to themed walks, including a Spring Flower Walk and an American Wildflower Walk. A few picnic tables are on the premises, and catering is available for special functions, but otherwise visitors must bring their own provisions. Follow Route 2 on Mayo Road to get here. ⌂ *839 Londontown Rd., Edgewater, ☎ 410/222–1919.* ⌷ *$5. ☼ Mar.–Dec., Tues.–Sat. 10–4, Sun. noon–4.*

SOUTHERN MARYLAND

Numbers in the margin correspond to points of interest on the Southern Maryland map.

South of Annapolis and Washington, DC, the Western Shore peninsula of Maryland is prominently cleft by the Patuxent River, a 110-mi tributary of Chesapeake Bay, which separates Calvert County in the north from St. Mary's County in the south. The river's name, in the language of the original natives, meant "where tobacco grows," and it was this stinking "sotweed"—along with the seafood industry—that supported the local economy for centuries. Tobacco and cornfields commonly border the highways across the flat terrain of this coastal plain region, an area for touring and fishing. Calvert County also has a couple of rare bay beaches.

Chesapeake Beach

⑪ *32 mi south of Annapolis (via Rte. 2).*

In Chesapeake Beach, a bayside town in northern Calvert County, the **Chesapeake Beach Railway Museum** stands as a reminder of the town's glory days as a seaside resort. The 1898 railroad station contains a poignant collection of relics from a brief heyday. Chesapeake Beach was founded in 1900 as a business venture, a seaside resort linked by rail to Washington, DC, and Baltimore. In time, the decline of train travel and of the traditional middle-class Chesapeake Bay vacation led to the town's demise as a business. Grand hotel, racetrack, casino, and boardwalk attractions are gone. ⌂ *Rte. 261, Chesapeake Beach,* ☎

410/257–3892. ▣ *Free.* ◷ *May–Sept., daily 1–4; Apr. and Oct., weekends 1–4.*

Dining

$$ ✕ **Penwick House.** You'll get the feeling you've entered another time zone when you visit the Penwick House. Glowing candlelight, fresh flowers, Oriental rugs, waiters in historic costumes, a garden and an enclosed patio, and a fireplace offer an atmosphere that almost equals the food. Enjoy the heritage that embodies Maryland cuisine, which includes hearty soups, fresh seafood, beef, pork, and chicken cooked southern-Maryland style. Along with your entrée, try the pumpkin muffins, and after your meal at least share one of the homemade desserts. This is also a great place for Sunday brunch (10:30–2). ⊠ *Rte. 4, Pennsylvania Ave. extended at Ferry Landing Rd., Dunkirk,* ☎ *301/855–5388 or 410/257–7077. Reservations essential. AE, D, MC, V. Closed Mon.*

$$ ✕ **Rod and Reel.** As its name implies, this is *the* place for anyone who enjoys fishing and its rewards. In business since 1946, the family-owned eatery has five bars, one outside, and a large dining room that overlooks the Chesapeake Bay. In addition to hosting an annual fishing tournament—and offering fishing charters and slips for boaters—the restaurant serves some of the best seafood around. Rockfish, in season, is among the specialties. Crab is served every which way: crab balls, crab imperial, crab cakes, and crab quesadilla. ⊠ *Rte. 261 and Mears Ave., Chesapeake Beach,* ☎ *410/257–2735. AE, D, MC, V.*

Outdoor Activities and Sports

GOLF

Twin Shields Golf Club (⊠ Rte. 260, Dunkirk, ☎ 301/257–7800) is 8 mi northwest of Chesapeake Beach.

TENNIS

Dunkirk Park (⊠ Rte. 4, Dunkirk) has four tennis courts.

Sunderland

⑫ *6 mi southwest of Chesapeake Beach; 28 mi southwest of Annapolis.*

All Saints Episcopal Church (1775), a mile south of Sunderland, is the redbrick replacement for a log building that served as the sanctuary of an Episcopal parish founded in 1692. Traffic noise from the highway junction mars the calm of the hilltop site, yet the trees create a calm among the 18th-century tombstones that mark the family plots, all fenced with wrought iron. Indoors, the clay-tile floor, classic white box pews, and plain windows set off the subtle blue-and-rose stained-glass window over the altar. ⊠ *Jct. Rtes. 2 and 4, Sunderland,* ☎ *410/257–6306.* ◷ *Daily 10–5.*

Prince Frederick

⑬ *10 mi south of Sunderland; 38 mi south of Annapolis (where Rte. 2 merges with Rte. 4).*

Prince Frederick, a town of only 1,800, is the Calvert County seat. Three times the town has been destroyed by fire; each time, the county courthouse went up in flames. The current courthouse, on Main Street, is a white-columned, redbrick building with a green tin roof, dating from 1916.

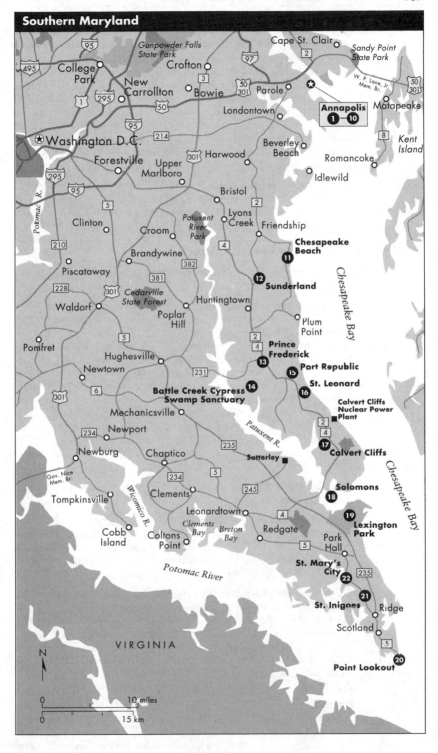

Dining

$$$ ✕ **Old Field Inn.** This wood-frame house was built in 1885 by a branch of the Briscoe family that once owned Sotterley Plantation in St. Mary's County. In two of the three dining rooms, Oriental rugs cover the wood floors; the tables in all three rooms have linen cloths and candlelight in the evening, and old family portraits hang on the walls. The menu is classic, the food high-quality. Try the Veal Wellington, stuffed veal wrapped in a pastry and served with a tomato-and-wine sauce. The seafood sampler—an appetizer prepared for two—includes clams casino (with bacon, cheese, and vegetables) and stuffed mushroom caps. ⊠ *485 Main St., Prince Frederick,* ☎ *410/535–1054. AE, D, MC, V. No lunch weekends.*

Outdoor Activities and Sports

The Calvert County Department of Parks and Recreation (☎ 301/535–1600) supervises four courts at **Hollowing Point Park** (⊠ Rte. 231, Prince Frederick).

Battle Creek Cypress Swamp Sanctuary

🐾 ⑭   *6 mi southwest of Prince Frederick; 44 mi southwest of Annapolis (via Rte. 2/4)*

With the northernmost stand of bald cypress trees in the United States, Battle Creek Cypress Swamp Sanctuary is a place to glimpse the forest primeval. The 10-acre swamp, thick with the 100-foot members of an ancient species, can be comfortably inspected from a ¼-mi elevated boardwalk at the bottom of a steep but sturdy column of steps. Attendants at the nature center alert visitors to the seasonal permutations of the vegetation and the activities of squirrels, owls, and other wildlife. Indoor exhibits focus on the area's natural and cultural history and include a working beehive under glass. ⊠ *Rte. 506,* ☎ *410/535–5327.* ⊞ *Free.* ⊙ *Apr.–Sept., Tues.–Sat. 10–5, Sun. 1–5; Oct.–Mar., Tues.–Sat. 10–4:30, Sun. 1–4:30.*

Port Republic

⑮   *5 mi east of Battle Creek Cypress Swamp Sanctuary; 41 mi south of Annapolis (via Rte. 2/4).*

In Port Republic, **Christ Episcopal Church** (1772) is notable for its biblical garden planted with species mentioned in the scriptures. Look for the Madonna lily and the Judas tree. The congregation was founded in 1672 in a log cabin. ⊠ *3100 Broomes Island Rd. (Rte. 264), Port Republic,* ☎ *410/586–0565.* ⊞ *Free.* ⊙ *Dawn–dusk.*

The **Port Republic School No. 7,** near Christ Episcopal Church in a small grove of trees, is a classic one-room schoolhouse built in the 1880s. Until 1932 a single teacher taught children in seven grades here. The schoolhouse has been restored and furnished with archetypal desks, inkwells, and a school bell. Since 1868 the grounds have been a venue for jousting—the oldest state tournament of the official state sport— on the last Saturday in August. ⊠ *3100 Broomes Island Rd. (Rte. 264), Port Republic,* ☎ *410/586–0232.* ⊙ *June–Aug., Sun. 2–4.*

Dining

$ ✕ **Stoney's Seafood House.** This off-the-beaten-path restaurant in ★ Broomes Island is worth the detour for its crab cakes alone. The larger-than-usual portions are all back fin, no filler. Oyster sandwiches and Stoney's Steamer—handpicked selections of fresh crustaceans—are among the popular seafood choices. Desserts are homemade, and like the crab cakes, their portions are extra large. The restaurant overlooks

Island Creek, a tributary of the Patuxent River; evenings and weekends you'll find it crowded with sailors, boaters, and locals. ⊠ *Oyster House Rd., Broomes Island,* ☎ *410/586–1888. AE, MC, V.*

St. Leonard

⑯ *2 mi south of Port Republic; 43 mi south of Annapolis (via Rte. 2/4).*

Behind 2½ mi of scenic Patuxent riverfront stretch 512 acres of woods and farmland on which more than 70 archaeological sites have yielded evidence of 9,000 years of human habitation. At the **Jefferson Patterson Park and Museum** in St. Leonard, visitors follow an archaeology trail to inspect artifacts of the successive hunter-gatherer, early agricultural, and plantation societies that exploited the resources of this area. Primitive knives and axes, fragments of Native American pottery, and Colonial glassware are among the items that have been recovered and are on display here. Stroll along the nature trails to take a look at wildlife, antique agricultural equipment, and fields of crops. ⊠ *Mackall Rd., Rte. 265, St. Leonard,* ☎ *410/586–0050 or 410/586–0055.* ☞ *Free.* ☉ *Apr. 15–Oct. 15, Wed.–Sun. 10–5.*

☙ **Flag Ponds Nature Park,** on the eastern side of the peninsula, is one of the few Chesapeake Bay beaches in Calvert County open to the public. In the first half of this century this was the location of a busy fishery. Now its attractions—in addition to the shoreline and its fishing pier—include 3 mi of gently graded hiking trails, observation decks at two ponds, a boardwalk through wetlands, and indoor wildlife exhibits. Fossil hunting also is a popular activity here. As the 327 acres contain both marshland and cliffs, they hold a diversity of plant and animal life, including indigenous wildflowers—notably the blue flag iris. ⊠ *Rte. 2/4, St. Leonard,* ☎ *410/586–1477 or 410/535–5327.* ☞ *Car $6.* ☉ *Memorial Day–Labor Day, weekdays 9–6, weekends 9–8; Sept.–May, weekends 9–6.*

Outdoor Activities and Sports

Breton Bay Country Club (⊠ Rte. 243, ☎ 301/475–2300), southwest of Leonardtown, has an 18-hole golf course.

Calvert Cliffs

⑰ *6 mi southeast of St. Leonard; 49 mi south of Annapolis (via Rte. 2/4).*

☙ **Calvert Cliffs Nuclear Power Plant,** the first such plant in the state, is ¼ mi south of Flag Ponds Nature Park; its generator towers, rising before the cliffs, make an incongruous sight. Atop the cliffs, overlooking the reactor and Chesapeake Bay, a restored barn from 1818 has bundles of strong-smelling tobacco hanging from the ceiling and stuffed into hogshead barrels; it also houses sophisticated exhibits on atomic energy. A computer quiz linked to a scale-model reactor allows visitors to manipulate the fuel rods (it buzzes to signify human error). Youngsters can burn off excess energy at stationary bicycle-generators. On the grounds are the foundations of a 19th-century farmhouse and a heavily populated wildlife sanctuary whose inhabitants include spectacular snowy egrets, wild turkey, and white-tail deer. Some 80 acres of this land are still under cultivation, producing wheat and corn. From the observation deck on a clear day observers can spot the Eastern Shore. ⊠ *Rte. 2/4, Lusby,* ☎ *410/260–4676.* ☞ *Free.* ☉ *Daily 10–4.*

★ ☙ **Calvert Cliffs State Park** is the site of the Calvert Cliffs, famous for the fossils they contain. Dating from the Miocene era, which began 15–

20 million years ago, the 600-plus species of fossils are on view at the nuclear plant visitor center. Visitors can scavenge for, and keep, shark's teeth and other fossils along the beach, which is reached on foot by a 2-mi trail from the parking lot of the 1,600-acre park. Access to the cliffs, which range from 40 to 100 feet, is prohibited because of the danger of landslides. A children's playground has swings, a slide, and a jungle gym. Fishing and picnicking are permitted. *Rte. 2/4, Lusby,* ☎ *410/888–1410.* ☉ *Fri.–Sun. 10–6. Schedule for rest of wk varies; call for additional hrs.*

<table>
<tr><td>OFF THE
BEATEN PATH</td><td>**MIDDLEHAM CHAPEL** – This small redbrick cruciform structure was erected in 1748 on the foundations of a "chapel of ease" (a chapel situated in a convenient location for the dispersed population) that was built in 1684. Visitors must park carefully on the highway and climb a dozen steps to the sanctuary, whose acute roofline and lack of ornament lend it a storybook cuteness from the front. Indoors the atmosphere is cozy but solemn. Among the exposed beams in the ceiling hang anachronistic fans, which are used on summer Sundays in this swampy climate. The chapel is surrounded by tall hickory trees and tombstones from as far back as the 18th century. A bell given to the congregation in 1699 still calls the faithful to worship. ✉ *Rte. 765, Lusby,* ☎ *410/326–9507.* 🖾 *Free.* ☉ *By request.*</td></tr>
</table>

Nightlife and the Arts
Vera's White Sands (✉ Rte. 4, Lusby, ☎ 410/586–1182) has a comfortable lounge overlooking the St. Leonard's Creek marina.

Outdoor Activities and Sports
There are four lighted tennis courts at **Cove Point Park** (✉ Rte. 765, Lusby).

Solomons

🔞 *7 mi south of Lusby; 59 mi south of Annapolis (via Rte. 2/4).*

On the tip of the peninsula, where the Patuxent empties into the Chesapeake, Solomons is a tranquil, relaxed town that attracts many sailors and boaters, who rate its charms on a par with St. Michaels and Annapolis.

★ ♻ The aptly situated **Calvert Marine Museum** recounts the histories of both the river and the bay. The bright and spacious exhibition hall contains models and life-size examples of business and pleasure boats that represent phases in local maritime history; blacksmith and ship's carpenter shops have been re-created; and a 15-tank estuarium shows the diversity of marine life on the bay and the Patuxent River, where river otters can be spotted at play. In the supervised Discovery Room, children may sift through a tray that has shark's teeth and other fossils among the sand and gravel, and then use microscopes to examine them. Outside, small craft of different periods are on display in a waterside shed, and visitors are welcome to take cruises on a converted 1899 bugeye sailboat. The greatest spectacle, however, is the restored Drum Point Lighthouse, built in 1883 and transported here in 1975: It is of the squat yet graceful screw-pile design, a hexagonal house poised like an insect on six slender legs. Tours of the cramped quarters are somewhat strenuous; senior citizens, preschoolers, and people with heart problems are discouraged from taking them. ✉ *Rte. 2/4 at Solomons Island Rd., Solomons,* ☎ *410/326–2042.* 🖾 *$3.* ☉ *Daily 10–5.*

Affiliated with the Calvert Marine Museum is the **J. C. Lore & Sons Oysterhouse,** a processing plant built in 1934 and converted to a museum of the local seafood industries, displaying the tools of the trades and illustrating the work of oystermen, crabbers, and fishermen. The oyster house, a short walk south from the museum, is on the harborfront strip of Solomons Island Road, where visitors find restaurants, antiques shops, and plentiful parking. ⊙ *Memorial Day–Labor Day, daily 10– 5.*

Dining and Lodging

$$$ ✕ **The Dry Dock.** Grilled rockfish in béarnaise sauce and grilled blackened tenderloin are among the choices at this small restaurant on the second floor of a boat house overlooking Solomons Harbor. The theme is nautical: Flags hang from the ceiling; pictures of ducks and waterfowl adorn the walls. The mood is intimate and informal. ⊠ *Box 760, Solomons,* ☎ *410/326–4817. AE, MC, V.*

$$$ ✕ **Lighthouse Inn.** The first-floor dining room has a view of Solomons Harbor on Back Creek; from the nearly floor-to-ceiling windows of the second floor, diners look onto the creek toward the Patuxent River. Indoors, the polished wood tables are illuminated with gas lanterns, the ceiling beams are exposed, and the floors carpeted. Fishing nets and pictures of old Solomons set the mood, and the bar is a replica of an oyster boat. The chef seasons his crab cakes following a recipe that is closely guarded in the competitive crab market. The catch of the day, which can take inventive form, is frequently sautéed. In the warm months, the harbor can be watched from the partially covered "quarterdeck," where lighter fare is served. ⊠ *Solomons Island Rd., Solomons,* ☎ *410/326–2444. AE, D, DC, MC, V. No lunch Mon.–Fri. Lunch outdoors on weekends, weather permitting.*

$$ ✕ **The CD Cafe.** Formerly the Main Street Grill, the CD Cafe describes itself as a coffee house with a bistro flair. Fresh flowers on every table create an inviting atmosphere. The menu is limited but inventive: Try the pan-seared chicken breast with pecans, apples, onions, and deglazed apple schnapps. Vegetarian, pasta, and seafood dishes are also fine, and the homemade desserts are spectacular. The restaurant overlooks the main road into Solomons and the Patuxent River. ⊠ *14350 Solomons Island Rd., Solomons,* ☎ *410/326–3877. MC, V.*

$$$ ▥ **Solomons Victorian Inn.** On the Back Creek side of narrow Solomons Island stands this three-story, white wood-frame house built by a local seafood magnate in 1906 and operated as a bed-and-breakfast since 1985. Four rooms look onto Solomons Harbor and two face the yard. All are furnished with period antiques and reproductions in comparable proportions, and every room has an ornate armoire; none has phone or TV. A third-floor suite offers a panoramic view of the harbor. Afternoon refreshments and breakfast are served on a screened porch. ⊠ *Charles and Maltby Sts., Box 759, Solomons 20688,* ☎ *410/326–4811. 5 rooms, 1 suite. MC, V.*

$$ ▥ **Back Creek Inn.** Behind this wood-frame house built by a water-
★ man in 1890 are an outdoor deck and a Jacuzzi; beyond that the lawn leads to the very edge of Back Creek. A cottage on the grounds holds a one-bedroom apartment, and an extension to the main house completed in 1986 contains two suites. In the guest rooms colorful quilts cover the beds, three of which are brass. Three rooms enjoy views of either the Patuxent or Back Creek; the others face a lovely perennial garden or a quiet street. The suites and the cottage have TVs. Breakfast is served in the dining room or in the garden, which has a lily pond. The kitchen's chocolate chip cookies are addictive. ⊠ *Calvert and Alexander Sts., Solomons 20688,* ☎ *410/326–2022. 4 rooms, 2 suites, 1 cottage. MC, V. Closed mid-Dec.–mid-Feb.*

$$ 🏨 **Holiday Inn Select Conference Center and Marina.** In this five-story waterfront hotel, every guest room has a water view (if you count the swimming pool); rooms look onto the cove, the open creek, or the court-yard. Designed to accommodate plenty of convention and meeting business, the hotel provides amenities such as whirlpools in some suites. Rooms are heavily booked, so early reservations are advised. ⊠ *155 Holiday Rd., Box 1099, Solomons 20688,* ☎ *410/326–6311 or 800/356–2009,* FAX *410/326–1069. 326 rooms. Restaurant, 2 bars, pool, sauna, 2 tennis courts, exercise room. AE, D, DC, MC, V.*

Nightlife and the Arts

At **Solomons Pier** (⊠ Solomons Island Rd., Solomons, ☎ 410/326–2424) a DJ spins pop tunes of the 1960s and 1970s and lighter recent hits.

Outdoor Activities and Sports

BICYCLING

Cycle 90 (⊠ Solomons Island Rd., Solomons, ☎ 301/326–2864) rents bicycles.

BOAT RACES

Zanhiser's Sailing Center (☎ 410/326–2166) has details of the annual powerboat and sailing-yacht races that are held at Solomons in August.

Shopping

Grandmother's (⊠ Dowell Rd., Dowell, 2 mi northeast of Solomons, ☎ 301/326–3366) showcases restored trunks and country oak furniture; its branch store, **Grandmothers II** (Solomons Island Rd., Solomons, ☎ 301/326–6848), is in a complex of similar shops at Harmon House.

OFF THE
BEATEN PATH

SOTTERLEY – While it hardly ranks with Shirley and its James River neighbors in Virginia, this distinguished plantation house does not deserve to be overlooked by visitors and guides, as it is. Not only is the house surrounded by the only working 18th-century plantation in Maryland open to the public, it is the earliest known (1727) posted-beam structure in the United States: In place of a foundation, cedar timbers driven straight into the ground support it. Sotterley is a sampler of architectural styles and interior design from the last two centuries, and the walls are hung with portraits of the successive owners. Like the secret closet built to conceal children from pirates, each feature of the house presents its own history lesson. On the grounds, one of the original slave cabins has been restored. Sotterley overlooks the Patuxent; if you're sailing past on a boat you may dock, telephone, and be picked up and brought to the house by station wagon. ⊠ *Rte. 245, near Hollywood,* ☎ *301/373–2280.* ☜ *$5.* ⊙ *Apr.–May and Nov.–Dec. by appointment; June–Oct., Tues.–Sun. 11–4.*

Lexington Park

🅱 *9 mi southeast of Solomons; 68 mi south of Annapolis (via Rte. 2/4 to Rte. 235).*

The **Naval Air Test and Evaluation Museum** is the only facility in the country for testing naval aircraft. Vintage aircraft are parked along-side automobiles in the front lot, among them an imposing 25-ton twin-turboprop Hawkeye. Indoors, visitors are welcome to climb into an F-4 cockpit procedures trainer. An exhibit on contraptions that failed their tests includes the improbable Goodyear Inflatoplane: One of the portable rubber aircraft, fully inflated, is on display. The museum shop stocks a wide assortment of airplane models and accessories. ⊠ *Rte. 235, Three Notch Rd., Lexington Park,* ☎ *301/863–7418.* ⊑ *Free.* ☉ *Fri.–Sat. 11–4, Sun. noon–5.*

Lodging

$$ ⊞ **Patuxent Inn.** This three-story hotel, built in 1982 on an overdeveloped strip of Route 235 near the Patuxent Naval Air Test Center, is charming compared with its surroundings—and the best equipped of its impersonal type in St. Mary's County. Guest rooms are furnished with mock-Colonial furniture, and their windows face either the highway or the woods in back. Many guests are those with business at the air base, and that tends to keep rates to the government's per diem level. Since the mood here is hardly that of a resort, it's a surprise to find a pair of lighted tennis courts, a jogging trail, and a pool. ⊠ *Rte. 235, Box 778, Lexington Park 20653,* ☎ *301/862–4100. 120 rooms. Restaurant, bar, pool, 2 tennis courts, jogging. AE, DC, MC, V.*

$$ ⊞ **Potomac View Farm.** Construction of this white wood-frame "tele-
★ scope" house (built in progressively smaller sections) began in 1830. It's emphatically a farmhouse, not a manor, and is furnished accordingly with handsome but simple oak furniture and decorative quilts. Yet there are elegant touches in some rooms, such as the 10-foot ceilings with crown moldings. One of the restored outbuildings, originally the gardener's cottage, is now a room with its own bath. A one-bedroom kitchenette apartment attached to the main house but entered through a separate door also has its own bath. The remaining rooms share five baths, so there is rarely a wait. As its name suggests, the inn sits by the water on working farmland: 120 acres planted with corn and soybeans. The proprietors also operate the marina, where guests may arrange excursion charters. A full breakfast is included in the price. ⊠ *Rte. 249, Tall Timbers 20690,* ☎ *301/994–0419. 5 rooms, 1 cottage. Restaurant, bar, pool, beach. AE, MC, V.*

Point Lookout

❷⓿ *20 mi south of Lexington Park; 88 mi south of Annapolis (via Rte. 235 to Rte. 5).*

Point Lookout State Park, at the farthest tip of the peninsula, was the site of a Union prison during the Civil War. The prison was so placed because of the point's convenient location, just across the Potomac River from the Confederate state of Virginia. Conditions in the penitentiary evidently fell short of the standards of the much later Geneva Convention, for nearly 3,500 Confederate soldiers died here in the last two years of the conflict. All that remains of the prison are some earthen fortifications, partially rebuilt and known as Ft. Lincoln, with markers noting the sites of hospitals and other buildings. Park attendants and psychics report sightings of the ghosts of Confederate soldiers who, they believe, were imprisoned here. On the approach on Route 5, two memorial obelisks remind vacationers of the bloody background of this place, and a small museum within the park supplies some of the details. Today the place has resumed its antebellum function as a recreational area; the 500-acre state park offers camping year-round, as well as boating facilities, nature trails, and a beach for swimming. The RV campground, with hook-ups, is open year-round; tent camping facilities close in winter months. ⊠ *Rte. 5, Point Lookout,* ☎ *301/872– 5688.* ⊑ *$2 (weekends and holidays only).* ☉ *Park: 8 AM–11 PM. Museum: Apr.–Memorial Day and Labor Day–Oct., weekends 10–6; Memorial Day–Labor Day, daily 10–6.*

Dining

★ ✕ **Spinnakers Restaurant at Point Lookout Marina.** Established by former students from St. Mary's College, this burgeoning restaurant has brought all the best of southern Maryland to the shores of Smith Creek. When partners John Spinnichia (a.k.a. "Spinach") and Michael Gould aren't in the kitchen baking bread or cooking what *Nightline* commentator Ted Koppel has called "the world's best gold-medal crab cakes," they're probably behind the bar mixing drink specials such as Outriggers (peach schnapps and orange juice) and Russian Quaaludes (coffee liqueur, cream, and Irish whiskey). Contributing to Spinnakers's friendly atmosphere are the subdued lighting, fresh flowers, and linen-covered tables, but really it's the genuinely enthusiastic staff that makes dining here such a comfortable experience. When in season, the soft-shell crabs caught fresh from the creek outside are a sure bet, especially when complemented by a glass of wine from Catoctin Vineyards, in the mountains of Maryland. Sunday brunch here has fast become a tradition. ✉ *Point Lookout Marina, 32 Millers Wharf Rd., Ridge,* ☎ *310/872–4340. D, DC, MC, V.*

Outdoor Activities and Sports

Scheibel's, in Ridge (✉ Wynne Rd., ☎ 301/872–5185), south of Lexington Park, will arrange yacht charters.

St. Inigoes

㉑ *9 mi northwest of Point Lookout (via Rte. 5); 77 mi south of Annapolis.*

St. Ignatius Church, built in 1758 by Roman Catholics (Maryland's first settlers were Catholics, and the 1649 Toleration Act guaranteed religious freedom in the colony), is all that survives of the pre-Revolutionary plantation of St. Inigoes. A church dating from the 1630s had stood where this church stands now; the graveyard is one of the oldest in the United States. Several veterans of the Revolution are buried here, alongside Jesuit priests who served at this church named for the founder of their society. To see inside the church, ask for the key at the sentry box of the naval installation next door. ✉ *Villa Rd., off Rte. 5, St. Inigoes,* ☎ *410/863–2149.* ✉ *Donation.* ☉ *Daily 9–4.*

St. Mary's City

㉒ *4 mi northwest of St. Inigoes (via Rte. 5); 73 mi south of Annapolis (via Rte. 2/4 to Rte. 235).*

Historic St. Mary's City is Maryland's birthplace. In 1634, the first colonists stepped ashore at St. Clement's Island, a short distance away on the Potomac River, and celebrated a thanksgiving mass under Father Andrew White. Here, too, the first act of religious tolerance in the New World was enacted, guaranteeing the freedom to practice whatever religion one chose. The settlement served as Maryland's capital city until 1695, when the legislature moved to Annapolis. The county seat was then moved to Leonardtown, and St. Mary's City disappeared from the maps.

In the early 1970s, a vast archaeological/reconstruction program began. A project that has been carried out in earnest since its earliest days has to date revealed nearly 200 individual sites that have been explored or are in the process of rediscovery. The entire 800-plus acres have be-
★ come a living-history museum called **Historic St. Mary's City,** and although the city is less well-known than Virginia's Williamsburg, its project is no less ambitious.

The historic complex includes several notable restored buildings. The **State House of 1676,** like its larger and grander counterpart in Williamsburg, has an upper and a lower chamber for the corresponding houses of parliament. This is a 1934 reproduction based on court documents from the period; the original was dismantled in 1829 and many of the bricks were used for Trinity Church nearby. The small square-rigged ship docked behind the State House is a reproduction of the *Maryland Dove,* one of two vessels (the other being the *Ark*) that conveyed the original settlers from England. The nearby **Farthing's Ordinary** is a reconstructed inn.

The nearby **Godiah Spray Tobacco Plantation** shows life on a 17th-century tobacco farm in the Maryland wilderness. Interpreters portray the Spray family—based on a real Maryland family that lived about 20 mi away—and its indentured servants, by enlisting visitors in such daily household chores as cooking and gardening or in working the tobacco field. The buildings, including the main dwelling house and outbuildings, were constructed with period tools and techniques. ⊠ *Rte. 5,* ☎ *301/862–0990 or 800/762–1634.* ▱ *$6.50.* ☉ *Late Mar.–late Nov., Wed.–Sun. 10–5.*

St. Mary's College is an intimate state-run liberal arts school that, among other roles, functions as the cultural center for the surrounding community. Overlooking the St. Mary's River (which feeds into the Chesapeake Bay), the peaceful campus makes a delightful place for a picnic, especially in fall or spring, when the humidity level is low and the breeze blows off the water. In summer you can sunbathe along the beach and watch sailboarders catching crosswinds from the Bay. Although the river is warm and safe for swimming, beware of sea nettles that lurk below the water's surface. Their sting can be quite painful.

ANNAPOLIS AND SOUTHERN MARYLAND A TO Z

Arriving and Departing

By Car
Annapolis is normally 35–45 minutes by car from Washington, DC, on U.S. 50 (Rowe Blvd. exit), but during the evening rush hour, after 3:30 PM, the trip can take two hours. From Baltimore, following Route 3/97 to U.S. 50, travel time is the same. (Note that Route 3/97 is heavily patrolled by unmarked cars with radar.) To tour Southern Maryland, follow Route 2 south from Annapolis, and Route 4, which continues through Calvert County.

By Bus
Maryland's Mass Transit Administration (MTA) offers regularly scheduled bus service from Baltimore to Annapolis (about 1 hour and 20 minutes one way from downtown—exact fare is required). Bus No. 210 departs from the Baltimore State Office Building Complex at Preston and Eutaw streets several times daily. One-way fare is $2.85. For schedules, call 410/539–5000.

Getting Around

By Bus
Annapolis Department of Public Transportation (☎ 410/263–7964) has shuttle bus service (30¢) to the downtown area every hour between from 6:30 AM until 8 PM.

By Car

On-street parking is scarce in the historic downtown areas of Annapolis. The lot at the Navy–Marine Corps Stadium is on the right of Rowe Boulevard as you come into town from Route 50. Avoid Route 50 and other roads leading into Annapolis during morning and evening rush hours. Throughout the rest of Southern Maryland, well-marked two- and four-lane highways make driving a pleasure.

Contacts and Resources

Emergencies

Throughout the region, dial **911** for emergency assistance.

HOSPITALS

Anne Arundel Medical Center (✉ Cathedral and Franklin Sts., Annapolis, ☎ 410/267–1260).
Calvert Memorial Hospital (✉ Rte. 4, Prince Frederick, ☎ 410/535–4000).
St. Mary's Hospital (✉ 234 Jefferson St., Leonardtown, ☎ 410/475–8981).

Guided Tours

Historic Annapolis Foundation Tours (✉ Old Treasury Building, State House Circle, ☎ 410/267–8149) and **Three Centuries Tours** (✉ 48 Maryland Ave., ☎ 410/263–5357 or 410/263–5401) offer two-hour walking tours with similar itineraries that may include the State House, St. John's College, the Naval Academy, the Hammond-Harwood House, and the Chase-Lloyd House. Three Centuries guides wear Colonial dress.
Maryland State House Tours (✉ State House Circle, Information Desk, ☎ 410/974–3400) are offered free of charge daily at 11 AM and 3 PM, except Thanksgiving, Christmas, and New Year's Day.

Visitor Information

Annapolis and Anne Arundel County Conference and Visitors Bureau (✉ 26 West St., Annapolis 21401, ☎ 410/280–0445).
Calvert County Dept. of Economic Development (✉ County Courthouse, Prince Frederick 20678, ☎ 410/535–4583 or 800/331–9771).
Charles County Division of Tourism (✉ 8190 Port Tobacco Rd., Port Tobacco 20677, ☎ 800/766–3386).
St. Mary's County Tourism (✉ Box 653, Leonardtown 20650, ☎ 410/475–4626).

10 Maryland's Eastern Shore

Cross the bridge from Annapolis to the Eastern Shore and you enter another world. This is a land dominated by the Chesapeake Bay, where—with the exception of the flamboyant coastal resort of Ocean City—historic towns and fishing villages carry on a slow pace of life, largely based on seafood and shipping. Here 18th- and 19th-century churches, cottages, and courthouses coexist with quirky museums of maritime history and wildfowl art.

THERE IS NO LIFE WEST OF THE CHESAPEAKE BAY reads the bumper sticker on a pickup truck crossing the Chesapeake Bay Bridge to Maryland's Eastern Shore. You need to spend only a little time in this region to understand that it is a unique area whose natives are cut from a different cloth: They're committed to their land and their bay and are fiercely independent people (yet dependent on the bay). Most, in fact, would probably not be too disappointed if the counties east of the bay were to secede from the state, and many have never ventured off this peninsula.

Captain John Smith, who explored the Chesapeake Bay region in 1607–8, may have expressed it best when he noted in his diary that "Heaven and earth never agreed better to frame a place for man's habitation . . . truly a delightsome land." Of the bay's resources he recorded, "That abundance of fish, lying so thicke with their heads above the water, as for want of nets . . . we attempted to catch them with a frying pan . . ."

The Chesapeake Bay—in actuality, the drowned valley of the Susquehanna River, which before the last ice age flowed directly into the Atlantic Ocean—is unquestionably Maryland's major natural resource, the focal point of an immense seafood, shipping, and recreational industry. It's the largest estuary in the United States and one of the most productive bodies of water in the world. Comprising 3,237 sq mi, the bay is 195 mi long—if straightened, the shoreline would reach from Baltimore to Honolulu, with a few hundred miles to spare—and 37.5 mi across at its widest point, near the mouth of the Potomac River. At the William Preston Lane Jr. Memorial Bridges, its narrowest point, it is but 4 mi across.

In addition to the Chesapeake Bay, the Eastern Shore offers beautiful historic towns and fishing villages that have little changed over the years, and a distinctive shore hospitality unequaled in most other East Coast regions. The long, flat roads with nicely paved shoulders provide a good surface for long bike rides and exploring, and there are numerous cozy bed-and-breakfasts posted between towns. Also, there's Ocean City, an ever-growing, flamboyant Atlantic resort town, as well as more modest hamlets with good quiet beaches.

Exploring Maryland's Eastern Shore

Maryland's Eastern Shore comprises most of the Delmarva Peninsula, a land mass between the Atlantic Ocean and the Chesapeake Bay—a peninsula shared at its northern end with Delaware and at its southern end with Virginia. In between these two points are historic towns such as Easton, Cambridge, Salisbury, and St. Michaels; surviving watermen's villages such as Tilghman Island, Hoopers Island, and Crisfield; and Ocean City, a resort town that rivals other East Coast communities with its multimillion dollar hotels, miles of sandy beaches, and entertainment.

QUEEN ANNE'S COUNTY

Numbers in the margin correspond to points of interest on Maryland's Eastern Shore map.

Small towns, each with its share of historic churches and homes, remind visitors of this region's Colonial past. Even its name, which honors Queen Anne of Great Britain and Ireland, is a nod to Colonial times. As in the past, Queen Anne's County thrives on maritime activity.

Stevensville

❶ *10 mi northeast of Annapolis (via Rte. 50/301).*

Stevensville is the largest town on Kent Island, which in turn is the largest island in the bay. The island has been a thriving trading post since 1631, when it became the first permanent settlement in Maryland. Access to the island is via the William Preston Lane Jr. Memorial Bridges, which reach into Chesapeake Bay from Sandy Point State Park. The bridge toll of $2.50 for cars is collected at Sandy Point.

The oldest surviving building in Stevensville, **The Cray House** was completed in 1815. The two-story, mansard-roof cottage of post-and-plank construction is set in a little yard surrounded by a picket fence and furnished with period pieces, providing a glimpse into the middle-class life of the early 19th century. ⊠ *Cockey's La.,* ☎ *410/758–2300.* ⊿ *Free.* ☉ *May–Oct., Sat. 1–4, and by appointment.*

Christ Episcopal Church is the sanctuary for what could be the state's oldest continuous religious congregation, one that dates from the settlement of the island. The curious Carpenter's Gothic structure, built in 1880, is mostly of wood, but the lancet chimney (a gap in the center has the shape of a lancet window in a medieval church) is made with bricks from a church of 1652 that stood nearby. ⊠ *Rte. 18,* ☎ *410/643–5921.* ☉ *By appointment.*

Dining and Lodging

$$$ ✕ **The Narrows.** The atrium dining room, with a mix of uncovered wood and Formica tables, is decorated with potted ficus trees and stuffed waterfowl. Large windows on three sides (and, in spring and fall, a glass-enclosed "greenhouse") allow diners to watch the activity of the fishing and pleasure craft on the waterway that separates Kent Island, opposite, from the mainland. In warm weather, meals are also served on the deck, where sailors can tie up their vessels before dinner. Cream of crab soup contains one pound of crabmeat per gallon, along with chicken stock and heavy cream. Strip steak Quimby, named for a prominent local family, is prepared with a sauce made of brandy, onions, freshly ground black pepper, and cream. ⊠ *Rte. 50 at Kent Narrows, Grasonville,* ☎ *410/827–8113. AE, DC, MC, V.*

$$ ✕ **Harris Crab House.** The restaurant's location, on the mainland side
★ of Kent Narrows, enables boaters to sail up and dock their boats at slips provided by Harris's; open-deck dining offers expansive water views. Seafood here is purchased directly from watermen at the restaurant's docks. Cream of crab soup and back-fin crab cakes are among the best around—and the crabs are spicy enough to promote plenty of beer drinking. A nautical theme prevails in the large dining room, and a collection of oyster cans and other relics from an adjacent oyster house add local flair. An oyster-processing plant next door is still in use. ⊠ *433 Kent Narrows Hwy., Grasonville,* ☎ *410/827-9500. MC, V.*

$$$ ✕▥ **Kent Manor Inn.** Although it's just off the main highway leading
★ to Ocean City and the beaches, this impressive 19th-century home remains hidden from passersby. The original wing was built in 1820 and a west wing was added in 1987. Ownership of the property, a 226-acre working farm on Kent Island, can be traced well back into the mid-17th century. The entire farm is visible from an eight-window cupola on the roof. A complete renovation brought four-poster beds, Victorian reproductions, and impressionist paintings to hang above the marble fireplaces. Half of the rooms face Thompson Creek. Rooms on the first and second floors open onto verandas; those on the third floor have sloped ceilings and dormer windows. The dining room has pink

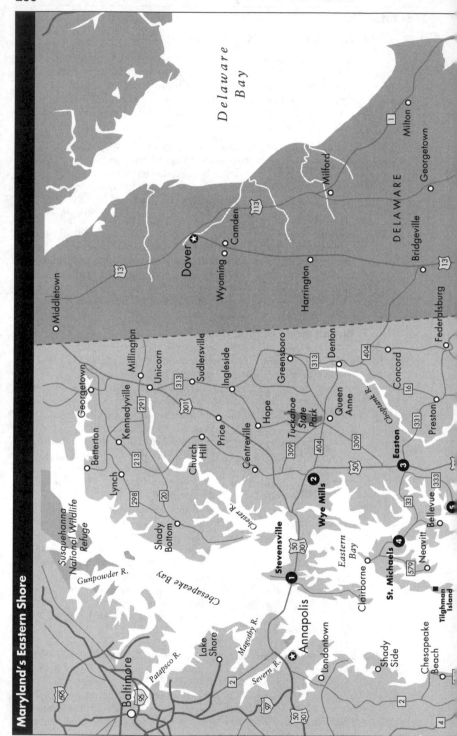

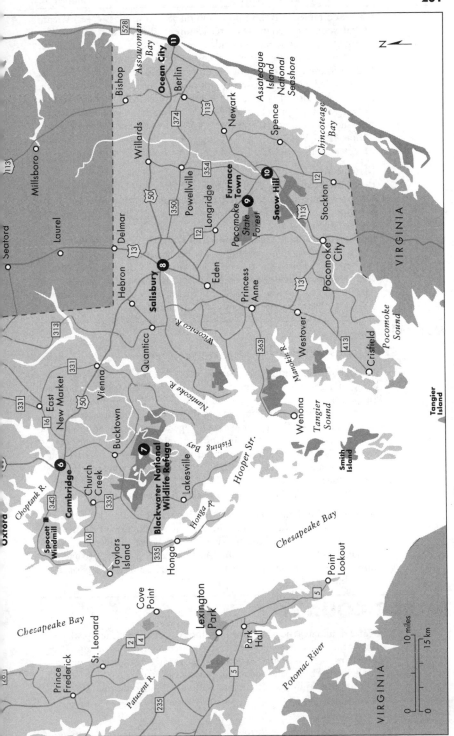

walls and tablecloths, and porcelain displayed in glass cases. Cream of crab soup is served in the Eastern Shore tradition—accompanied by a shot of sherry. Also recommended are the pesto-crusted rack of lamb served with shiitake mushroom-and-raspberry compote; and Elizabethan Scampi, shrimp stuffed with horseradish, wrapped in bacon, and drizzled with tomato-vermouth sauce. The wine list is extensive, and the chef also offers guests "flights," which includes four samples of wine, sherry, port, cognac, or single malts for a single price. Room rates include Continental breakfast. ⊠ *500 Kent Manor Dr., Stevensville, 21666,* ☎ *410/643–5757. 24 rooms, some disabled-accessible. Restaurant, bar, pool, croquet, horseshoes, volleyball. AE, MC, V.*

Shopping
Carvel Hall Cutlery (⊠ Rte. 50, Queenstown, ☎ 410/827–6904) is a unique outlet for the famous Crisfield manufacturer, offering heirloom-quality utensils and seafood tools at factory prices. The store is open daily 9:30–6.

Chesapeake Village Outlet Center (⊠ Rte. 50, near Grasonville, ☎ 410/827–8699), 10 mi east of the Bay Bridge, is composed of 19 "factory direct" labels, among them Liz Claiborne, Capezio, and Nike.

Kent Narrows Factory Stores (⊠ Piney Narrows Rd., Chester, ☎ 410/643–5231), on Kent Island, is a complex of 29 merchants, including American Tourister, Anne Klein, and Corning Glass.

Wye Mills

❷ *14 mi east of Stevensville; 28 mi east of Annapolis (via Rte. 50/301).*

Named for a gristmill built in 1671, the village of Wye Mills is something of a ghost town today, but its historic mill is worth seeing. Sitting on the line between Queen Anne's and Talbot counties, both of which claim it as a landmark, the mill has been reconstructed twice, in 1720 and 1840. During the War of Independence, Washington's troops at Valley Forge ordered flour and other supplies from here. The present structure is powered by a waterwheel, and visitors can watch the mill's gears turn and apparatus grind: Cornmeal, whole wheat, and buckwheat flour produced here are on sale. ⊠ *Rte. 662,* ☎ *410/827–6909 or 410/685–2886.* ⌨ *Free.* ☉ *Apr.–Dec., weekends 11–4.*

Wye Oak, Maryland's State Tree, is an imposing landmark some yards south of the Wye Mills, on the other side of the junction of Routes 662 and 404. The 450-year-old tree is 95 feet tall and 37 feet around its thickets; its branches spread out 145 feet, casting plenty of shade on sunny days. A 29-acre park with a picnic area and tables is open to the public.

TALBOT COUNTY

Water dominates the landscape of Talbot County. The Chesapeake Bay forms the its western border, and the meandering Choptank River slices through the Delmarva Peninsula, forming the southern and eastern borders. Fishing and sailing villages dot the waterways: St. Michael's, Oxford, and Tighlman Island are popular day-trip destinations.

Easton

❸ *13 mi south of Wye Mills (via Rte. 50); 36 mi southeast of Annapolis (via Rte. 50/301 to Rte. 50).*

The affluent town of Easton has a well-preserved downtown full of buildings dating from Colonial through Victorian times. On the second full weekend in November, the whole town erupts in the Waterfowl Festival (⊠ 40 S. Harrison St., Box 929, Easton 21601, ☎ 410/822–4567), a convention of decoy carvers and painters. Their work, which draws on the wildlife of the area, is offered for sale in galleries and at auction. Related events include goose- and duck-call competitions and demonstrations by retrievers. Proceeds benefit waterfowl conservation efforts all over the United States; the festival has donated more than $3.3 million in its 26-year history.

The **Historical Society of Talbot County** (⊠ Box 964, 25 S. Washington St., Easton 21601, ☎ 410/822–0773) offers walking tours of the town's historic district.

The **Talbot County Courthouse** of 1794, still in use, is one of two courthouses in the state built in the 18th century (the two wings were added in 1958). Its two-tier cupola topped by a weather vane recalls Colonial Williamsburg. Rebellious citizens gathered at the courthouse to protest the Stamp Act in 1765 and to adopt the Talbot Resolves, a forerunner of the Declaration of Independence. ⊠ *Washington St.,* ☎ *410/822–2401.* ☉ *Weekdays 9–5.*

The **Third Haven Friends Meeting House,** built by Quakers in 1682, is the oldest building in Maryland and one of the oldest wood-frame houses of worship in the country. No doubt it is the oldest still in use; meeting takes place Sunday at 10 AM and Wednesday at 5:30 PM. The Quaker William Penn and the Catholic Lord Baltimore are among those who have attended over the centuries. The white building is strikingly plain inside and out, with the simplicity that the sect reveres. The building remains unheated; a stove was deemed a frippery. ⊠ *405 S. Washington St.,* ☎ *410/822–0293.* ☉ *Daily 9–5.*

A federal town house is now the home of **the Historical Society of Talbot County,** a source of information on the Eastern Shore and a starting point for guided tours of the area. The restored three-story brick structure, with a fourth dormered story under the roof, was built by a Quaker cabinet maker in 1810. An adjacent museum shows changing exhibits of local history. The small wood-frame house in the garden behind was built in 1795. ⊠ *25 S. Washington St.,* ☎ *410/822–0773.* ⌷ *$4.* ☉ *Tues.–Sun. 10–4.*

Lodging
$$ ⌂ **John S. McDaniel House.** This three-story white clapboard house with green roof and shutters, built in 1890, is dominated by an octagonal tower. A circular turret room on each floor is distinctively Victorian. All rooms were renovated in 1988 and furnished with period reproductions. The beds have quilts, and pictures of waterfowl hang on the white-with-gray-trim walls. Ceiling fans augment the central air-conditioning. Rocking chairs and other wicker furniture invite guests to enjoy a wraparound porch. Room rates include Continental breakfast. ⊠ *14 N. Aurora St., 21601,* ☎ *410/822–3704. 8 rooms. AE, MC, V.*

Nightlife and the Arts
Avalon Theatre (⊠ Dover and Harrison Sts., ☎ 410/822–3355), a restored venue for the performing arts, is in an especially attractive building. It is home to the Talbot Chamber Orchestra and the Eastern Shore Chamber Music Festival, and host to other performances as well.

The **Historical Society of Talbot County** (⊠ 25 S. Washington St., ☎ 410/822–0773) sponsors occasional concerts.

At the **Washington Street Pub** (✉ 20 N. Washington St., ☎ 410/822–9011) the Saturday-night acts are more or less countrified.

St. Michaels

❹ *9 mi west of Easton (via Rte. 33); 49 mi southeast of Annapolis.*

Historically a shipbuilding center because of the abundant timber nearby, the harborside village of St. Michaels was a focus of attack in the War of 1812. During one attack, citizens diverted British fire from strategic targets by adroitly placing lanterns in the fog.

Just one house in "the town that fooled the British" was struck during the shelling in 1812. That structure, known as the **Cannonball House,** built in 1805, is privately owned and not open to the public, but you can see it on Mulberry Street at the northwest edge of St. Mary's Square. This square, dedicated to public use in perpetuity, is the core of a neighborhood whose architecture has remained largely unchanged since the 19th century.

A 17th-century cabin of axe-hewn half-timber houses is part of the **St. Mary's Square Museum,** which preserves local artifacts. Most prominent in the collection is a shipyard bell that still rings at the start of the workday, at lunch, and at quitting time. The museum also occupies the adjoining Teetotum Building, a yellow clapboard house of the Civil War era named for a children's toy it was thought to resemble. ✉ *St. Mary's Sq.,* ☎ *410/745–9561.* 🎫 *Donation.* ☉ *May–Oct., weekends 10–4.*

Talbot Street, St. Michael's main drag, is lined with seafood restaurants and boutiques that sell summer fashions, crafts, bowls of potpourri, and the like. Even the hardware store is also a gift shop.

★ The **Chesapeake Bay Maritime Museum** at Navy Point is a complex of six exhibition halls on 17 acres. Tracing the history of the bay and its traditions in boat building, commercial fishing, navigation, and waterfowling, the exhibits include a restored log-bottom bugeye (a two-masted skipjack native to the Chesapeake Bay and used for oyster dredging), a skipjack, and a racing log canoe. In the Bay Building, artifacts and illustrations, including a dugout canoe hewn by Native Americans and a later crabbing skiff, recount the history of the great estuary. The Waterfowl Building contains carved decoys and stuffed birds, including wood ducks, mallards, and swans. The lighthouse on the pier, built in 1879 at Hooper Strait (in the southern bay) and moved here in 1966, is of screw-pile design (a hexagonal house poised on six slender legs and used for marking shoals) and virtually identical to the one at Solomons Island in Southern Maryland (☞ Chapter 9); the interior is a surprisingly spacious apartment with wood floors and quaint stoves. ✉ *Navy Point,* ☎ *410/745–2916.* 🎫 *$7.50.* ☉ *Jan.–Mar., weekends 10–4; Apr.–Oct., daily 10–5; Nov.–Dec., daily 10–4.*

Dining and Lodging

$$$ ✕ **Lighthouse.** Paneling and captain's chairs are of traditional design, but the blond wood lends a light, contemporary appearance to this restaurant's interior. Tables are set with mauve tablecloths and candles. Large windows and an outdoor deck allow diners to watch the comings and goings in the marina below. Following an appetizer (perhaps shrimp with Dijon mustard sauce) or a soup (lobster bisque with brandy), a sorbet is served. Among the entrées, stuffed soft-shell *choron* is a pair of soft-shell crabs stuffed with crab imperial and shrimp, then lightly breaded and fried. *Saumon en papillote* is salmon cooked with

celery, white wine, and lemon. The dessert cart carries a large selection. ⊠ *101 N. Harbor Rd., ☎ 410/756–9001. AE, DC, MC, V.*

$$$ ✕ **Michael Rork's Town Dock Restaurant.** Every seat in Michael Rork's restaurant overlooks the water, and pictures of sailboats and local landmarks celebrate the Chesapeake Bay. The dining room accommodates up to 350 diners, and a deck overlooking the Miles River seats another 75. Seafood is the specialty: Try crab cakes, fried oyster sandwiches, Maryland crab soup, and bouillabaisse. Desserts are homemade and served with strawberries. Eastern Shore–brewed beer is on tap. ⊠ *125 Mulberry St., ☎ 410/745–5577. AE, D, DC, MC, V.*

$$$$ ⊞ **Inn at Perry Cabin.** An early 19th-century Colonial Revival farm-
★ house was expanded, renovated, and opened as an inn in 1990. The proprietor is the widower of the designer Laura Ashley, and the inn is a showcase for the rich yet restrained fabric designs she popularized. With its handsome but cozy library and spectacular gardens, this place feels like an English country house. Afternoon tea and fresh flowers in guest rooms and common areas are distinctive touches; many rooms have heated towel racks and private balconies. The inn sits on 25 acres of property along the Miles River. Call ahead to arrange boat rides, fishing excursions, or golf outings. ⊠ *308 Watkins La., 21663, ☎ 410/745–2200 or 800/722–2949. 11 rooms, 8 suites. Restaurant, bar. AE, DC, MC, V.*

$$$ ⊞ **St. Michaels Harbor Inn and Marina.** A favorite with bay boaters, this multigable clapboard structure, built in the mid-'70s, is a postmodernist takeoff on the town's Victorian architecture. Part of the waterfront complex is the 60-slip marina that sits just across the harbor from the Maritime Museum. Most rooms in this all-suite facility have dockside patios or verandas and—on the third floor—large dormer windows and cathedral ceilings. Some suites have Jacuzzis. Interiors are soothingly spare: white walls, a mirror here, a botanical print there; fabrics have muted floral or simple geometric patterns; a brass ceiling fan is the most colorful element. Rooms have a wet bar and refrigerator. The odd angles and slopes in many ceilings add interest, and the views of the sailboats in the harbor are diverting. ⊠ *101 N. Harbor Rd., 21663, ☎ 410/745–9001 or ☎ 800/955–9001, FAX 410/745–9150. 46 suites. Restaurant, bar, pool, exercise room. AE, D, DC, MC, V.*

$$$ ⊞ **Tilghman Island Inn.** Location is the name of the game at this intimate resort on the water, across the busiest drawbridge in the country, at the confluence of the Chesapeake Bay and Choptank River. Other assets are its fine restaurant and private tennis court, swimming pool, croquet court, biking, fishing, and boating facilities, and dock. The modestly priced menu at the restaurant specializes in seafood, but there's a good variety of other items that you'd probably expect to find in a big-city bistro, not a small-town place like Tilghman. To top it off, everything is well prepared. ⊠ *21384 Coopertown Rd., 21671, ☎ 410/886–2141. 20 rooms. Restaurant, pool, tennis court, croquet, dock, boating, fishing, bicycles. AE, D, MC, V.*

$$$ ⊞ **Victoriana Inn.** Originally built as a private residence by Dr. Clay Dodson, a U.S. army officer during the Civil War, this two-story wood house, white with blue trim, is across a footbridge from the Maritime Museum. Guest rooms, which face the cove or the inn's own gardens, are furnished with 19th-century antiques; one has a canopied four-poster bed. All rooms have rocking chairs and air-conditioning, and hand-woven floral rugs lie on polished wood floors. The sunroom, where breakfast is served, has a VCR. At the center of tourist and maritime activity, with a view of the harbor's picturesque sailboat traffic, this inn is a haven in an increasingly popular town. Rates include full breakfast. ✉ *205 Cherry St., 21663,* ☎ *410/745–3368. 5 rooms, 1 with bath. MC, V.*

$$$ 🏨 **Wades Point Inn.** Amid fields of corn and gladioli, on a 120-acre farm 5 mi south of St. Michaels, stand three adjoining brick Colonial and wood-frame Victorian buildings. The oldest structure was built in 1820 by Thomas Kemp, the Baltimore shipwright who built the famous Baltimore clipper ship, *The Chasseur* (nicknamed "The Pride of Baltimore"). The newest part of the property was added in 1989 by the present innkeepers, John and Betsy Feiler. The houses are about 100 feet from the Miles River, and some rooms have views of the Chesapeake Bay. Wood floors and painted walls are the rule in some guest rooms; others have a carpet and wallpaper. Some rooms have four-poster beds, and one has a canopied bed; two rooms have intricate moldings around the ceiling; most guest quarters have a private porch or balcony. Two brightly sunlit corner rooms in the summer wing provide the closest look at the water. A 1-mi trail through the property accommodates joggers and bird-watchers. If you're seeking solitude and lots of fresh salt air, you'll find no better location in Maryland. Rates include Continental breakfast. ✉ *Wades Point Rd., Rte. 33, Box 7, 21663,* ☎ *410/745–2500. 24 rooms, 15 with bath. MC, V.*

$$ 🏨 **The Oaks, a Country Inn.** Set on Oak Creek in Royal Oak, 3 mi from St. Michaels, the Oaks is a tranquil choice for families, receptions, bicycle touring, conferences, and weekend getaways. Guests can borrow a rowboat, canoe, paddleboat, or bicycles, or use the horseback-riding facilities about 7 mi away. The property consists of a 240-year-old mansion (currently undergoing renovation) and guest cottages, all owned and operated by Schwaben International. Amenities include a full country breakfast, and à la carte American dinners are available nightly to guests and to the public. Smoking is not permitted in the guest rooms but is allowed in a lower-level public room and on the porches. ✉ *Box 187, 25876 Royal Oak Rd., Royal Oak, 21662,* ☎ *410/745–5053. Restaurant, pool, boating, bicycles. MC, V.*

Nightlife and the Arts

Longfellow's (✉ 125 Mulberry St., ☎ 410/745–2624) has Top-40 programs on Saturday night.

Outdoor Activities and Sports

BICYCLING

Town Dock Marina (✉ 305 Mulberry St., ☎ 410/745–2400) rents bicycles.

FISHING

For fishing on the Chesapeake Bay, contact **Eastern Bay Charters** (✉ Box 452, 21663, ☎ 410/745–2329).

SAILING

Town Dock Marina (✉ 305 Mulberry St., ☎ 410/745–2400) rents sailboats, runabouts, and pedal boats.

Shopping

The **Blue Swan** (✉ 200 Talbot St., ☎ 410/745–9346) sells seashell ornaments, wood Santas and elves, crystal, glass, and other furnishings for the holiday season—all year long. The store is just one in a neighborhood of curiosity shops.

En Route   Bellevue, 7 mi south of St. Michaels via Routes 33 and 329, is the departure point for the **Oxford-Bellevue Ferry,** believed to be the oldest privately owned ferry in continuous operation in the United States. In 1683 the Talbot County Court "pitcht up on Mr. Richard Royston to keepe a Ferry," and it has been running across the Tred Avon River ever since. ✉ *N. Morris St. at the Strand, Oxford,* ☎ *410/745–9023.* 🎫 *Ferry rates: $4.50 car and driver one way, $7 same-day round-trip; 50¢ car passenger, $1 pedestrian, $1.50 bicycle, $3 motorcycle.* ⊙ *Operates weekdays 7 AM–sunset, weekends 9 AM–sunset. Extended hrs June, July, Aug. Closed mid-Dec.–Feb.*

Oxford

❺ *7 mi southeast of St. Michaels; 44 mi southeast of Annapolis.*

Oxford, founded in 1683, is one of the oldest towns in Maryland, but few of the buildings put up before the middle of the 19th century still stand. The prevailing style is Victorian Carpenter's Gothic. One exception is the Robert Morris Inn, at Morris Street and the Strand, on the rise overlooking the ferry terminal. The inn, expanded gradually from a four-room core from 1710, was once the house of the Liverpool merchant Robert Morris and his son. The junior Morris signed the Declaration of Independence, enlarged the family fortune, helped to finance the Revolution, and ended up in debtor's prison after failing at land speculation.

On the riverbank, the **Customs House** is a Bicentennial replica of the shed from which Jeremiah Banning, the first federal collector of customs, kept track of the traffic in and out of this crucial 18th-century port. Often immobilized by gout, Banning watched the ships through a spyglass. The replica version is simply but comfortably furnished with antiques of the period and attended by a docent who will tell the story of the port and direct visitors to points of interest in the town. The original structure, built in 1777, stands on private property across the harbor. ✉ *N. Morris St.,* ☎ *410/226–5122.* 🎫 *Free.* ⊙ *Apr.–Oct., Fri.–Sun. 3–5.*

The **Oxford Museum,** an unusually well-maintained local museum, is three blocks down Morris Street, adjacent to the town offices at Market Street. On display are models and pictures of sailboats, some constructed at the Cutts and Case shipyard, which is still in business. Oxford was the site of one of the first Chesapeake regattas (1860), hence the full-scale racing boat that sits by the door. Other artifacts include the lamp from a lighthouse on nearby Benoni Point, a sail-maker's bench, and an oyster-shucking stall. Docents elaborate on the exhibits, which set the context for a walking tour of the blocks nearby (tour booklet $1 here and at most local merchants). ✉ *Morris and Market Sts.,* ☎ *410/226–5122.* 🎫 *Free.* ⊙ *May–Oct., Fri.–Sun. 2–5.*

Opposite the Oxford museum is the **Town Park,** a leafy area with benches and an unobstructed view of the Tred Avon River.

Dining and Lodging

$$ ✗ **Pope's Tavern.** A pressed-tin ceiling and large display windows remain from when this restaurant was a grocery store. Ship models decorate both dining rooms, where the hardwood floors are uncarpeted and fireplaces provide warmth in cold weather. Blue-and-gray linen cloths on the tables are covered with glass, candles, and fresh flowers. Try shrimp and crab Norfolk, sautéed in white wine and butter, or chicken Patricia—a boneless chicken breast sautéed in white wine with a sauce of green peppers, mushrooms, scallions, and butter. Sunday brunch is known for meaty crab cakes and freshly baked muffins. A mostly Californian wine list includes a selection of Australian vintages. ✉ *Oxford Inn, 1 S. Morris St.,* ☎ *410/226–5220. MC, V. Closed Tues.*

$$ ✕🖫 **Robert Morris Inn.** Situated near the Bellevue-Oxford Ferry terminal on the Strand, this friendly inn offers a convenient location. Accommodations include efficiencies, river cottages, and simple bedrooms, some with bay windows, others with porches. In addition to simple comfort and quiet hospitality, the inn is known for its excellent food. The main dining room has crystal chandeliers and murals depicting 18th-century river scenes; there are also a pine-panelled Tap Room with nautical prints and a more casual tavern with oak panels and slate floors. All three eateries serve noteworthy seafood cakes au gratin—a mix of crab and shrimp, baked with Monterey Jack and cheddar cheeses. Author James Michener, who often dined here while working on his epic novel *Chesapeake,* was especially fond of the inn's crab cakes and still has them air-mailed to his home. ✉ *Box 70, 21654,* ☎ *410/226–5111. Restaurant, dining room, pub. AE, MC, V.*

$$$ 🖫 **Oxford Inn.** Built as a private home in 1872, this inn served as a watermen's bar during the seafood industry boom in the early part of this century, and later as a grocery store. The innkeepers renovated the rooms in 1990; they also raised the roof and added a third floor, so that guests can spy Town Creek from the dormer windows. The furniture is a collection of antiques, mostly early 20th-century American; rocking chairs and quilts are standard. Public tennis courts and a children's playground are across the street. Rates include Continental breakfast. ✉ *1 S. Morris St., Box 627, 21654,* ☎ *410/226-5220. 13 rooms, 7 with bath. Restaurant. MC, V.*

Nightlife and the Arts
Tred Avon Players, a versatile community theatrical troupe, performs musicals, comedies, and melodrama at the Oxford Community Center (✉ Rte. 333, ☎ 410/226–5904).

Outdoor Activities and Sports
BICYCLING
Oxford Mews (✉ Morris St., ☎ 410/820–8222) rents bicycles.

Fishing
Eastern Shore Yacht Charters (✉ Box 589, 21654, ☎ 410/226–5000) charters fishing trips on the Chesapeake Bay.

OFF THE
BEATEN PATH

TILGHMAN ISLAND – Although commercialism has begun to creep into the Eastern Shore communities of Easton, Oxford, and St. Michaels, Tilghman Island, on Route 33, remains mostly untainted. This is an authentic waterman's village where in the spring and summer you'll see skipjacks (oyster boats) tied, awaiting the beginning of the oystering season (September–April). These indigenous boats are the only working fleet of sailboats in North America. In the 1800s there were about 1,500 of them sailing the bay; today there are fewer than 30. Just a short drive beyond the Knapps Narrows Bridge, on the one small road on the island, is Harrison's Chesapeake House–Country Inn and Sportfishing Center, on the left (☎ 410/886–2123), where "Captain" Buddy and his wife Bobbie Harrison oversee every detail of the 100-year-old restaurant-provisions center, geared mostly to hunters and outdoorspeople. The Harrisons exude friendliness and work hard to accommodate their guests: For example, they have devised the "Buddy Plan," which includes all the elements needed for goose- and sea-duck–hunting packages, and fishing packages for parties from one to 100. The moderately priced restaurant offers an equally hospitable atmosphere, and on the menu is a variety of seafood specialties—only a handful of dishes are nonseafood. You'll be hard-pressed to find fresher fish anywhere in these parts. Dress is casual, and sometimes bluegrass and country music are featured; the tone is always relaxed here.

DORCHESTER COUNTY

South of Talbot County, Dorchester County is best known as the home of the expansive Blackwater National Wildlife Refuge. Much of Tidewater Maryland's Colonial history can be found in the county's historic communities such as Cambridge, Vienna, and East New Market.

Cambridge

❻ *15 mi southeast of Oxford (via Rte. 50); 55 mi southeast of Annapolis (via Rte. 50/301 to Rte. 50).*

On the south shore of the Choptank River, Cambridge is the second-largest port in Maryland, used heavily by the seafood-processing plants nearby. Work on the revitalization of the port area, now called Sailwinds Park, was scheduled to begin in early 1997. The complex will eventually comprise a visitor center and museum complex, a hotel, a marina, a shopping area, a playground, and a park. The Festival Hall hosts public events and concerts (☎ 410/228–7245). In addition, the **Antique Fly-In,** a convention of vintage aircraft including World War I biplanes, takes place in mid May on the grass landing strip of the former Francis Du Pont estate at Horn Point, 4 mi northwest of Cambridge. The Dorchester Heritage Museum (☎ 410/228–1899) has up-to-date information.

The **Meredith House** (1760) is a three-story, redbrick Georgian structure housing the collections of the Dorchester County Historical Society. This regional museum features artifacts of Native Americans and colonists; a child's bedroom has antique toys and dolls; and the Governor's Room holds personal effects of the six Maryland chief executives who sprang from the county. A smokehouse, a blacksmith's shop, formal gardens, and a medicinal herb garden have been restored. ⊠ *Greenway Dr. and La Grange St.,* ☎ *410/228–7953.* 🎫 *Free.* ☉ *Thurs.–Sat. 10–4.*

The **Wild Goose Brewery** is the Eastern Shore's only microbrewery. Take the tour and see every step of the operation—then sample some of its highly regarded ale, amber, or lager. ⊠ *20 Washington St.,* ☎ *410/221–1121.* ☉ *Tours Mon.–Sat. 10–3.*

OFF THE BEATEN PATH

OLD TRINITY CHURCH – Seven miles west of Cambridge near the town of Church Creek, tiny Old Trinity Church is possibly the oldest Episcopal church in the country in continuous use. Built in 1675 and extensively altered in the 19th century, the church has been restored to its 17th-century appearance. On display is a Table of Marriages, a chart that details proscribed relationships. The silver chalice given by Queen Anne and the cushion she knelt upon when she was crowned are sometimes exhibited. In the churchyard are the graves of four governors of Maryland and several members of the distinguished political and clerical Carroll family. ⊠ *Rte. 16, near Church Creek,* ☎ *410/228–2940.* ☉ *Mon., Wed., Fri., Sat. 10–4; Sun. 1–4.*

SPOCOTT WINDMILL – The only existing post windmill for grinding grain in Maryland is 6 mi west of Cambridge on Route 343. Unlike stationary Dutch windmills, English post windmills can rotate 360 degrees. Although they were common in England as early as the 1100s, it wasn't until the early 17th century that they became common in Virginia and Maryland—particularly in the eastern counties where the terrain is generally flat. This is an authentic replica of one destroyed in a great blizzard in 1888. Also on the property and open to the public are the miller's tenant house, a country store from the 1930s, and a one-room schoolhouse dated 1868. The windmill is operated from May to October. ⊠ *Rte. 343,* ☎ *410/228–7090.* ⊠ *Free; donations accepted.* ☉ *Mon.–Sat. 10–5.*

Dining and Lodging

$$ ✕ McGuigan's Pub. Look for the golden retriever resting on the lawn in front of this turn-of-the-century home-turned-pub in Cambridge. Owner Gerry Boyle, retired from the British Army, has achieved a cozy British atmosphere, with wood floors, fireplaces, and Tiffany windows. Eastern Shore's Wild Goose beers are the specialty here; four variations are on tap at any time. If you're hungry, try the savory steak pie, with chunks of round steak cooked with onion, or the Scotch pie, filled with ground spicy lamb. Beer-battered fish-and-chips are wrapped in British newspapers. ⊠ *411 Muse St.,* ☎ *410/228–7110. AE, D, MC, V.*

$$$$ ⌑ Glasgow Inn. Built in 1760 and restored in 1987, this white brick plantation house sits in a 6-acre park across the street from the Choptank River. The look is purely Colonial: There's a clapboard wing; inside, prints of the period and four-poster beds carved with rice designs or turned to resemble spools enhance the effect. Some rooms have quilted hangings; one room contains French provincial furniture, white with hand-painted detailing. The ample common space includes a screened porch that faces the river, with a daybed on which guests have been known to choose to spend the night. The grounds are practically a refuge for birds, and eight public tennis courts are a block away. Room rates include full breakfast. ⊠ *1500 Hambrooks Blvd., 21613,* ☎ *410/228–0575. 7 rooms, 3 with bath. MC, V.*

$$ ⌑ Loblolly Landings and Lodge. Essentially a retreat for lovers of the great outdoors, this unique B&B is near the Blackwater Wildlife Refuge, among 170 acres of loblolly pines. At present, there are only four rooms available in the main lodge, though the owners plan to have a total of 10 rooms ready by mid-1997. Bicycles and canoes are available for rental, and there is an archery course on the property (bring your own bow and arrows). An adjacent 3,500-foot grass runway is available for guests who want to fly in. Well-behaved dogs are allowed. ⊠ *2142 Liners Rd., Church Creek 21622,* ☎ *410/397–3033. Archery, boating, bicycles. AE, D, MC, V.*

Blackwater National Wildlife Refuge

❼ *8 mi south of Cambridge (via Rte. 16 to Rte. 335); 63 mi southeast of Annapolis.*

Nearly 22,000 acres of marshland, woodlands, open water, and farmland are protected by the Department of the Interior at this wildlife refuge—a winter haven for songbirds and migratory birds. Canada geese are prominent among the waterfowl that winter here; the fish-eating osprey hatches its offspring in June; the bald eagle, as seen on the national coat of arms, makes frequent appearances. Another (less majestic) endangered species on the premises is the fox squirrel; white-tail deer and sika deer can also be found. Drivers and cyclists follow a 5-mi road through several habitats; pedestrians follow a network of trails. Exhibits and films in the visitor center provide background. ⊠ *Rte. 335 at Key Wallace Dr.,* ☎ *410/228–2677.* ⊠ *$3 car, $1 pedestrian or cyclist.* ☉ *Drive: daily sunrise–sunset. Visitor center: June–Labor Day, weekdays 8–4; Sept.–May, weekdays 8–4, weekends 9–5.*

WICOMICO AND WORCESTER COUNTIES

Wicomico and Worcester counties form Maryland's border with southern Delaware. Wicomico County is named after the slow-moving Wicomico River, along which lies Salisbury, the Eastern Shore's largest city and second busiest port. In neighboring Worcester County is the busy seaside village of Ocean City.

Viewtrail 100, a specially marked 100-mi biking circuit in Worcester County, uses secondary state and county roads between Berlin and Pocomoke City, supervised by the University of Maryland Extension Service (⊠ Box 219, Snow Hill 21863, ☎ 410/632–1972).

Salisbury

❽ *32 mi southeast of Cambridge (via Rte. 50); 87 mi southeast of Annapolis (via Rte. 50/301 to Rte. 50).*

Salisbury is the largest city and, with the barge traffic along the Wicomico River, the second-largest port on the Eastern Shore. Twenty thousand people live here; one in eight of them packages chickens for a living.

Though Salisbury is an industrial city, it does have a six-block historic district around the intersection of Elizabeth Street and Poplar Hill Avenue; a brochure with a walking tour is available from the Chamber of Commerce (⊠ 300 E. Main St., Box 510, 21803, ☎ 410/749–0144). These are Victorian houses: Few buildings survived the fire of 1886.

One structure that remained after the fire of 1886 was the wood **Poplar Hill Mansion,** built in 1805 by a Revolutionary officer. The Federalist house is notable for a large Palladian window and a 12-foot-wide arched front hallway. ⊠ *117 Elizabeth St.,* ☎ *410/749–1776.* 🎟 *$1.50.* ☉ *Sun. 1–4.*

★ **The Ward Museum of Wildfowl Art** illustrates the history of decoy carving, whose beginnings are traced to the wildfowl hunters who made primitive decoys to lure unsuspecting waterfowl. The Ward brothers of Crisfield, Maryland, were the first to bridge the gap between hunter and artist; here their studio is recreated, with more than 2,000 works of art and related artifacts on display. Visitors walk through recreated marshlands, listening to the calls of duck and geese on their migratory paths. Replicas of simple 1,000-year-old figures made from reeds by Native Americans share space with lifelike works of the 19th and 20th centuries. The 30,000-square-foot structure includes exhibition and gallery spaces, a gift shop, a library, and research areas. Artists from all parts of the world participate in the World Championship Carving Competition held in April in Ocean City. This is a craft whose premium pieces have commanded hundreds of thousands of dollars at auctions. ⊠ *3416 Schumaker Pond at Beaglin Park Dr.,* ☎ *410/742–4988.* 🎟 *$4.* ☉ *Mon.–Sat. 10–5, Sun. noon–5.*

Salisbury Zoological Park, said to be one of the finest small zoos in North America, offers spectacled bears—distinguished by light fur around their eyes—of a small (5- to 6-foot) South American species. Also dwelling on the 12 acres are animals native to Maryland, in addition to monkeys, prairie dogs, lions, panthers, alligators, llamas, bison, bald eagles, and plenty of waterfowl. ⊠ *750 S. Park Dr.,* ☎ *410/548–3188.* 🎟 *Free; donations accepted.* ☉ *Daily 8–7:30.*

Shopping

At **Salisbury Pewter** (⊠ Rte. 13, between the town of Salisbury and the Delaware border, ☎ 410/546–1188), visitors can watch craftspeople turning pewter by hand at the factory showroom and select from a variety of Early American designs for sale at very reasonable prices.

OFF THE
BEATEN PATH

SMITH AND TANGIER ISLANDS – These two fishing communities, both in the Chesapeake Bay, each with fewer than 1,000 residents, are actually in two different states: Smith Island (☎ 410/651-2968 for a self-guided tour brochure) is in Maryland, while the Tangier Islands are officially part of Virginia. One of the most remarkable characteristics associated with both islands is that the natives have not lost the accents of their 17th-century English ancestors, and they are very difficult to understand. A midday visit by passenger ferry will allow plenty of time for a leisurely meal and a stroll around the island; large areas of wildlife refuge are not open to visitors. While you're here, take advantage of whatever seafood is in season: Some of the local specialties served at the islands' inns include soft-shell crabs, crab cakes, crab soup, oysters, and clam fritters. The Smith Island Center, which opened in the summer of 1996, offers visitors a glimpse of island life with a 20-minute film. Exhibits, not yet completed, will include waterman's boats and tools as well as historical and environmental information. The *Captain Tyler 2* departs from Somers Cove Marina in Crisfield for the one-hour, 10-minute cruise to Smith Island. Visitors receive a seafood luncheon and island tour as well. To reach Crisfield follow Route 13 south from Salisbury. Turn at Westover and take Route 413 south to Crisfield. ⊠ *Tyler Cruises: Box 41, Rhodes Point, MD, 21824,* ☎ *410/425-2771. For a tour to Tangier, contact Tangier Island Cruises, 10th and Main Sts., Crisfield, MD, 21817,* ☎ *410/968-2338.*

Furnace Town

❾ *19 mi southeast of Salisbury (via Rte. 12); 96 mi southeast of Annapolis.*

This is a re-creation of a 19th-century industrial village, complete with broom house, blacksmith shop, smokehouse, print shop, and church company store. The village sprang up around the huge outdoor Nassawango Iron Furnace (1828–50), which is now inactive. A visitor center has background information and exhibits. In addition, there are nature trails, bird watching, living history programs, and an elevated boardwalk that traverses the cypress swamp. Mosquitos are a nuisance in summer. ⊠ *Old Furnace Rd., Rte. 12,* ☎ *410/632-2032.* ⌨ *$3.* ☼ *Apr.–Oct., daily 11–5.*

Snow Hill

❿ *18 mi southeast of Salisbury (via Rte. 12); 106 mi southeast of Annapolis.*

The Pocomoke River port of Snow Hill is no longer the shipping center it was in the 18th and 19th centuries, but the summertime cruise-tours that depart from Sturgis Park (☎ 410/632-0680 or 800/345-6754) recall the river's importance.

The story of the town is told in the **Julia A. Purnell Museum,** where spinning wheels, mousetraps, and other miscellany illustrate the 100-year life of the woman for whom it is named, an ordinary citizen who died in 1943. ⊠ *208 W. Market St., Snow Hill,* ☎ *410/632-0515.* ⌨ *$2.* ☼ *Weekdays 10–4, weekends 1–4.*

The redbrick **All Hallows Episcopal Church,** completed in 1756, occupies the site of an earlier sanctuary at Church and Market streets. Inside is a Bible that belonged to Queen Anne. The church is one of the Snow Hill historic structures that appear in a walking-tour brochure available at the Purnell Museum or, on weekdays, at Town Hall (⊠ Green and Bank Sts.).

Outdoor Activities and Sports

Nassawango Country Club (⊠ 3940 Nassawango Rd., ☎ 410/632–3114 or 410/957–2262) has an 18-hole golf course.

Ocean City

🕕 *29 mi east of Salisbury (via Rte. 50); 116 mi southeast of Annapolis (via Rte. 50/301 to Rte. 50).*

Ocean City lies on the Atlantic side of the peninsula, spreading along a ¼-mi-wide strip of barrier peninsula that extends north into Delaware; to the west are the Isle of Wight and Big Assawoman bays. Coastal Highway (Hwy. 1) is the main artery through town; "Olde Towne" Ocean City is on the south end of the island, and "Condo Row" runs from 90th to 110th Street. The large residential areas of Little Salisbury and Caine Woods are home to approximately 7,500 year-round residents. This population often swells to more than 250,000 on summer weekends, however, when vacationers flock to the 10 mi of white-sand beach and 3-mi boardwalk with shops, pubs, restaurants, hotels with big decks and rocking chairs, a restored 19th-century carousel, water parks, a fishing pier, and stomach-churning amusement rides. Along the lower boardwalk—below 1st Street—are stores selling Dolles and Candy Kitchen saltwater taffy, Thrasher's french fries, and Fisher's caramel popcorn—traditional souvenirs to take home from Ocean City. Although this is a resort town, service and friendliness are quickly disposed of during the busy summer months. Expect heavy crowds along the Coastal Highway and the boardwalk. To the south of Ocean City lies the narrow, barrier island, Assateague Island National Seashore (☞ *below*).

🔄 **Trimper's Amusement Park,** at the south end of the boardwalk, has a number of rides, including a double-loop roller coaster. Of special interest is the Hirschell Spellman Carousel, dating from 1902. The outdoor portion of the amusement complex is open when there are crowds and has a double Ferris wheel; the indoor portion is open year-round, but on weekends only November–March. ⊠ *Boardwalk and S. 1st St.,* ☎ *410/289–8617.* 🎟 *Pay per ride.*

🔄 The **Jolly Roger Amusement Park** has two miniature golf courses, a water park, a roller coaster, kiddie rides, a petting zoo, and miniature racing cars. ⊠ *30th St. and Coastal Hwy.,* ☎ *410/289–3477.* 🎟 *Park: free; rides and golf: priced individually.* ⊙ *Easter–May 1, weekends noon–midnight; May–Sept., daily noon–midnight.*

Dining and Lodging

$$$ ✕ **Atlantic Hotel Inn and Restaurant.** Ten miles from Ocean City in the
★ picturesque town of Berlin, this restored late-19th-century hotel is worth the 20-minute drive: Its dining room is one of the best-kept secrets in Maryland's ocean resort area. Plush chairs and oversized tables bring a Victorian elegance to the small but formal dining room. The American regional menu is limited but choice: Try the tournedos of beef—twin medallions of filet mignon rubbed with green peppercorns and deglazed with brandy. Rockfish, crab sauté, and Cajun shrimp are among the seafood entrées. Desserts are a must—espe-

cially the Austrian sacher torte topped with a Chambord ganache. ⊠ *2 N. Main St., Berlin,* ☎ *410/641–3589. AE, MC, V.*

$$$ ✕ **Fager's Island.** The fun begins at the end of the day when
★   Tchaikovsky's *1812 Overture* accompanies every sunset over the As-
sawoman Bay. The restaurant and bar create an American café–style
atmosphere, with a beautiful bayside setting. There are more than 100
beers on the menu, including one brewed especially for Denise and John
Fager, the hospitable owners. Major wine publications agree that the
wine list is, unexpectedly, one of Maryland's best. In the dining room,
where plenty of windows overlook the water, sun, and waterfowl,
you'll enjoy some of the area's finest seafood, as well as prime rib with
fresh-shaved horseradish. Also recommended are the crab cakes, fla-
vored with garlic, and a semi-boned roast duckling with orange sauce,
a house favorite. Desserts are homemade. As the night progresses, the
adjoining bar comes to life and the crowd gets younger, but old-timers
won't ever feel out of place here. ⊠ *60th St. at the bay, Ocean City,*
☎ *410/723–6100. Reservations essential. AE, DC, MC, V.*

$$ ✕ **The Hobbit.** Dedicated to Bilbo Baggins and other literary creations
of J. R. R. Tolkien, the dining room has murals depicting scenes from
the classic novel, and wood table lamps are carved in the shapes of individual hobbits. The room's wedge shape affords a view of Assawoman Bay and surrounding marshland from two angles, and New
Age or classical music plays in the background. A bayside deck is popular with summer diners. Veal with pistachios is sautéed in a sauce of
Madeira wine, veal stock, prosciutto, mushrooms, shallots, and heavy
cream. Hobbit Catch is the fish of the day (typically swordfish, tuna,
or salmon) sautéed in butter with white wine, artichoke hearts, capers,
and mushrooms. Light fare is served in the adjoining bar as well as in
the café. A gift shop sells Hobbit–related T-shirts and gifts. ⊠ *101 81st
St.,* ☎ *410/524–8100. Reservations essential. MC, V.*

$ ✕ **Lombardi's.** With a consistent reputation for being the best pizza
kitchen in Ocean City, Lombardi's produces a consistent thin-crust pie
baked with the traditional toppings. The one unusual option is the white
pizza: mozzarella, olive oil, garlic, and onions not accompanied by
tomato sauce. A summer pizza of sliced tomatoes and fresh basil is popular, too. Homemade lasagna, cheese steaks, and cold-cut sandwiches
are the alternatives to pizza. The dining room furnishings, cozy wood
booths and tables, are augmented by photographs of Ocean City; the
adjacent solarium provides additional seating. Full bar service includes
a fairly priced selection of beers. ⊠ *9203 Coastal Hwy.,* ☎ *410/524–
1961. Reservations not accepted. MC, V.*

$$$$ 🏨 **Hotels at Fager's Island: Coconut Malorie Hotel and Lighthouse
Club Hotel.** These hotels, connected by boardwalks and nearly surrounded
by water and marshland, occupy Fager's Island, an oasis in a busy, noisy
resort town. The Coconut Malorie Hotel is an 85-suite Caribbean-style
hotel with full amenities and stylish decor, including marble bathrooms and Haitian art. Offering a different ambience is the Lighthouse
Club Hotel, a 23-suite maritime inn designed to represent a typical
Chesapeake Bay lighthouse. No creature comfort has been overlooked
at either accommodation. The Coconut Malorie, named after one of
the owner's daughters, features a Grecian white-marble lobby, palm
trees, and a waterfall. The Lighthouse "Lightkeeper" suites are ultra-
spacious with fireplaces and double marble Jacuzzis, four-poster beds,
and other luxurious amenities. The Lighthouse Club Hotel is connected to Fager's Island by an arched, lighted footbridge. ⊠ *56–60th
Sts. at the bay, 21842,* ☎ *410/723–6100 or 800/767–6060,* FAX

410/723–2055. 85 suites at Coconut Malorie, 23 at Lighthouse Club. Restaurant, bar, pool, health club. AE, MC, V.

$$$$ ⊞ **Merry Sherwood Plantation.** A wealthy Philadelphian built this
★ mansion "of suitable proportions" for his future bride, the daughter of a prominent Berlin family, in 1859. Since then the classic Italianate-style home has had several owners before being restored as a country inn in 1992. Occupying 18 acres, the plantation is surrounded by a rose garden, a topiary garden, and perennials. A wraparound porch entices guests to relax on white porch rockers. Loblolly pine floors and a mahogany rail and staircase greet visitors entering the home. In the formal dining room, carved rosewood furniture makes a statement—the table and chairs once belonged to the Vanderbilt family. A hand-carved rosewood chair made for Queen Victoria sits in the elegant ballroom. A full gourmet breakfast, often including apple pancakes, is served in the formal dining room, complete with china, crystal, and silver. Guest rooms are on the second and third floors and are full of antiques. ⊠ *8909 Worcester Hwy., Berlin, 21811,* ☎ *410/641-2112. 8 rooms, 6 with bath. Dining room. MC, V.*

$$$ ⊞ **Dunes Manor Hotel.** It's hard to miss this 11-story pink stucco building with a peaked roof that looks like a Victorian seaside inn even though it was built in 1987. Guest quarters are pink and green, with botanical prints and light oak furniture that includes an armoire to hide the TV. Each room has a refrigerator, an ocean view, and a private balcony. Every day at 3:30 the owner presides over afternoon tea in a lobby notable for a large double staircase and a brass chandelier. ⊠ *28th St. at the oceanfront, 21842,* ☎ *410/289–1100 or 800/523–2888. 160 rooms, 10 suites. Restaurant, bar, indoor-outdoor pool, exercise room. AE, DC, MC, V.*

$$$ ⊞ **Dunes Motel.** Half the rooms are oceanfront efficiencies in this five-story building of 1978, with windows that slide open for access to the beach or (on the upper story) to admit the sea breeze. Rooms in the older three-story building have a small refrigerator and no view of the water. The motel is dependably clean and conveniently located at the north end of the boardwalk. ⊠ *27th St. and Baltimore Ave., 21842,* ☎ *410/289–4414. 103 rooms. Restaurant, pool, wading pool. AE, MC, V.*

Nightlife and the Arts

Ocean City offers entertainment for everyone in the summer, ranging from refined to rowdy.

DANCING

Ocean City Convention Center (⊠ 4001 Coastal Hwy., ☎ 410/289–2800 or 800/626–2326) presents big-band dances and star entertainers throughout the year.
Bonfire (⊠ 71st St. and Ocean Hwy., ☎ 410/524–7171) plays slow tunes for an over-30 crowd.

MUSIC AND ENTERTAINMENT

Northside Park Recreation Center (⊠ 125th St. at the bay, ☎ 410/250–0125) is frequently the site of free outdoor concerts.
Under 21 Club (⊠ Boardwalk at Worcester St., ☎ 410/289–6313), for dancers 16–21 only, has a DJ whose sets are occasionally interrupted by a live act. No alcohol is served.
Tiffany's (⊠ 24th and Philadelphia Sts., Ocean City, ☎ 410/289–3322) rocks with live entertainment for the young set.
Paddock (⊠ 17th St. and Coastal Hwy., ☎ 410/289–6331), and the **Purple Moose** (⊠ 108 S. Boardwalk, ☎ 410/289–6953) are heavily booked all summer long with diverse bands and DJs.

Outdoor Activities and Sports

BICYCLING

Ocean City has designated a portion of the bus lanes on Coastal Highway for the use of bus and bicycle traffic. Traffic does get heavy, however, so exercise caution. Bicycle riding is allowed on the Ocean City boardwalk from 5 AM to 10 AM in summer and 5 AM to 4 PM the rest of the year. A bike trail connects Ocean City with Assateague Island, and the island itself is crisscrossed by a number of clearly marked paved trails.

On the **boardwalk,** try Caroline, 1st, 2nd, 6th, 9th, 14th, 15th, 16th, 17th, 21st, 23rd, 26th, 28th, and 72nd streets for rentals.

FISHING

Free public fishing piers on the Assawoman Bay and Isle of Wight Bay are at 3rd, 9th, 40th, and 125th streets and at the inlet in Ocean City. Other fishing and crabbing areas include the Route 50 bridge, Oceanic Pier, Ocean City Pier at Wicomico Street and the boardwalk, and Shantytown Village.

Several charters leave the Talbot Street pier and Dorchester Street pier in South Ocean City daily. In addition to arranging private charters, **The Fishing Center** (⊠ Shantytown Rd., West Ocean City 21842, ☎ 410/213–1121) sends out groups of 20 to 100 day-trippers on the *Ocean City Princess* and *Miss Ocean City,* both head boats. They also run the *Bay Queen* for quieter (and closer) bay fishing. **Bahia Marina** (⊠ 21st St. at the bay, Ocean City 21842, ☎ 410/289–7438) will arrange deep-sea charters to fish for marlin, shark, and tuna. This is the home of the head boat *Judith M.*

GOLF

There are 10 excellent golf courses in the Ocean City area. For a complete listing of courses and details, contact Worcester County Tourism or the Ocean City Public Relations Office. **The Bay Club** (⊠ 9122 Libertytown Rd., Berlin, west of Ocean City, ☎ 410/641–4081) has 18 holes. **Ocean City Yacht Club** (⊠ 11401 Country Club Dr., Berlin, ☎ 410/641–1779) has 36 holes.

TENNIS

Ocean City's public tennis courts (☎ 410/250–0125) are located on 41st and 61st streets and require reservations. Courts on 14th, 94th, and 136th streets are first come, first served.

VOLLEYBALL

The **Eastern Volleyball Association** (☎ 410/250–2577) coordinates a series of professional and pro/am tournaments on the beach at Ocean City each summer.

WATER SPORTS

Ocean City Public Relations Office publishes a guidebook called *Sea for Yourself* and a small brochure entitled "Get Hooked On Ocean City," which lists information on charter fishing and head boats, marinas and boat rentals, scenic cruises, diving charters, speedboat cruises, sailing yachts, and public boat ramps. The office has also published a brochure entitled "Camping In and Around Ocean City," which lists campgrounds, RV parks, camping stores, and bike and canoe rentals.

Sailing, Etc. (⊠ 5305 Coastal Hwy., ☎ 410/723–1144) rents sailboats, catamarans, and Windsurfers, and teaches sailing and windsurfing.

Shopping

Ocean City's 3-mi-long boardwalk is lined with T-shirt, souvenir, candy, and other stores. Several shopping malls also can be found along the Coastal Highway, which runs the length of the peninsula.

OFF THE
BEATEN PATH

ASSATEAGUE ISLAND NATIONAL SEASHORE – This immaculate untamed 37-mi-long barrier island extends south into Virginia (☞ Chapter 6). Swimming, biking, hiking, surf fishing, picnicking, and camping are permitted in the national park, and there is a bayside boat launch. A visitor center with aquariums and informative exhibits on the birds and wild ponies that inhabit Assateague is at the entrance, 6 mi south of Ocean City. It's important to note that the ponies that roam the dunes really are wild and should not be ridden, fed, approached, or played with. ⊠ 7206 National Seashore Ln. (Rte. 611), ☎ 410/641–1441. ☞ $4 cars, $2 per person for bicycles and pedestrians. ⊙ Visitor center: Daily 9–5; Park: daily 24 hours.

MARYLAND'S EASTERN SHORE A TO Z

Arriving and Departing

By Car

To reach the Eastern Shore from Baltimore or Washington, DC, cross the Chesapeake Bay by the toll bridge (toll collected eastbound only, $2.50) northeast of Annapolis; continue on U.S. 50, a divided four-lane highway in good repair with a 55 mph speed limit. A car is indispensable for touring the Eastern Shore, except within Ocean City—and even there it's your most effective means of transportation.

By Bus

Carolina Trailways (☎ 800/231–2222) makes several runs daily in both directions between Baltimore or Washington and Easton (FastStop Convenience Store, Rte. 50, 2 mi north of town, opposite airport, ☎ 410/822–3333), Cambridge (⊠ 501 Maryland Ave., ☎ 410/228–4626), Salisbury (⊠ 350 Cypress St., ☎ 410/749–4121), and Ocean City (⊠ 2nd St. and Coastal Hwy. at the Rte. 50 bridge, ☎ 410/289–9307).

By Plane

Cambridge/Dorchester Airport (☎ 410/228–4571) is 3 mi east of Cambridge on Bucktown Road.

Easton Municipal Airport (☎ 410/822–8560), 2 mi north of Easton on Route 50, is served by Maryland Airlines (☎ 410/822–0400) from Baltimore-Washington International Airport. Other services are offered by Easton Jct (☎ 410/820–8770) and East Coast Flight Services (☎ 410/820–6633).

Ocean City Airport (☎ 410/289–0927) is 6 mi southwest of Ocean City on Route 611.

Salisbury-Wicomico Regional Airport (☎ 410/548–4827), 5 mi north of Salisbury off Route 50, is served by USAir (☎ 800/428–4322).

Getting Around

"The Bus" (☎ 410/723–1607) travels the 10 mi of Coastal Highway 24 hours a day, with service about every 10 minutes. Bus-stop signs are posted every other block, and there are shelters at most locations. A $1 ticket is good for 24 hours.

Contacts and Resources

Emergencies

Dorchester General Hospital (⊠ 300 Byrn St., Cambridge, ☎ 410/228–5511).

Easton Memorial Hospital (⊠ 219 S. Washington St., Easton, ☎ 410/822–1000).

Peninsula General Hospital (⊠ 100 E. Carroll St., Salisbury, ☎ 410/543–7101).

LATE-NIGHT PHARMACIES

CVS Pharmacy (⊠ 11905 Coastal Hwy., Ocean City, ☎ 410/524–5101) is open daily until 9 PM in winter and daily until 10 PM in summer.

Rite-Aid Drugs (⊠ 94th St. and Ocean Hwy., Ocean City, ☎ 410/723–2425) is open until 9 PM, 10 PM Memorial Day–Labor Day.

Guided Tours

The paddle wheeler **Maryland Lady** (⊠ Box 316, Salisbury 21803, ☎ 410/543–2466) takes sightseeing, lunch, brunch, and dinner cruises on the Wicomico River.

The Patriot (⊠ Box 1206, St. Michaels, 21663, ☎ 410/745–3100), a 65-foot motor yacht, departs three times daily (at 11, 1, and 3 PM) for 90-minute cruises on the Miles River, from May to October. It passes many magnificent estates that front the river, including Bel Aire, Perry Hall, Wheatlands, the Anchorage, and the Willows.

The Ocean City Public Relations Office has information on boats that make scenic cruises of ½–2 hours from Ocean City, taking 25 to 150 passengers.

Visitor Information

Caroline County Commissioner's Office (⊠ Box 207, Denton 21629, ☎ 410/479–0660).

Dorchester County Tourism (⊠ 501 Court La., Room 103, Cambridge 21613, ☎ 410/228–1000 or 800/522–8687, ℻ 410/228–1563).

Kent County Chamber of Commerce (⊠ 118 N. Cross St., Box 146, Chestertown 21620, ☎ 410/778–0416).

Ocean City Public Relations Office (⊠ Dept. of Tourism, City Hall, 4001 Coastal Hwy., Box 158, Ocean City 21842, ☎ 410/289–2800 or 800/626–2326).

Queen Anne's County Visitors Service (⊠ Kent Narrows Center, 3100 Main St., Grasonville 21638, ☎ 410/827–4810).

Somerset County Tourism (⊠ Box 243, Princess Anne 21853, ☎ 410/651–2968 or 800/521–9189).

Talbot County Chamber of Commerce (⊠ 805 Goldsborough St., Box 1366, Easton 21601, ☎ 410/822–4606).

Wicomico County Convention & Visitors Bureau (⊠ Civic Center, 500 Glen Ave., Salisbury 21801, ☎ 410/548–4914).

Worcester County Tourism (⊠ 105 Pearl St., Box 208, Snow Hill 21863, ☎ 410/632–3110 or 800/854–0335).

11 Portraits of the Chesapeake Region

The Road to Appomattox

Pleasures of the Islands

THE ROAD TO APPOMATTOX*

THE THINNING Confederate lines around Petersburg finally extended fifty-three miles. Grant's force had grown to 125,000. Lee's had dwindled to 35,000. "My own corps was stretched," John B. Gordon remembered, "until the men stood like a row of vedettes, fifteen feet apart. . . . It was not a line; it was the mere *skeleton* of a line." Soon the gaps between the men stretched to twenty feet.

Lee's only hope lay in moving his army safely out of the trenches and to the southwest, to link up with Johnston in the hills of North Carolina.

Grant wanted to ensure that he did not get away.

Lee moved first. On March 25, Confederates under Gordon mounted a sudden night assault that briefly won possession of an earthwork called Fort Stedman before superior Union firepower drove them off. It was merely "a little rumpus," Lincoln reported to his Secretary of War.

Grant counterattacked, sending Phil Sheridan, two infantry corps, and 12,000 cavalry racing around Lee's flank to block Lee's exit at a crossroads called Five Forks. There, on April 1, they routed a Confederate division under George Pickett, taking 4,500 prisoners. "They had no commanders," a northern newspaperman noted, "at least no orders, and looked for a guiding hand. A few more volleys, a new and irresistible charge . . . and with a sullen and tearful impulse, five thousand muskets are flung upon the ground."

When Grant got the news he simply said, "All right," and ordered an all-out Union attack all along the Petersburg line for 4:30 the next morning. Slowly, relentlessly, his men drove the Confederates out of their trenches. Among the southern dead left behind were old men and shoeless boys as young as fourteen.

A. P. Hill, who had served Lee faithfully in a dozen battles and had staved off disaster at Sharpsburg, could do nothing for him now. Two Union infantrymen shot him through the heart as he rode between the lines. "He is at rest . . ." Lee said, "and we who are left are the ones to suffer."

As the Union columns started into Petersburg, Lee's army slipped across the Appomattox. "This is a sad business," Lee told an aide. "It has happened as I told them in Richmond it would happen. The line has been stretched until it is broken."

Jefferson Davis was attending ten-o'clock services that Sunday morning at St. Paul's Episcopal Church in Richmond. His wife and children had already left the city for safety farther south. The sexton handed him a message from his commander. A woman seated near Davis watched him read it: "I plainly saw the sort of gray pallor that came upon his face as he read [the] scrap of paper thrust into his hand."

"My lines are broken in three places," the note said. "Richmond must be evacuated this evening."

Davis hurried from the church, and ordered that his government move to Danville, 140 miles to the south. He took only a few belongings with him, but entrusted a heroic marble bust of himself to a slave, instructing him to hide it from the Yankees so that he would not be ridiculed.

The President of the Confederacy and his cabinet boarded the last train—a series of freight cars, each bravely labeled "Treasury Department," "Quarter Masters Department," "War Department." It was "Government on Wheels," said one man who watched it pass.

A slave dealer named Lumpkin failed to get his coffle of fifty chained slaves aboard the crowded train. A soldier with a bayonet barred him, until he unlocked his $50,000 worth of property in the street and let them go.

Chaos was all around them. Much of Richmond had been set afire by retreating Confederates. Mobs plundered shops,

---

This account is drawn from The Civil War, *based on the documentary film script by Geoffrey C. Ward, Ric Burns, and Ken Burns.*

broke into abandoned houses. "Fierce crowds of skulking men and coarse . . . women gathered before the stores . . ." an eyewitness remembered. "Whiskey ran in the gutters ankle deep; and half-drunken women, and children even, fought to dip up the coveted fluid in tin pans, [and] buckets."

Rear Admiral Raphael Semmes blew up all that was left of the Confederate fleet anchored in the James, the shock shattering windows throughout the city. Then the fire on land spread to the Confederate arsenal, filled with gunpowder and artillery shells. A Confederate captain, on his way out of the city, described the bedlam left behind:

Every now and then, as a magazine exploded, a column of white smoke rose . . . instantaneously followed by a deafening sound. The ground seemed to rock and tremble. . . . Hundreds of shells would explode in the air and send [down] their iron spray. . . . As the immense magazines of cartridges ignited, the rattle as of thousands of musketry would follow, and then all was still, for the moment, except the dull roar and crackle of the fast-spreading fires.

Union troops occupied the city the next day, cheered by ecstatic crowds of blacks, and did their best to restore order. "Our . . . servants were completely crazed," a Richmond matron noted. "They danced and shouted, men hugged each other, and women kissed. . . . *Imagine* the streets crowded with these people!"

Two Union officers spurred their horses to the deserted Confederate Capitol. "I sprang from my horse," remembered Lieutenant Livingston de Peyster of New York, "first unbuckling the Stars and Stripes [from my saddle], [and] with Captain Loomis L. Langdon, Chief of Artillery, I rushed up to the roof. Together, we hoisted the first large flag over Richmond and on the peak of the roof drank to its success."

"Exactly at eight o'clock," a Richmond woman noted, "the Confederate flag that fluttered above the Capitol came down and the Stars and Stripes were run up. . . . We covered our faces and cried aloud. All through the house was the sound of sobbing. It was as the house of mourning." Nearby, another woman remembered, "We tried to comfort ourselves by saying in low tones (for we feared spies even in our servants) that the capital was only moved temporarily . . . that General Lee would make a stand and repulse the daring enemy, and that we would yet win the battle and the day. Alas, Alas, for our hopes."

Mrs. Robert E. Lee, too disabled by arthritis to travel, remained in Richmond. The Union commander posted a guard before her house to ensure no harm came to her—a black cavalryman. Mrs. Lee complained that the presence of a black soldier on her doorstep was "perhaps an insult," and was assigned a new guard, a white Vermonter—to whom she sent out meals on a little tray.

—Geoffrey C. Ward with
Ric Burns and Ken Burns

PLEASURES OF THE ISLANDS

THE WATER WAKES long before the land. A raucous hen mallard, sassing the dawn, sails from behind a point of marsh, trailing gouts of liquid fire wherever first light catches her ripples on the cove's black, silken surface. A flight of quick-winged teal circles to land, pinions flailing a sound of far-off jingle bells from the chill air. Now the cove mirrors seamlessly the frosty gold thawing into day on the eastern horizon. The teal coming down could as well be flying up through the water's depths, like the ducks embedded in expensive crystal paperweights. A burst of wind ruffles the illusion, and the breeze chuckles softly as the stiff marsh grass scratches its belly; then it is gone and the stillness of the island is pierced by one of the wildest songs on earth.

The geese are aloft, piping their haunting obligato to the grander, slower cadence of winter's coming. It is music that sets dogs to frenzied yelping along the great migration routes from Labrador to North Carolina, and makes people on the streets of large cities pause, cock an ear, and look skyward, stirred by a longing so old and deep we cannot articulate it much better than the dogs. Just as an old, popular tune on the radio can activate a hundred associations from one's youth, so does goose music evoke places and times out of some ancestral consciousness, when the flights heralded changing seasons to prehistoric hunters on these same shores—signified the glad prospect of roast goose in a season when the land would be otherwise lean. The tune no longer has survival value, but we still find it thrilling.

The same elemental shifts of season and weather that tug geese southward, and goad fish across whole oceans toward their natal streams, also whisper to something in our genes that it is time to be moving. We needn't heed such atavism, of course, but an impending snowstorm still sends us flocking to the supermarket with an almost delicious anticipation, to lay in stores well beyond any strictly rational need; and who could deny, watching the flow of Florida-bound Mercedes and Cadillacs on Interstate 95 each winter, that as soon as we are able to afford our druthers, we resume migrating?

The pleasure of migration is part of why I try faithfully to return each spring and fall to camp on islands like South Marsh in the Chesapeake Bay. The other reason has to do with the special nature of islands. South Marsh Island is five miles from the Somerset County mainland and consists of about three thousand low acres, owned by the state of Maryland, which with rare wisdom leaves it pretty much alone. Norfolk lies to the south, Wilmington to the north, and Baltimore and Washington to the west. Ocean City's teeming beaches on the east complete the circle. Six million people, conservatively, are busy carrying on the business of modern civilization within a hundred-mile radius of us. It is obscenely satisfying, in the midst of the conurbation, to be foraging for supper with our bare hands on this utterly lonesome, permanently unpeopled sweep of marsh. Not more than ten feet from shore, in the olive water off the camp, lies a trove of plump, salty oysters. To collect a bushel is the work of minutes, and the toughest chore is deciding how to eat them. We bicker, and then settle on steamed, raw, fried, and stewed. A short canoe trip to a nearby point of land yields an equal harvest of striated mussels. Gouged fresh from the peaty shore and steamed, they retain a delicate earthy taste that is the very essence of the tide marsh, a sort of estuarine equivalent of a mushroom. Fresh drinking water bubbles up sweet and pure from a rusting pipe sunk eight hundred feet deep here decades ago by a wealthy duck-hunting club. It taps a mammoth aquifer that runs beneath the bay, sloping west to east. Tonight we will wash down our fresh seafood with swigs of rain that fell on Appalachian slopes thousands of years ago, filtered a few inches a century through the geologic strata of half a state. In truth, we have also ferried over a case of beer to ease our transition to the natural life. Still, there is something heady and fulfilling about even so dilletantist a reversion to hunter-gatherer status.

Perhaps because they physically bound one's experiences and insulate the senses from the mainland's distractions, islands concentrate and render more vivid everything that happens on them. South Marsh and its neighbors, for example, might strike you as plain with their monolithic vegetational stands of needlerush and spartina grasses; but the rich light of a late afternoon sun can charge such places with a purity and strength of color to shame van Gogh's palette, floating golden as Eldorado between blue blazes of autumn sky and water. On hot summer afternoons I have seen them, backlit before an approaching thunderstorm, glowing like neon emeralds. Without its islands, the bay would lose a vital texture.

Island communities are the original alternative societies, says the author John Fowles, and "that is why so many mainlanders envy them. Some vision of Utopian belonging, of social blessedness, of an independence based on cooperation, haunts them all." Even a cursory review of literature would show that, from the *Odyssey* to *Robinson Crusoe*, through *Misty of Chincoteague,* islands have commanded attention all out of proportion to their tiny share of the earth's land mass. In a complicated world, they seem alluringly defined and comprehensible. Special things, we feel, are bound to happen there. It seems no oddity that two of television's biggest hits in the past, insipid though they may have been, were "Fantasy Island" and "The Love Boat" (boats, after all, are the ultimate islands). Mythically, islands are places of origins, which does not surprise me in light of my growing kinship with islands in the bay. Sometimes on still, clear evenings, it is possible to lie supine on South Marsh, cerebral cortex pressed into the damp peat and eyes locked on the starry galaxies, and complete a sort of primal circuit. Lulled by the amnion bay's gentle suck and glut in every indentation of the marshy edge, you may come close to re-experiencing the pleasures of the womb.

The Chesapeake Bay is favored with about fifty of the world's estimated one-half million islands. They range from Garrett in the mouth of the Susquehanna at bay's head, to Watts, a deepwater rendezvous for 17th-century pirates in Virginia. Uses of the islands include preserves for ducks, like South Marsh; preserves for the wealthy, like Gibson Island on the Magothy; isolation chambers, like heavily diked Hart-Miller, for the shiploads of polluted spoil that must be dredged constantly from Baltimore harbor's channels; and military bombing ranges, like cratered Bloodsworth Island in Dorchester County. It is from other islands—Smith, Deal, Tilghman, Kent, Hoopers, Tangier—that the watermen who harvest most of our seafood still choose to operate.

ON THE ISLANDS elements of our human and natural heritage have been able to flourish well past the time they could still exist, unsullied, on the mainland. Water, even in the jet age, remains a surprisingly efficient barrier. If you doubt that, compare the cultures of Crisfield, where they say *aryster,* and St. Mary's County, where they say *oistuh;* or the Eastern Shore fishing community of Rock Hall with Baltimore City. Neither pair is separated by much more than a dozen miles, but they are water miles, and the insulation they provide is blessedly effective. This essential characteristic of islands enforces an interdependence, trust, and cooperation among their residents that we envy. It sometimes confounds me how the word *insular* ever got its slightly pejorative connotation.

I am convinced we are now living in the best of times—and probably the last of times—for appreciating the bay's islands. It is only in the last generation or two that the growth of road and bridge access, and of leisure time for boating and day-tripping, has begun allowing frequent and easy travel there for most of us. Modern bug repellents have also helped a lot, for these are often low and marshy places. At the same time, forces are at work that probably will extinguish, or greatly diminish, the islands' special qualities in many of our lifetimes. A number of bay islands already have vanished or dramatically receded from wind and wave erosion in the last century. That retreat will only accelerate as our profligate incineration of fossil fuels warms the global atmosphere and melts more of the polar icecaps, causing the sea level to rise at a rate unprecedented in many thousands of years. Right now it appears to be coming up at a foot a century, fast enough to doom thousands of precious island acres in a span of a few decades. It will not take long until the islands are actually inundated. Long before that happens, storms riding in atop an elevated sea level will cause more erosion and property damage than they ever did in the past.

And perhaps even before physical forces decide the issue, the bay's declining nat-ural-resources base, on which many wa-terfront communities depend for a living, could depopulate the islands. Already the difficulty of making a living on the water is reinforcing a trend toward gentrification of some islands, as growing numbers of city folks find the low price and avail-ability of second homes there too good to pass up. On Tilghman Island in Talbot County, the man who owns both the biggest oyster company and a burgeoning tourist complex calculates that between 1978 and 1984 the former enterprise de-clined 40 percent, while the latter grew by 300 percent. So much of what is happen-ing to the bay islands smacks to me of the irreversible. My advice is to revel in our favored-generation status, and celebrate them while we still can.

—Tom Horton

A native of Maryland's Eastern Shore, Horton is a writer and analyst for the nonprofit environ-mental group the Chesapeake Bay Foundation. This essay appears in his book *Bay Country*, winner of the John Burroughs Medal for nature writing in 1988.

INDEX

NOTES

NOTES

NOTES

NOTES

NOTES

Fodor's Travel Publications

Available at bookstores everywhere, or call 1–800–533–6478, 24 hours a day.

Gold Guides
U.S.

Alaska	Florida	New Orleans	Santa Fe, Taos, Albuquerque
Arizona	Hawai'i	New York City	
Boston	Las Vegas, Reno, Tahoe	Pacific North Coast	Seattle & Vancouver
California		Philadelphia & the Pennsylvania Dutch Country	The South
Cape Cod, Martha's Vineyard, Nantucket	Los Angeles		U.S. & British Virgin Islands
	Maine, Vermont, New Hampshire		
The Carolinas & the Georgia Coast		The Rockies	USA
	Maui & Lana'i	San Diego	Virginia & Maryland
Chicago	Miami & the Keys	San Francisco	Washington, D.C.
Colorado	New England		

Foreign

Australia	Europe	Montréal & Québec City	Scotland
Austria	Florence, Tuscany & Umbria		Singapore
The Bahamas		Moscow, St. Petersburg, Kiev	South Africa
Belize & Guatemala	France		South America
Bermuda	Germany	The Netherlands, Belgium & Luxembourg	Southeast Asia
Canada	Great Britain		Spain
Cancún, Cozumel, Yucatán Peninsula	Greece	New Zealand	Sweden
	Hong Kong	Norway	Switzerland
Caribbean	India	Nova Scotia, New Brunswick, Prince Edward Island	Thailand
China	Ireland		Tokyo
Costa Rica	Israel	Paris	Toronto
Cuba	Italy		Turkey
The Czech Republic & Slovakia	Japan	Portugal	Vienna & the Danube
	London	Provence & the Riviera	
Eastern & Central Europe	Madrid & Barcelona	Scandinavia	
	Mexico		

Fodor's Special-Interest Guides

Alaska Ports of Call	Halliday's New England Food Explorer	Rock & Roll Traveler USA	Wendy Perrin's Secrets Every Smart Traveler Should Know
Caribbean Ports of Call		Sunday in New York	
The Complete Guide to America's National Parks	Halliday's New Orleans Food Explorer	Sunday in San Francisco	Where Should We Take the Kids? California
	Healthy Escapes	Walt Disney World for Adults	Where Should We Take the Kids? Northeast
Disney Like a Pro	Kodak Guide to Shooting Great Travel Pictures		
Family Adventures		Walt Disney World, Universal Studios and Orlando	
Fodor's Gay Guide to the USA			Worldwide Cruises and Ports of Call
	Nights to Imagine		

Special Series

Affordables
Caribbean
Europe
Florida
France
Germany
Great Britain
Italy
London
Paris

Bed & Breakfasts and Country Inns
America
California
The Mid-Atlantic
New England
The Pacific Northwest
The South
The Southwest
The Upper Great Lakes

Berkeley Guides
California
Central America
Eastern Europe
Europe
France
Germany & Austria
Great Britain & Ireland
Italy
London
Mexico
New York City
Pacific Northwest & Alaska
Paris
San Francisco

Compass American Guides
Alaska
Arizona
Canada
Chicago
Colorado
Hawaii
Hollywood
Idaho
Las Vegas

Maine
Manhattan
Montana
New Mexico
New Orleans
Oregon
San Francisco
Santa Fe
South Carolina
South Dakota
Southwest
Texas
Utah
Virginia
Washington
Wine Country
Wisconsin
Wyoming

Citypacks
Atlanta
Hong Kong
London
New York City
Paris
Rome
San Francisco
Washington, D.C.

Fodor's Español
California
Caribe Occidental
Caribe Oriental
Gran Bretaña
Londres
Mexico
Nueva York
Paris

Exploring Guides
Australia
Boston & New England
Britain
California
Caribbean
China
Egypt
Florence & Tuscany
Florida
France

Germany
Ireland
Israel
Italy
Japan
London
Mexico
Moscow & St. Petersburg
New York City
Paris
Prague
Provence
Rome
San Francisco
Scotland
Singapore & Malaysia
Spain
Thailand
Turkey
Venice

Fodor's Flashmaps
Boston
New York
San Francisco
Washington, D.C.

Pocket Guides
Acapulco
Atlanta
Barbados
Budapest
Jamaica
London
Munich
New York City
Paris
Prague
Puerto Rico
Rome
San Francisco
Washington, D.C.

Mobil Travel Guides
America's Best Hotels & Restaurants
California & the West
Frequent Traveler's Guide to Major Cities
Great Lakes

Mid-Atlantic
Northeast
Northwest & Great Plains
Southeast
Southwest & South Central

Rivages Guides
Bed and Breakfasts of Character and Charm in France
Hotels and Country Inns of Character and Charm in France
Hotels and Country Inns of Character and Charm in Italy
Hotels and Country Inns of Character and Charm in Paris
Hotels and Country Inns of Character and Charm in Portugal
Hotels and Country Inns of Character and Charm in Spain

Short Escapes
Britain
France
Near New York City
New England

Fodor's Sports
Golf Digest's Best Places to Play
Skiing USA
USA Today The Complete Four Sport Stadium Guide

Fodor's Vacation Planners
Great American Learning Vacations
Great American Sports & Adventure Vacations
Great American Vacations
Great American Vacations for Travelers with Disabilities
National Parks and Seashores of the East
National Parks of the West

WHEREVER YOU TRAVEL, *H*ELP IS NEVER FAR AWAY.

From planning your trip to providing travel assistance along the way, American Express® Travel Service Offices are always there to help.

Virginia

American Express Travel Service
1100 South Hayes Street
Pentagon City
Arlington
703/415-5400

Enterprise Travel (R)
Main Reservation Center
400 East Main Street
Charlottesville
804/296-7500

American Express Travel Service
1846 Tysons Galleria
McLean
703/893-3550

American Express Travel Service
1412-A Starling Drive
Richmond
804/740-2030

American Express Travel Service
6640 Springfield Mall
Springfield
703/971-5600

Gibson World Travel (R)
279 Independent Boulevard
Virginia Beach
804/499-2333

Maryland

American Express Travel Service
67 Annapolis Mall
Annapolis
410/224-4200

American Express Travel Service
32 South Street
Baltimore
410/837-3100

Travel

http://www.americanexpress.com/travel

American Express Travel Service Offices are located throughout the United States. For the office nearest you, please call 1-800-AXP-3429.